PEACE, FAITH, NATION

MENNONITE EXPERIENCE IN AMERICA SERIES

The Mennonite Experience in America series attempts to tell with disciplined integrity the history of the first three centuries of Mennonite and Amish in America. There are four volumes:

1. *Land, Piety, Peoplehood: The Establishment of Mennonite Communities in America, 1683-1790*
by Richard K. MacMaster, 1985.

2. *Peace, Faith, Nation: Mennonites and Amish in Nineteenth-Century America*
by Theron F. Schlabach, 1989.

3. *Vision, Doctrine, War: Mennonite Identity and Organization in America, 1890-1930.*
by James C. Juhnke, 1989.

4. *Mennonites in American Society, 1930-1970*
by Paul Toews, 1996.

The Mennonite Experience in America, Volume 2

Peace, Faith, Nation

MENNONITES AND AMISH IN NINETEENTH-CENTURY AMERICA

Theron F. Schlabach

HERALD PRESS
Scottdale, Pennsylvania
Waterloo, Ontario

Library of Congress Catologing-in-Publication Data

Schlabach, Theron F.
Peace, faith, nation.

(The Mennonite experience in America ; v. 2)
Bibliography: p.
Includes index.
1. Mennonites—United States—History—19th century.
2. Amish—United States—History—19th century.
3. United States—Church history—19th century.
4. Minorities—United States—History—19th century.
I. Title. II. Series.
BX8116.M46 vol. 2 289.7.73 s 88-28443
ISBN 0-8361-3102-9 [289.7'73]

On the Cover: **John Unruh's threshing crew from Goessel, Kansas, ca. 1900.** Photo courtesy of Mennonite Library and Archives at Bethel College.

PEACE, FAITH, NATION

Library of Congress Catalog Card Number: 88-28443
International Standard Book Number: 0-8361-3102-9
Printed in the United States of America
Design by David Hiebert

05 04 03 02 01 00 99 98 97 10 9 8 7 6 5 4 3 2

To those
nineteenth-century
Mennonites and Amish
who were determined
to be faithful.

CONTENTS

SERIES INTRODUCTION

In 1683, when the Mennonite experience in America began, there was no American nation. Like their fellow Americans, Mennonites and Amish came to the New World at different times for different reasons, and spoke different languages and dialects. They along with other immigrant groups began eventually to ask who they were as a people. They searched for identity, and for mission. And, in provincial and fragmented fashion, they began to tell their stories. Recently they have become more and more aware that separate Mennonite and Amish stories are one interwoven story, closely intertwined with national history.

For Mennonites, history has always been a statement of faith, a tracing of the ways of God with God's people. The intention for the Mennonite Experience in America books is that they be also a history with disciplined integrity, portraying both shadow and light.

In four volumes, the series savors the meaning of three hundred years of Mennonite history in the New World. The authors tell not only of Mennonites, but also of America. The relation to America is one of paradox and promise. The four volumes are an invitation to come, read, learn tales never before told, and reflect on the story of Mennonites through three centuries of growing nationhood.

In this volume the account of Mennonites in America moves through the nineteenth century. As it moves, the pace quickens. New waves of immigrants arrived from Galicia, Volhynia, West Prussia, the Ukraine, and elsewhere. Rooted in distinct cultural and religious traditions, each Mennonite or Amish group found its own ways to confront the claims of a new and rapidly changing society. A modernizing America offered pluralism and choice, individualism and professionalism, technology and industrialism, nationalism and revivalism.

This book offers a significant and alternative reading of the American experience by telling of a people who both resisted and yielded to the imperialism of American culture and American values. Lines of the poet William Butler Yeats suggest the Mennonites' dilemma:

> Things fall apart; the centre could not hold. . . .
> The ceremony of innocence was drowned. . . .

Yet the center did hold. That is the story of the two volumes yet to come.

Robert Kreider
Chairperson, Editorial Committee
The Mennonite Experience in America
North Newton, Kansas
November 1987

EDITOR'S FOREWORD

One of the least-studied periods of American Mennonite history is the nineteenth century. The publication of this volume by Theron Schlabach will begin to cure that deficiency.

Beginning the story at 1790, Schlabach tells of a century of Mennonite and Amish immigration, migration, settlement, and resettlement. For Americans in general the nineteenth century was a time of expansion, formation, and consolidation. Out of the ferment came an American nation—powerful, rich, and ebullient.

One focus of this volume is on how the rural, pious Mennonites responded to such an environment. How quiet were the quiet in the land? Did the corrosive acids of nationalism and individualism affect the piety of these gentle sectarians?

A second concern is how these inheritors of the sixteenth-century Radical Reformation were developing as a religious community. Were the gentle breezes of Pietism still changing Mennonite worship, devotion, and practice in the nineteenth century? How did the Mennonite emphasis on humility contrast with the mood of the country, and with the activism of revitalistic Protestants?

Mennonites struggled for unity but often did not succeed. Therefore an important part of their story is the fraying of their churches' fabrics. In Schlabach's account, Mennonites' schismatic tendencies become comprehensible examples of spiritual vitality and renewal. Mennonites were homogeneous, but not monolithic. They were diverse. Given the serious and central role they and their polity gave the church, some shifting and shaking was inevitable.

At mid-century the U.S. civil war proved a severe test for Mennonites and their sectarian identity. Mennonites found themselves making compromises while showing acts of conscience and courage in danger—a fascinating study of faith under stress.

One purpose of the Mennonite Experience in America series is to offer readers in today's era of Mennonite history a resource of biographical and anecdotal memory. For that, this volume will serve well. Schlabach introduces interesting characters who lend their times a personality which until now has not been present.

A rich story is that of the coming of Mennonites from the Russian empire in the 1870s and '80s. Today there is much interest in merger of the "old" or "MC" Mennonite church (largely of Swiss-German heritage) and the General Conference or "GC" Mennonite church (substantially of so-called Russian heritage). With that interest, the rich and detailed account of the 1870s and '80s has possibilities for inter-Mennonite understanding. In those decades American Mennonites of Swiss-German descent responded to the needs of the Russian immigrants. Mennonites of the two streams clearly enjoyed a common spiritual identity. Yet, clearly, there was also corrosion produced by three hundred years of separate history. Schlabach's story offers necessary perspective on the shared American experience of the last one hundred years.

An area to which this book offers fresh research is the nature of Mennonite and Amish communalism. The pervasive role of the church in Amish and Mennonite community life is evident. The community was grounded in a religious self-understanding. That understanding made the church—or, better, the congregation—the context for spiritual experience and the arbiter of community life.

The book also confirms the rural, agricultural setting of the community. Despite intense communalism, the economy of Mennonite and Amish community was largely a replica of the normal American form of agriculture. Yet there was a matter of scale: even in agriculture, Mennonites did not develop large economic enterprises. The sociological glue of Mennonite and Amish communal life clearly was religious—a pervasive mutuality which conditioned economic activity just as it did other aspects of life.

By the end of the century, American culture was making its presence felt among Amish and Mennonites. Yet the changes were minor. The author calls the changes a "quickening," implying a new tempo and spirit. And so it was. But the roots of sectarian consciousness remained and pervaded. It would be not the nineteenth century but the twentieth, with its violence and technology and theological controversies, which would rend and reconstitute the fabrics of Mennonite identity and practice.

Nineteenth-century Mennonite history is an important window through which to view present Mennonite experience.

Albert N. Keim
Eastern Mennonite College
November 1987

AUTHOR'S PREFACE

If this book has value, many people have helped create it. Behind the author is the MEA Editorial Committee: Robert Kreider as chairman, Cornelius J. Dyck, Leonard Gross, Peter J. Klassen, John A. Lapp, Wesley Prieb, Willard Swartley, and Carolyn C. Wenger. These people have given shape to the MEA project, worked through policy questions, and in some cases read manuscripts. Not least, they searched and found that crucial ingredient, money.

Behind them have been many financial contributors. At the risk of being unfair to others who have strained to give, I will thank some of the principal ones. These include Paul and Barbara Detweiler, C. J. and Wilma Dyck, John E. Fretz, Merle and Phyllis Good, David and Mary Groh, Walton Hackman, Gerald and Gwen Hartzel, Dwight and Ellen Hartman, Albert and Leanna Keim, Robert and Lois Kreider, Horace C. Longacre, Michael Loss, Richard and Betty Pellman, Wesley Prieb, Herbert and Louise Regier, John and Rebecca Rutt, Willard and Verna Smith, Edward C. Snyder, Will Stoltz, Carolyn C. Wenger, and Lloyd Zeager.

Many other persons have contributed through organizations. We in the project greatly appreciate sizable grants received from the Commission on Education of the General Conference Mennonite Church; Schowalter Foundation; Mennonite Central Committee; Mennonite Mutual Aid; Goodville Mutual Insurance Company; the Franconia, the Indiana-Michigan, the Ohio, and the Virginia conferences of the Mennonite Church; Associated Mennonite Biblical Seminaries; Mennonite Historical Society; Eastern Mennonite Associated Libraries and Archives; the two Centers for Mennonite Brethren Studies at Pacific and Tabor colleges; Lancaster Mennonite Historical Society; Illinois Mennonite Historical and Genealogical Society; Iowa Mennonite Historical Society; and Mennonite Historians of Eastern Pennsylvania.

A special thanks also to the Institute of Mennonite Studies, and particularly to Willard Swartley as director, for managing the project's finances.

Goshen College has provided me a steady flow of modest research allowances over the years, in addition to office space, equipment, secretarial services, and cooperation to arrange research leaves. Along with the Associated Mennonite Biblical Seminaries, the college has also contributed greatly to the project by supporting the Mennonite Historical Library. So have Bethel College with its Mennonite Library and Archives, Tabor and Fresno Pacific colleges with their Centers for Mennonite Brethren Studies, Eastern Mennonite College with its Menno Simons Historical Library, the Mennonite Church with its Archives, and the Lancaster Mennonite Historical Society and the Mennonite Historians of Eastern Pennsylvania with their respective libraries and archives.

One cannot begin to mention all the generous, service-minded people in these centers, so one name will be symbolic for all: Lena Lehman, administrative assistant of the historical library at Goshen College. The depth of her knowledge of the MHL collection, her attitude of making resources quickly available, her ability to sense the right questions, and her readiness with personal help are a model for all professionals everywhere.

For a few persons my thanks are even more personal. One of the great rewards of this project has been the chance to work with my fellow MEA authors—Richard MacMaster, James Juhnke, and Paul Toews. Albert Keim, editor of this volume, has taken a similar place on this team. Less formally, Marion Wenger edited and improved my use of German (and occasionally my English).

There has also been a string of student assistants. How fortunate I have been in the caliber the project has attracted! Of the many who deserve it, I must mention four: Joseph C. Liechty, who at the outset put his keen intelligence to sifting the chaff from the worthwhile sources; Joyce Peachey, who aided greatly in changing to computerized note-taking; Edward Zuercher, who collected and prepared photographs; and Timothy A. Schmucker, who worked mightily and competently with various details, not least to put notes and bibliography into shape.

Most of all, I thank my wife, Sara Kauffman Schlabach, who supported the book more than anyone. She did so by accepting a reduced family income, few vacations, and a husband buried in his work for months and years on end. Hardly anyone but other authors' spouses can fully appreciate how much she gave.

As do most endeavors, writing this book has posed problems with no perfect answers. One problem was terminology. What term shall we use for the largest Mennonite branch, often called simply "the Mennonite Church (MC)"? That label, with its suggestion that this group is *the* Mennonite church, is flatly inaccurate. At the risk of confusion with old-order varieties I have returned to a longtime popular usage and accepted the phrase *the "old" Mennonites* with *old* in quotation marks since it is not part of the official name.

And what shall we call those Mennonites who immigrated, or whose ancestors immigrated, from the Russian empire beginning in the 1870s? *Russian Mennonites*, the standard term, is not a very good label. Although living in the empire changed them, culturally they remained essentially German, never Russian. Nor did they ever really live in Russia. They only lived in lands controlled by the Russian czars, principally the Ukraine. Originally I put the word *Russian* in quotation marks. But some readers found that solution clumsy and full of more questions than it solved. In the end I deleted the quotation marks, however imprecise and misleading that choice.

There are other dilemmas which some careful scholars might have solved differently. Within the available space should interaction with the U.S. as a nation have been an even stronger topic, with less of Mennonites' own views of life? Should the humility theme have been treated more in one place instead of woven throughout? How can one be fair to the larger Mennonite groups without becoming obscurantist regarding the smaller ones? Has there been a proper balance in presenting the various views of differing Mennonites?

Some readers will differ with certain choices, as well as with presuppositions and conclusions. Let them join the discussion. It is not the aim of this series to be the final word on the Mennonite experience in America. It is to lay the groundwork and open the issues.

Theron F. Schlabach,
Goshen, Indiana
November, 1987

PEACE, FAITH, NATION

CHAPTER

1

MENNONITES AND AMISH IN A NEW NATION

"What a joy to hear sudden news of peace!" wrote a Mennonite deacon in 1816 to relatives in Europe. Martin Mellinger of Lancaster County in eastern Pennsylvania was rejoicing that England and the United States had just ended the war of 1812. But while he was glad, he also was uneasy. "We Americans" needed also to learn peace of soul, the deacon reflected. A decade later he feared that "in our highly praised America . . . sincerity is gone" and "integrity is at a low level." It seemed that "humility" was "spoiled" and that "justice has disappeared."[1]

Mellinger had immigrated in 1772[2] and lived through the American revolution. Now, in the teens and 1820s, using words such as "we Americans," he identified with the new United States. Yet he was also a Mennonite, member of a church whose people were skeptical of the world's political structures. In his call for humility he sounded different from the assertive, modern nationalism of the new United States. No wonder he felt uneasy!

ORIGINS AND DIFFERENCES

Mennonites took their name from a sixteenth-century Anabaptist church reformer named Menno Simons; but whereas Menno had lived in Holland, the spiritual roots of most Mennonites in America went back to Anabaptism in Switzerland and south Germany. The original Anabaptists had varied considerably. The ones whom Mennonites counted as forebears had been pacifists who insisted that Christians had no business resorting to war, violence, and "the sword." Another emphasis was that a person could not become a Christian, a true disciple of Jesus, except by a decision which was personal and voluntary. Believing that no one could "make" Christians by force or by baptizing babies, the Anabaptists baptized only persons who were old enough to decide and apparently had decided to be Christian.

Such Anabaptists also called on the church to separate clearly from the worldly order of politics, civil society, and state. On other points—such as salvation by faith, authority of Scripture, or the nature of redemption—they taught much as did Martin Luther, John Calvin, and other Protestant Reformers. Yet they were preoccupied somewhat less with deliverance from prior guilt and somewhat more with the regenerated life after conversion. At the heart of their faith was rigorous discipleship and faithful Christian living.[3]

Anabaptists thoroughly frightened Europe's people of power. Many were outspoken and missionary about their faith, and insisted forthrightly that European society and institutions were not really Christian. To authorities they seemed sectarian and divisive. Their worldview pitted the faithful remnant of true Christians in hard struggle against the established churches and against the vast majority of "Christians" who did not live righteously. So churchmen and rulers, both Catholic and Protestant, considered them dangerous to social solidarity and order. Some Anabaptists in fact did use violence against authority, particularly a faction who captured Münster, Germany, in 1534-1535. But the authorities hunted down peaceful as well as armed ones, and women and youths as well as men. For decades many, many Anabaptists were brought to trial, imprisoned, tortured, and frequently executed by drowning or burning.[4] Such persecution taught them and early Mennonites another point: to be faithful meant to suffer.

From the sixteenth century onward, to flee persecution or for other reasons, Anabaptists and Mennonites in Europe frequently moved and resettled. Local princes or large landowners sometimes tolerated and protected them, especially where they moved onto marginal lands and made the soil productive. The main Mennonite migrations formed two patterns: a movement northward along the Rhine River from Anabaptist clusters in Switzerland and south Germany; and a movement eastward from Holland across northern Europe, which eventually turned southward into the Russian empire. As for America, in the seventeenth century a few Mennonites, mainly Dutch, made their way to New Amsterdam or Long Island. Others began settling in William Penn's Pennsylvania.

In 1683 at Germantown, just north of Philadelphia, a northern European group from Krefeld, Germany, established the Mennonites' first permanent settlement in America. Some from Germantown soon moved about thirty miles northwest to a place called "Skippack" and began what became a series of rural communities spreading out from there. In 1710 new immigrants took up land also some fifty miles farther west, near Lancaster. Before the end of the colonial and revolutionary period Mennonites had moved southwestward into the Cumberland and Shenandoah valleys of Maryland and Virginia.[5]

In Europe in the 1600s and 1700s Anabaptists and Mennonites changed considerably. One change was to share in Pietism, a movement among Protestants who sought warmer, inner spirituality. Pietism deeply affected sermons, devotional books, hymnody, and perceptions of faith. Having drunk deeply of Pietism in Europe, Mennonites who went to America shared much of the religious language and outlook of Pennsylvania-German Lutheran and Reformed neighbors.[6] But if Europe's Mennonites broadly accepted Pietism, they were not all alike. Diverse in origin and scattered by migration, they developed differently. For instance, compared to Mennonites elsewhere some of those in Holland were soon much more urban. From 1577 onward their rulers granted a degree of toleration. Relatively accepted, urbanized Dutch Mennonites began rather early to re-integrate into society as business persons, medical doctors, or artists. In 1735 Dutch Mennonites established a seminary for training ministers. However, before the 1870s not many of such acculturated northern European Mennonites migrated to America. Most immigrants arrived from south Germany and Switzerland, and from rural villages.[7]

After the 1690s one major difference was between Mennonites and Amish. In some European communities a quarrel erupted in that decade around the person of a Swiss minister named Jakob Ammann. The dispute was not about theology so much as about degrees of discipline and separation. Ammann wanted stricter rules concerning attire and other matters. To bring erring ones to repentance he wanted more rigorous use of shunning (systematic social ostracism) and the ban (excommunication). He gained fol-followers especially in Alsace, the Palatinate, and Switzerland, followers who became known as the *Ammansch* or "Amish."[8]

By 1736, or perhaps a decade earlier, Amish began settling alongside (and sometimes among) Mennonites in eastern Pennsylvania, especially in eastern Lancaster and adjacent Berks counties.[9] Thereafter most Amish lived near Mennonites, but not fully integrated into Mennonite communities. When Amish sought more and cheaper land they did not, like some Mennonites, migrate southward into Virginia. Instead some went to central or western Pennsylvania and then to Ohio. There too they usually lived near Mennonites. In the twentieth century most Amish would graft into one or another Mennonite branch. Amish history and Mennonite history in America are inseparable.

SEPARATE FROM THE "WORLD"?

As the nineteenth century began, Mennonites were somewhat buffered from the world. In eastern Pennsylvania, where most resided, one buffer was English-speaking Quakers and other fellow pacifists. Even more effectively they lived in a womb of Pennsylvania-German culture. Scholars write of different kinds of Pennsylvania Germans: the "church" people (primarily Lutheran and Reformed); sectarians (mainly Mennonites, Dunkers, Amish, and Schwenkfelders); and, by the 1790s, the revivalists (Methodist-oriented groups, especially the United Brethren, and after 1800 the Evangelical Association).[10]

Such distinctions are often useful, yet they can make the Mennonites and other "sectarians" seem more separated than they were. With other Pennsylvania Germans, Mennonites shared a dialect learned in the Palatinate and known in America as "Pennsylvania German" or "Pennsylvania Dutch." Religiously they shared broadly the language of Pietism. Sometimes they shared pulpits, especially at funerals. In their schools (often in or by their meetinghouses) they frequently cooperated with Pennsylvania-German neighbors, including the "church" people. The schools in turn taught the language and outlook of Pietism. Intermarriage was extensive, with intricate family networks across church and sectarian and revivalist lines. And in daily life Mennonites and Amish constantly mixed with their neighbors in mills, distilleries, markets, and shops.[11]

Even attire and pacifism did not draw formidable lines. At the turn of the nineteenth century Mennonite ministers preached against fashion and in 1805 at least one revivalist, Jacob Albright, main founder of the Evangelical Association, warned Mennonites and Dunkers in Pennsylvania's Lebanon County that neither their "large farms and earthly possessions" nor their "peculiar dress and outward plainness" could save them. Yet there is not much evidence that clothing caused early-nineteenth-century Mennonites and Amish to stand out sharply. "Church" as well as sectarian ministers preached against superfluity and display, and their people responded.[12] As for pacifism, the general mood of Pietists was pacific even if most did not make nonresistance a doctrine the way Mennonites, Amish, and some other sectarians did. The phrase "the quiet in the land" has been used for Pietists as well as for Mennonites. Records of fines during the American revolution show that in eastern Pennsylvania not only pacifist sectarians but many "church" Germans declined to fight.[13]

If Mennonites and Amish had much in common with fellow Pennsylvania Germans they shared also in the new nation's life and expansion. As the revolution and the war of 1812 opened lands for settlement beyond the Allegheny Mountains, some of them moved west. Consider Amishman Joseph Schantz, or "Johns," founder of Johnstown, Pennsylvania. In 1767 as a young man of about eighteen he immigrated, apparently from Switzerland, and went almost immediately to southwestern Pennsylvania, to the Somerset region and a place called "Glades." There he accumulated land. Then in 1793 he sold it and moved a few miles north into Cambria County, where he purchased more than five hundred acres. Here he built a cabin and in 1800 laid out the beginnings of the city which now bears his name. But he himself remained a farmer and moved some ten miles away.[14] He did not give Johnstown his own name but used an Indian one, "Conemaugh."[15] Perhaps his choice reflected Amish humility. Yet as a land developer he followed an American pattern. What was more American than to possess Indian lands?

About 1790 other Amish people stopped farther east, in Mifflin County—along a tributary of the Juniata River in central Pennsylvania's Kishacoquillas Valley. There, in what the Amish call "Big Valley," they established one of the most thriving (and schismatic) of Pennsylvania's Amish settlements.[16] Throughout the nineteenth century central and western Pennsylvania communities such as Big Valley and Glades and nearby Garrett County in western Maryland were notable departure points for Amish moving west.

Mennonites also shared in early U.S. expansion. As the eighteenth century closed they established several rather strong settlements in western Pennsylvania along a stream known as Jacob's Creek. Farther west than the Amish, the Jacob's Creek communities were in Westmoreland and Fayette counties, about forty miles southeast of Pittsburgh. Just before the American revolution Scotch-Irish people had pushed into the area. Mennonites went with a second settlement line. Yet some of them, arriving by the mid-1780s, apparently were only about five years behind the retreat of Indians.[17]

In the 1790s more came, arriving from Bucks, Chester, Berks, Lancaster, and Northampton counties in eastern Pennsylvania; Bedford County in central Pennsylvania; Maryland; and Europe.[18] Economically, they soon prospered. For instance, after arriving in 1799, a Christian Stoner started a saw mill and eventually added

Nützliche und Erbauliche

Anrede an die Jugend;

Von der wahren Buße, von dem Seligmachenden Glauben

an JEsu CHristo, und der reinen Liebe zu

GOtt und seinem Nechsten.

—

Nebst
der Gehorsame der Worte GOttes, und der reinen
übergab der Seelen, an die Hand GOttes.
Vorgestellt in Frag und Antwort.

Wie wird ein Jüngling seinen Weg unsträfflich gehen?
Wenn er sich hält nach deinen Worten. Psalm 119, v. 9.

Gedruckt im Jahr
M DCCC IV.

Courtesy of Mennonite Historical Library

Title page of Christian Burkholder's *Nützliche und Erbauliche Anrede an die Jugend* (Useful and Edifying Address to Youth—first printed 1804).

cabinetmaking, coffin-making, and undertaking.[19] In 1800 an immigrant's son named Henry Oberholzer arrived from Bucks County with a veritable tribe: his wife, twelve sons and daughters, seven sons- and daughters-in-law, and thirteen grandchildren. One son, Jacob Overholtzer (or "Overholt," as the name evolved), became a skilled veterinarian.[20] Another, Abraham, built a steam-powered flour mill and established a distillery that eventually made "Overholt" a well-known brand of whiskey. Although apparently his children all left the Mennonite church, distiller Overholt remained in the congregation and was one if its trustees.[21] As craft and business people (and as farmers), early nineteenth-century Mennonites in new western communities were part of the nation's expansion.

However, some moved to Canada. In 1786 a few Mennonites from eastern Pennsylvania began migrating to "Upper Canada" or what later became eastern Ontario. After 1800 more went, especially to neighborhoods in the region of present-day Kitchener. Mennonite lore—for instance, an 1895 history of Ontario's Waterloo County by a Mennonite named Ezra Eby—has said that a major reason they moved was loyalty to the British crown. It is true that during the American revolution Mennonites had little quarrel with the British and little enthusiasm for revolutionary slogans and issues. Staunchly pacifist, they sometimes felt the wrath of patriots. But since few of them left for Canada until after 1800 the timing hardly suggests that many went as British loyalists. Their greater motive was land. Their moves were not much different from other moves to western Pennsylvania or Ohio.[22] Having migrated over much of Europe, Mennonites easily ignored a political boundary in North America. They were Mennonites far more than nationalists.

As the nineteenth century began, other Mennonites and Amish moved into Ohio. In 1802 members of a Virginia family named Sager began buying land in the state's extreme northeast corner, Trumbull County. For down payment they used $300 worth of silver coins they had carried from the Shenandoah Valley in saddlebags. Family folklore says that at first Trumbull County was so raw that it took three days' walking through the wilderness to go to town and back for flour. The line of Indian removal was so close that for five or ten years Indian people occasionally stepped into Mennonite houses. At least one Indian spoke enough German to pronounce "*Messer*" when he wanted a knife.

In 1808 the Sagers' father, Gabriel, a minister, moved from Virginia at age 74. He organized Ohio's first Mennonite congregation, albeit one which disbanded about 1816. Meanwhile in 1810 from the Sagers' Virginia community there came some Dunkers (fellow Pennsylvania-German pacifists with Anabaptist and Pietist roots). The Dunkers began a congregation that thrived, partly by winning over quite a few of the Mennonites.[23] The Trumbull County experience was typical: movement as extended family; a struggling congregation, even one that failed; intertwining with other pacifist Pennsylvania Germans; and following the frontier closely enough to profit quite directly from Indian removal and national expansion.

Amish also moved closely on the heels of Indian removal. Folklore of Holmes County in eastern Ohio says that in the early days Amish settlers traded bread to Indians for venison. The tradition says they considered the meat unsanitary and threw it away, yet traded in order to have good relations.[24] In any case in 1808 and 1809 in Holmes and neighboring Wayne and Tuscarawas counties a few families settled and began what eventually became the world's largest Amish community. The first arrivals were not from eastern Pennsylvania but from the Somerset region. Meanwhile Mennonites and Amish transplanted themselves also to other Ohio counties—for instance, Columbiana and Stark, beginning in 1806 and 1810. Soon more and more were coming to Ohio directly from Europe. By 1819, Amish families from the Alsace region of France had established themselves as far west as Ohio's Butler County, north of Cincinnati.[25]

Back in Switzerland in the rugged Jura Mountains, where Anabaptists had settled earlier to escape persecution, the decade 1810-1820 was a time of famine and hunger. So quite a few Mennonites emigrated. A family or two settled in Pennsylvania but others took the advice of some Amish and went directly to eastern Ohio. There they began a community in Wayne County.[26] Their choice set new patterns: moving directly from Europe to the West without first settling in Pennsylvania; and continuing the Swiss dialect rather than learning Pennsylvania German. But if the Jura Swiss began new patterns they also benefited from an old one: Amish and Mennonite mutual aid. The first four Jura families received help en route from a Mennonite minister in Holland. Arriving in the U.S. they stayed with Mennonites in Pennsylvania's Lancaster County at least long enough to clean off their trip's accumulation of lice, and sent news back to Europe that Lancaster Mennonites had generously given them "butter, meat, bread, and vegetables." From Lancaster they went to Mifflin and Somerset counties, to Amish people who also gave them "much to eat" and took no pay.[27] Mutual aid transcended longstanding Mennonite divisions: north-European versus Swiss, and Mennonite versus Amish. The treatment of those Jura families foreshadowed a massive generosity in the 1870s to aid a different kind of Mennonites, some 18,000 who arrived in North America from the Russian empire.

Moving with the nation's expansion led some Mennonites and Amish away from their faith. In 1784 a Jacob Nessley, reared Mennonite, settled near the Ohio border in what is now West Virginia. He and his wife became Methodists. In 1806 near Charleston in present-day West Virginia there lived a Mennonite widow named Ruffner—probably Ann Hiestand Ruffner, formerly of Virginia's Shenandoah County. One of her sons became a Lutheran and another a Presbyterian, or at least he married one. Some of her grandsons became Presbyterian ministers.[28] Thus did some Mennonite families see their offspring drawn to the American mainstream.

As in Trumbull County, Mennonite congregations sometimes failed. Others succeeded, more or less. In Pennsylvania's Somerset County one congregation, Blough, developed well. But another, at Springs, near the Maryland border in the same county, almost died out. Founded in the 1780s, the congregation was reasonably healthy until about 1808. But by then two of its early ministers had died and in that year a third, Joseph Gunty, joined the revivalistic United Brethren. The congregation survived but for decades was rather sickly.[29]

Mennonites and Amish who migrated as the nineteenth century began did not try to build communities radically separate from neighbors, or radically communal. Unlike later "Mormons" they did not seek out remote valleys to be alone; and they bought land individually or as families rather than as congregations. To be sure, in 1815 a half-dozen Lehigh County, Pennsylvania, Mennonites, led by one Andrew Ziegler, formed a joint-stock company to raise $100,000 to buy the holdings of a commune named Harmony in western Pennsylvania. (The Harmonists were moving to Indiana to establish New Harmony, the more famous community they later sold to the Scottish utopian Robert Owen.) But Ziegler's venture languished—partly, it would seem, because the investors preferred to divide the land and live on separate farms rather than in the settlement's town.[30] In many other places Mennonites and Amish settled densely enough to form what may be called Mennonite or Amish communities. Yet they did so within the flow of American westward migration and with ordinary American patterns of landholding. They were not highly separated.

REVIVALISM AND HUMILITY

If some currents pulled Mennonites and Amish toward mainstream economics, others pulled toward mainstream religion. Especially revivalism. But in religion Mennonites were more resistant. They altered their theology to express a fresh dissent both from revivalism and from much of the mood of American life.

Revivalism in America had begun in the 1720s and '30s and in various places had produced a "Great Awakening." The colonial awakening's first wave affected Mennonites and Amish only indirectly.[31] But by the late 1700s some were being attracted. Two notable converts were Martin Boehm and Christian Newcomer. Boehm, born in 1725, grew up in a Mennonite congregation called Byerland, several miles south of Lancaster, Pennsylvania. There he became one of the congregation's ministers and in 1759 its bishop. Yet he worried that he lacked a real message and assurance of salvation.

According to an account he wrote much later, one day while he was plowing the word *verloren, verloren!* (lost, lost!) kept coming to him with every round of the furrow. In desperation he stopped his horses, knelt in the field, and begged God to save him. Thereupon a "thought or voice" assured him, " 'I am come to seek and to save that which is lost.' " Boehm later remembered that he experienced a new joy. Soon he described his experience to his Mennonite congregation, moving many persons to tears. Now, he later recalled, Scripture which had seemed "mysterious, and like a dead letter to me, was plain of interpretation.... Like a dream, old things had passed away, and it seemed as if I had awoke [*sic*] to new life, new thoughts, new faith, new love."[32]

Christian Newcomer, born in 1749, a resident of Maryland who had been reared Mennonite and joined the faith in Lancaster County, Pennsylvania, gave a similar testimony. He too spoke of conversion alone in a field, although with variations such as calling on God as he was choking on a peach stone and afraid he might die.[33] Actually Boehm's and Newcomer's conversion testimonies followed a rather standard revivalist pattern: desperate feeling of lostness, being alone while in crisis, a voice from heaven, and sudden experiential assurance of salvation. Such accounts are similar enough to suggest that, over time, the memories of even honest and sincere people may have reshaped themselves a bit to fit the pattern.[34]

In any case neither Boehm nor Newcomer found a place as a revivalist within the Mennonite church. Boehm's fellow bishops and the Byerland congregation let him preach apparently for more than a decade after his experience at his plow, but about 1777 the bishops silenced him. He claimed later that his offense had been to associate with English-speaking Christians. But the bishops' formal charges at the time were rather different. The charges ranged from an obscure one that Boehm had taught that Satan was of benefit to humans to a more understandable one that he had united with Christians who "allow themselves to walk in the broad way." He was aligning himself, his fellow bishops said, with those who swore oaths and practiced warfare "in direct opposition to the truths of the Gospel and the teachings of Christ."[35]

Boehm did associate closely with Methodists and with a like-minded Reformed minister named William Philip Otterbein. Gradually a "United Brethren" denomination emerged with Otterbein and Boehm as its founding bishops. In time Christian Newcomer also became a U.B. bishop, and a much-traveled and beloved circuit-riding leader. On his journeys he often stayed with Mennonites or Amish. Some Mennonites and Amish followed him into the U.B. fellowship, especially in settlements away from the larger Mennonite and Amish communities, settlements mainly in central or western Pennsylvania or Maryland.

Among those who joined the U.B. were some preachers, for instance, Joseph Gunty at Springs. In at least one case, in Pennsylvania's Lebanon County, almost a whole congregation made the change. Meanwhile a colorful horse racer named Samuel Huber, reared Mennonite, became a vigorous U.B. camp meeting preacher. Unhumbly and aggressively, Huber liked to tell stories of bodily tossing out rowdies or of talking down pompous, unawakened clergymen.[36] Early in the century revivalism had not yet entered the Mennonite and Amish churches: those who chose its style and theology had to depart. But it was a challenge, drawing some away.

At least partly in response to revivalism, Mennonites restated and subtly altered their theology—by a new emphasis on humility. Through much of the coming century humility theology would dominate. The outlook of that theology was quite at odds with the mood and emphasis of revivalism. More broadly but less directly it was at odds also with a youthful, boastful, expansionist U.S. nation.

Adequate research on the roots of humility theology has yet to be done. No doubt a main root leads back to the Pietism which Mennonites brought with them from Europe. One has only to read parts of *Wahres Christenthum* by Johann Arndt, an early German Pietist who died in 1621, to find phrases which became code words for the humility talk of Mennonites in nineteenth-century America—words such as *Armuth* (weakness, poverty), *Sanftmuth* (meekness), and

Demuth (humility itself), or on the negative side, *Hoffart* (pride, arrogance) and *Weltliebe* (love of the world).[37] But careful study will almost certainly show differences between Pietistic and Mennonite use of those words. It will probably show that most Pietists used the words more subjectively—in connection with initial repentance and yielding to God, or what they emphasized as the *Busskampf* (repentance-struggle)—whereas nineteenth-century Mennonites used them quite *objectively*, testing humility more by observable criteria such as styles of life, work, attire, furnishings, political approach, and other practical expressions.

Most Pietists were still children of the Protestant Reformers whose main concerns had been the forensic-salvation ones of initial forgiveness, justification, and renewed relationship with God. Mennonites were children of Anabaptists. Anabaptists also had been concerned with those initial steps. But their somewhat greater concern was what followed: namely, Christians' objective new life and walk.[38]

If one root of the humility theology proceeded from Pietism, a second no doubt grew out of Mennonite and Amish experience. At mid-eighteenth century the first and most important Mennonite author in the colonial era, a Franconia-area bishop named Heinrich Funck (d. 1760), had hinted of what was to come. In a short section of a book published posthumously in 1763, he had asked why nonresistant Christians were no longer suffering. His answer: they should live more humbly and quit striving for political power and other forms of status. Then, inevitably, they would clash with the world and suffering would return. Funck's test of faithfulness was still the old Anabaptist one of suffering. To him, humility was only a means. However, his words were ironic. He himself was a man of wealth and stature in his community and by no means a sufferer. That irony must have made him uneasy.[39]

Fifty to a hundred years later Mennonites and Amish had shifted to making humility itself the central test of faithfulness.[40] No doubt lack of suffering helped bring the change. Suffering as the test of self-giving, self-yielding discipleship just did not fit the American experience. Shortly after Funck wrote, Mennonites and other pacifists did suffer a bit in the American revolution, as patriots ostracized and fined them and restricted their voting and other civic freedoms.[41] However, such suffering hardly compared to sixteenth-century Anabaptist loss of home, loved ones, and life itself. Still, if a theology of suffering was hardly relevant in America, a theology of humility was relevant, and ever more so. National rhetoric and law favored unhumble eighteenth-century ideas of individualism, enterprise, and emergent, aggressive nationalism. In America the marks of humility could be the objective signs of Christian faithfulness. They could be signs that Christians were standing against the ways of the world.

In 1804 a Mennonite bishop named Christian Burkholder, living in the Lancaster County, Pennsylvania, Mennonite heartland, published the century's most important document of the new humility motif. Or rather he and fellow Lancaster conference ministers published it, for it appeared bearing the endorsement of twenty-seven ordained men. The small book, actually written in 1792, took the form and had the title of an *Address to Youth.* In it Burkholder had a hypothetical but perceptive youth pose earnest questions he wanted answered before he would join the Mennonite church. Burkholder provided the answers—in a manner simple and pastoral yet often profound and sometimes eloquent.[42]

Burkholder's *Address* became a basic Mennonite document for the humility era. In its first year it came out in a second printing.[43] Throughout the nineteenth century it would reappear often: in eight more printings in German, and, beginning in 1857, four in English.

Clearly a purpose of Burkholder was to strengthen Mennonites against revivalism. Yet in a day of harsh religious polemic the author's tone was loving and gentle. Nor did Burkholder oppose the revivalists at every point. He himself was quite Pietistic[44] and wrote as if to instruct his hypothetical youth in personal, individual salvation. Pointedly, he explained the new birth. But by emphasizing humility he gave the new birth a certain meaning. He did the same with conversion, the salvation process, holy living, and devotion to Jesus.

Replying to revivalists he resisted the idea of public testimonies and all tendency to measure new birth and conversion much by inner, subjective experience. "Boasting much of ourselves is the work of the old man," he warned; "the enemy tempts us with self-exaltation . . . in the divine life, trying to persuade us that we have had much experience, much more than we really have had."[45] As evidence for new birth Burkholder instead put forward a list of objective fruits. Heading his list was a shift from pride to humility.[46]

Along the way Burkholder included venerable Mennonite themes such as nonresistance; nonconformity in clothing and other appearance; discipline according to Jesus' words in Matthew 18; reminder of past Anabaptist and Mennonite suffering, persecution, and scorn; and obedience and faithfulness to Jesus.[47] Concerning salvation he used the language of Christ's shed blood. But he used it to point to Christ's love[48] more than, as a revivalist might, to describe a formal transaction between the sinner and God. For a symbol of salvation Burkholder looked to Jesus' lowly manger at least as much as to his cross.

Concluding a section on new birth and regeneration he invited readers to that manger. To it, he beckoned, "we are to direct our course." For Christ "has given us in His birth, doctrine, and life, an example of childlike humility. Those who are born of Christ have become partakers of His nature and virtues." In that message God extended his mercy and gave Christians " 'a lively hope.' "[49] Such was the call of Burkholder and the Mennonite leaders who endorsed or reprinted his work. They called people to come to Jesus, the example for humble living, as much as to the Christ sacrificed at Calvary.

Until about the 1870s humility would be a key to the way Mennonites and Amish thought about Christian faith—and about themselves in relation to the world. Of course nineteenth-century revivalists also spoke of humility. But like the Pietists, revivalists were more likely to emphasize the subjective: the inner, spiritual submission necessary for initial repentance.[50] While not ignoring its application to repentance Mennonites saw humility more as a foundation of obedience and a righteous Christian life.

* * *

The humility emphasis and its anti-aggression put Mennonites somewhat at odds not only with revivalism but with the mood and character of the American nation. In the colonial period, North America had been kind to Mennonites and Amish. There, as in few places in Europe, they had found not only freedom from outright persecution but also a place to establish peaceful communities. There they had been able to interweave faith, political protection, social acceptance, and modest but real economic well-being into an integrated and attractive whole. To a degree the American revolution had interrupted that well-being. Yet as wartime leaders go, the patriots had been remarkably tolerant and well-being had returned.

Mennonites and Amish appreciated the new American nation. Yet they also retained a strong sense of being a called-out people of God. And their humility outlook was at odds with much of American religion, individualism, and nationalism. So they began the nineteenth century with a mood like that of deacon Mellinger: desire for peace and hope for the nation, yet with mixed feelings toward it.

CHAPTER

2

LAND, WEALTH, COMMUNITY

"Nebraska is a nise country," wrote a young Mennonite woman named Saloma Overholt about 1885, to a young man, her cousin, who lived at her former home in a rural area north of Philadelphia. "I no you would likit hear." He might get a farm for half the cost back home and not "haft to work haf as hard." And "their is lots of good Looking young Ladyus hear."[1]

As the U.S. nation expanded westward in the nineteenth century, Mennonites and Amish moved with it. Their motives varied and so did their movements. Their eyes were open for economic gain and on the whole they prospered. Yet there were limits to their economic desires, limits imposed partly by faith. Especially, they were cautious about going into business.

LAND AND OTHER MOTIVES

If one word had to explain the westward migration of Amish and Mennonites, it would be *land*. Yet the impulses were not simply economic. That was true both of those who moved within North America and of new arrivals. New arrivals came mainly from south Germany and Switzerland. In the early nineteenth century Swiss immigrants continued to come from the Jura Mountains in the canton of Bern. Continuing a pattern of not stopping in Pennsylvania or learning Pennsylvania German as most earlier immigrants had done, they built up their Swiss-speaking communities around Kidron in Ohio's Wayne County and established new ones farther west at Bluffton in Ohio and at Berne in Adams County, Indiana.

Their immediate reasons for leaving Switzerland were economic: severe crop failure in 1816 and then several years of high prices and a "hunger year" in 1819, plus heavy taxes and lack of land for expanding families. Other changes also helped them move. With the close of Europe's Napoleonic wars and America's war of

1812, movement across the ocean became easier. Some Swiss laws continued to discriminate against Mennonites despite some legal reforms. And although a Swiss law let them hire substitutes, Mennonites chafed at a military draft.[2] Even the economic problems went back to religion. Their ancestors had moved to the Juras' poor land largely to escape persecution.[3]

If the Bernese felt pushed by conditions in Europe, some immigrants also felt America pulling them. Red-blooded youth sought adventure. In 1854 or 1855 an eighteen-year-old Gotthard Althaus left Switzerland and eventually settled near Bluffton, Ohio, where he married a daughter of Mennonites, Elizabeth Steiner. But community lore says that before he settled he traveled to Chicago and Wisconsin and elsewhere to see the West and Indians.[4] Twenty years later Mennonites from the Russian empire had solid reasons for coming. Yet some of their emigration fever arose because in 1872 four young men from wealthy Mennonite families of the Ukraine traveled to America, partly just to travel.

A few Mennonites or Mennonite-reared youths openly headed west to make their fortunes. Mennonites and Amish seldom spoke the language of pure self-interest, but in 1863 a young son of Mennonites in Pennsylvania's Bucks County did just that. He was Abraham (A. K.) Funk, a brother and future partner of John F. Funk, who in a few years would become a publisher and the "old" Mennonites' strongest progressive leader. In 1863 the U.S. was deep in civil war. A. K. Funk explained to his brother that if he stayed in Pennsylvania he would have to pay a hefty fee for military exemption. So, he said, to move would be "for my own interest—concerning nobody but myself." And he would stay "as long as prudence or self interest dictate."[5]

A half-dozen years earlier John F. Funk himself had moved west to lusty young Chicago to make his fortune. There he felt pulled two ways. With building and other activity booming he joined a prospering lumber business, dressed smartly, and attended a commercial college and various clubs and political rallies. The young man did not live simply. Yet at times he criticized wealth and reflected that the "followers of the meek and lowly Jesus" should keep themselves "plain and untarnished."[6] In 1859 he committed himself to be a follower of Jesus. He did so in a city Presbyterian church; but for baptism (and eventually for a wife) he returned to Bucks County and his Mennonite congregation.

Later, in 1864, he began a Mennonite paper in English and German editions: the *Herald of Truth* and *Der Herold der Wahrheit*. After three more years he moved to Elkhart, Indiana, near communities of "old" Mennonites and of Amish, and took up publishing full-time. In that move he surely put service to the church ahead of fortune. But earlier, even after his conversion, he was quite frank about pursuing wealth. In 1861, encouraged by his Mennonite father, the twenty-six-year-old Funk promised to "spare no effort and omit no exertion in the endeavor of accumulating a fortune." But (again with his father's prompting) he said he would do so only "by honorable means with industry and economy."[7]

Few admitted self-interest as boldly as did the Funks. Yet there were probably many who migrated for motives closer to that of the Funks than they admitted.

If fortune was one lure, another was to follow friends and relatives. A married half-sister of Funk was already in Chicago when he went, and he joined her husband as a partner in business. Pursuit of friends often was pursuit of mates. In 1864 a young Salome Kratz Funk went west as Funk's new bride. Her move was typical, except that most others went to farms, not to a city. Another prod for moving was dissatisfaction with one's church congregation. And more positively, from about mid-century onward, an occasional Mennonite or Amish voice (by century's end quite a few of them) said a reason for moving was to spread the gospel.

By 1866 a son-in-law of prominent Mennonite bishop Peter Burkholder of Virginia, Harry Rexrode, had moved apparently from Virginia to Indiana and then recently on to Missouri. Later he would go to Texas. From Missouri he reminded a friend that "Christ says go out in all the world and preach the gospel to evry [*sic*] creature." What was the gospel? Rexrode did not really say. But writing from Goshen, Indiana, in 1865 he had denounced crusaders against slavery. Referring to civil war times he was happy to say that at least "our church & the Amish," unlike other churches, "did not preach negro in this county."[8] To Rexrode and apparently to others, Jesus' words of liberty for captives did not imply literal freedom for black slaves.

More often than for evangelism, Mennonites or Amish moved because of home-church conditions. Among the descendants of Anabaptists the search for a more perfect and literal version of God's church went on and on. In 1851 Jacob and Barbara Oesch Schwarzendruber, immigrants from Germany, moved their family from Garrett County, Maryland, to Johnson County, Iowa. Soon ordained to be bishop, Jacob would be a strong Amish leader. According to tradition the couple moved partly to get away from unmarried couples' "bundling" (visiting in bed), a practice common among Amish in western Maryland and nearby neighborhoods in Pennsylvania.[9] Others moved for less colorful but more or less similar reasons. To move was a means of conflict resolution. Especially to the Amish a harmonious congregation was a large part of what faithful Christianity was about. And for both Mennonites and Amish, had not flight and migration often been their way of handling conflicts with worldly powers? So (whether theologically ideal or not) why not do the same to resolve their own conflicts?

In 1865 Mennonite bishop John M. Brenneman of Elida, Ohio, worried that his people were spreading too thinly. Materialism was causing too many to scatter in the West. Probably he could increase his own wealth by going, the bishop told a friend; but if a day like Noah's was coming, what good was more worldly treasure?[10] Although a somber man, Brenneman was a kind and gentle shepherd who saw keenly how scattering endangered the flock. He saw because he constantly traveled to serve the scattered. Due to his wide contacts, in the third quarter of the century he was as close as anyone to being leader of North America's largest Mennonite branch, the "old" Mennonite church. In his travels he sometimes served Amish, also. In 1873 he wrote publicly that too many Mennonites settled "one family here, and another there." They behaved too much like the biblical character Lot, choosing the best land no matter what Sodoms and Gomorrahs lay nearby.[11]

It would be much better, Brenneman continued, to go only where there was "a sure prospect of immediately organizing a church."[12] As the century progressed Mennonites became more mission-minded and soon turned the question of settlement into a low-key debate. For evangelism, was it better to move in clusters or more individually? In 1893 "D. Kauffman" (probably Daniel Kauffman, just emerging as a strong church leader) agreed with Brenneman. Writing in Funk's paper Kauffman admitted that some who scattered had built up prosperous congregations. But for every case of success "dozens of families have been lost sight of [and] their children carried off into popular churches."[13]

Leaders might warn. But if any nineteenth-century Amish and Mennonite people considered the ethics of migration, not many of them left a record of their ideas. A quest for land, land, and more land continued. Letters of Mennonites, men and women, continually returned to land, land prices, and land purchases.[14] At the end of the century when the U.S. government opened "Indian Territory" and began to build the state of Oklahoma some Mennonites, still hungry for land, took part in the famous Oklahoma land "runs."[15]

Yet Mennonites and Amish did not seek land simply for individual wealth. Unlike their religious cousins, the communal Hutterites, they accepted individual landowning. No doubt many moved mainly for profit. And surely quite a few accumulated much more acreage than they and their sons and daughters needed. Nevertheless, their reason for garnering land was not fortune for its own sake so much as to accommodate expanding families and communities. They wanted space for their kinds of communities—agrarian communities, and ones in which faith and a sense of peoplehood would remain strong. In many ways the communities were wholesome, offering a less fragmented existence than do most modern ones. They did not provide *shalom* for American Indians whom they displaced. Yet for its own people the Mennonite and Amish vision for community reflected something of the biblical ideal of people living in peace and well-being under their own vines and fig trees.

Unfortunately, real Mennonite and Amish communities were not in balance with nature. The successful ones expanded and demanded ever more soil. That imbalance and the constant engrossment of soil might have stimulated Mennonites and Amish to have deep second thoughts about how they were relating to God's creation and to fellow humans. This was especially true since they were so staunchly pacifist. Paradoxically, they often engrossed land recently acquired for whites in a frontier process that used considerable violence or the threat of it, or in which governments broke promises to American Indians or got land through scarcely disguised bribes to greedy or dispirited Indian or half-breed leaders.[16]

Benefiting from that process did not trouble Mennonites and Amish as it might have. In 1835 an immigrant Amish minister named Frederick Hage wrote back to Europe saying that several years earlier he had bought land in Ohio. Hired help was costly: $1 per day. The land itself was "nothing but forest." The government had only recently purchased it from "the Indians or wild people." But "if a man has youngsters or his own people, he soon has a nice farm."[17]

Often in other countries and other centuries Mennonites and Amish had moved to flee outright persecution or simply to survive. Under those circumstances if they moved onto land recently taken by violence perhaps their responsibility was not heavy. But in nineteenth-century America they made their own choices. Their communities were expansive. They seem not to have many second thoughts about participating in American expansion and benefiting from its violence.

MIGRATION PATTERNS

The way Mennonites and Amish followed the nation's migrations might appear chaotic. Yet there were some broad patterns. Overwhelmingly, Mennonites and Amish chose the North. A few may have chosen the upper South by following an eighteenth-century pattern of moving from eastern Pennsylvania and Maryland into Virginia's Shenandoah Valley; but others—like Harry Rexrode—left Virginia for the Midwest. Another pattern was not to make much of the border between the U.S. and Canada. Certainly some Mennonites showed political preferences for one nation or the other, or crossed the border deliberately for reasons such as to escape the U.S. civil war draft. But many moved across the international border as if merely to another state or province.[18] Their own Mennonite or Amish group had always meant more to Mennonites than had any political nation. Still another pattern was that in the nineteenth century small clusters and streams of immigrants arrived from abroad and went directly to Ohio or Illinois or elsewhere. Nevertheless, in the first half of the century most of those newcomers settled among or quite near Mennonites or Amish who did have eastern Pennsylvania roots. And in so doing they joined still another pattern.

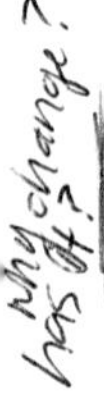

That larger pattern was to move along a path which extended straight west from Pennsylvania as far as Iowa, but from Illinois and Iowa bent down through Missouri and into Kansas. To be sure, by century's end Mennonites and Amish of Swiss and south-German origin would establish some communities along other paths: in northwestern New York, Canada, Nebraska, North Dakota, Idaho, Oregon, and elsewhere in the West. Mennonites and Hutterites coming in the 1870s from Prussia and the Russian empire would stray from the main route even more. But most of the internal migration followed that path.

In 1800 a Mennonite elder named David Funk and his wife, Catherine Godshall Funk, moved from Bucks County on the New Jersey border to settle in Westmoreland County in western Pennsylvania. The Funks had eight children, all but one or two of whom eventually moved on and left Pennsylvania entirely.[19] Such movement was quite typical. But there were other kinds of movements—for instance that of Frederick Hage, the Amish minister who wrote in 1835 of buying land acquired recently from "wild" Indians. Hage and his wife, Varone Asche (or Esch) Hage, had immigrated through Philadelphia in 1826. For five years they had lived in eastern Pennsylvania but had decided that land there was too expensive. Hage considered Canada, but that idea puzzled his neighbors. If he wanted to live under a monarch why had he left Europe? Besides, land was available in Ohio for only 2 florins, 57 kroner ($1.25) per acre. In 1835, $1.25 was the price of a bushel of wheat.[20] The various settlers, whether migrants like the Funks or immigrants like the Hages, helped to fill many a new locality. Eventually, for instance, the one where the Hages stopped—Holmes County, Ohio—became a large Amish community.[21]

By the middle third of the century many migrants were leaving not like David and Catherine Funk from the old communities of southeastern Pennsylvania but from newer ones such as in Mifflin, Somerset, or Westmoreland counties farther west in Pennsylvania or from western Maryland, eastern Ohio, or Upper Canada (present-day Ontario). In 1840 four Amishmen named Miller and Speicher traveled by riverboat from Somerset County to the lower tip of Illinois, up the Mississippi River to Iowa, then overland back across Illinois and Indiana. They favored northern Indiana, where the Indians had ceded the land only ten years earlier. So in 1841 two Miller and two Borntreger families (twenty-four persons) loaded wagons, went west, and began what became populous Amish communities in Indiana's Lagrange and Elkhart counties.[22]

A generation later in an economy inflated by the civil war a Lagrange County Amishman named Samuel Mast thought land was still cheap at $55-$60 an acre. Tell Joseph (probably his brother) to come and buy, he wrote back to Holmes County, Ohio, in 1865. The Amish had begun church meetings in his neighborhood, albeit "a little more old fashen" than "our old meeting in ohio." If Joseph planned to come soon, Mast would plant him some cabbage.[23]

In Elkhart County west of the town of Goshen and some twenty miles west of the Amish was a community called Yellow Creek. There Mennonites, not Amish, had settled. The first family arrived in 1839 and many more in the next decade. Thirty families settled in 1848 alone, at least twenty-four of them from Ohio.[24] Some stayed and some soon moved on. Careful study of early Yellow Creek families, their origins, and their movements probably tells much about Mennonite and Amish patterns in many another midwestern community. Yellow Creek Mennonites kept a strong sense of community. But the bonds were to fellow Mennonites, not to particular plots of soil.[25]

Thirteen early Yellow Creek families who stayed for some years became the core of the Mennonite community. Two of their male family heads were immigrants from Germany but most were from Pennsylvania, Ohio, and Upper Canada (Ontario). At arrival most of those men were from thirty to fifty years old. Many were relatives. The majority had been born in Pennsylvania but had children born in Ohio. Of the two immigrants the wives had been born in Pennsylvania and their older children in Ohio. Before stopping at Yellow Creek some settlers had made three major moves, and by 1860 six of the thirteen families had moved on. Yet all those moves were from one Mennonite settlement to another. The Yellow Creek Mennonites were not individualists—not Daniel Boones alarmed at seeing the smoke of neighbors' chimneys.[26]

The Yellow Creek Mennonites continually bought and sold land. At first they purchased modest tracts 20 to 160 acres in size, and by 1852 ten of the thirteen families owned from 54 to 480 acres. When the average for all rural Indiana was 130 acres their average was 182, although half still owned fewer than 130. Probably the main reason for continual land purchases was large families: the thirteen original ones had an average of 5.6 children, compared to 4.3 in all of rural Indiana. Mennonite households were not only couples and their children. Five of the thirteen included hired men or women, a grandparent, a boarder or family friend, or children of other surnames.[27]

Nor, apparently, did Yellow Creek Mennonites try to establish family estates which they might preserve generation after generation. Throughout America, Mennonites and Amish generally divided their wealth quite equally among all sons and daughters (or sons-in-law), thus dispersing their holdings;[28] and the Yellow Creek settlers did the same. Also, quite a few Yellow Creek sons took up trades or business—printing, painting, operating a sawmill, dealing in livestock or lumber, or keeping stores in the township center or a nearby town, Nappanee.[29]

The settlers' wills exerted little pressure on sons and daughters to stay in the community, and many of Yellow Creek's Mennonites moved away. But almost all who left went to another Mennonite community. Thus they showed that their sense of community was a bond of peoplehood, not attachment to hallowed soil. In the words of a scholar who studied the community carefully, they "carried their own sort of rootedness with them as they moved."[30]

The early Amish of Elkhart County were more or less similar. A researcher who studied thirteen of their core families (mostly in Clinton Township) confirmed that most of them had also lived in Ohio but had roots in Pennsylvania. When the settlers arrived most of their children had been born in Ohio. The parents arrived younger than did the Yellow Creek Mennonites. The average age of male family heads was only 33, female only 28. Perhaps because of their youth the Clinton Amish, once established, owned fewer acres on the average than did Yellow Creek Mennonites: 148 compared to 182. In 1850 their total wealth per person was an average of 43 percent above that of all Clinton Township. However without the holdings of one wealthy member named Schrock, the average would have been about the same as their neighbors'.[31]

From Ohio to Iowa and eventually beyond, Amish and Mennonites established other communities with innumerable variations. Until the 1870s, when new kinds of Mennonites arrived from Prussia and the Russian empire, almost all in North America were of Swiss and south German ancestry and most spoke Pennsylvania German. But of course those Bernese added their Swiss.[32] Moreover quite a sprinkling of new immigrants, especially some Amish, arrived via New Orleans and the Mississippi River rather than via the East. Some of those Amish went directly to Illinois (where Amish and Mennonites began to settle in 1830, even earlier than in northern Indiana). Others went elsewhere, especially to Butler County, Ohio, near Cincinnati and river transportation; but quite a few Butler County settlers moved to Illinois.

By 1860 a dozen Amish or Mennonite communities in Illinois were strong enough to have congregations. Almost all were in a belt whose length crossed the state east to west and whose width was from about mid-state to halfway to the Wisconsin border. A few Mennonites settled nearer Wisconsin, notably at Sterling and Freeport.[33]

In Iowa, Mennonites and Amish went first to Lee County, in a region in the state's extreme southeastern corner well served by Mississippi River transport. Mennonites arrived by 1839 and Amish by 1843. Like the Amish in Illinois quite a few early settlers were from Europe: Mennonites from the Palatinate or Bavaria and Amish from German-speaking areas of France (usually Alsace or Lorraine). Here too some Amish came via Ohio's Butler County.[34]

Quite a few of the Lee County settlers soon moved on to other places in Iowa, in Missouri, or eastward in Illinois. One reason was uncertain land titles left by vagueness in the way that Congress arranged for transfer of land from American Indians to whites in events closely tied to the so-called Black Hawk War of 1832. Meanwhile in the 1840s Amish land scouts, for instance Joseph Swartzendruber of Maryland's Allegany County and Daniel Guengerich of Ohio's Fairfield County (son and stepson of future Iowa bishop Jacob Schwarzendruber), began to promote what are now Johnson and Washington counties in Iowa. Joseph Swartzendruber admitted that it was a place where Indian bands still roamed, people were poor, and ague and other sicknesses were all too common. Nevertheless during the 1840s quite a few Amish peoople moved there. According to folk memory the Indians got on well with at least some of the Amish. The wife of a minister named Christian Raber favored them with pumpkin-butter bread and they liked the services of a blacksmith named William Wertz.[35]

Thus a broad Mennonite and Amish path from Pennsylvania to Illinois and Iowa was established. Even most of the immigrants from Europe found places somewhere along it. About mid-century the path bent southwestward. By 1870 there were seven congregations in Missouri—five Amish and two Mennonite, including a Swiss-speaking one.[36] Thence to Kansas. Soon most Mennonites in Kansas would be immigrants of north European origin, coming from the Russian empire and Prussia. But before the Russians, Mennonites of Swiss and south German origin began probing the state. By 1873 there were or had been scattered Amish and Mennonites in at least nine different Kansas counties. In one, McPherson County near the state's center, there was a Mennonite congregation. Soon the state had many more.[37]

Mennonite and Amish movements fit into much larger national and international migrations. And off the major path were those lesser ones. In the 1830s to 1850s a number of immigrants named Krehbiel plus relatives and neighbors with other surnames arrived from the Palatinate and Bavaria and—after establishing homes in upstate New York; Lee County, Iowa; Summerfield, Illinois; and elsewhere—went on to become important early leaders in the General Conference (GC) Mennonite branch. One, Daniel Krehbiel, with his wife, Mary Leisy Krehbiel, settled at Cleveland in Ohio. Yet even from that urban center he managed to be a GC conference leader.[38]

There were others with individual stories, for instance, Christian Reeser. Born in 1819 to an Amish family in Lorraine, Reeser left Europe in 1838 or 1839, traveling with three brothers and a sister, pushed by compulsory military service, pulled by opportunity. Being a draft evader he went as a stowaway. After disembarking at New Orleans he made his way upriver to Ohio's Butler County. There he worked for a time as a farmhand then moved to Delaware County in east-central Indiana, built a log cabin, and married a neighbor named Barbara Zimmerman.[39] Eventually railroad promoters bilked Reeser of some acreage and by 1857 he convinced a reluctant Barbara that they should sell the remainder, 380 acres, and move to Illinois. A friend of Christian Reeser had settled in Woodford County east of Peoria so the family went there.[40]

Ten years later, in 1867, Christian Reeser was ordained as an Amish minister. Yet even as he grew old he was restless and bought land in Arkansas with an idea of moving there. This time Barbara Reeser said no. Two Reeser sons moved but the parents did not.[41]

In a long life the Reesers established a home, enjoyed an honored place in their community, saw twelve of their thirteen children grow to adulthood, and accumulated at least 296 acres in Illinois plus 160 in Arkansas. Christian Reeser lived to be 103.[42] His longevity was not typical for Amish and Mennonites but other facets of his life were: residence in two or three states, setbacks, and hard work to survive and become established rather than for high consumption, all ending in moderate success. Success, but on the land: not mainly in business, not with a large fortune, and not with much abstract paper investment and wealth.

Many stories were sadder. In Iowa's Lee County starting a congregation took some time partly because robbers murdered the preacher, one John Miller.[43] In various places whole settlements and congregations fizzled. In the 1840s a Lancaster County Mennonite bought land in Pennsylvania's Mercer County, near the Ohio border at Youngstown. By 1848 he had attracted ten Mennonite families for a congregation of twenty. But the group was mainly an extended family named Bixler. Moreover potential leaders, Bixlers and others, soon moved on to Ohio, Indiana, and in this case even Tennessee. In 1862 the bishop, Joseph Bixler, fell on the blade of his sawmill and died. About the same time a brother and sister-in-law of the bishop lost seven children to diphtheria. Other families moved away—one of them to Ohio, then Tennessee, then Kansas, then back to Ohio. Remaining members gathered now and then for worship but gradually the congregation disappeared.[44]

Most false starts were farther west. In 1853, through contact with non-Mennonite Hollanders in southern Michigan, nineteen families left a very conservative congregation in the Netherlands and moved to near New Paris in Indiana's Elkhart County. As Mennonites directly from Holland they were, culturally, a lone group and apparently unique in all nineteenth-century America. The original members tried more or less to fellowship with Mennonites at Yellow Creek but with time their children dispersed and the settlement disappeared.[45] Elsewhere Mennonites suffered along with other Americans. In Kansas and Colorado in 1889 John Baer, a minister appointed by the GC church to serve scattered members, remarked on the conditions that were breeding populist protests in the West. Some regions, he said, had "absolutely out-boomed themselves." If people only would believe that "Godliness with contentment is great gain" there would be less spiritual despair.[46]

Women often bore the heaviest burdens of migrations. Barbara Zimmerman Reeser was surely quite sensible when she resisted uprooting. Yet she suffered far less than did Susanna Heatwole Brunk Cooprider. Born in 1839 and reared in Virginia's Shenandoah Valley, Heatwole married a Henry Brunk. During the U.S. civil war her husband hid to escape the draft. Meanwhile a small son died, and with time Henry escaped to Hagerstown, Maryland. Susanna heard of his whereabouts, took their baby daughter, made a hazardous wartime journey, and joined him. At the war's end the Brunks moved to Illinois. Then in 1873, eight years and five children later, Henry Brunk and a brother of Susanna, Reuben (R. J.) Heatwole, decided upon Kansas. So the family boarded wagons and traveled laboriously to a spot near Marion Center, about fifty miles west of Emporia.

Along the way Henry contracted typhoid fever, and in Kansas he managed only to build a crude shelter. Then he died. A month later the newly widowed Susanna Brunk had the "joy" of bearing a son. Within the next three weeks two daughters aged 5 and 11 also died. A two-year-old son, George R., came so near dying that his mother gave up and quit giving him medicine. Some time later an older son, Joseph, although still a child, was working and lost his left hand in the rollers of a cane mill. With the help of her brother R. J., Susannah Brunk struggled for her family's survival.

Then in 1878 she married again, this time to a widower named Matthias Cooprider. Cooprider had been United Brethren but now joined the Mennonites and eventually became a Mennonite minister. He brought three children to the marriage. Together the couple had three more children and, with the harshest days of pioneering past, lived together into old age.[47] In the twentieth century the son George R. Brunk became a prominent "old" Mennonite church leader, and a granddaughter, Florence Cooprider (later Friesen), became a medical doctor and an able and respected "old" Mennonite missionary in India.

Susanna Heatwole Brunk suffered more than most, yet other women also carried heavy loads. Sarah Gross was reared in comfortable Bucks County, Pennsylvania, but after moving with her husband, Samuel Lapp, to south-central Nebraska about 1876 or 1877 she had to run a boarding house for the meager funds it would bring. Relatives in the East hinted that the couple must not be managing well; but Sarah Lapp protested in 1878 that she and Samuel were "as savin as we could be" and their children were without Sunday clothes.[48] The young woman Saloma Overholt, who

Courtesy of Elaine Sommers Rich, *Mennonite Women* Herald Press, 1983

Susanna Heatwole Brunk Cooprider (1839-1909), woman of many difficult times in civil war Virginia and frontier Kansas.

praised Nebraska as a "nise country," bore a different burden. She was a niece[49] of the Lapps and so was with relatives, but she was sad. If only she could visit back in Pennsylvania when fruits were in season! In Nebraska, fruit was just too expensive. She did housework for "hie tone bankers" in a nearby town, and after a half-dozen years she grew tired of it. And she lamented that leap year 1884 passed without romance. Finally in 1888 she married a Thomas Higby, surely not a Mennonite. He was, said Sarah Lapp, "an entire stranger to us." Soon the couple moved 500 miles west into Colorado, away from the young woman's relatives.[50] Such were the burdens migration brought to Sarah Lapp and Saloma Overholt and many others.

The settlers helped fill and build a nation and the movement helped Mennonites and Amish spread their faith. The costs could be heavy. The Saloma Overholts and sometimes whole families or clusters of them were lost to Mennonites and their faith. Other settlers found strength in the faith. Sarah and Samuel Lapp reared four sons all of whom became Mennonite bishops. But many settlers still bore heavy burdens of work and financial despair.

Nonetheless a strong fabric of Mennonite faith and Mennonite community survived across the distances. And the migrations added richness and texture to that fabric. They especially made room for greater progressivism. It was in what was then the West that John F. Funk began to publish for an "old" and Amish Mennonites readership and to inject various ideas for change. Some of the new immigrants were quite conservative, for instance, the Iowa bishop Jacob Schwarzendruber. Yet on the whole they were probably more literate than Mennonites and Amish reared and educated in America.[51] And some, notably the Mennonite Krehbiels and some Amish who settled in Ohio's Butler County or in Illinois and Iowa, arrived with relatively progressive ideas.[52] Mennonites who came from Prussia and the Russian empire in the 1870s added another ethnicity and other experience and ideas to the texture, often ideas somewhat progressive

PROSPERITY?

How did New World Mennonites and Amish fare economically? Overall, did they prosper? Some hardly prospered. As the century neared its end the West betrayed a group of Amish who had moved in the 1880s to Lyons County, Kansas. A scholar who lived there as a lad later wrote that his people had been enticed by "land agents, free trips to Kansas, and glowing accounts of the fertility of the soil." However true his words, those Amish of course suffered also from the conditions that were just then driving many western farmers to populism. Like many others, the Lyons County Amish lacked drought-resistant strains of wheat and skill at dry farming. What crops they grew were often ravished by floods, insects, and dry winds. Because of a hidden lien on their title a bishop from Ohio and his family lost their land with buildings they had built. Most of that family moved eastward to Missouri. Other Lyons County Amish moved back to Ohio. Some who found an Ohio move too costly went to Nebraska.[53]

But Nebraska could be just as cruel. If salvation were not free few Westerners would be saved, mused one of those four Lapp sons, Daniel, in 1895. As a young traveling evangelist Lapp was seeing too many poor. The people had suffered two years of crop failure and were out of money for food, feed, and seed. Banks would lend no more and state aid went only to farmers who could put up some funds of their own. Lapp's own congregation sent a member east to seek aid. Its people did not like to beg, but seemed forced to. Whether the trip produced much truly Mennonite aid is not clear; but some of the Lapps' relatives sent $15, family-to-family. That was more than they expected, said the Lapps; the money would buy flour. Besides, it had begun to rain.[54]

Western poverty was a result not only of weather but of

expanded wheat production worldwide which brought falling international prices. Moreover some Mennonite and Amish people were poor at other times and places also. Times were hard, wrote William and Sarah Hendricks from northeastern Indiana in 1859. The family needed wheat, corn, and potatoes, and the price of flour was up to $3.50 per hundred pounds. To make ends meet, two single daughters were working in nearby Ft. Wayne. Two years later William Hendricks wrote to an eastern Ohio deacon named Jacob Nold and his wife, Catarina, telling of Sarah Hendricks' death. Others had paid for the funeral, he said, because he had no money.[55]

Life could be hard enough even in eastern Pennsylvania. In 1878 Mary Geil Landis, daughter of influential Mennonite minister John Geil of New Britain in Bucks County, had been a widow for twenty years. Meanwhile her children had grown to adulthood and marriage. Advising them she remembered how she and her husband had suffered from money problems forty years earlier. Only semiliterate but quick of mind, Mary Landis was more class-conscious than were most Mennonites. At the death of a certain woman she observed that "the rich must have thare share of trubl as well as the pore," and she lamented that her brother Samuel Geil, a cripple, was "as pore as poverty." But oh well, Christians could look forward to heaven, and "if we have to sufer here in this world it is nothing to wat our saver suferd fore our sake."[56]

Mary Landis did not want her sons to move west. By the latter 1870s she herself had gone to Elkhart, Indiana, to live with her only daughter, Anna, married to publisher Funk's brother and associate, A. K. With her intellectual vigor Landis was free with economic and other advice to both the men and the women of her family.[57] "I dont want eny more of my chilrun here in this malara [malaria] contry fore it is hard to be sick all the time," she counseled a daughter-in-law and a son (a farmer and former schoolteacher) in 1878. "I have studed the matter over care full." To come west "wouldind make maters any better." "It takes aman his life time before he has enny thing like he was use to have it at home." The son and daughter-in-law stayed in the East.[58]

Mennonites and Amish in nineteenth-century America might have become richer if they had pursued large fortunes more single-mindedly. After carefully analyzing eighteenth-century data a scholar named James T. Lemon has decided that eastern Pennsylvania's Mennonites and Amish (and some others) sought comfort and modest prosperity but were not modern capitalists going after every possible pound and shilling. They were not economic maximizers.[59]

In general Lemon's statement fits Mennonites and Amish in the nineteenth century as well.

Quite a few did go into business. But scholar David Apter, a student of modern business attitudes, has pointed out that in certain stages of a nation on its way to modernity many business people are neither traditional nor yet fully modern. They are not fatalistic about economic well-being, yet neither do they view wealth abstractly as if deeds and stocks and other bits of paper are wealth in themselves. Apter believed that along the road to modernity some business people stand between, connecting traditional groups in one part of the economy with more modernized ones in another.[60] Probably most Mennonites and Amish who took up business in nineteenth-century America were such intermediaries.

In any case such business people seem not to have been maximizers. Consider deacon Jacob Nold of Ohio. Born in 1798, in 1817 he moved with his parents and others from eastern Pennsylvania to Columbiana County in eastern Ohio. There his father, Jacob, Sr., became Ohio's first Mennonite bishop and a vigorous leader. In the Mennonite scheme the son's becoming a deacon fit nicely with being a successful farmer and businessman.

By his thirty-fifth year deacon Nold had acquired 250 acres whose taxable value was nearly $1000. Besides land, he owned mills, a distillery, and a press, to produce flour, whiskey, and linseed oil. By his early forties he owned more than 600 acres plus his mills, although in 1841 he quit distilling.[61] Tradition says he took at least one load of flour and apple butter downriver to New Orleans where he sold both boat and cargo. Another report says he shipped flour via New Orleans to Philadelphia. Documents show that in 1853, with the opening of state canals, he checked with a Pittsburgh firm for the cost of shipping flour east that way.[62] If Nold used the Ohio-Mississippi River route or the new canals he fit right into the patterns of American trade.

The American temperance movement may also have affected Nold's business. A report says that his father the bishop thought a nip of whiskey improved his preaching—but that Jacob the deacon quit distilling out of conviction. The tradition is that he stopped after one of his sons imbibed too much.[63] If he developed that new conviction he probably was listening to national voices as well. In the 1840s the American temperance movement was growing strong and shifting its message from moderation to total abstinence.

Temperance was not new to Mennonites, but for most, total abstinence was. Sixteenth-century Anabaptists had stoutly opposed alcohol's abuse. Christian Burkholder in his 1804 *Address to*

Youth had advised strongly against letting strong drink "become a habit" if it seemed to be one's weakness. For drunkenness produced "much evil," including discord and hatred. But by mid-century some Mennonite members and leaders were accepting the temperance movement's position.[64] As for the Amish their leaders addressed the question especially at a historic ministers meeting in 1866. Those leaders did not demand total abstinence; but, much like early Anabaptists, they warned against public drinking houses. They also opposed the making and selling of strong drink for profit. Yet indirectly they took note of the prohibition crusade, for they expressed sorrow that on this issue government seemed ahead of the church.[65]

Whatever Nold's reasons for getting rid of his distillery, in general he seems to have backed away from expanding his businesses. As he passed through his forties (and the 1840s) he apparently quit trying much to increase his fortunes. His taxable holdings leveled off. Then in the 1850s he lost some acreage,[66] no doubt as he helped sons and perhaps daughters and sons-in-law get established. (At the time of his death in 1864 he and Catarina had six daughters and six sons.) Perhaps his wealth leveled off because he declined in health. But the pattern appears also to be that of a person who sought tangible rather than abstract wealth, and who knew when he and his family had enough. He accumulated property but evidently not profit for its own sake. He was not a maximizer in business; and in that respect he was like many other well-established Mennonites and Amish.[67]

Among nineteenth-century Mennonites and Amish there were various church reformers, some of whom sought spirituality through stricter discipline. Strongly emphasizing humility, such reformers were generally skeptical of business and pursuit of wealth. Abraham Landis, a founder of a small "Reformed Mennonite" church in Pennsylvania's Lancaster County in 1812, complained that among other Mennonites "one brother sought the advantage of the other in trade" to the point of fraud.[68] At mid-century David Beiler of the same county, an Amish bishop who expressed an emerging Old Order view, warned against trying to serve God and mammon. As an aging man in 1862 he wrote longingly of bygone days when Amish supposedly had been less covetous and not so bent toward splendid and well-furnished barns and houses. Meanwhile the first major Old Order Mennonite, Jacob Stauffer, also of Lancaster County, complained in an 1850 book that even at the door of the meetinghouse Mennonite men talked only of crops, prices, and markets. Stauffer and others began a small, strict Mennonite branch that among other disciplines forbade members from demanding security when lending money to fellow members. After all, members of a body were bound to help each other. Nor were members to insure buildings through worldly companies, for Jesus had called his people out of the world. John Holdeman of Wayne County, Ohio, chief founder of the "Church of God in Christ, Mennonite" in 1859, shared similar ideas although with a touch of Methodistic revivalism. In addition he showed a streak of class-conscious populism and complained of landlords. Why he asked, should the landowner get half the crop? One-fifth would have been more right.[69]

By 1876 Holdeman and his church decided also that the Bible forbade lending at interest. Meanwhile in 1866 the Ohio conference of "old" Mennonites from which Holdeman had broken passed a rule to limit interest to 6 percent, and recommended none at all for loans to the "honest poor and needy." In 1874 and 1891 the Indiana Mennonite conference and the western Amish Mennonite conference ruled against exceeding "legal" or "lawful" interest rates.[70]

Not all those pronouncements were direct attacks on Mennonites' being in business. But they were surely less friendly to business than were some key decisions of more progress-minded Mennonites. The first major Mennonite church reformer on the progressive side was John H. Oberholtzer. In 1847 Oberholtzer supporters and the Franconia "old" Mennonite conference of eastern Pennsylvania parted ways, with the reformers creating a conference that later would join the GC Mennonite branch. In Canada about the same time, a minister named Daniel Hoch led a somewhat more revivalistic but also progressive movement. Neither Oberholtzer nor Hoch aimed especially to bring socioeconomic change; their interests were church renewal. Yet they struck some tones friendlier to business. For instance, Oberholtzer wanted the conference to keep records in modern fashion—much as modern business was rationalizing its methods.[71]

More directly, Oberholtzer and his supporters adopted a constitution for their new conference which said explicitly that members might call upon government "as God's minister" for "protection." Mennonites had long taught against suing at law. But Oberholtzer and his progressive conference permitted an appeal to the courts if the member and the church decided the cause was just. A written discipline of Hoch and his church repeated the Oberholtzer point almost exactly.[72] The new logic was the very American one of "rights" rather than the traditionally Mennonite one of accepting suffering. Lancaster area "old" Mennonite leaders sharply rebuked Oberholtzer for the change, insisting that it was "totally contrary to the teachings, life, and walk of our Savior and his Apostles."[73] Scarcely any change could have done more to let Mennonites enter modern business.

To Mennonite progressives some affinity with modern business was almost automatic. That was true both in a new conference such as Oberholtzer's or later among progressives who stayed in the "old" Mennonite and Amish churches.

In the century's last several decades, amid great business expansion, many Americans looked eagerly to businessmen as models for success, with glowing references to the "self-made man." Some Christians added to the din by insisting that economic success came through Christian virtue.[74] Among those voices Mennonites were usually quiet. Yet their progressive papers, especially a GC one called *The Mennonite* and an "old" Mennonite or "MC" one called the *Young People's Paper*, put in some words. Like other Christian papers they sometimes criticized business people they deemed ruthless, dishonest, or harsh toward the poor. But rather often they also reprinted articles by non-Mennonite authors who espoused the myth of the self-made man. An article in *The Mennonite* of 1897 declared that biblical principles were "universally acknowledged as indispensable in a prosperous businessman" and that practical businessmen turned to the Bible before "any other book as a guide in the management of their affairs." Articles in the *Young People's Paper* praised hardworking paperboys because, as one writer suggested, "they will make what everybody admires—self-made men."[75]

The progressives' words were not typically Mennonite. Much more typical was a Mennonite Brethren (MB) conference resolution late in the century. The MB church had originated about 1860 in the Ukraine as a Mennonite renewal movement under strong influence from European Baptists and continental Pietists. In 1883 their North American conference said yes, ignorance about business and desire to become rich often brought members to embarrassment and shame. But no, the church could not really forbid living in town or entering business. Just let the businesses remain simple. Let members not get too entangled, especially not in debt.[76] The MB resolutions expressed well the attitude of most nineteenth-century Mennonites and Amish toward business

BUSINESS, MENNONITE-STYLE

With that attitude quite a few Mennonites and Amish entered business in modest ways. In the mid-to-latter part of the century in Wayne County, Ohio, lived John Smiley (1822-1879), an Amish

Courtesy of the Archives of the Mennonite Church

Christian Zook (C. Z.) Yoder (1845-1939) of Wayne County, Ohio, progressive Amish Mennonite farmer, businessman, and church leader.

minister. His Irish surname had become an Amish one as an Amish family in Somerset County, Pennsylvania, had reared an orphan who became Smiley's father. At least in his latter years Smiley was a man of some wealth, not only in land but also with surplus cash. For instance, in April of 1868 he recorded that the taxable value of loans he had made to various people was $8,738. The names on his list suggest that some borrowers were Mennonites or Amish and some were other.[77] In a rudimentary way Smiley provided financial services which banks in his community would soon provide more formally and institutionally.

So also did Smiley's bishop, John K. Yoder (1824-1906). As an able religious leader Yoder led his large Wayne County Amish congregation, Oak Grove, with some caution. Yet, in a process from the 1860s to the 1890s which sorted emerging Old Order Amish from more progressive Amish Mennonites, he and his congregation took the progressive side. Yoder kept careful records. Business transactions he recorded in reasonably good English. Religious ones—baptisms and marriages—he noted in German.[78] No doubt the difference reflected his nurturing for each role. It also suggested a certain separation of religion from life.

Still, as a businessman he, like Smiley, operated in a rather rudimentary and pre-modern way, for he easily mixed roles as both an economic and a moral leader for his community. He built up accounts with many neighbors for grain he sold them or for services such as hauling or threshing. He seems also to have served as a guardian for various semi-dependent persons, keeping an account for each person or family showing advances of beef, pork, mutton, potatoes, sugar, salt, calico and muslin cloth, shoes, and occasionally coffee and tobacco. Some accounts were for persons with "Amish names," such as Yoder or Schrock; others were for people with English or Irish or Scotch-Irish names, such as Culbertson, Daughty, or McFaden.[79] John K. Yoder was in business, but perhaps not mainly for business' or profit's sake. Quite probably he did business mainly to carry on his larger role as religious and moral leader in church and community.

Somewhat more modern was Christian (C. Z.) Yoder (1845-1939). Yoder was a son of the bishop and the bishop's wife, Lydia Zook Yoder, and a son-in-law of minister Smiley and Mary Conrad Smiley. He also was a prominent promoter of Sunday school and other change. Late in life his church made him a deacon and then a minister. Meanwhile he carried on some of his father's and his father-in-law's roles as careful guardian of community dependents and lender of money. However, apparently more than did the earlier generation, he worked through the local Wayne County National Bank. In matters of farming and business he was thoroughly progressive, writing for farm magazines and promoting farmers institutes to improve agriculture. He experimented, especially with garden crops, and developed a thriving greenhouse business.[80]

Not all Mennonites and Amish, not even all leaders, did so well. In the 1850s just as John K. Yoder was getting established in Wayne County, an earlier bishop of his congregation, a Jacob Yoder, drew upon himself a shady reputation as a horse trader. Jacob Yoder eventually went bankrupt and moved to Indiana.[81] But Smiley and John K. and C. Z. Yoder managed to be in business in ways that fit their community and its values. They were leaders of both religious and economic life, and the status they enjoyed from one activity no doubt reinforced their leadership in the other. As Amishmen they could not have backed up their lending with lawsuits or threats to sue. No doubt most of their lending was to neighbors whom they knew and trusted or who needed help. Besides, in their kind of community Smiley and the Yoders surely could rely on social pressures far more subtle than the courts.

Other Mennonites moved to town; but even in town they were almost never at the front of economic modernization. In eastern Pennsylvania along the Bucks-Montgomery County line, the town of Souderton gradually emerged. It did so on land owned mainly by Mennonites. Many of the town's early business leaders were from two Mennonite families whose head males were Jonathan Hunsberger and Henry O. Souder, born 1804 and 1807. Although situated only about thirty miles north of Philadelphia, Souderton was slow to develop. In the 1820s it was still a town of small mills and crafts, not factories, not even rudimentary ones. About 1830 young Henry Souder began to build up a sawmill and lumber company. Wanting the railroad to come through and open wider markets, he offered land if a rail line would pass by his property. One came, but not until late in the 1850s. It was 1876 before the town got a bank. Until then Mennonites and others did business much as Smiley and John K. Yoder were doing in Ohio. Yet Souder and other Mennonites developed some key early businesses: saw and planing mills, a hotel, feed and general stores, and firms which bought hay from farmers to ship out and resell as horse feed in Philadelphia.[82]

In the 1870s and 1880s Souderton's pattern—a core of Mennonite businessmen in a town serving a rural area—reappeared also among Russian and Prussian Mennonites who settled on Western prairies. For them the pattern was all but inevitable. In the

Ukraine most of them had lived in Mennonite colonies which had begun to develop extensive milling, farm machinery production, and other agriculture-related businesses.

In America they settled in the West when the railroads were new and towns were sprouting. Often they settled so compactly that if they were to have supplies, farm implements, lumberyards, mills, marketing, and banking, then Mennonites would have to supply them. At the town of Mountain Lake in Minnesota, Mennonites began arriving in 1873 when by one scholar's account the town was only "about a dozen houses, three stores, and a railroad station." By 1900 nearly three hundred Mennonite families settled there. After 1874 most of the town's businesses were begun by Mennonites. By 1878 Mountain Lake had sixteen businesses from blacksmith shops to a saloon to two grain elevators. Of the sixteen, Mennonites owned nine (not the saloon).[83]

In Kansas, where most of the newcomers went, Russian and Prussian Mennonites, plus some earlier ones from the Palatinate and Bavaria, quickly established small businesses in towns such as Halstead, Hillsboro, Burrton, and Walton. It took more time to dominate Newton, a settlement already thriving as a rough cattle town located where at that time the historic Chisholm trail made its connection with the railroad. But with time Mennonites became prominent even in Newton's businesses. A few even moved beyond the usual lumberyards, implement stores, and local mills. In 1888 a Cornelius F. Claassen founded a finance company. A Herman Suderman began in 1886 to work in a local bank, left for some years to work in a Kansas City bank, then returned in 1902 to be vice-president of another Newton bank. In 1893 a "Mennonite Mutual Fire Insurance Company," first formed at Halstead in 1880, moved its address to Newton.[84]

Newton's most notable "Mennonite" in business was Bernard Warkentin. Son of a wealthy Mennonite miller in the Ukraine, in 1872 and 1873 Warkentin traveled extensively in America and sent back reports which helped stimulate fellow Mennonites to emigrate. Being very able he was soon a key figure in the immigration which followed. Meanwhile he started a mill at Halstead in 1873, and succeeded well. In 1886 he moved his main operation to Newton. There he became one of the wealthiest men in Kansas. By 1908, when he died, he had extended his milling businesses into Oklahoma, become president of a new bank in Newton, served as director of several companies ranging from a Halstead bank to a mill-insurance company in Chicago, and obtained stock in other corporations.[85]

However, Warkentin's story suggests subtle conflict between Mennonitism and modern corporate business. Long before he died, Warkentin broke with his Mennonite church. In 1875 he married a Methodist woman. She joined a Mennonite congregation before the wedding but in 1887 as the couple moved from Halstead to Newton they became Presbyterians. The Halstead congregation was progressive; yet even there, whoever entered the Warkentins' departure in the congregation's records added cryptically: "*Man war reich geworden!!*" (People have gotten rich!!) In Newton Warkentin still worked closely with some Mennonite leaders and supported institutions such as a new GC Mennonite college. But his own son attended Wentworth Military Academy in Missouri and his daughter an elite eastern institution, Bryn Mawr.[86]

Warkentin moved much deeper than most Mennonites into modern corporate business. Yet he remained largely what scholar David Apter described as an intermediary, operating between modernity and a more traditional community. By and large it was the same with Mennonite business people in the East. At Souderton, Mennonites only touched high finance and large-scale industry. From the 1860s onward the town did develop several cigar factories, apparently with Mennonite Henry Souder putting up some of the money for the first one. (Cigars, if not cigarettes, were acceptable to the town's churches, whether Lutheran, Reformed, "old" Mennonite, or "new" "Oberholtzer" Mennonite.) In 1885 Mennonite Michael Bergey opened a stocking factory. From its beginning in 1876 the town's bank included quite a few Mennonites among its owners and officials.[87] But of course such businesses were very different in kind and size from the steel, oil, financial, railroad, and other empires being built just then by people named Carnegie, Rockefeller, and Morgan.

Some Mennonites were close enough to cities and large enterprise that they could have participated in big business—had Mennonite culture groomed them for it. Near the end of the century, at the town of Scottdale precisely where Mennonites had settled along Jacob's Creek, a man named Henry Clay Frick grew rich supplying coke to nearby Pittsburgh's burgeoning steel industry. Eventually he became one of steel-maker Andrew Carnegie's most trusted lieutenants. Only two generations earlier some of Frick's ancestors were Mennonite. His mother's father was Abraham Overholt, the wealthy Mennonite distiller. One of his great-grandfathers was Abraham Stauffer, the community's first Mennonite preacher and bishop.[88] But apparently Mennonite values and culture did not fit Frick's kind of career.

David Hiebert

Label of brand of whiskey established by Mennonite Abraham Overholt of West Overton, near Scottdale, Pennsylvania.

Earlier in the century a Matthias Pennypacker had lived in Chester County, Pennsylvania. He was a Mennonite and son of a prominent Mennonite bishop. In 1814 he furnished money to republish his church's 1632 confession of faith. A decade later Matthias Pennypacker became president of what would evolve into the Reading Railroad. He also served in the Pennsylvania Assembly. But he married a woman of a decidedly non-Mennonite family: English, Episcopalian, Masonic, and military. And apparently none of his children chose his faith.[89]

A different story was that of Shem Zook (1798-1880). A progressive Amishman of Mifflin County, Pennsylvania, Zook gained a reputation wide enough that a Pennsylvania senator once lauded him from the U.S. Senate floor.[90] He promoted local public schools and published or helped publish various Amish-related writings, some from his own pen and some from others' (including a new German-language edition of Mennonites' ancient *Martyrs Mirror*).

Zook also helped promote a railway, at a time when no enterprise lay closer to the nation's development and modernization. At least oral tradition has said that he was the Pennsylvania Railroad's agent as it bought right-of-way for a set of tracks through his county. The tradition has said further that the company wanted him to run for governor—but that he refused, saying his faith would not allow it. In light of his activities and writings, the tradition is plausible. Obviously he was enough in touch with the Amish and Mennonite faith to believe that a nonresistant Christian could not wield governmental authority, especially over police or militia.[91] Perhaps he also knew how dismal were the ethics of nineteenth-century railroad politics.

Evidently Zook was closer to the nation's economic modernization than were most Amish. But like most Mennonites and Amish in business, he recognized a point where his faith set limits. A classical theory of Max Weber, early twentieth-century German sociologist, asserts that capitalist behavior grew out of a "Protestant" work ethic and Protestant unease about uncertainty of salvation.[92] By that theory nineteenth-century America should have had many prominent Mennonite and Amish capitalists. Mennonites and Amish certainly believed in the virtue of work; and for the most part they rejected nineteenth-century revivalism's offers of near-absolute assurance of salvation. But they did not produce such capitalists. Part of the explanation may be their Germanness.

Several scholars have looked into the social origins of top U.S. industrial leaders of the 1870s. Despite the myth that any ambitious boy could rise and become "a self-made man" they have found that only 2 percent were of German stock. (The other 98 percent, with exceptions too few to form a percentage, were of British ancestry.)[93] Careful study would probably also show that German-Americans generally had an attitude of wanting to pass on "a competency" and nothing more.[94]

But holding back from being large capitalists surely came also from Mennonite faith. Operating in the manner of the Pennsylvania Railroad or John D. Rockefeller or Henry Clay Frick meant wielding political and economic power in ways which did not fit with nonresistance and rejection of lawsuits. More subtly, those ways did not fit with humility. A strong theology of humility underlay the warnings of an Old Order thinker such as Jacob Stauffer against insurance, interest-taking, and preoccupation with markets, crops, and trade. The majority of "old" and Amish Mennonites did not apply the theology as strongly as did Stauffer; yet they believed and tried to practice it. Mennonites and Amish may have benefited from empire. But their theology was not suited to its front-line battles, whether the empire was the American West or the Standard Oil Company.

* * *

Indirectly, of course, Mennonites and Amish did help build those empires. They used railroads and kerosene. Above all they occupied land. Thus they helped build the American nation and its economy. But they did so without much idea of building a nation. Their vision was to build farms, families, communities, and congregations. That vision and the ties it created often survived even over long distances. Mennonites who stayed in the East may have tied their ideas of community to particular plots of soil. But many of those who moved showed that their sense of community lay more with the Mennonite and Amish people than with particular soil or place.

Yet the Mennonite and Amish idea of community required more and more land. In America the descendants of harried Anabaptists no longer moved to escape persecution or civic discrimination. Nor did they move simply to increase fortune for its own sake. They wanted enough land for comfortable community. The vision did not produce *shalom* for the peoples displaced. But for its own people it was something close to the biblical hope of everyone living peacefully on the family's own plot. Some caught a vision also of pursuing that comfort through business, but their German ways and their ethics of nonresistance and humility set limits to that pursuit. The vision was very agrarian. And Mennonite and Amish families were too large to be in balance with the land. So they sought more land, and moved.

CHAPTER 3

THE INNER LIFE

"When I was a child we spun our own wool and wove our own cloth," remembered Rosina Mosser Gerber, born in 1842, a daughter of Swiss immigrants in eastern Ohio. To clean and full it we spread it on the floor inside a circle of chairs and poured on warm soap suds. Then "the men and boys rolled up their trousers and . . . would kick and kick." When they got tired from laughing and kicking, others took their place. Or at apple cuttings, "after cutting about 10 bushels, we young folks would play games for two or three hours." And on butchering day four or five men chopped meat into sausage around one large block. As they worked "they would sing and laugh and have a big time."[1]

Inner life for nineteenth-century Mennonites (and Amish) was not mainly a matter of the struggles or ecstasies of individual souls. They were not individualists. Their ancestors had not imbibed much from the eighteenth century's so-called Enlightenment, so not many of them operated from the key ideas which underlay the American nation. Especially, they hardly held the eighteenth-century notion that individuals came before society. Nor did they have a concept that a person entered into relationships with others, or into the "social contract," only far enough for the individual's own convenience and advantage. Two central ideas of Mennonite theology worked strongly the other way. One was emphasis on the church, less as a mystical body than as a living, redeemed people of God finding its way in the real world. The other was humility. Leaders often invoked humility to instill submission to the group.

Both ideas worked against individualism and some members chafed. But few chafed as much as people steeped in eighteenth-century ideas of individual rights might expect. Nineteenth-century Mennonites and Amish hardly knew where the individual stopped and the group began.

What bound this or that Mennonite group together and gave its members a common inner life was not only piety and church discipline, but also folk pleasures and diversions. Nineteenth-century Mennonites and Amish lived lives that seem somber to entertainment-saturated people of the twentieth-century. But in fact they did "sing and laugh and have a big time."

LEICHTSINNIGKEIT

They did so against certain odds. Amusement as a gift to the human spirit was not an Amish or Mennonite idea. "A merry heart doeth good like a medicine" was not a favorite text. Quite the opposite. Preachers and other keepers of the faith constantly warned about merriment. Certainly the most discipline-minded did so. One complaint of Reformed Mennonites when they formed in 1812 was that leaders of the old church did not keep their people from playing cards or attending fairs and horse races. They further charged that even preachers drank at inns, places of disorder.[2] About mid-century Jacob Stauffer, David Beiler, John Holdeman, and others made similar charges.[3] Stauffer included a lament that Mennonites were playing "all kinds of musical devices to pass the time and amuse the sinful flesh." However, he wrote as if even his Mennonite opponents recognized that card-playing, horse racing, shooting matches, and going to dancing or fencing schools were sin.[4]

If such diversions were not positively harmful Mennonites thought they showed *Leichtsinnigkeit*, that is frivolity or (literally) light-mindedness. Of course many people in America—religious and other—warned against frivolity. But perhaps Mennonites and Amish were especially persistent, conditioned as they were by centuries of suffering and then a certain amount of Pietism.

Warnings against *Leichtsinnigkeit* came not only from strict traditionalists and disciplinarians and not only from long-settled Easterners such as Stauffer or Beiler. Some of them came from progressives and from late immigrants from the Russian empire. In 1849 the conference recently begun by John H. Oberholtzer and his supporters, the most progressive Mennonite conference in America, gave quite a strict ruling: that a congregation could discipline a person for merely attending a place whose main purpose was "foolishness," even without proof that the member had done anything which was bad in itself.[5]

In the mid-to-latter years of the century progressives began to publish periodicals and often included pieces with the anti-frivolity message. Many times they borrowed the pieces from non-Mennonite religious journals. In 1892 the GC branch's English-language *The Mennonite* quoted a New York clergyman who had written against church entertainment committees and other such "grinning ghastliness." Ministers, he said, should know that "lost men have more serious business than to laugh at so much an hour."[6] GC writers in particular were not inclined to mark Mennonite separation from the world by restrictions on clothing, furnishings, and such like. But anti-frivolity was acceptable for the purpose. Not to dance, play cards or billiards, attend the theater, etc., became their version of Mennonite nonconformity to the world.[7]

Progressives and traditionalists stood side-by-side against frivolity but their postures were not the same. Progressives were calling people away from folk culture to a more systematized and institutional Christianity. So they sometimes warned against pastimes on which traditional communities thrived. According to one scholar, Amish in Ohio's Logan County in the 1860s had made visiting "such a deep-rooted custom" that traditional ones treated it as "a duty with almost religious significance." But progressives who wanted Sunday schools on Sunday afternoons began to oppose the habit.[8] In 1889 Nathaniel (N. B.) Grubb, an outstanding GC progressive and pastor of one of the few urban Mennonite churches (in Philadelphia), spoke similarly. "Sunday visiting is not courted in my family," Grubb told a Sunday school convention; "it is an evil," he said flatly, "and only an evil."[9] Traditional communities wove piety with folk activity; progressives wove theirs with being active in programs and institutions.

Yet as they lived closer to a newer and more urban America with more institutionalized patterns, progressives recognized that new ways brought their own temptations. In the 1890s, as baseball was rapidly becoming an organized business,[10] progressives at the "old" Mennonites' first city mission (in Chicago) spoke out against playing on Sunday for money.[11] Meanwhile by the late 1880s Sunday school picnics aroused warm debate in *The Mennonite*.[12] The picnics were being avidly promoted by some people in the interdenominational American Sunday School Union,[13] and those who expressed doubts in *The Mennonite* probably felt threatened because they knew that Mennonite progressives often copied such organizations' ways. The doubters were afraid of turning religion into mere socializing and entertainment. And their imaginations told them what could happen if young people roamed among the bushes and woods. In 1897 one writer recounted that he had been at a picnic where the adults in charge ended up "leading young drunken men from the grove."[14]

Also, progressives were inclined to rely on teaching and nurture where traditionalists would go further and use church discipline. Speaking of what amusements and games to allow, an editor of *The Mennonite*, Anthony (A. S.) Shelly, told a GC ministers conference in 1895 that the way to proceed was not to draw "definite lines" but instead define "some underlying principles by which each individual must decide the question for himself." According to Shelly, one principle was never to choose amusements just to kill time. Pastimes should "serve . . . the higher end of physical or mental recreation and development." They should cultivate one's "social nature" in a healthy way.[15] Shelly's words would have pleased the American Ben Franklin much more than the Amishman David Beiler.

Yet in a broad sense traditionalists and progressives agreed against *Leichtsinnigkeit*. And if they agreed, so of course did the many "old" Mennonites and Amish who stood between. Their conferences made many a comment and ruling. In 1897 the Indiana "old" Mennonite body summed up what was a general consensus. It urged "that our people refrain from such amusements as croquet, baseball, birthday parties; also from visiting questionable places such as pool rooms, horse races, etc." Christians, the conference said, should "spend their time in things more profitable, such as Christian work, visiting the sick, relieving the distressed, [and] reading the Word and prayer."[16]

In 1876 the outstanding Ohio "old" Mennonite bishop, John M. Brenneman, even published a piece entitled "Christians Ought Not Laugh Aloud."[17] Unfortunately, some modern Mennonites with their twentieth-century biases seem to remember the able, hard-working, and deeply pastoral leader for that and nothing else.[18] In fact, his writing suggests that his fellow Mennonites were often quite merry. Else why was he concerned?

Brenneman enjoyed his own kinds of pleasure. In 1867 after one of his numerous visits to the scattered in the West, he recounted that among Swiss-speaking Mennonites in Missouri "we had three meetings and enjoyed ourselves well." Despite some ethnic difference the Swiss had received him kindly. Moreover they had sung so nicely that Brenneman wished all Mennonites would sing as well.[19]

MUSIC

Warnings against *Leichtsinnigkeit* did not stop nineteenth-century Mennonites and Amish from having good times. A few did so with musical instruments. In 1839 Joseph Funk, compiler of songbooks in Virginia, admitted that his son Joseph, Jr., had "prevailed on me to . . . get a violin" and had won the father over by "promising to devote it to sacred music." Since then the lad had learned to produce "sweet sounds . . . highly gratifying and cheering"—sounds that Joseph Funk said were good if they turned people toward heavenly hosts "harping on their harps and singing hallelujahs." What a shame, said Funk, that instruments were too often "perverted and abused to the vilest purposes!"[20]

Funk was not a typical Mennonite. A grandson of Heinrich Funck, the outstanding eighteenth-century bishop and Mennonite author, he himself became a printer (not to be confused with John F. Funk of Indiana, a cousin). More important, he worked with music theory and significantly refined American musical notation. And rare for Mennonites, he was an individualist. Thus he stubbornly refused the foot-washing rite even though Virginia Mennonites practiced it. After his first wife, a Mennonite, died, he married a woman named Rachel Britton, who was Presbyterian or Baptist and seems never to have joined Funk's church. Yet somehow Funk managed to stay in the Mennonite fellowship.[21] He was after all a man of obvious piety and gentle temperament.[22] Besides, his music won him a great following.

When Funk wrote his remarks about instruments no Mennonites or Amish in America used them in their churches. Many did not even allow them in their homes. One report says that Funk once had a visit from a bishop and several ministers who heard his sons play and did not have their thoughts turned heavenward. Instead they were quite critical.[23] Their logic may have been the literalist one that in the New Testament model for the church neither Jesus nor the apostle Paul had mentioned instruments and that Paul's instructions were to sing with spirit and understanding.[24] Or maybe they thought, as the "old" Mennonites' Indiana conference said officially in 1875, that rather than leading toward "humility," instruments fostered "pride and display."[25]

A great many Mennonites and Amish with Swiss and south German roots opposed musical instruments on such grounds. Yet others had them. One day in 1837 John Gehman, a farmer-preacher in Pennsylvania's Montgomery County, recorded spending $8 for "*ein hand orgel*" (a hand organ). Twenty-four years later he paid one George Kraus to fix what was probably the same instrument. With a touch more English he now called it "die Cordian." Meanwhile some Amish who immigrated from the German territory of Hesse to Butler County in Ohio arrived with pianos among their freight.[26]

Immigrants who arrived in the 1870s and '80s from the Russian empire also gave different answers about musical instruments. A small *Kleine Gemeinde* ("little church") group which in 1812 had broken away from the "big" Mennonite church in the Ukraine flatly forbade them—along with other frivolities such as smoking, drinking, and playing cards. But the MBs, from a later renewal movement and schism, thought instruments were quite all right and used them even for worship. In at least one Ukrainian village MB worshipers played a drum, "organs, flutes, violins, guitars and musical triangles" so loudly that the Mennonite mayor, no MB sympathizer, confiscated the drum. And among non-MB Russian Mennonite emigrants was the family of Cornelius Jansen, an emigration leader. Although thoroughly pious, in the Ukrainian port city of Berdyansk they had had a piano in their home. For their new home (at Mt. Pleasant, Iowa) they found a harmonium.[27] However, the Jansens were more wealthy, educated, and cultured than were many Russian immigrants.

While Mennonites in the Russian empire disagreed about instruments, they also disagreed about new tunes and new forms for vocal music. Early in the century apparently most congregations sang in unison and allowed disharmonies and flourishes which purists believed were not worthy of worship. As a result some schoolteachers and others introduced notation in forms known as *Zahlengesang* or *Ziffemgesang*—number or cipher singing, so called because the notation designated tones by numbers. The new forms were controversial, partly because many new tunes were much like popular, secular ones. Youths might like them but about the 1860s one music teacher recorded occasion after occasion when older persons walked out of church because of the new style. Nevertheless by the 1870s when Russian Mennonites began to emigrate to America, singing in harmony with one or another form of notation was taking hold. Some congregations, especially MB ones, were also beginning to use choirs.[28]

Meanwhile group singing with harmony and a different kind of notation was catching on also among Mennonites in America. They accepted such changes much more readily than they accepted instruments. Indeed singing was one activity which nineteenth-century Mennonite and Amish leaders let develop into something systematic and organized. Maybe that was because it obviously added to a sense of peoplehood. Words of historian Paul Wohlgemuth with regard to MBs could apply to Mennonites and Amish generally. Youths often gathered in homes "for an evening of singing," he said. The music "seemed to act as an important

Nr. 121. VM 16.

Es-dur, a=24. Thüringer Volksweise 1840.

1. Gott ist die Lie - be, läßt mich er - lö - sen, Gott ist die
2. Du füllst mit Freu - den die mat - te See - le; du füllst mit
3. Ich will dich prei - sen, du ew - ge Lie - be; dich will ich

Schlußreim.

Lie - be, er liebt auch mich.
Freu - den mein ar - mes Herz. Drum sag ich noch ein - mal:
lo - ben, so - lang ich bin.

Gott ist die Lie - be, Gott ist die Lie - be, er liebt auch mich.

[illegible]

Courtesy of Mennonite Historical Library

"Gott ist die Liebe," an example of Russian Mennonite cipher singing, 1840.

catalyst for . . . fellowship" and to serve a "spiritual ministry." And, "since participation in 'worldly amusements' was frowned upon," it also "served a vital social function."[29]

Two functions, social and spiritual. One evening in 1859, in Medina County, Ohio, a young Emaline Meyers attended a party of about forty young folks and later that night a "sparking frolic." Just what sort of "sparking" (flirtation, courting, love-making) went on she did not say. But she did record that on the next day, Sunday, she went to meeting, then to singing school in the afternoon, and then "to Henry Kindys," where she "staid all night and there was 12 young folks together there."[30] Was the "singing school" more like church meeting or more like the parties? In fact, gatherings for singing varied widely, ranging from "singings" to "singing schools." The "singings" were likely to be folkish social events of a still traditional people, the schools more often goal-oriented and devoted to rationalized order in keeping with emerging modernity.

In the singings the social function was exceedingly strong. In the schools and classes the functions came in various mixtures. A certain country merchant was paying attention to "Miss Annie," a friend wrote to young Mennonite John F. Landis of eastern Pennsylvania in 1867. He had brought her to singing school and it appeared that the two might be thinking of "embarking."[31] The great master of Mennonite-run singing schools was Joseph Funk in Virginia, especially in the 1840s and '50s. He thoroughly intended his classes to be educational and they were; but no doubt they also served the mating function. And a religious one: like virtually all singing-school masters Funk used and promoted hymnody. Later, in 1883, a certain Christian (C. H.) Brunk, one of Funk's Virginia successors, traveled to Mennonite communities of Indiana and Ohio to teach singing. When he did, John F. Funk's *Herald of Truth* endorsed him saying that "the church very much needs his services."[32]

Mennonite-run singing schools flowered especially in Virginia. No doubt Virginia led because: (1) there, much more than in eastern Pennsylvania and many other places, Mennonites were moving beyond Pennsylvania-German culture; (2) they did so when a singing-school movement much broader than Mennonites had recently taken root in the state; and (3) Joseph Funk.

Funk's home was in Rockingham County. Because of his work the tiny spot where he lived eventually was called "Singers Glen." Singers Glen was in the heart of a Mennonite community; but culturally and religiously Funk lived more on the margins. For instance, having a non-Mennonite wife, he seemed unperturbed if his children took up with local Presbyterians rather than with his church. And in his letters he sometimes referred to God as "Providence," "Omnipotent Love," or "Nature's God"—names which smacked more of eighteenth-century rationalism or later romanticism than of Anabaptist-Mennonitism.[33] Yet he was a son of a Mennonite preacher as well as grandson of Heinrich Funck. So he communicated between the nation's culture and Mennonites.

Doing so, he also did what virtually no other Mennonite of the nineteenth century ever did: deliberately and formally, not simply in folk-art fashion, he helped develop an American art form. The form was vocal harmony. Specifically, Funk helped develop musical notation from a "fasola" system of four shape notes to the do-re-mi system of seven.[34] In so doing he did not offer anything particularly Mennonite to the nation. But in the other direction he helped immeasurably to transmit a popular American tradition to Mennonites.

Songmasters had founded singing schools in America at least as early as the 1720s in New England, at first mainly to preserve Puritans' psalm-singing. The schools spread along with new settlement and by the early 1800s grew especially strong in the upper South. Church music was constantly yielding to all sorts of folk rendition; songmasters hoped to make it orderly and rational. Yet the schools themselves became a kind of folk institution. More and more the songmasters worked in village and country rather than in larger towns. Some city sophisticates looked upon the songmasters as crude rustics at best, greedy opportunists at worst. Yankee peddlers, one critic called them in 1848: charlatans who claimed to produce a singer for a dollar but mostly corrupted people's tastes.[35]

Joseph Funk was no charlatan. And in 1848 he was at the apex of his career. Born in 1778, in 1816 he had published his first book, *Choral-Music*, in German. *Choral-Music* taught three-part harmony, even though up to then Mennonites normally sang in unison. In 1832 Funk began publishing much more ambitiously and in English, with a substantial work named *A Compilation of Genuine Church Music: Comprising a Variety of Metres All Harmonized for Three Voices Together with a Copious Elucidation of the Science of Vocal Music*.

Eventually he and his successors sold the book as a singing-school text in thirty or more Virginia counties and a dozen states and provinces, some as far away as Georgia, Missouri, and Ontario. Funk died in 1862. By then he and his sons had produced ten editions apparently amounting to some 40,000 copies. Thereafter his sons and others published at least a dozen editions more, some for four rather than three parts. From an 1851 edition onward the title was its better-known one, *Harmonia Sacra*. In 1847 the Funks began to do their own printing, on a small press installed in the springhouse of their farm. That same year Funk and others on a committee of the Virginia Mennonite conference produced a hymnbook called *A Selection of Psalms, Hymns, and Spiritual Songs*, drawing some tunes from *Genuine Church Music*. It was the first English-language hymnbook published officially by any Mennonites in North America; and for some of its later editions Funk was the printer.

Joseph Funk was the first Mennonite in North America to own and operate a press. He and his family also began a journal, *The Southern Musical Advocate and Singer's Friend*. And he was translator for a 457-page compilation by a Virginia bishop named Peter Burkholder, *Confession of Faith of Christians Known by the Name of Mennonites* (1837). In 1851 he also published the first translation of his grandfather's *A Mirror of Baptism, with the Spirit, with Water, and with Blood*.[36]

Funk also taught singing schools. He may have done so as early as 1825[37] but some of his letters suggest he began, or began anew, in the 1840s.[38] Through the years he and his sons taught in at least ten Virginia counties. Finally in 1859 they began to advertise for young men "of high moral character" to come, live at the Funk home, and (for room, board, and tuition fees of $9 per month) learn music.[39]

That he wanted "high moral character" is no surprise, for along with music Funk taught piety. A teacher, he once wrote, should offer music as "not merely an entertainment, a pastime or a means of support" but as a service to God. He said that while the schools themselves were not worship, teachers should conduct them to improve worship.[40] Not all Mennonites saw them that way. In 1860 the "old" Mennonite conference of Virginia was not sure that the schools should be held in its meetinghouses and decided that each of its three districts could decide for itself. And in Pennsylvania Jacob Stauffer and his supporters saw nothing good in them. "It is not allowed," they ruled, "to go to *Kampmieting* [camp meeting] or singing schools and similar kinds of things where there is disorder . . . either by day or by night." Stauffer explained that his Mennonite opponents argued that "to the pure all things are pure," and that the schools were a form of worship. But, thought Stauffer, how could a child of God, born anew, see any good where there was such *Hochmuth* (pride), self-promotion, and "*Leichtsinnigkeit*"?[41]

Not all singing-school teachers were pious, fatherly Funks. In eastern Pennsylvania's Montgomery County one of them in the 1840s was a youthful schoolteacher named Garret Kolb. His name and the names of families where his school sometimes met were "Mennonite" ones and he sometimes attended Mennonite services. But at other times he played organ in this or that non-Mennonite church, or went to camp meetings, or danced to band music.[42] Since in the 1840s the Franconia conference did not keep records, its official attitude toward singing schools in Kolb's day is not clear. But forty years later it enjoined parents not to let their youths go to "singing schools in halls."[43] Mentioning halls but not homes suggests that the schools became more questionable when they moved out of the folk community and into town.

Whatever the case, in the 1880s and '90s the conference also ruled or warned against: women's surprise parties ["zerpreis partys"] and ladies' fairs; brethren joining in horse companies, fairs, and gambling; traveling to Atlantic City with organized excursions and their "hard class" of people; going to any such outing on Sunday; drinking at public sales or at bees such as for shoveling snow or raising buildings; stopping at an inn to eat after a cornhusking; and letting Mennonite ministers preach in any chapel which had a choir or a Christmas tree.[44]

By century's end singing schools as well as singings had become tradition for many Mennonites and Amish Mennonites. In 1898 Abram B. Kolb, editor of the *Herald of Truth*, thought American families spent too much money for piano lessons and for teachers who taught solo performance but did not train for congregational singing. Let those with high tastes sing Haydn, Handel, and Mendelssohn, advised Kolb. And for ordinary people "give us back the old-fashioned singing school, that teaches the young people of the community to read music, and to sing it together."[45] To Kolb singing schools were a beloved tradition, a tradition that built community.

For Mennonites the singing schools were an institution completely borrowed, not their own. Yet as Funk and lesser teachers taught them the schools gave Mennonites a mighty tradition: entire congregations singing a cappella in four-part harmony. That such singing took root and thrived probably shows something of how communal some Mennonite groups still were and how much they preferred blending over individualism. It also shows that Mennonites and Amish were not as separatist as the myths sometimes say. In the arts as in economics they had little taste for the more abstract and sophisticated forms America had to offer, nor did they strive for high status and prestige. But if an American folk pattern offered pious enjoyment and enhanced their common life they readily accepted it.

THE SIMPLE PLEASURES

In essence Mennonites and Amish were not pleasure-oriented but serious. Yet even amid serious purpose they often found pleasure. Church itself offered some variety. If a visiting minister preached, even rather light-minded young people treated the event as news. They did so especially if the stranger preached in English, as happened often in the last third of the century.[46] Camp meetings offered a less Mennonite diversion, but various Mennonites or their sons and daughters attended. For instance in 1874 a young woman went to Lansdale in Pennsylvania's Montgomery County, a town surrounded by Mennonite congregations, and reported that she heard a "colored" man preach a "very good sermon."[47]

Better accepted were Sunday schools, which progressives began to establish after about 1860. The youngsters "around here all seem to take great delight in our sunday school" and she was very glad, wrote a daughter of Ohio bishop John M. and Sophia Good Brenneman in 1868.[48] At first Sunday schools were not "evergreen"; that is, they closed during winters. So on a bleak October day in 1878, as her Mennonite Sunday school in Pennsylvania's Lancaster County closed for the season, a young woman named Maria Hershy lamented: "but what shall I do with myself on sundays?"[49]

If visiting preachers, camp meetings, and Sunday schools broke monotony, so also did some official public events. In 1864 in Ohio's Medina County a local hanging so intrigued Emaline Nold (formerly Meyers) that she rushed to tell a friend the details. Authorities had given the condemned man, convicted of killing a girl or woman with a dagger, time for last words. He spoke up in a "clear tone without a treble or a treamer" to declare again that he was innocent and wished God's forgiveness for his executioners; and he repeated the same even when the victim's father mounted the scaffold. Then, Nold recounted, the sheriff put him in the drop-chair, drew down the man's cap, and put the rope around his neck. Mercifully, Nold spared her friend the details of the drop.[50]

Government offered comic theater as well as tragic, for instance during the campaign to elect James A. Garfield as U.S. president in 1880. At Elkhart, Indiana, Mary Geil Landis had recently died; but the family and relatives of publisher John F. Funk followed the election with interest, including Landis's daughter, Funk's sister-in-law, Anna Landis Funk. "Last Sat- night a week ago we [Republicans] had our Illumination and Pro[c]ession" (torch-light parade), she observed. "They had the finest show of fireworks I ever saw. I . . . think of Mother how she would have enjoyed this campaign."[51]

Traditional folks found diversion in the rhythms of deaths, marriages, and the seasons. In 1842 an English-named storekeeper at Morgantown, Pennsylvania, in the Conestoga Valley on the Lancaster-Berks county line, was quite impressed at what followed after the funeral of an Amish neighbor named Christian Hertzler. There was, he said, "a general and pressing invitation for all to stay and dine." One hundred fifty or two hundred people stayed. The menu included "two whole quarters of beef . . . some 30 odd fowl and other things in proportion." The merchant was impressed again several years later when the wife of a David Mast died. "Upwards of 100 sleighs" came to the Mast home, he reported, amid orders "to have a barrel of flour baked up into bread so that there should be no lack."[52]

At weddings Mennonites and Amish not only ate but made merry. According to someone's memory the ceremonies of Swiss-speaking immigrants and their offspring at Bluffton in Ohio were huge affairs with great feasts. They were huge because almost all in the community were relatives and everyone came. In Pennsylvania a Reformed Mennonite apologist was partisan but no doubt at least partly correct when he said that a reason for breaking with the "old" Mennonites in 1812 was that their weddings carried "feasting, drinking and noisy mirth . . . to great extremes." However in 1867 an "old" Mennonite made the same charge against an Amish double wedding in her neighborhood. "Unnecessary sport," Susan Ressler of near Strasburg in Lancaster County described the goings-on. More than a hundred folks had come for "great play in the evening of the marriage day" and had "feasted and played alternately all night." To Ressler it was so much "nonsense." If Christians wanted to celebrate, let them be merry "*in the Lord.*" Some Amish leaders agreed. In the 1860s bishop Jacob Schwarzendruber of Iowa advised fellow ministers that if a wedding included a meal "then it should be done with caution and thankfulness toward God, for his gift and not in such an excess as has already happened!"[53]

Even hard or repetitive work could be occasion for celebrating; hence those strictures against drinking at snow shovelings or against visiting a drinking house after a corn-husking. In 1857 Emaline Meyers enjoyed a "paring bee" where seven girls had the company of fourteen boys. (She also enjoyed a fair in Akron, finding "a great many hansom things.") In 1844 in Montgomery County,

Jan Gleysteen collection

An example of nineteenth-century Fraktur work. Artist: Esther Bechtel. Date: 1829

Pennsylvania, the same Garret Kolb who taught singing and went dancing also had fun at "an apple butter party at Abraham Markley's," where youngsters had stayed "till two oclock," and at "a Husken at Samuel Schwenk's of about one hundred boys and girls." At century's end in 1894 the progressive editor of the "old" Mennonite *Young People's Paper* endorsed progress and said new farm machinery was good. But he admitted they spoiled some good harvest fun.[54]

In less folkish fashion quite a few Mennonite youths pursued self-improvement. "A good education qualifies a person to associate in Society," wrote an Amish schoolteacher of Iowa, Samuel (S. D.) Guengerich, perhaps in 1864 as he attended a term of normal school in Pennsylvania. Reading, Guengerich said, brought "pleasure and contentment," while the uneducated were likely to use time in vulgar ways.

In 1868 on a Sunday evening in Ohio the family of John M. and Sophia Brenneman had a spelling bee with the father pronouncing the words. Bishop Brenneman may not have liked jest and laughter but his daughter told relatives that "I just wish you could have all bin here. . . . We had such a good time of spelling and singing duch [German, of course]."

In 1853 and possibly many other years, in eastern Pennsylvania near a point where Bucks, Berks, Montgomery counties join, young men with "Mennonite names" such as Gehman, Schantz, Moyer, and Stauffer participated with others in a "Speak School." To improve their rhetoric if not their spelling and word choice they met weekly for debate. Some questions were: "Which is the Usefulest, Cattel or Horse?" "Which is the distroyablest? Water or Fier?" Or more seriously, "Which live in the most Oppression, Indians or Africans?" Working and attending commercial college in Chicago in 1858 young John F. Funk joined with other students to create a "mutual improvement society." They also formed a debating club which they appropriately named their "Franklin Junto," and explored such topics as hanging v. life imprisonment. And they debated the policies of Democrat James Buchanan, the nation's president.[55]

Twenty years later, at Elkhart, Indiana, where her father had established his press, it was the turn of Martha Funk, thirteen year old daughter of John F. and Salome Funk. She joined with neighborhood friends, some evidently from Mennonite families and some not, to form their own club. In keeping with current ideals for refined females they gave theirs an artistic rather than a political name: the "Literary Club."[56] In 1882, from another cultural angle, young men in the nine-year-old Russian Mennonite community at Mountain Lake in Minnesota began a cultural and debating club and called it a *Schiller Verein* after a great German poet and writer. Some church leaders objected; so they disbanded their club or transformed it into a chapter of the "Christian Endeavor," a prominent interdominational Protestant youth organization.[57]

Most Mennonite and Amish diversions were not so deliberate, organized, goal-oriented, or modern. When winter weather made for good sleighing, young people made much of the good news.[58] In 1878 in Bucks County, Pennsylvania, a young woman named Annie Kratz communicated the warmth of her family circle to a sister who had moved to Indiana. Annie Kratz's life was often monotonous: chores at home and, when work was available, sewing coats and vests at 14 to 40 cents per garment in what economic historians call a "mill and putting-out stage" of pre-industrial production. One suspects that Kratz was mostly waiting for romance. But meanwhile she knew the joy of family. "Father and Emma are singing Sophia is knitting," she informed her sister. "Henry went to Naces Mother is in the kitchen. this has been a pleasant day."[59]

Mennonite and Amish pleasures were seldom individualistic. It was rare for an Amish or Mennonite community to produce a recluse who took pleasure in being alone to read, write poetry, enjoy nature, or whatever. In central Illinois in the 1860s, '70s, and '80s there was one such Amishman, a Joseph Yoder who changed his name to the more German "Joder" and had a bent for poetry and philosophy. A greater problem was that he embraced a theology of universalism (God will save all, damn no one). Eccentric as he was, he became so controversial among Amish that his case helped cause some relatively liberal Amish to break away and take a road leading eventually into the GC Mennonite fellowship.[60] But such individualists were few. Even the frowned-upon pleasures of the frivolous were almost always group activities.

At heart, Mennonites and Amish were not pleasure-oriented people. But they did make merry and find communal pleasure.

SEX AND MARRIAGE

"Cousin Mary I could not advise you always to stay Single for A Dear Husband is the Companion and Comfort of life," wrote a young woman who had migrated with her Mennonite parents from Pennsylvania to Nebraska. Now, in 1879, she was married to a man not Mennonite, a John Hill. And she was thoroughly happy. "I never had eny Ide or thoughts that I was worthy of being treated with So much Affection and kindness," she continued. Also, she appreciated a "Nice quilt" which a cousin had given her. "I have taken lots of comfort Sleeping with my Husband under" it.[61]

Few Mennonites or Amish, even in private correspondence, alluded so freely to their sexual intimacies. Strict ones sometimes suggested that even within marriage sex was not among God's highest blessings to humans. Some who advocated the *Meidung* for church discipline ("shunning"—systematic social ostracism of members guilty of more-or-less flagrant sins) even insisted that a Christian spouse had to withhold sexual intercourse from a partner being shunned. Defending the rule Jacob Stauffer argued at mid-century that the spiritual union of Christ and church was after all a more important relationship for the Christian than was earthly marriage. A few years later Daniel Musser, historian and theologian of the Reformed Mennonites, cited the New Testament statement that marriage is "honorable in all." Yet he gave marriage second-rate status. It was, he said, an ordinance which was merely "carnal"—as compared to those which were "spiritual."[62]

Whatever their theology Mennonites and Amish were not ascetics to the point of denying their sexual natures. Large families of seven or eight or even twelve or fourteen offspring were common, regardless of which Mennonite or Amish group or branch. Even larger were some blended families, formed as widows and widowers brought children to second or third marriages. Cornelius and Catherine Wiens Hiebert, immigrant parents of twentieth-century MB leader Peter (P. C.) Hiebert, had twelve children—eight born in Russia and four in Kansas where they settled. In 1887 five had died and seven were alive. Then the mother died of "dropsy" (edema). The next year the father traveled to Nebraska and married widow Elizabeth Petker. She brought five children, had three more with her new husband, and then died. In 1893 widower Hiebert had fifteen Petker and Hiebert children living, besides the five who had died. Thereupon he returned to Russia and married a Katherine Warkentin, who had five. By then two of Hiebert's older children were married; but the new family still had to set table for eighteen offspring plus the parents.[63]

Sexual union occurred outside of marriage. In a very few cases it got mixed up with religious turmoil or ecstacy. For instance in the early days of the MB group in the Ukraine, several extremists discredited themselves with sexual sins.[64] Also, future church reformer John Holdeman seems to have fathered a child premaritally during a time of spiritual turmoil before his final conversion.[65] Meanwhile Amish leaders had to deal with unmarried couples' "bundling."

Despite a reputation to the contrary, bundling was not unique to the Amish nor did it necessarily involve sexual intercourse. It was an old practice (in times of scarcely heated houses) whereby courting couples or other persons lay side by side under covers in bed. In colonial America immigrants from England, Wales, Scotland, and Holland as well as from Germany practiced it. But of course it easily led to sexual conduct. In 1837 some Amish ministers meeting in Pennsylvania's Somerset County tried to stop it. They noted "excesses practiced among the youth, namely that . . . [they] sleep or lie together without any fear or shame. . . ." Such behavior, they said flatly, "shall not be tolerated at all."[66] Yet to stop it was not simple. One problem was that youths in Amish families normally did not declare personal faith, receive baptism, and formally become part of the church until near marriage or later. Another was that some Amish argued about as twentieth-century youth wanting to camp together might argue—that bundling did not imply impure thoughts or deeds. To an immigrant Amish writer, George Jutzi, such reasoning was unrealistic. Apparently it was equally so to those ministers in 1837. Speaking more or less to both problems, the ministers held parents responsible. When the practice "takes place with the knowledge of the parents and something bad happens," they ruled, "the parents shall not go unpunished."[67]

In 1865, to a much broader Amish meeting with ministers present from various states, the Iowa bishop Jacob Schwarzendruber repeated the ministers' warning. "The boys go into the beds with the girls when they perhaps have drunk too much," he lamented, "and evil consequences follow." Congregations found it necessary to deal with the problem, and illegitimate children were the proof. Sometimes, the bishop lamented, mothers even helped prepare the beds. The ministers who gathered in 1865 backed him fully. Once more they urged "all Christian parents to prevent all indecent acts of the youth in their houses."[68]

But bundling was too entrenched. In some communities it continued into the twentieth century.[69] Amish church authority was very congregational. Ministers meetings could warn and advise but had little power unless local bishops and congregations decided to act. And some parents argued that they could hardly forbid what they themselves had done as youths.[70] Among a people with strong reverence for tradition, such logic carried weight. Old practices did not necessarily yield to new words.

No group had a monopoly on sexual sins. In 1857 in a Swiss-immigrant congregation in Ohio a minister noted cryptically that a certain Kathrina had not taken communion. The reason: she had fallen into adultery and been excommunicated. Near Whitewater, Kansas, was a GC-affilaited congregation, Emmaus, founded in 1876 largely by Prussian immigrants. In its first seven years it excommunicated three persons for "immorality."[71]

A few sexual cases here and there by no means suggest a general pattern of license. The opposite was much more important. Amish and Mennonites recognized deeply that courtship, marriage, and who married whom were matters of profound concern not just to the couples but to community and church.

To be sure, by century's end progressive journals such as the *Young People's Paper* and *The Mennonite* approached courtship more individualistically and often tried to instill personal standards. To do so they printed short morality stories, hortatory pieces borrowed from the evangelical Protestant press, and the like. The rather conservative Lancaster "old" Mennonite conference did much the same in catechetical question-and-answer books published in the 1880s for use in Sunday schools and other nurture.[72] To rely on internal standards and controls was of course to assume that the social system was fluid and that individuals were likely to act more from their own wills than from deference to group authority. Such reliance was different from those Amish statements which held parents responsible for youths' behavior.

A simple way in which different Mennonite groups expressed the more communal view was to continue an old European practice (by no means only Mennonite) of "publishing the banns." That is, they required a family to announce a forthcoming marriage to the congregation a week or two in advance to give time for comment or objection.[73] The tradition was not at all unique to Mennonites. In any case it said clearly that to be fully human was a matter of merging properly into the community. Yet as the century passed Mennonites let it erode. Among "old" Mennonites an Ohio conference statement in 1867 seemed to assume it was still intact. And in Pennsylvania a Lancaster conference ruling of about 1880 said that "when members wish to enter into matrimony it shall be announced in the congregation. But an 1881 discipline of the same conference had no such rule; and the Indiana conference, reaffirming the practice in 1875, observed that "in some places the custom has been neglected."[74]

To neglect the banns was of course to move toward American individualism. So it is no surprise that one of the first bodies to relax the practice was the East Pennsylvania conference—the body which was created in 1847 by reformer John H. Oberholtzer and others and which eventually became a part of the GC Mennonite branch. Immediately in 1847 the conference ruled that its ministers were free to marry couples who had not published the banns. By the end of the century some "old" and Amish Mennonites agreed. For instance, in 1892 the Kansas-Nebraska Mennonite conference left the matter up to the couples themselves.[75]

Yet on the whole Mennonites and Amish of the nineteenth century viewed courtship and marriage as community matters rather than mainly as romantic affairs between individuals. The Amish—especially those inclined to keep old ways—were quite concerned that marriages be properly arranged through the church. By 1852 and probably much earlier, perhaps already in Europe, an Amish ministers manual by a Joseph Unzicker passed from hand to hand. Referring to how Abraham in the Old Testament sought a wife for his son Isaac, the manual declared: "This shows us how a youth should not run and go courting himself." Couples who did, it suggested, often acted dishonestly or made "a secret marriage or promise to themselves with endearing words." The manual upheld an Amish discipline which went back at least to 1779-1781 in the German Palatinate. According to it a person who wished to marry was to go tell the ministers and probably the parents also. A deacon was to do the actual proposing, or if not a deacon, then a minister.[76]

The rules were more than just an ideal. One day probably about 1860 or 1870 a young man in the congregation of Amish minister Christian Reeser in Illinois came while the preacher was butchering. The fellow offered to do the butchering so that Reeser could go ask a certain young woman on his behalf. Reeser went. Since the woman lived a distance away either she had to give a quick answer or Reeser would have to stay overnight. Reeser hoped to return. But she asked for time, and he had to stay. The young man, fearful that she was not saying yes, spent a tense night. But the next morning she readily consented. According to the account Reeser later learned that she had known all along she would say yes—but that "a man should be kept waiting at least one day."[77] The young man had followed the proper steps. The young woman managed to enter marriage with a small show of independence.

With careful diplomacy, in 1864 Barbara Beachy of western Maryland also showed some independence. Sometime that year the Iowa schoolteacher S. D. Guengerich evidently wrote to her in a way to suggest matrimony. Replying, Beachy wrote first about her congregation installing a deacon and then about the weather and the hay crop. Finally she remarked that apparently Guengerich "was going to Iowa and would like to have me go along." She supposed that was "a question to me"; but, she wrote, "I am not planning to take such a trip at this time." Still, it might "happen after all if it is the Lord's will," and she welcomed further communication. Then switching from German to schoolgirl English she added: "If this you see/ remember me/ that I your friend will ever be." She ever was. During the following winter Guengerich wrote a proper request to Beachy's father and obtained consent. The couple married and lived together for 63 years, until he died at 94.[78]

In some groups young people made quite a game of keeping their courtships more or less secret until time for announcement. A generation before Beachy's and Guengerich's courtship an Amish youth in Wayne County, Ohio, wrote lightheartedly but chastely to friends about some pairing he supposed was taking place back at his former home, Mifflin County in Pennsylvania. Through a female cousin he also communicated discreetly with a certain Lydia Kurtz, whom he then married. Elsewhere, at Kidron, Ohio, Bernese Swiss played a similar game. So, apparently, had a GC immigrant named Heinrich Friesen when he had courted a young woman named Helena Duerksen back in the Ukraine in 1859. Even among quite progressive youth in eastern Pennsylvania a vestige of secrecy about engagement and marriage seems to have persisted. "Astonishing news," wrote a sister of Salome Kratz Funk from Bucks County in 1872. John Landis and Huldah Shaddinger had gotten married even though during a visit with friends the previous Sunday the young man had not said a word of it.[79]

John Landis and Hulda Shaddinger may have been secretive because Shaddinger was Methodist, not Mennonite. What of marrying outside the faith?

Landis and Shaddinger solved the problem by joining the East Pennsylvania conference of "new" Mennonites.[80] Those "new" Mennonites accepted American denominationalism and its central idea that most of the churches were just different branches of true Christianity. So they gave explicit permission for members to marry respectable Christians of other faiths.[81] However, almost all other Mennonite and Amish groups (as indeed, for instance, Methodists and Quakers early in the century[82]) tried to prevent interdenominational marriages.

The prohibition operated widely. Throughout most of the century Swiss congregations in Ohio and Indiana excommunicated members who married outside the faith unless the member confessed to wrongdoing. In 1837 the same Amish ministers who denounced bundling also advised strictly against marrying non-Amish. No longer, they said, could they easily reinstate a member who did so. The member would have to show "true repentance and change of heart" and bring the partner into the Amish fellowship.[83]

As the century continued, some regional conferences of the "old" Mennonite church began writing down their decisions; and as they did, they often recorded decisions against marrying outside the church. Usually, however, they called not for excommunication but for a halfway penalty: "setting back" the violator until he or she confessed error. To "set a member back" was to forbid him or her from participating in communion and in church counsels. The question also arose among the MBs, especially at the 1889 session of their North American conference. Conferees cited many cases of members having married outside the fellowship; but after "long, earnest discussion" they reaffirmed an earlier decision to allow marriages only within. A larger number of Russian Mennonites who joined the GC branch were apparently more tolerant. In 1882 a Kansas GC ministers meeting, with some south German and Prussian immigrants present, as well as Russian, took up the intermarriage question. But they made no decision. Nor did the annual Kansas conference take up the matter in the next few years—in contrast, for instance, to that of lodge membership, which it staunchly opposed.[84]

Most Mennonites and Amish rejected an easy mood of you-go-to your-church / and-I'll-go-to-mine / and-we'll-walk-along-together. Did they therefore mean to deny that people in other churches were Christians? One very exclusive group, the Reformed Mennonites, took that position.[85] But they were a tiny group.

Most other Mennonites and Amish rejected the central idea of American denominationalism by which most mainline Protestant churches more or less accepted each other's validity. Yet they tried not to judge harshly. Nobody stated their thinking better than did Christian Burkholder in his influential *Address to Youth* in 1804. Burkholder said that marriage should be only "with the counsel, knowledge, and will of the parents, and the ministers and elders of the church."

Then he asked: but why "only . . . amongst members of one's own church? Are there not also many pious, discerning christians, who do not belong to such church?" Was the rule scriptural? To reply, he first made clear that he did not mean to pass judgment against other churches. But yes, the rule was scriptural. First, without considering one tribe of Israel better than another, God had commanded marriage only within each tribe. Second, the rule helped protect Burkholder's favorite principle, humility. To intermarry displeased the Lord because it tempted "carnal-minded youth" to respond to those who were "of reputation, or in authority." Third, Burkholder reminded his reader of Matthew 18:15-17—of Jesus' words on how to deal with conflict and maintain discipline within the church. According to Burkholder those words established a church order "which we are bound to enforce."[86] In modern words Burkholder meant that if the church was to have discipline and be what its Lord intended, it had to have clear boundaries.

Humility, a cohesive and disciplined faithful church, and rejection of a too-easy American denominationalism—Burkholder wanted to uphold those principles, yet not say Mennonites were the only true Christians. He connected the case against intermarriage to some of the most central ideas of nineteenth-century Mennonite outlook and theology.

Despite such belief Mennonites and Amish or their offspring very often did marry outside the faith. The rule against intermarriage caught them in the snare that waits for all morally earnest people, that of idealism versus reality.

Even official church decisions compromised the rule. The usual compromise was that of setting back but not excommunicating. Although no doubt sensible, mere setting back seems often to have been a way to restore violators after only routine confessions. Apparently those Amish ministers in 1837 were speaking to that problem when they ruled that they could no longer accept anything less than evidence of true repentance plus bringing the spouse along into the church.[87]

Some "old" and Amish Mennonite decisions were unclear or seemed to permit intermarriage. The Mennonite church in Virginia, whose members began very early to mix with United Brethren, Methodists, Baptists, and others, was remarkably lax on the question. In 1837 Peter Burkholder and Joseph Funk published a catechism along with a confession of faith. The catechism said merely that both partners in a marriage should belong to "the church of Christ."

Four decades later the Virginia conference said that to marry fellow Mennonites was "in all cases preferred." But claiming to reaffirm an earlier ruling, it nevertheless allowed marriage to others who were "in good standing in society and possessed of good moral character." Oddly, it did not even specify that a partner had to be a Christian. In 1865 the Indiana Mennonite conference enjoined marriage only to "a believer or Professor of Christianity." But then it added that a Christian should wed "only a fellow believer of the same faith." Where was it drawing the limit? Only against non-

Christians? Against all non-Mennonites, even Amish or Dunkers? In 1892 an Amish Mennonite (not Old Order Amish) conference rejected marriage to members of "so-called popular churches." It said that to achieve unity in both church and home, members should marry others "of the non-resistant faith."[88]

Complicating the intermarriage question was the fact that young people often did not declare their faith or join the church until after marriage. So according to Mennonites' theology of believers baptism they married as unbelievers. Surely the original Anabaptists had not meant believers baptism to become a device for freeing young people from church control. But for reformers to see how their innovations may work out in future generations has always been difficult. Such freedom was a side effect. And often it remained so until a given Mennonite or Amish group accepted a revival which harvested their youth and brought them into the church much earlier, as adolescents or even as children.

Couples often had non-Mennonite ministers perform their legal ceremonies. In 1875 Annie Kratz of eastern Pennsylvania informed her Indiana sister that a J. Shaddinger and a Sara Fretz had gone to Doylestown on Tuesday and gotten "married at Rev. S. M. Andrews." She supposed however that the next Sunday they would show up at the "old" Mennonite meeting at Perkasie.[89] That pattern—or an even more troublesome one by which couples did not return to the Mennonite meeting—must have tempted many Mennonite and Amish ministers to go ahead and perform the marriages of the as-yet-unbaptized. But conferences warned against ministers' performing weddings of unbelievers.[90]

By 1890 Amos Herr, a prominent minister in the Lancaster "old" Mennonite conference, was ready for frank compromise. "Why must our menonite children when they are united in the bonds of matrimony, be sent to those least esteemed in the church?" he asked a bishop privately. "We try to raise them up in the nonresistent [*sic*] doctrine in our Sunday schools, but when they get married, we must send them to those war ministers to get married."[91]

Or, Herr continued, if the couples turned to other nonresistant preachers—River Brethren or Dunkers—too often those ministers tried to win them over. If Mennonite ministers were allowed to perform the weddings they at least could admonish the couples to unite with their church. One could hardly argue that such marriages not made "in the Lord" were invalid, Herr reasoned; for if a non-Mennonite minister performed the wedding Mennonites did not demand a new ceremony before accepting the couple into the church.[92]

In the Lancaster conference only bishops could perform marriages. So Herr thought a good.compromise might be to let ordinary ministers conduct non-members' weddings while keeping the rule that bishops could not. If anyone said, "Let them become members then we will marry them"—of course "who of us would not like this"? But Herr thought that "we must take things as they are, often not as we would like to see them."[93] His argument was a rare one for Mennonites. Few Mennonite or Amish leaders explicitly advocated such concession to realism. Anabaptist-Mennonite theology made little place for compromise.

Yet Mennonites even conceded to divorce. To be sure, more often they did not. An Amish ministers meeting in 1867 was controlled by leaders who were mildly progressive, yet it counseled that the husband of a divorcée had to separate from her (although continue to support her) if he wanted to join an Amish congregation. The Indiana "old" Mennonite conference of the same year made a similar ruling. And in 1868 a sister conference in Ohio ruled very uncompromisingly: it said the gospel neither allowed divorce, even for adultery, nor let the parties remarry. In 1883 the "old" Mennonite conference of southwestern Pennsylvania refused to accept a man married to a divorcee whose former husband was still living, even though in the divorce she had been the innocent party. Among Russian Mennonites, also in 1883, the MB North American conference ruled very similarly. At first the conferees seemed ready to allow such remarriage. But after a lengthy discussion which the record says was sometimes sharp and sometimes gentle, they warned against presuming too quickly to know which party was innocent. It might be better, they said, to wait until God himself made the innocence more clear by removing the guilty one through death.[94] Did they really mean God would strike down the sinner?

Whatever the answer, such absolutist rulings were not the whole story. Not everyone among the "old" Mennonites agreed with the Indiana and Ohio conferences' absolutism in 1867 and 1868. Just two weeks before the Indiana decision the Virginia conference had ruled quite opposite. Virginians reasoned that if Jesus' words about fornication allowed a man to put away his wife the same logic allowed him to marry again. Moreover not only Virginians but the prestigious John M. Brenneman of Ohio had been present. In a public article early in 1868 Brenneman admitted that he had helped shape the Virginia statement. With remarkable research he also argued that Jesus' exception for fornication was authentic, not a later insertion.[95]

But Brenneman soon retreated. The Virginia ruling disturbed

various readers of Funk's *Herald of Truth*,[96] and Brenneman decided he was not speaking for the church. At about the time of the Ohio ruling he published an article entitled "I Beg Pardon." In it, in good Mennonite fashion he said that he had not meant to carry out his ideas "without the counsel and consent of the brethren."[97] For the moment the absolutists had won. But in the next seven years a schism occurred in Indiana and Ohio which took some Old Order-minded people, supporters of an Indiana bishop named Jacob Wisler, out of the "old" Mennonite church. With them gone, in 1875 the Indiana conference decided more liberally.

A man applying to become a Mennonite member was married to a woman who had divorced a previous husband for drunkenness and other misdeeds. The conference ruled that if the applicant confessed his sin and showed true repentance the congregation could accept him. It did not demand that he separate from his previously divorced wife. Even more remarkably it went on to say that the woman's earlier marriage was not one the church had to recognize: it had not been a godly marriage of Christians but only something made and broken by civil authority. The conference did not spell out the implications of that interpretation; but a dozen years later it took up the case of another applicant who had divorced a wife for adultery and granted him permission not only to become a member but also to marry a Mennonite woman.[98]

However, such liberality was not a final "old" Mennonite position. "Old" Mennonites in the nineteenth century agreed that if a person who was already a member of their church was the guilty party in a divorce, he or she had to be disciplined. But on the tougher questions of remarriage they found no common position. Moreover the generally more progressive GC Mennonites had the same difficulty. In 1889 their Eastern District (formerly East Pennsylvania) conference pondered the divorce question. One report says the conferees answered it by citing various Scriptures; another says they tabled the item "for future consideration." If they tabled it they seem not to have taken it up again at any time soon.[99] Given the GC style of church government, silence meant letting each congregation deal with divorce and remarriage as it saw fit.

Divorce touched Mennonite and Amish communities enough to trouble their leaders and demand practical response, yet the cases were few and isolated. A much more important pattern was that family ties and feelings of responsibility ran strong indeed. Some of the ties were economic. Amish or Mennonite men wrote wills one after another that provided for surviving wives, recorded numerous loans and financial aid already given to sons or daughters or sons-in-law, and spelled out in detail the inheritances of widows and offspring.[100]

Yet the ties went much deeper than only self-interest. Especially impressive were concerns that young people felt for parents. A young male schoolteacher or a young woman at home was willing to shape plans and perhaps delay marriage for parents' sake. A youth in the West longed to return east to see not only friends and cousins but especially her grandmother. In 1868 a young Levi Ressler in Lancaster County, Pennsylvania, longed to go west at least to Ohio, yet hesitated. He said he had no problem parting with "earthly things," but that "I have Dear old Grandparrents and Parents who cared for me when I was yet helpless and should I not care for them now in return[?] Yes Dear brother it would go hard to part with them." Similarly, in 1872 future Kansas GC leader David Goerz wanted very much to move from the Ukraine to America but felt a strong sense of duty to a poor and sick father. He and his wife emigrated only when a trusted adviser convinced them that they could help the father more from America because they would have more money.[101] Family ties were strong.

* * *

In their deepest convictions Mennonites and Amish remained serious and sober. Frivolity as an overall attitude or style of life was quite contrary to their faith. Some of them may have been too afraid of fun and some leaders may have warned against *Leichtsinnigkeit* more than was good for spirit and soul. But if they did, they surely also drew many persons away from what was superficial and cheap, and led them toward the more profound and lasting enjoyments of faith and family and secure community.

Mennonites and Amish stood in a kind of triangle. At one point were those who watched and strove lest pleasures get out of hand and become enemies of piety. At another were others who let their pleasures became more or less vulgar. At the third were some who seemed not to need the constant warnings. The third kind knew how to merge faith with the rhythms of laughing and singing and loving. For personal living that triangle was probably more important than the continuum from progressive to traditional. In any case, neither progressives nor traditionalists all stood at the same spot in the triangle.

Amish and Mennonite people in nineteenth-century America laughed and sang and loved, amid deep piety. The laughing and singing and loving enriched their communities' inner life and strengthened its bonds.

CHAPTER

4

PATHS TO PIETY

Demuth ist die schönste Tugend,
Aller Christen Ruhm und Ehr;
Denn sie zieret unsre Jugend,
Und das Alter vielmehr.

Pflegen sie nicht auch zu Loben,
Die zum grossen Glück erhoben?
Sie ist mehr als Gold und Geld,
Und was ist herrlich in der Welt.

To be humble is a virtue;
  and the one most fair
Of all adornments
  Christians wear—
Embellishing one's youthful days,
And even more the time of age.

Do we not give our praise and best
To that in which we find success?
Yet she is more than wealth and gold
And all the fame the world may hold.

So began a Pietistic hymn which was a favorite among Pennsylvania Germans in the first half of the nineteenth century. Christian Burkholder used it to conclude his 1804 *Address to Youth.*[1] Appearing as a poem in schoolbooks, in song, and elsewhere, the hymn fit nicely with German Pietism. Pietism (of the "capital P" kind) came from Europe, from reformers' efforts in the seventeenth and eighteenth centuries to revive a Protestantism which they thought had degenerated into formal ritual and fine points of theology. Wanting a warmer and more inward, experiential faith, the reformers cultivated personal devotion, Bible knowledge, fellowship, and holiness.[2] With time Mennonites and Amish accepted much of Pietism's outlook.[3]

PIETISM

By 1800 Mennonites and Amish had accepted so much from Pietism that ever since, many perceptions of what is "Mennonite" are probably at least as Pietistic as Anabaptist. To a mid-twentieth-century scholar named Robert Friedmann, in his well-known book, *Mennonite Piety Through the Centuries* (1949), that was a tragedy. Friedmann recognized that some of the early Pietists drew on Anabaptist sources. Also he admitted that Anabaptism and Pietism had major points in common—especially biblicism, concern for inner transformation and the new birth, and insistence on practical holiness in one's life. Yet Friedmann thought the two were quite different. Often they seemed to use the same words but with different meanings. Anabaptists began with a collectivist aim, to bring the reign of Christ; Pietists began with individual justification. Anabaptists had invited people to follow the "bitter Jesus" of cross, obedience, and suffering; Pietists called people mainly to a "sweet Jesus" of personal salvation, inner victory, and warm embrace. Anabaptists, in one of Friedmann's favorite phrases, had worked for "radical world transformation"; if Pietists worked for the world's betterment their first concern was nevertheless the individual's relation with Christ.[4]

Nineteenth-century Mennonites and Amish still imbibed some of the sternness of Anabaptism. Especially, they read their ancient book of martyr stories, the *Martyrs Mirror* (or, by its longer, more literal title, *The Bloody Theater, or Martyrs Mirror, of the Defenceless Christians . . .*). At least their more articulate leaders read it, and as the century progressed they helped reprint it three times in German and twice in English. Often they absorbed it and used it as an authority to the point that they cited exact pages much as they referred to Bible references. From it they absorbed an understanding of history which emphasized faithful remnants of Christians who had lived as beleaguered minorities among the vast majority whose Christianity was false. The remnants, a continuous string of them since the time of Christ, were various groups who had followed him in being weaponless (*waffenlos*) and defenseless (*wehrlos*). In other words the faithful were those who let themselves

Der
Blutige Schau-Platz
oder
Martyrer
Spiegel der Tauffs-Gesinnten
oder
Wehrlosen-Christen,
Die um des Zeugnuß JEsu ihres Seligmachers willen
gelitten haben, und seynd getödtet worden, von Christi Zeit an
bis auf das Jahr 1660.
Vormals aus unterschiedlichen glaubwürdigen Chronicken, Nachrich
let und in Holländischer Sprach heraus gegel
von T. J. V. BRAGHT.
Nun aber sorgfältigst ins Hochteutsche übersetzt und zum erstenm

EPHRATA in Pensylvanien,
Drucks und Verlags der Brüderschafft. Anno MDCCXLVIII.

THE
BLOODY THEATRE,
OR
MARTYRS MIRROR
OF THE
DEFENSELESS CHRISTIANS,
who baptized only upon Confession of Faith, and who suffered and died for the testimony of Jesus, their Savior, from the time of Christ to the year A. D. 1660.

COMPILED FROM VARIOUS AUTHENTIC CHRONICLES, MEMORIALS, AND TESTIMONIES, BY

THIELEM J. VAN BRAGHT.

TRANSLATED FROM THE ORIGINAL DUTCH OR HOLLAND LANGUAGE FROM THE EDITION OF [illegible],
BY JOSEPH F. SOHM.

ILLUSTRATED.

ELKHART, INDIANA.
MENNONITE PUBLISHING COMPANY.
1886.

Title pages of Martyrs Mirror. Inset: 1886 English edition published by the Mennonite Publishing Company in Elkhart, Indiana. Above: 1748 German edition published by the Ephrata Cloisters in Ephrata, Pennsylvania.

be vulnerable and suffer rather than be assertive and do harm. They were a sort of apostolic succession of the nonresistant.[5]

But unlike Friedmann, nineteenth-century Mennonites saw little conflict between martyrdom and Pietism. Some read a book of sermons first published in 1730 by a thoroughly Pietistic Mennonite minister of near Hamburg in Germany, Jakob Denner. Or they read books of verses, meditations, and stories for devotion and edification—a kind dear to Pietists. For a century Mennonites had produced such writings, with clearly Pietistic titles. A book printed in 1702 in Switzerland was called *Golden Apples in Silver Vessels, or Words and Sayings Beautiful and Useful to Godliness.* It easily mixed the martyr theme with sweeter Pietist ones.

Also in 1702 another Hamburg-area Mennonite minister, Gerrit Roosen, published a question-and-answer nurture book whose title translates as *Christian Conversation on Spiritual, Saving Faith and Knowledge of Truth.* Roosen mainly offered non-controversial Protestant doctrines and pious *Stillen im Lande* (quiet in the land) ethics rather than the earlier Anabaptist mood of vigorous dissent. He gave only token space to the ideas of being nonresistant and vulnerable, aggressive in faith, and ready to suffer.[6] Nevertheless, Mennonites in nineteenth-century America liked his work so well that they reissued it a dozen times, eight editions in German and four in English. Usually they bound it with reprints of Burkholder's *Address to Youth.*

More devotional than Roosen's book was another called *Die ernsthafte Christenflicht* . . . or (in full and in English) *The Earnest Christian's Duty: Consisting of Beautiful, Spiritually-Rich Prayers, Wherein Pious Christian Hearts at All Times and in Every Need May Find Solace.* Published as early as 1739 in southern Germany, and in America in 1745, the book included writings from the Bible and from Anabaptists and Mennonites, plus some from Pietists and spiritualists.[7] In the 1800s Mennonites and Amish or printers related to them reissued the work in the U.S. and Canada seventeen times. Not, however, in English: apparently it was more a favorite of traditionalists than of progressives.

Such works conveyed Pietism of a mild sort. Some Mennonites and Amish wanted more radical versions and read (among others) two prominent German Lutheran Pietists named Gottfried Arnold and Johann Arndt.[8] In the 1850s the reform-minded Mennonites John H. Oberholtzer and Daniel Hoch apparently collaborated to reprint a work by Arnold. Its title meant "Experiential Theology."[9] Meanwhile even schoolchildren read Arndt's works, for instance, a 1605 meditation and prayer book entitled *Wahres Christentum*

(*True Christianity*). In it Arndt had emphasized that "the Kingdom of God is within you" and had made the imitation of Christ very much an inward, devotional matter.[10] Not every schoolchild caught Arndt's piety. In 1811 a boy in Pennsylvania's Lancaster County, a Jacob Scherg, apparently from a Mennonite home, decorated his copy of *Wahres Christentum* with a most undevotional sketch of a jaunty fellow strolling along in top hat and striped coat. In his hand the fellow carried a whip or stick and in his mouth a huge, fuming cigar.[11] Nor did mature Mennonite authors cite writers such as Arndt nearly as often as they did two early Anabaptist ones, Dirk Philips and, of course, Menno Simons.

Yet nineteenth-century Mennonites and Amish simply did not see the conflict Friedmann would see. Was the difference due to the fact that they were not rigorous rationalists and therefore did not see the conflicts between incompatible ideas? Or, as Friedmann suggested, had Pietism seduced them? Surely Friedmann was correct when he implied that Mennonites had lost sixteenth-century Anabaptism's prophetic and confrontational mood. But he was less convincing when he implied that Pietism caused that loss. For he did not seem to ask whether Pietism might instead have filled a vacuum left by changes within Anabaptism and Mennonitism. Nor did he explore whether Pietism and Anabaptism complemented each other more than conflicted. Perhaps Mennonites accurately sensed that their own tradition lacked some important ingredients for a full-orbed, fully developed Christian faith.[12]

A prime carrier of Pietism was hymns. Pietists were prolific hymn-writers. Mennonites and Amish had their own songbook called the *Ausbund*. First published in Anabaptist days, it was (and is) a collection largely of martyr ballads and other songs of sufferings. But well before 1800 Mennonites (less true of Amish) were often singing not from the Anabaptist book but from more mystical and Pietistic ones printed by Dunkers, Lutherans, or Reformed. By 1803 and 1804 Mennonites of the two large eastern-Pennsylvania conferences, Franconia and Lancaster, replaced the *Ausbund* with collections made up largely of newer Pietistic numbers—the first new hymnals that Anabaptists or Mennonites anywhere had compiled in 250 years. For obscure reasons (which Lancaster area deacon Martin Mellinger claimed were not hostile), each conference printed its own. The Franconians named theirs *Die Kleine Geistliche Harfe* (*The Little Spiritual Harp*) and included 30 psalms and 475 hymns. The Lancastrians' offering was an *Unpartheyisches Gesangbuch* (*Non-denominational Hymnbook*), with 62 psalms and 390 hymns.[13]

The Franconia hymnal scarcely differed from hymnbooks used by state churches in German lands and by Reformed or Lutheran churches in America. Its foreword was practically a copy of one in a Reformed hymnal. In Pietistic language the foreword promised spiritually enriching and upbuilding songs. Very likely both introductions were written by a Lutheran who printed both the Reformed and the Mennonite books. In almost state-church language the Mennonite introduction commended the collection to all "evangelical congregations in this land." As for the songs and how the Franconians' "little spiritual harp" grouped and labeled them, there were only hints of uniquely Mennonite theology or tradition.

The collection included only four *Ausbund* hymns out of its 475, and those were not about martyrs. Some of its headings did convey Anabaptist-Mennonite understandings: for instance, *Von der christlichen Kirche* ("of the Christian church") became *Von der wahren Gemeinde Gottes*. The latter phrase is difficult to express in English, but it indicated that God's true church was not the institution; instead, the church was the fellowship, the people. More subtle was a certain emphasis on the somber. A Dunker songbook of the day expressed an effervescent side of Pietism with a section whose name meant "Joyousness of Faith"; the Mennonite book had no such section but did have one on "Cross and Sorrows." Yet a careful analyst named Ada Kadelbach has said that even in such a section the book replaced the old martyr ballads with a "baroque and pietistic interpretation" of those somber themes.[14]

The Lancastrians' hymnal was rather more Mennonite. More of its headings had a Mennonite ring. And of 390 hymns, sixty were carried over from the *Ausbund*. The book's introduction said the church needed to keep the memory of the fathers and pious martyrs alive. Yet except for the sixty *Ausbund* numbers the collection was very much like that of the Franconia book. The very name, "Non-denominational Hymbook," suggested that Mennonite music would not be unique. Nor did the book's introduction preserve the Anabaptist idea that Christians stand at odds with the world's evil structures. Instead, it warmly praised a government that "does not begrudge us full freedom of conscience." One scholar has suggested that after such an introduction even the *Ausbund* numbers bespoke patriotism. For by recalling past persecutions they highlighted the goodness of present rulers.[15]

Yet the collection's strong theme was Pietism, not patriotism. As Kadelbach has shown, Pietistic poets predominated and the great majority of the non-*Ausbund* hymns were from Pietism's great era, the seventeenth and eighteenth centuries. With a third edition in 1808 the Lancastrians began to add compositions by one of their own, a middle-aged bishop named Christian Herr. In his lifetime Herr wrote some twenty-five hymns, but not peculiarly Mennonite ones. In general he followed German church-song tradition. In particular his theme was Pietist subjectivism with emphasis on "I" and "you" and inner experience rather than on the collective side of worship or on liturgy. In Kadelbach's words, he wrote mostly of "sin, repentance, conversion, following after Christ, resignation of one's own will and natural desires, obedience, humility, love of Jesus, and sickness and death"—themes which Pietist writers had already "belabored a thousand-fold."[16] Of course in themselves such themes were not new to Mennonitism: the newness was in emphasis.

Even then, at least in Kadelbach's analysis, Herr's kind of hymnody departed less from Mennonite emphases than did some English-language, invitational songs which Mennonites (particularly bishop John M. Brenneman and a problematic brother of his, Daniel) wrote at mid-century or later. Pietism's calls to the sinner were typically gentle, drawing people to God's mercy and reconciliation. According to Kadelbach the English-language invitations, drawing more from American revivalism, tended more to be aggressive and use threats of damnation.[17]

The gentler, spiritualized kind of piety ran deep among Mennonites and Amish in nineteenth-century America. They referred constantly to the world as a vale of tears, the brevity of life, the glory of heaven, personal hope in a sweet Savior, and other Pietistic themes. In private letters ordinary folk as well as preachers made a ritual of long greetings and closings couched in standard Pietistic phrases. Thus in 1877 Lizzie Brubaker of Lancaster County addressed a Franconia area couple as "Beloved fellow pilgrim's," thanked them for a "very kind and pious letter," and rejoiced that "we are yet spared in the land of the living." In these "our day's of grace" God was honored if friends wrote to "admonish and encourage one another," she continued. After all, the grave was ever near, "where there is no rependance." But the "dear Saviour" had "through love laid down his life for us" and Christians should feel "inwardly . . . touched by a feeling that we can not express." As the poet had said,

The pleasures of earth I have seen fade away
  They bloom for a season but soon they decay
But pleasures more lasting in Jesus are given
  Salvasion on earth and in mansion in heaven.[18]

At the time Brubaker wrote, Mennonites from the Russian empire were settling in North America. With American Mennonites the Russian immigrants shared not only Anabaptist origins, nonresistance, and a name; they also shared Pietism. Even future businessman Bernhard Warkentin used its idioms, however worldly he would be in later life. In 1868 as a 21-year-old in Russia he advised a young friend that "if only we could accept our Lord and Saviour as our guide ... we could face the threatening future ... without constant grief." If persons were more sensitive to God's leading they would not worry half as much about the future in "this earthly pilgrimage."[19]

Here was personal, inward-looking piety but different from that of many American revivalists. Persons such as William Gross, a schoolteacher in Bucks County, Pennsylvania, or Jacob Mensch, a minister in Montgomery County, carried on correspondence filled with Lizzie Brubaker's kind of expression, yet rejected revivalism. Near century's end an aging Gross wrote quite negatively to the foremost "old" Mennonite revivalist, John S. Coffman, saying that many of the new, zealous activists did not know God's will for themselves because they did not understand much "of silent waiting on the Lord."[20] Gross's objections did not arise from any lack of deeply personal faith in Christ or from a faith that was dry and formal. Rather, he sensed a conflict. At century's end among some Mennonites and Amish a clash was occurring between the Pietism absorbed quietistically from Europe and the more aggressive piety of American revivalism.

Mennonites accepted much from Pietism but did not abandon their own traditions. Much that Mennonites absorbed from Pietism fit rather well with what their ancestors had taught from Anabaptist days onward: personal, voluntary decision; yieldedness and obedience; rejection of worldliness; and even (despite the individualism of Pietism) a delight in communal Christian fellowship.[21] It is possible to draw distinctions between Anabaptism and Pietism too sharply.

It is possible especially if real flesh-and-blood Mennonites were less-than-perfect examples of pristine Anabaptism. Church of the Brethren scholar Dale Brown has criticized Friedmann's work for a common mistake: comparing a theoretical and idealized version of one's own faith with the actual, messy working-out of others' beliefs.[22] In practice the Anabaptist-Mennonite faith requires strong, determined conviction. Surely in nineteenth-century America Pietism helped many Mennonites come to such conviction. By helping them deepen their convictions it made them more earnest in their faith. So it helped lay a groundwork for commitment to Mennonite tradition. Moreover Mennonites and Amish could and did select what they borrowed from Pietism. The Franconians did so when they chose the more somber of Pietism's hymns. And in emphasizing humility Christian Burkholder borrowed a theme with an Anabaptist-like potential for challenging the ethos of surrounding society.

THEOLOGY OF HUMILITY

A question larger than Pietism was to what degree Mennonites would be Protestant. That was a question not only of theology but also of how the nation related to one of its minorities. Cultural leaders in the United States often saw their nation as Protestant, with Protestant denominationalism as the American way in religion. So to become more Protestant was also to become more a part of the nation.[23]

Earlier Anabaptists and Mennonites had not rejected Protestants' central doctrines. They certainly believed in justification by faith, salvation by grace, and redemption through the atoning work of Christ on the cross. But where Protestants saw in these doctrines the essence of God's reconciling work, the Anabaptist-Mennonite saw them more as parts of a larger process by which God was forming a reconciling new community, his church. Anabaptists shared the Protestant principle of *sola scriptura* (Scripture the only authority). But where Reformer Martin Luther had said that the church existed where God's Word was proclaimed, Anabaptists and Mennonites were more inclined to say that it existed only where Christians formed a community who discerned and obeyed God's Word.[24]

The main questions surrounding Mennonites and Amish in nineteenth-century America were: Would they become more like Protestants who were quite individualistic in their understanding of God's message and its proclamation? And, would they shift their focus more to the forensic processes of individual forgiveness, justification, and atonement? Many Protestants (especially English-speaking revivalists) had largely tied the word "salvation" to these processes.[25]

If Mennonites and Amish were going to keep their own more corporate and holistic understandings of gospel in the nineteenth century, they probably needed some reformulation of how to go about it. Authorities in America did not harass them, so they could no longer make their point by accepting persecution, banishment, and suffering. The humility theology of Christian Burkholder was a reformulation. After Burkholder wrote, Mennonites had a choice. They might keep humility primarily as an adorning virtue and become more Protestant. Or they might make humility into a central theme of what it meant to be faithful disciples of Jesus and the new people of God. In the second lay an alternative to human greed, self-aggrandizement, and war. Humility theology could offer a prophetic message against such evils.

Burkholder himself did not spell out the choice so clearly. He wrote nothing that a non-Mennonite Pietistic Protestant absolutely could not have written. Nevertheless, implicitly, he offered it. He declined to make the forensic process of justification and atonement completely central. At one point he said that "the whole doctrine of Christ leads into a course of self-denial, and separation from the world." He wrote of the new birth and said it was indeed "something very necessary, and ... a chief article of salvation." Yet he hoped that others would "advance further in the new birth than I have done." In other words, regeneration was a matter of growth. And he did not try to say exactly how justification and atonement come about.[26]

When he wrote of God's reconciling act on the cross Burkholder connected it clearly with the ethic of nonresistance. He recalled that on the cross Christ had prayed that God would forgive his enemies. Throughout the ordeal God was "reconciling the world unto himself." Christ had "suffered his blood to be shed" for his enemies as well as for his friends.[27] As for the new birth, Burkholder made humility its chief sign. For him the evidences of repentance and conversion were not subjective experience but objective, visible, ethical fruits. He pointed to fruits such as love, chastity, honesty, and not being covetous, but first of all to a shift "from pride to humility." As the pastor ended his lesson on the new birth he called the penitent not to the cross but to the manager, and to humility.[28] Thus he put humility at the center of God's work of salvation more clearly than he did the processes of justification and atonement.

For the first six or seven decades of the nineteenth century in America, humility saturated ordinary Mennonite and Amish discourse. Seek first the kingdom of God, a Wayne County, Ohio, Mennonite named Henrich Martin wrote to his brother-in-law in 1819. To Martin the words meant that parents were to nurture their children in the ways of the Lord, keep them from bad company, and not let them become proud through wearing what he called strange or uncustomary ("*fremden*") clothing. For, Martin quoted, God resists the proud and gives grace to the humble.[29]

For such ideas Burkholder's *Address to Youth* was a main

source but not the only one. For instance, there was also the so-called "Elbing catechism," first printed in 1778 in Germany and reprinted in North America some fourteen times throughout the nineteenth century. It did not make humility as central as in Burkholder's address yet it warned the child not to be puffed up with knowledge. Instead, "be humble and diffident." And pray,

> Blessed Jesus, meek and mild,
> Stoop to hear a little child; . . .
> In my childhood may I be
> Gentle, meek and pure, like thee. . . ."[30]

A more American source was a treatise by Abraham Godshalk, a minister at Doylestown, Pennsylvania. In 1837 and 1838, in German and in English, Godshalk published a small (77-page) book on regeneration. Humility was not his central theme; mainly he wrote to refute revivalist perfectionism and to argue that Christian maturity came only gradually, through growth. But when he listed commands that mature Christians obeyed he listed first coming to faith or belief, second repentance, and then "meekness and lowliness of heart." Meekness would make Christians long-suffering, interested in their neighbors' welfare, etc. Further in Godshalk's list were nonconformity to the world, not being slothful, being nonresistant as was Christ on the cross, and other points. Thus the minister connected humility to Christians' day-to-day conduct, not mainly to the process of repentance as Pietists and revivalists often did. And he made it more or less a foundation of Christian ethics.[31]

The most systematic theology book of any "old" Mennonite in the nineteenth century was by a nephew of Christian Burkholder, Virginia bishop Peter Burkholder. In 1837 the younger Burkholder and his translator, Joseph Funk, published *The Confession of Faith of the Christians Known by the Name of Mennonites*. . ., a compilation covering 461 pages. Parts of the book were Peter Burkholder's own, parts were borrowed from previous Mennonite authors. Half the volume was an edited version of a 33-article confession of faith written about 1600 by a Dutch Mennonite named Pieter Jansz Twisck and kept in print in various editions of the *Martyrs Mirror*.

Overall, the book was explicitly doctrinal and at points gently polemical. So in contrast to his uncle's nurture book Peter Burkholder's volume dwelled more on subjects such as why not believe in predestination, how Christ's atonement covered unbaptized infants, or why infant baptism was wrong. The Virginia bishop wrote

THE
CONFESSION OF FAITH,
OF THE CHRISTIANS KNOWN BY THE NAME OF
MENNONITES,
IN THIRTY-THREE ARTICLES;
WITH A SHORT EXTRACT FROM THEIR CATECHISM.

TRANSLATED FROM THE GERMAN,
AND ACCOMPANIED WITH NOTES.
TO WHICH IS ADDED
AN INTRODUCTION.

ALSO,
Nine Reflections,
FROM DIFFERENT PASSAGES OF THE SCRIPTURES,
ILLUSTRATIVE OF THEIR
Confession, Faith & Practice;
BY PETER BURKHOLDER,
Pastor of the Church of the Mennonites;
Written by him in the German Language, and from his manuscript translated, together with the foregoing Articles,
BY JOSEPH FUNK.

"And are built upon the foundation of the Apostles and Prophets, Jesus Christ himself being the chief corner stone." Eph. 2: 20.

Winchester:
PRINTED BY ROBINSON & HOLLIS.
—1837.—

Title page of Peter Burkholder's *Confession of Faith* (1837).

forthrightly of repentance, new birth, and conversion—and also of Jesus' kingdom of peace.[32] To reinforce pacifism he included the *Martyrs Mirror* interpretation which assumed that Mennonites stood in the line of Waldensians, Albigensians, and others in the succession of nonresistant martyrs who were God's faithful remnants in history.[33] In Peter Burkholder's book humility was only one of various themes.

Nonetheless, when it came to the nature of the new birth, salvation, and the fruits which marked them, the Virginia bishop stayed with his uncle's way of thinking. He made clear that he was writing of heart religion, not merely of outer form. So at points he treated humility mainly as a matter of spirit or of contrition before repentance. Yet he rejected the idea that "if the heart's right all's right."

To him as to his uncle the test of conversion was not subjective experience but objective, observable fruits. And again the most important fruit was humility. Although he did not list it first he listed it twice. And as he elaborated he used the phrase "meek and lowly" five times in nine lines of text! In a warning against false prophets he said that impostors managed to imitate some evidences of true religion—but never "the meek, lowly and humble life of Christ which is so despicable in the sight of the world."

Also he tied humility closely to the ideas of separation from and rejection by the world. And he made a clear connection between it and the kingdom of peace: Jesus' humble followers were lambs among the world's wolves.[34] All of Peter Burkholder's points formed one whole: conversion, the cross, clear distinction from the world, readiness to bear scorn, the way of peace, and humility. He did not put a plan of salvation in one compartment and obedient Christian living in another. Humility was not everything but he put it near the heart of Christian faith. To him as to his uncle it was much more than only the fairest of Christian virtues.

Since they tested so much by practical marks of faith, nineteenth-century Mennonites and Amish saw nothing odd in a leap such as Henrich Martin made when he jumped directly from the kingdom-of-God idea to clothing. God's people were not an abstraction; they were to be visible and easily identified. In admonitions about clothing, then, two ideas easily mixed: (1) humility, and (2) separation from the world, or avoiding worldliness. They mixed easily because of a third idea: that (along with vulnerability and defenselessness) humility was a key mark of the people of God. Thus a conference of "old" Mennonites in southwestern Pennsylvania resolved in 1882 that "we learn by the Scriptures that the people of God were, from the beginning, a plain, common, and humble people modest in their apparel."[35]

Clothing and other visible applications were very important in the theology of humility—important for issues larger than just themselves. An Indiana conference resolution of 1864 was typical. It admonished "that brethren and sisters observe, according to the doctrine of Christ to be humble and plain in their manner of dress, excluding therefrom all needless ornaments, hoops, laces, jewelry, artificial flowers, and other things which tend to pride. . . ."[36] The word was "tend" to pride. Despite the concrete meaning Mennonites and Amish gave to humility they did not quite say that plainness and humility were one and the same.

Practical applications covered more than clothes. Mennonites and Amish invoked humility against frivolity and useless decoration in everything from house furnishings to barn decorations to bells on horses. Funeral practices often evoked admonition, and not only from traditionalists. In 1850 even the progressive East Pennsylvania conference warned against excesses in funeral preparations.[37] Meetinghouse architecture was another application. We do not plan "a mignificent temple, with ornamentations, erected for pride," declared the Salford "old" Mennonite congregation in Montgomery County, Pennsylvania, in 1850. Instead, the standard was "what is useful, orderly, becoming, and lasting." And in 1868 in an Amish heartland—Mifflin County, Pennsylvania—progressives who built the area's first Amish meetinghouse were careful to extend a raised platform for speakers so that it would include the "amen" corners. They did not want to lift their ministers above the laity.[38]

The most deliberate statement of the humility theology was an English-language pamphlet by bishop John M. Brenneman of Ohio. Published in 1867 (and in later editions, some in German), the booklet was titled *Pride and Humility: A Discourse Setting Forth the Characteristics of the Proud and the Humble.* Historian Joseph C. Liechty, after studying John F. Funk's "old" Mennonite paper the *Herald of Truth,* has observed that the pamphlet said nothing new. According to him Brenneman only said "well and fully what his peers said fumblingly and partially."[39] If so the Ohio bishop met a favorite Mennonite test of good theology: not to be original but to express the mind of the church.

Often Mennonite or Amish preachers and writers tried to retell the whole sweep of salvation history. They began with Adam, moved through the patriarchs and perhaps the prophets, and found a climax at the life and cross of Jesus. Then they moved into church history, especially to the faithful martyrs. The sermon might end

The Casselman Mennonite Church built this structure in 1889. Other congregations in Springs, Pa., and Grantsville, Md. areas, as well as Johnstown, Pa., used this 19th century meetinghouse architectural pattern.

with a present-day application. On the one hand the preachers offered a high view of Christ, for they emphasized his divinity and made him and his going to the cross the fulcrum of all history. On the other they presented Christ as sufficiently human to be the model for flesh-and-blood Christians. Brenneman followed the tradition but with a special theme: God having to deal with human pride. So Jesus was a master of humility. Brenneman drew special attention not to the manger-Jesus but to the Christ who stooped to wash his followers' feet and who humbly accepted death.[40]

Jesus' act of washing feet made humility specific. Moreover, Brenneman offered a wide range of other real-life applications, from not owning fancy carriages or costly furniture to avoiding overly elaborate meals. Like others, he wrote at length about clothing, citing Menno Simons as authority and writing to men as well as to women.

He also warned against polite manners "in imitation of the higher and fashionable classes of the world."[41] Few Mennonites or Amish belonged to such classes, and that fact no doubt helped to shape Brenneman's remarks. In fact he believed in manners but of a different sort. The humble person, he wrote, "is usually of a quiet, meek and gentle disposition knowing when to be silent and when to speak." Such a person was willing to yield to others and let them express opinions. In social situations the humble were modest, not seeking the best seats at the table. As for classes, *Pride and Humility* recognized only two: the proud and the humble. Brennemen treated the two categories as if there were no others, and no mixtures or gradations.[42]

Writing his pamphlet Brenneman faced a dilemma all Christians face if they try to make their faith explicit and practical: how to keep conscientious living from becoming legalism. He clearly felt stung by charges that Mennonites preached a religion of works. So while he called for humility he denied that outward form was the essence. "There are persons who say that the religion of the Mennonites consists entirely in their manner of dress," he observed; but if that were true, Mennonites "would not have any [religion] at all." It was just that "a genuine and true Mennonite" did not see how a "humble and regenerated heart" could produce "fruits of pride."[43]

Like most Mennonites and Amish of his day Brenneman simply could not separate the process of repentance, regeneration, and receiving of God's grace from putting on the outer marks of humility. He tied his humility theme so closely to repentance and conversion that he even turned it into an evangelistic invitation. The central text of his booklet was was 1 Peter 5:5: "God resisteth the proud, and giveth grace to the humble." The bishop implored any reader "sunk and enveloped in the wickedness of pride" to "repent quickly and be converted. . . . Seek grace in humility . . . ."[44]

In its social and political implications the humility theology carried a paradox. On the one hand it cultivated a deferential and self-effacing kind of personality. Brenneman wrote that "the humble man feels small, poor, bowed, cast down, and unworthy within himself, and esteems others more highly than himself."[45] It was almost as if he hoped deliberately to make late-twentieth-century people cringe, indoctrinated as they are with the language of self-realization and self-fulfillment. Yet the humility doctrine also bolstered a stubborn, steely will to resist if government or society demanded anything contrary to Mennonite belief.

Thus it reinforced the trait which had kept Mennonitism from extinction through the centuries. For instance it helped Brenneman prepare a civil war petition to send to U.S. president Abraham Lincoln, pledging loyalty but also insisting that Mennonites simply would not fight. Paradoxically, humility theology instilled

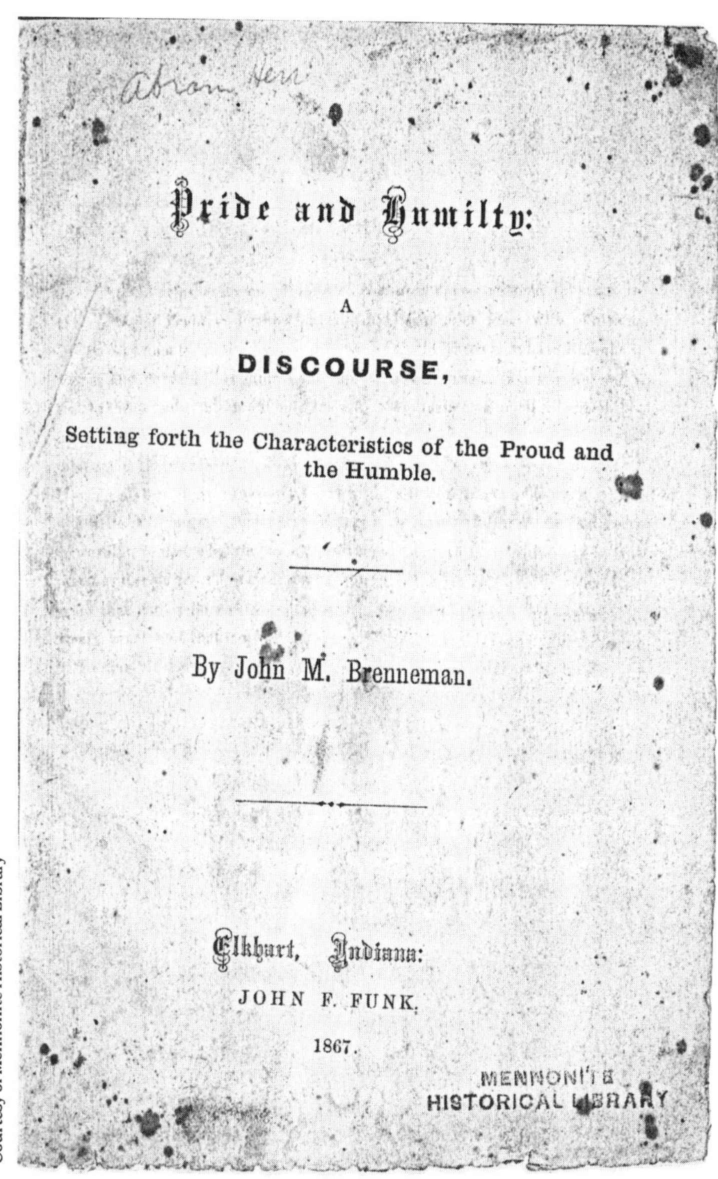

Pride and Humilty:

A

DISCOURSE,

Setting forth the Characteristics of the Proud and the Humble.

By John M. Brenneman.

Elkhart, Indiana:

JOHN F. FUNK.

1867.

Courtesy of Mennonite Historical Library

Title page of John M. Brenneman's *Pride and Humilty* (first published 1866-1867).

deference yet taught its people not to be awe-struck by the rich or the powerful.[46]

A sociologist might say that Mennonite and Amish leaders used humility for boundary maintenance and social control. Clothing and other humility symbols marked who was in the group and who was out. Calls to humility were often calls to obey and be subordinate to the group. Christian Burkholder told his fictional inquirer that uneasiness with church rules came "from the old, unregenerate nature." Seven decades later Brenneman seemed even less open to American notions of individual rights. Specifically for clothing he rejected an enforced uniformity. His only test, he said, was that clothing "should be plain and simple according to God's word." Yet he left almost no room for different opinions about how to express humility. Instead, he assumed that the church should exert strong control. Invoking a common phrase, he strongly challenged ministers to be "watchmen of Zion." As watchmen they should warn against pride.[47]

Yet Brenneman and other humility-minded leaders were not simply autocrats. As on that question of divorce the Ohio bishop yielded if the common mind of the church did not support him. He yielded quickly, gracefully, and publicly.[48]

Liechty has suggested that the style and practice of humility made for resolution of conflict. He said that contrary to how an individualist might see the case, the type of personality Brenneman cultivated and exemplified did not fear conflict. Instead, "personal humility functioned as a technique for Christian confrontation." Strong leaders set forth their ideas but did not dig in their heels for a fight. On the other hand Canadian Mennonite historian Frank Epp has emphasized that mid-nineteenth-century Mennonites suffered schisms because they had not learned conflict resolution. Actually both points are correct. Indeed there were schisms. Humility did not always succeed, a fact Liechty had to admit.[49]

No one can say how many divisions and schisms were avoided by sincere practice of the humble style. It is hard to prove a negative. For instance, in that controversy over divorce humility surely helped to resolve conflict.

The theology had its failures. During its era Mennonite and Amish had no theory that differences of opinion might be legitimate and even enriching and healthy. Almost always, with their strong doctrine of visible church, Mennonites and Amish saw differences only as lack of unity. And lack of unity meant spiritual decline. Against any dissenter it was all too easy to make the sweeping charge of pride.[50]

An even larger failure was that Mennonites and Amish did not develop their humility ideas into a vigorously prophetic witness. The failure was tragic, for the humility emphasis was exactly what Americans needed. A youthful United States needed it to counter an arrogance which expressed itself in exploitive expansion, injustices toward blacks and other poor, and talk of a God-given "manifest destiny" which justified aggression against American Indians and Mexicans.[51] Americans needed it to dampen their cocksure, idolatrous assertions about the total superiority of their political and economic system and about America being God's favorite.

But Mennonites and Amish were not ready to challenge the nation so boldly. Humility reinforced by Pietism became one more reason to be "the quiet in the land." Of course, to turn humility theology into an aggressive prophetic message would have been a paradox: to Mennonites and Amish any kind of aggressive assertion would not have seemed humble. But humility theology offered an alternative system of values with prophetic possibilities. Not using it prophetically was perhaps early-nineteenth-century Mennonites' greatest failure.

Whatever its failures, humility theology helped Mennonites and Amish answer a host of questions. It spoke eloquently to the essential nature of human sin, and to how humans abuse power and status. It clarified God's way of dealing and his redemptive work in history. It helped explain the nature and example of Christ within the redemption story. And it undergirded Mennonite pacifism. Humility was a Siamese twin of lamb-like vulnerability and non-vengeance. Together with pacifism, humility went far to explain what it meant to be God's people rather than the world's.

Moreover, humility theology offered an authentic substitute for the suffering theme that America had removed from Mennonite experience. In peace and prosperity it helped Mennonites and Amish keep a vision of discipleship. It taught them how to live as God's people both in their inner attitude and in ways which were very open, visible, and specific. For better or worse, it helped them resist being Protestantized and Americanized. In a society with great power of assimilation, that was quite a feat.

REFORMED MENNONITE AND HOLDEMAN PERFECTIONISM

Not all Mennonites and Amish of the humility era were happy with their churches. Some dissenters zealously embraced the theology but wanted stricter practice. Others thought practice too strict, or refused to make humility so central, or both. An interpreter can only suggest, not prove, what moved the reformers. Often, no doubt, they simply made different choices at points where there were internal tensions within Mennonite thought[52]—for instance tension between voluntarism and church discipline. Therefore dissenters, as well as their "old" Mennonite and Amish opponents, often invoked the *Martyrs Mirror*, Menno Simons and Dirk Philips, and ancient Mennonite confessions.

In almost every dispute each party could claim that it stood on Anabaptist and Mennonite principles. But often the dissenters were listening also to one or more voices from outside Mennonitism. They listened to radical Pietism; to American revivalism; to Protestants who saw "salvation" almost entirely in terms of initial justification and individual, forensic atonement; to American denominationalism and its desire for full acceptance across the different churches' boundaries; and to others. No researcher can say conclusively who borrowed from where. Neither Mennonites on the one hand nor Pietists or revivalists on the other were uniform or consistent enough in their thinking to allow anyone to trace influences and ideas precisely. Yet the evidence offers some suggestions.

The first dissenters to create a new fellowship after 1800 were the Reformed Mennonites in 1812. The main founder was a John Herr of near Strasburg in Lancaster County, Pennsylvania. Herr inherited his dissent: his father, Francis Herr, had disputed with his Mennonite congregation and gathered some followers who met in the Herr home. Some immediate issues were what the Herrs thought was laxity in "old" Mennonite discipline, plus a rumor, probably quite false, that Francis Herr had cheated in a horse deal.[53] A deeper issue seems to have been that the Herrs and their followers were influenced by a radical Pietism. To achieve a Pietistic spirituality they turned to some Mennonite ideas and tried to invoke them very absolutely.

The radical Pietism showed itself in various ways. Repentance-and-conversion accounts of the Herrs followed standard Pietist emphasis on *Busskampf* (the repentance-struggle) interspersed with times of ecstasy.[54] Groups that began to meet around the Herrs fit a Pietistic pattern of *collegia pietatis*—small groups meeting apart from the larger church, for Bible study, fellowship, and mutual support. If the Reformed Mennonites were Pietistic they were radically so. Unlike milder Pietists they were quite ready to break with their old church. They used favorite language of radical Pietists, roundly denouncing others' churches as "Babel" and "the whore of Babylon."[55] (To be sure, such language was also in the *Martyrs Mirror*.[56])

As for Mennonite ideas used absolutely, the Reformed Mennonites carried the doctrine of the church and of being God's separated new people to the point of total exclusivity. Daniel Musser, a bishop of the group who wrote in the 1860s and '70s, argued that Herr and those around him had *formed*, not *re*-formed the church. Reformed Mennonites refused to recognize anyone else as true Christians. If they found themselves listening to others' sermons, for instance at a neighbor's funeral, they put their fingers in their ears to show their rejection.[57]

Herr and his followers were a species of Christian perfectionists. Their recipe to reform the church and bring persons to spirituality was rigorous, uncompromising discipline. So they took ancient Mennonite doctrines of the ban (excommunication) and shunning (*Meidung*—social ostracism of offenders) to the very limits. Virtually all Mennonites believed in excommunicating for gross and unrepented sins; but there was disagreement about what sins deserved it, and even more about shunning. Among sixteenth-century Anabaptists Menno Simons in the Netherlands had taught shunning but others farther south had not. By the nineteenth century, Amish still practiced it to one degree or another but most Mennonites applied it only by holding "close" communion—that is, by allowing only members in good standing to eat and drink with them at the Lord's table.[58]

Furthermore, it seems that many bishops and other leaders carried out discipline with a degree of compromise. Much as parents may stop short of absolute principle in order to have peace with adolescent children, church leaders softened discipline to keep peace in the church. Indeed, bishops often spoke of their role as *Haus halten*—"to keep house." Yet nineteenth-century Mennonites had more literature available from north European Anabaptists, especially Menno Simons' *Fundamentbuch* (*Foundation Book*), than they had from non-shunning Anabaptists in lands farther south. And certainly they had no explicit theology for compromise. So the discipline-minded among the reformers revived shunning as an ancient Mennonite teaching. John Herr did so in 1812, Jacob Stauffer in the 1840s, other Old Order people thereafter, and John Holdeman in the 1850s. The Reformed Mennonites, perfectionists par excellence, carried shunning very far indeed.

Among Reformed Mennonites there was a certain clarity of thought, as there often is among people who carry ideas to their limits without qualifying them or trying to reconcile them with other ideas which also seem valid. In the generic sense of the word the Reformed were the most "fundamentalist" of Mennonites.[59]

Most Mennonite leaders of the nineteenth century, especially in the large "old" and Amish Mennonite branches, used Scriptures with a certain loose artistry. To twentieth-century people, preachers such as Christian Burkholder or Jacob Schwarzendruber might seem to have used them as proof texts, ad infinitum. Yet more careful reading will show that they were not building tight proofs so much as taking practical insights and guidance. They used Scriptures more as wisdom literature than for strict argument. Thus their theology was more a mosaic than a logic-tight system.

By contrast John Herr used Scriptures as flat, self-evident pronouncements and indisputable proofs. Daniel Musser did so even more.[60] Musser was rather a phenomenon. He was a physician in a church whose men were mostly farmers and craftsmen. He wrote with remarkable style, vocabulary, and evidence of reading. And even when he was very polemic he had a knack for sounding gracious.[61] Whatever the merits of his ideas, he was perhaps the most systematic theologian of any nineteenth-century Mennonite group. A booklet he published on nonresistance in 1864 once fell into the hands of Russian philosopher and novelist Leo Tolstoy. Tolstoy liked it and commented at some length. Closer home John M. Brenneman read the same booklet and commented that Musser was "certainly a Sharp kind of man."[62] Musser was indeed sharp, with the clarity of a fundamentalist whose mind recognizes no ambiguities.

With its discipline and its exclusivism, Herr's and Musser's church never grew large. Near the end of the century its membership reached a peak of perhaps 2,500; seventy-five years later it was only 725.[63] Yet in the nineteenth century it was significant. If nothing more, it showed what Mennonitism with an admixture of radical Pietism might become, if a group was thoroughly perfectionist and fundamentalistic and carried Mennonite concepts of church, separatism, and discipline to their limits.

A reformer somewhat like John Herr was John Holdeman, an Ohioan who broke with the "old" Mennonites in the 1850s. The similarity was not complete. If Herr borrowed from radical Pietism, Holdeman probably took more from American revivalism. Very probably he was influenced early in life by a certain John Funk (not the publisher) who was a preacher where Holdeman lived in Wayne County in eastern Ohio. Although formerly a Mennonite, Funk preached for a revivalistic group called "Winebrenners" or more officially the "Church of God."[64] Holdeman himself eventually was cautious about revivalistic exuberance. He wrote that "conversion is not a shouting for joy" or "the moving of the outward body in jumping and shouting." Yet his understanding of salvation was more revivalist than traditionally Mennonite, for he distinguished sharply between initial forgiveness or justification and the Christian obedience that was to follow. Discussing baptism, he even said that the use of water symbolized the one and the subsequent laying on of hands symbolized the other. But if Holdeman was touched by revivalism he still had much in common with John Herr. He too (like many another Pietist or revivalist) testified of having lived through a long personal spiritual struggle, which for him lasted from about age twelve until young adulthood.[65] Also both men's theologies seemed quite Protestant at points, for instance, putting stronger emphasis than did most Mennonites on human depravity.[66] And like Herr, Holdeman began his preaching by gathering relatives and others in his home apart from the official life of the church.[67]

That was in 1858, when Holdeman was twenty-six. In 1859 he and those he attracted broke with the "old" Mennonites and began a new branch.[68] Perhaps partly from Winebrenner influence they named it the "Church of God in Christ, Mennonite." More common are shorter labels: "the Holdemans" or "the Holdeman church." Unlike the Reformed Mennonites the new group never claimed to be the only true church.[69] But like Herr's church John Holdeman adopted shunning and a very strict discipline against a variety of offenses. Holdeman's list ranged from marrying a non-Mennonite or accepting non-Mennonite baptism to taking usury or engaging in politics or using government for lawsuits and other self-defense. It also forbade lightning rods.[70] In 1878 his group lost a troublesome $2,500 lawsuit brought by a Joseph Liechty of Williams County in western Ohio. The church had excommunicated Liechty for drunkenness and had required his wife to shun him to the point of refusing to eat or have sexual relations with him. As the suit put it, the church caused her "not to live and cohabit with him as his wife and to abandon and desert his bed and board."[71]

The "Holdemans" established only a few struggling congregations until the mid-1870s, when some rather leaderless Mennonites arrived from "Polish Russia" and joined them. Then they founded a string of congregations on the Western plains, especially in Kansas, Nebraska, and Manitoba. Those developments made the church rather different ethnically from John Holdeman and his original followers. But the church succeeded as a small, separatist Mennonite branch (700 to 800 members in 1900, about 10,000 in the 1980s).[72] Like the Reformed Mennonites, it was a case of Mennonite perfectionism. Much like John Herr's, John Holdeman's recipe for church reform and deeper spirituality was a more or less revivalistic kind of conversion followed by strict discipline.

MENNONITE REVIVALISTS: HOCH, BRENNEMAN, AND EGLY

About the 1850s reformers appeared who were much more clearly influenced by revivalism—reformers who called especially for clear-cut conversions. For decades, some Mennonites and Amish who sought a more definite religious experience or greater Christian vitality or assurance of salvation had been crossing over to the United Brethren and others. But now some reformers tried to bring revivalism to Mennonitism itself and fuse it with Mennonite theology. Two such leaders were Daniel Hoch of Upper Canada (today's Ontario) and Daniel Brenneman at Yellow Creek in Indiana, a brother of the notable Ohio bishop. They began groups which eventually would merge with others to form the Mennonite Brethren in Christ (MBC), which later became part of the Missionary Church. Another was Henry Egly, an Amish elder (or bishop) of Adams County, Indiana. Egly began a group which took the name "Defenseless Mennonite Church." The odd label "defenseless" was a literal translation of the German *wehrlosig*, now usually translated "nonresistant." Since 1948 the name is "Evangelical Mennonite Church."[73]

Hoch, Brenneman, and Egly accepted revivalism more clearly than did Holdeman. And concerning discipline, they started off in a different direction. Instead of invoking it as a means to purity and spirituality, they were inclined to see its rules as dead, outward form. So they or their successors relaxed Mennonite rules about matters from clothing to lawsuits and sooner or later even about pacifism. In so doing they usually went toward Methodism and what was becoming American Protestantism's "holiness" wing. Surely there was logic in Mennonites being attracted more to Wesleyan revivalism than to more doctrinal and Calvinistic varieties. Moreover the Methodist style offered an emotional warmth which Mennonitism rather lacked. Was the lack due to the stern legacies of martyrdom and costly discipleship, plus perhaps stolid Swiss-German ethnicity? Or was it due, as revivalists believed, to spiritual deterioration and an onset of formalism?

Whatever the answer, perhaps another fact was at work: compared to Calvinism, Wesleyan theology was closer to Mennonite and Amish people's own understandings of gospel. Its salvation message dwelled rather less on formal justification, atonement, and correct belief and rather more on regeneration for practical holy living.

Of course Wesleyan and Mennonite understandings differed, also. The Methodist tradition gave inner experience a larger role in judging holiness and was more individualistic. Nor did it understand nonresistant pacifism to be central to how God wanted his people to live and deal with evil. But reformers or their followers could treat the experiential element as an improvement, scarcely even recognize the issue of individualism, and judge Mennonite pacifism to be merely an option or a legalism or merely the special emphasis of an odd sect.

Daniel Hoch, Daniel Brenneman, and others began vital new movements that came together and in 1883 took the name Mennonite Brethren in Christ. Hoch, ordained in 1831, was a Mennonite minister in a congregation about twenty miles west of Niagara Falls. Although he and his supporters lived in Canada their area was not entirely different from one just east of them in upstate New York. There in the 1820s, '30s, and '40s revivals flamed and smoldered until the region won the nickname "the burned-over district."[74]

By 1848 Hoch was quite at odds with his bishop, one Dilman Meyer, and more or less so with the "old" Mennonite conference in Canada. Surely part of the problem was a personality clash. Although Meyer had the backing of his congregation, no doubt he was quite a bit as Hoch saw him: rigid and stubborn. Hoch also helped make the dispute personal. He wrote acid polemics making Meyer out to be a villain and even penned several balladlike "hymns" with passages such as:

> *"Der Dilman Meyer liebt es nicht,*
> *Wenn Jemand von Bekehrung spricht. . . .*"[75]
> (Dilman Meyer shows aversion,
> When someone talks about conversion.)

If Hoch had been a patient, sweet-tempered man like, for instance, John S. Coffman, pioneer "old" Mennonite revivalist later in the century—and if Dilman Meyer statesmanlike and ready for some change like, say, John M. Brenneman—then there may have been no rupture in Canada. Yet to dismiss the affair of Hoch or the later one of Daniel Brenneman as hardly more than a personality clash, or perhaps failure of conflict resolution,[76] is too easy. Such explanations ignore important historical currents.

Among the issues was the nature of authority. One strong and broad-minded bishop in the Canada conference, Benjamin Eby, seems to have seen some merit in Hoch's calls for reform, yet the conference believed enough in congregationalism that it hesitated to impose a solution on Meyer and his local church.[77]

On his side, Hoch spoke the modern language of individual and constitutional rights, saying he should not have to "prostrate myself" before Meyer and the congregation "as before Divine authority." Moreover he mixed the rights idea with a hint of direct revelation, suggesting that he and his supporters could not yield "Christian rights" gained by "superior light." And as John H. Oberholtzer had recently done in Pennsylvania, he and his supporters demanded that church decisions be put in writing. Thus he wanted to replace traditional personal authority with a more modern, rationalized kind. In similar spirit such reformers sometimes seemed to cite Scripture as if it were a modern legal contract.[78] Finally, political authority on both sides of the border in North America (as well as Anabaptist precedent) made it easy for Hoch, Brenneman, and others to form a new denomination.

Other issues stemmed more directly from revivalism, as hinted in Hoch's words about aversion to conversion. The dispute could hardly have been about conversion itself: traditional Mennonites believed in the new birth and used its language. Rather, the controversy was over revivalistic patterns of thinking and speaking about such matters. Hoch and his friends had constantly to argue against charges that they were Methodistic. Their standard reply was that the opponents had not proven their case. In a formal sense they were correct. Hoch and those around him continued to cite Menno Simons and declare themselves Mennonites. And although they relaxed on some points such as marrying non-Mennonites or using lawsuits for just cause, a new constitution they wrote in 1850 upheld standard Mennonite positions on believer's baptism, pacifism in wartime, refusal to swear oaths, and the rite of foot washing.[79]

But of course the charge of Methodism referred not so much to formal doctrine as to emphasis and style. In his writing Hoch referred to "new measures," a phrase very current especially among followers of revivalist Charles G. Finney in the "burnt-over district." And he referred to Dilman Meyer's followers as "that portion of the congregation which resisted the reviving and converting Spirit of God."[80] Thus he clearly identified with revivalists, for he used their code phrases.

In the immediate case the key issue was one of the main institutional forms of revivalism, the prayer meeting. Hoch and his supporters held prayer meetings. For Mennonites, prayer meetings seemed noisy and disorderly. Such, at least, were the rumors.

Moreover women often participated in ways which traditionalists saw as violating Paul's New Testament words that they should keep silent in church (1 Cor. 14:35).[81] The fact was, prayer meetings had become symbols—one of the first signposts along revivalism's path. They were advance agents for new forms of religious organization and authority, or in modern jargon, "parachurches." Thus they signified more than simple gatherings for prayer. Perhaps, as revivalists believed, they signaled exactly the changes which Mennonites and Amish needed. Whether or not the revivalists were correct, traditionalists were shrewd in sensing that the prayer meetings were signals of greater change.

In 1847 Canada's "old" Mennonite conference cautiously approved prayer meetings if held "on gospel principles." But Hoch's opponents, fearing the parachurch pattern and no doubt anxious to keep control, said the gatherings should be limited mainly to people who were sick or otherwise unable to attend regular church services. More specifically the opponents charged that in the prayer meetings held by Hoch and his party there was disorder. Moreover Mennonites mixed with Methodists and Catholics.[82] Hoch of course looked on the meetings as revitalizing both individuals and the church. And from his side he leveled charges such as that Meyer preached too much about clothes. To the charge of mixing he and his associates replied time and again that they accepted any people as brothers and sisters[83] if they were "born again of the incorruptible seed that is the living word of God." They accepted them "regardless of which church-party they wish to be in."

Those of course were admirable words from some points of view. But whatever their merits they assumed that Mennonites should make radical changes in their thinking about church—about how they "kept house," marked who was in and who out, exercised discipline, and maintained convictions on matters such as pacifism. Hoch and his supporters would use lines laid down by revivalism for the church's boundaries. And they accepted the denominationalist idea that churches were only different Christian parties.

Daniel Brenneman's case was a bit different. In 1849 the Canadian conference expelled the Hoch party without doing the same to Meyer. But in 1872, two years before it expelled Brenneman, the Indiana conference censured Brenneman's chief opponent, Old Order-minded bishop Jacob Wisler.[84] Nor were Brenneman and most other founders of the MBC group as polemical and concerned for self-vindication as was Hoch. Yet the deeper issues in Brenneman's break with the "old" Mennonites were much the same as in Hoch's. The formal charges against him were that he had supported a minister who had baptized without the approval of his bishop, that he had let women speak at public meetings in violation of Scripture, and that he had refused to take counsel. Ministers whom Brenneman had supported included John Krupp of Branch County, Michigan, and Solomon Eby of near Berlin (present-day Kitchener), Ontario.

Eby soon formed a union with the church Hoch had started, as Brenneman and his Indiana followers soon did as well. The public meetings in question were prayer meetings and revival meetings.[85] In 1874 Daniel Brenneman and his followers were expelled from the "old" Mennonites. The Indiana conference censured them even though they continued at the outset to espouse specific Mennonite teachings including nonresistance.[86] It expelled Brenneman even though he clearly wanted a deeper and more vital spirituality and was an attractive preacher, popular among youths and others.[87]

As for Methodism, Brenneman later recounted that he and his Indiana supporters decided quite soon not to join either the Methodistic Evangelical Association (as one preacher and a deacon at Yellow Creek had already done[88]) or the Free Methodists. He said they refrained because those groups allowed warfare, baptized infants, and neglected the foot-washing rite. The Evangelical Association also allowed lodge membership.[89] However, in 1880 the Brenneman group adopted a device Methodists (and others) had often used, namely camp meetings. A year earlier John F. Funk's "old" Mennonite paper had printed a borrowed item accusing camp meetings of luring people away from churches on the Sabbath to places where hucksters hawked their wares and where many people went only "to gratify curiosity and for mere pleasure." In 1889 the same paper would declare flatly that "the camp meeting is a thing unknown among orthodox Mennonites," whose "discipline ... absolutely prohibits it."

In words suggesting the clash of older Pietism with newer revivalism, the *Herald* said that the Christian who wanted to "edify his soul and enjoy communion with God" "in quietude" would go to "God's house" rather than to camp meetings. Camp meetings, the paper complained, usually included "boistrous and exciting scenes." To put the words "Mennonite" and "camp meeting" together was a contradiction. But whatever Funk's *Herald* might say, Brenneman's group did begin a more or less Mennonite version of camp meetings. Brenneman stood for a fusion of Mennonitism and Methodism. As a whole the new denomination took on a Wesleyan holiness flavor. A friendly historian of the group has written that from its beginning the new denomination's doctrine was "highly evangelistic and strongly Wesleyan, laying a deep emphasis on the experience of entire sanctification."[90]

In 1883, as it took the label "Mennonite Brethren in Christ," the denomination considered a name without the word Mennonite. But it kept the word so as not to lose military exemption in Canada.[91] In the latter-twentieth century, with the word dropped, only a few Missionary Church people seem conscious of Mennonite origins. From a Mennonite perspective the denomination seems to have evolved into a fairly standard North American "evangelical" if not "Fundamentalist" one, with virtually no pacifism or other particularly Mennonite convictions. Might their congregations still be Mennonite if church leaders in the 1840s to '70s had treated Hoch, Brenneman, and other MBC founders more tolerantly and diplomatically? Perhaps. But the forces for change ran far deeper than mere diplomacy or personal conflict.

The third group, the Defenseless Mennonite Church, grew out of issues that were partly revivalistic but also partly very Amish ones. In 1865 Henry Egly differed with part of his own congregation and with other Amish leaders and was censured. Soon he gathered supporters and in a number of Amish communities "Egly Amish" congregations appeared. The immediate issue was that Egly had extended membership to some persons whom other Amish congregations had disciplined and were shunning.[92] A less immediate fact was that Egly, born in Germany in 1824, had come to America with relatively liberal Amish who had gone to Butler County, Ohio, and never settled in Pennsylvania. Congregations who supported him were generally in communities of more or less similar immigrants—in northwestern Ohio, eastern Indiana, and central Illinois.[93] So the quarrel was a very Amish one. Yet it also showed revivalistic influences.

Egly said he doubted that the original Amish baptisms of the persons in question had been based on genuine conversions and new birth. So he reasoned that those persons were like new Christians, not errant church members. In that case shunning did not apply. For about a decade Egly had been preaching much about the new birth, with some emphasis on inner experience as a criterion.[94]

The dispute broke out just as Amish people were sorting themselves into Old Order Amish and more progressive Amish Mennonites.[95] Egly and his early followers were moderately progressive. For instance they built meetinghouses, yet were not the first Amish to do so. And at least until about 1890 they dressed plainly and kept Amish-Mennonite beliefs.[96] Except for some new emphasis on conversion and inner experience they did not change doctrine, practice, and cultural traits faster than most other Amish Mennonites who did not become Old Order. In Egly's lifetime his people appear to have learned from revivalism without departing radically from Amish faith and practice.

Then in 1890 he died and the group took a different path. During the 1890s a young evangelist named Joseph Ramseyer changed Defenseless Mennonite history. A product of the revivals in Canada which had helped shape the Mennonite Brethren in Christ, he was the kind of revivalist who testified of a sudden personal conversion while he worked in a field. He held revival meetings in Kansas in 1894, where he gained wide attention because people collapsed as if suddenly struck down. In 1896, attending a Christian and Missionary Alliance convention, he had himself rebaptized by immersion to replace his Amish-Mennonite baptism by pouring. He also taught a premillennial eschatology. Perhaps most importantly he emphasized the holiness doctrine of "second work of grace" or "entire sanctification"—an empowering baptism of the Holy Spirit separate from the original baptism of repentance from sin. By 1898 Joseph Ramseyer and others (including Egly's son Joseph, another of the church's leading ministers) formed a new group, the Missionary Church Association.

Later the Association would merge into the Missionary Church. Yet losses to that Association did not divert the Egly group, the "Defenseless Mennonite Church," from its new path. Many of its members became increasingly revivalist and Protestant and, in the twentieth century, Fundamentalist.[97] By mid-to-latter twentieth century only a minority of its people remained pacifist.[98] Nevertheless, the group retains a Mennonite identity and name, being in the 1980s a Mennonite branch of about 3,700 members. It originated partly from internal Amish tensions and partly from the effects of American revivalism.

CHAPTER 5

PATHS to PIETY: PROGRESSIVE MOVEMENTS

> [Yes,] Jesus commanded, . . . "Peace be with you." . . . But this peace of Jesus does not call wrong things right. . . . As long as I can remember, many ministers and, I think, the majority of the congregations have believed that various customs which are kept up among us ought simply to be dropped, and that the proceedings of the Conference should be written up. . . .
>
> —"New" Mennonite Abraham Hunsicker to "old" Mennonite bishop Christian Herr, 1848.

> [An old bishop told me,] "You know that if we would adopt their new constitution and discipline, then we would confuse and destroy our congregations." . . . Why did you not much rather take in hand the teaching of Jesus in Matthew 18, especially from the 21st verse to the end of the chapter, and keep house accordingly?
>
> —Christian Herr, in reply.[1]

On October 7, 1847, sixteen ministers and bishops, attending the regular fall session of the Franconia Mennonite conference, walked out of the meeting and soon began the East Pennsylvania Mennonite conference. Franconia was the oldest of Mennonite conferences in America, one of the two major conferences of the eastern Pennsylvania heartland. Those who walked out did so over issues of church renewal. But unlike Daniel Hoch and Daniel Brenneman they did not choose revivalism and emphasize inner experience as their means. They did want a faith that seemed less formal and they hoped to instill a deeper piety.

Within a decade like-minded Mennonites elsewhere in the U.S. would found another new conference, the General Conference of Mennonites in North America, which eventually became a new

"General Conference" (GC) Mennonite denomination. The "GC" body, built up from East Pennsylvania congregations and many others, became the second-largest Mennonite branch in North America. Its appearance offered Mennonites a different option. More than "old" Mennonites, the GC congregations were activist in matters such as missions and education. They also went much further in accepting two American patterns: denominationalism and progressivism.

Progressivism was faith that change—new institutions, new practices—usually meant improvement, not a falling away. It was faith in "progress."

JOHN H. OBERHOLTZER AND THE REFORM MOVEMENT IN EASTERN PENNSYLVANIA

Revivalism was not much of an influence on the man who was probably the most important of all mid-nineteenth-century Mennonite church reformers, John H. Oberholtzer. Oberholtzer strongly agreed with Hoch, Daniel Brenneman, and other revivalists about some of the "old" church's shortcomings: slow-tongued ministers and dull sermons; rigid, reactionary, and arbitrary authority; fixation with clothing and external trivia; and need for deeper and more inward piety. He agreed also that Mennonites were too separatist and slow to fellowship with other pious Christians. Sharing certain ideas, Hoch and Oberholtzer and their supporters mistook each other for being like-minded.[2] Oberholtzer even ordained Hoch to be bishop of the new group in Canada. But he was no revivalist.

Oberholtzer's way to deeper piety was not experiential conversion so much as nurture. In 1844 he reprinted the Elbing catechism and in 1847 he began a *Kinderlehre*, a sort of Sunday school. Moreover he and his supporters responded partly to secular, not strictly religious, impulses.[3] Perhaps Mennonites needed some secular influence, especially to help them be less preoccupied with their own inner life and more ready to go into the world with their understanding of the gospel. At the outset, Oberholtzer was as preoccupied with internal Mennonite issues as were traditionalists. Nor has anyone proven that changes such as relaxing rules about clothing ever helped Mennonites fulfill their mission.[4]

In any case Oberholtzer and his supporters quickly chose to be more in the world, culturally. Compared to the "old" Mennonites of the 1840s, they gave a somewhat different answer to a longtime Mennonite and Amish (really a Christian) dilemma: how to be, as a Scripture says, in the world but not of it.

John H. Oberholtzer was born (1809), grew up, and lived at Milford Square, Pennsylvania—on the northern edge of the large Franconia conference Mennonite settlement. He became a blacksmith, locksmith, schoolteacher, preacher, and printer. In 1852, five years after breaking with the "old" Mennonites, he began the first Mennonite periodical in America of any consequence. His role as a Mennonite leader began more or less with his ordination as a minister in 1842, in a congregation named "Swamp." One report says that the first time he preached someone remarked that his sermon had been "*eine studierte*"—that is, a "studied" or prepared one. In a day when Mennonites often warned against clergy who relied on learning, the remark must have been a barb. Yet as a preacher Oberholtzer was soon popular, among Mennonites and others.[5]

Within two years of his ordination the new preacher was deep in controversy. From 1844 to 1846 the Franconia conference, highest Mennonite authority in his area, barred him from having voice in its sessions. Then in 1847 he led a reform movement which permanently split the Mennonite church in his region. Superficially the issues were three:

> (1) For almost five years after he was ordained in 1842, Oberholtzer all but refused to wear a certain style of "round coat" expected of ministers.
>
> (2) Then he wrote a church constitution and with a group of fellow ministers proposed that the old conference adopt it.
>
> (3) Oberholtzer wanted the conference to keep written minutes so that there could be no question about its rulings.

Opponents saw his innovations as departures from the "old foundation."[6] Also they saw a constitution and records as inviting a sort of litigation.

To conference leaders the coat issue was not just about garb but about humility and submission.[7] As the controversy over a constitution and minutes heated up, Oberholtzer put on the "round coat." But in so doing was he being humble and obedient? acting prudently and properly for unity's sake? or making a play for power, ironically by manipulating a symbol of humility?

An adviser who encouraged him to accept the coat at a late date was a Skippack congregation minister named Abraham Hunsicker. Hunsicker was a liberal man. Surely he cared little for prescribed garb. But he was political, having once been reprimanded by church authorities for getting too deep into county politics.[8] Was his advice to wear the coat merely a political maneuver? If one suspects so, what about his tradition-minded opponents? Perhaps they also manipulated the symbols of humility as a means to power. Ten years earlier a neighboring Mennonite preacher had quoted words from the European Pietist Gerhard Tersteegen to say that a show of humility is often a front for pride.[9]

Whatever the answers, Oberholtzer donned the round coat too late to win the conservatives' trust, and the coat issue became moot. More important was his constitution. He and his supporters offered it to the conference as it met in May of 1847. The conference did not give it a public reading. Traditionalists later charged that the conference moderator, bishop John Hunsicker, an Oberholtzer supporter, hoped to ram it through without a reading. Reformers complained that conferees had voted it down without open debate. What clearly happened was that a conference majority voted not to have it printed for wider distribution and consideration. Hurt by that, Hunsicker said: "This is party spirit, it will be printed after all." His words were fateful. Submission to the group was at the very heart of what traditionalists understood as the "old foundation."[10]

After the conference, traditionalists refused to meet formally with Oberholtzer supporters; and, despite the conference ruling, the Oberholtzer party had the constitution printed. Distrust multiplied when most of the copies mysteriously disappeared while being shipped from the printshop by stage. Then a half-year later at the regular autumn meeting of the conference Oberholtzer and fifteen ministers and bishops who supported him seated themselves as a bloc. The conference decided that they had been disobedient and voted to deny them a voice in the proceedings. With that, on that October day in 1847, the sixteen walked out. Leading them was the venerable John Hunsicker—who died only six weeks later.[11] The schism was fact.

Beneath the surface were deeper issues. For better or worse, Oberholtzer's constitution proposed some basic changes. Two important ones were to allow suing at law in cases deemed clearly just, and to permit marriage across denominational lines. Another clause suggested salaries for ministers—a pattern traditionalists were sure had brought corruption to the Christian church through history. A vague passage allowed acceptance of other churches' baptisms; traditionalists read it, probably incorrectly, as accepting baptisms performed on infants.[12] A less doctrinal, more general issue was at least as momentous: the changes in procedures and patterns of authority implied by a constitution and minute-keeping. Underlying every issue was the way traditionalists viewed change: not as progress, but as leaving the "old foundations."

Two notions of authority were at work. After the walkout the old conference voted to forgive the dissidents if the dissidents would admit they had violated "the old gospel regulations." Thereupon the conference would accept them "in love" and even restore them to their ministerial offices. Given the seriousness with which they viewed disobedience, the traditionalist majority must have thought their offer quite generous. But the reformers thought it was most arbitrary and unjust for the conference to say, without debate, that the constitution departed from the old foundations. They insisted they were the ones true to New Testament and Mennonite teaching. To recant would be to violate conscience. With that attitude the reformers met on October 28 and adopted the constitution.[13] A new "East Pennsylvania" Mennonite conference was born. Eventually, as part of the "General Conference" Mennonite church, it would be renamed the "Eastern District Conference."

Such were the events; the dynamics ran deeper. The reformers were more from the edges of the Mennonite community, the traditionalists more from its center, known as *Menishteland* (Mennonite country).[14] In outlook the reformers were not notably humble. They might consider humility a fair virtue but they did not make it central to their theology, ethics, and personal styles. Abraham Hunsicker's political activities were one indication. Another was an urge for a self-improving kind of education. Over the previous decade Pennsylvania had been establishing a system of public schools. Most Mennonites opposed the change. But the "new" Mennonites (as those in the East Pennsylvania conference were soon called) gained a congregation at Bowmansville in Lancaster County which had been formed by advocates who supported public schools—and who, in a dispute about the issue, had resorted to a lawsuit.

In the Franconia district itself the liberal-minded minister Abraham Hunsicker and his family were especially education-minded. In 1843 they had named a newborn son for the noted public-school crusader Horace Mann; and in 1848 they began an academy which (with political overtones) they named "Freeland." It was the first Mennonite-related post-elementary school in North America.[15]

The 1840s were a time when self-improvement associations flourished in America; and both Hunsicker and Oberholtzer helped promote something called "The Skippack Association for the Promotion of Useful Knowledge."[16] Writing to friends in Germany in 1849, Oberholtzer lamented that American Mennonites were in a "low state of ignorance." He was glad to say also that his group had "some of the most skillful speakers (thank God!)." In the old church, he said, four preachers out of five were failures in the pulpit. Yes, the first consideration for a minister was a "blameless walk," but congregations should also choose men who could speak in "a clear, distinct voice" and with "natural fluency."[17] Surely his advice fit New Testament principles of discerning gifts in the church. But it might have been more acceptable if he had warned also that such preachers had to stay humble.

Oberholtzer's figure of "four out of five" may have been hyperbole. Only about a fourth of Franconia's Mennonites chose the new conference. The old church kept some able leaders, for instance, a schoolteacher-minister named Henry Nice and another preacher named John Geil. Geil was so attractive that a decade after the schism his presence helped keep bright, educated, ambitious John F. Funk in the old church.[18] Yet it was true, the "lot" in the old church was selecting some preachers of slow tongue and limited appeal.

Also true, no doubt, were some of Oberholtzer's other charges—for instance, that "old" Mennonites often baptized applicants routinely, without special instruction in "the way of salvation." The old church did need reform. It was not articulating its theology, outlook, and ethos in ways to make them very prophetic and inviting—not to people of the world, and often not even to its members' own sons and daughters.[19]

The reformers might have leveled even stronger charges had they challenged the old church more on its own ground. At its best the old-style Mennonite community should have sent someone to Oberholtzer with kindly, face-to-face counsel before it resorted to official reprimand. Yet, as historian John Ruth has pointed out, it seems never to have done so.[20] In the case of the coat the reformers might have asked why a minister was supposed to dress differently from other members. More generally, they might even have asked about pride. Were leaders of the old conference really using power in ways consistent with Mennonite humility?

But the reformers seldom spoke of humility.[21] At the extreme their words were quite the opposite. Man, "being a progressive creature, must rise gradually," wrote Abraham Hunsicker, previously president of the new conference, in 1851; "nor is there a limit set this side of infinity, to which the perseverance of man, ever directed to improvement, may not attain." Few in the reform party would have gone that far; in fact, Hunsicker published those words as part of a self-defense after even his "new" Mennonite congregation at Skippack had censured him. But if Hunsicker went beyond the limits, much of the reformers' language smacked more of the assertive mood of progress than of humility theology.[22]

Some of Oberholtzer's reforms are clear examples of what scholars have seen within Western society's process of modernization. According to students of modernization, pre-modern authority is largely personal rather than attached to constitutional systems and documents, except perhaps to some ancient and sacred documents which personal authorities then guard and interpret. Also, traditional authority lies with persons more than with the offices they hold. Modern authority, by contrast, is precisely as Oberholtzer was demanding. It is "rationalized"—that is, formally defined, deliberately spelled out, limited by constitution, and not left to personal discretion. It rests on documents, such as constitutions and minutes.[23]

In the same vein Oberholtzer and his supporters applied the ideas of due process: the right of individuals to hearings and to answer accusers, etc. Modern concepts of protecting one's rights underlay their change regarding lawsuits. The same modern ring was in their statement that to recant would be to violate conscience. Indeed the statement sounded not only modern, but quite American. Of course it also reminds one of another group who asserted the rights of conscience: the sixteenth-century Anabaptists.[24]

In theological terms the differences about authority raised questions of biblical interpretation and of legalism. On matters such as the coat Oberholtzer and his supporters said they were bound only to rules that had clear backing in Scripture or, at least, ancient Mennonite teaching. Responding, the old conference seems at one point to have resolved to be guided only by "gospel" standards—but then, on second thought, to have rescinded.[25] Of course a phrase such as "gospel standards" solved nothing. Would "gospel standards" include prescribing a coat as a symbol of humility and obedience? The conference seems not to have been really rigid on the matter of ministers' coats: it allowed newly ordained ministers to wear their ordinary coats until the garments wore out.[26]

But, understandably, Oberholtzer saw the issue as one of legalism, or what he called *Nebengesetz*, a word implying a proliferation of rules about nonessentials.[27] But were Oberholtzer's plans for due process and appeals to minutes and a constitution any less legalistic? Or his assumptions about appeals to Scripture? The question has no simple answer. The traditionalists sensed that the Bible did not always speak without the church's interpreting and applying it. Oberholtzer did not elaborate a theory about Scripture, but in practice his view seems to have been the rather fundamentalist one that Scripture's meaning is self-evident, and that to interpret and apply the Bible requires little more than to consult it. Such a view, of course, is an invitation to treat the Bible as one treats a code of law.

Nevertheless, Oberholtzer had raised valid issues which any Christian group must confront if it insists on practical righteousness. However petty the immediate questions, he and his supporters addressed some of the genuine issues the Christian church continually faces: the nature of church and its authority, the relation of grace and works, the nurturing of new generations in the faith, and how to translate God's rule into everyday practice. Moreover they touched on the relation of Christians to government, to the American faith that change brings progress, and to the nation's pattern of denominationalism. And with their concerns about constitutionality, due process, and checks on arbitrary rule they shared some of the nation's central political concerns.

Unfortunately, the East Pennsylvania conference soon found that its ideas of authority and procedure did not resolve all dilemmas. Having created an institution to conserve, "new" Mennonite leaders soon acted like conservatives. Indeed they had always been reformers and modernizers more than liberals. So while they offered new protections to individuals, they by no means abandoned the Mennonite idea of a disciplined church. Their constitution specified excommunication for quite a list of offenses: "false doctrine, blasphemy, contentiousness, false witness or perjury, theft, fornication, adultery, lying, drunkenness, quarrelsomeness, malice, deception, violence, unrighteous seeking for financial gain, luxury, gross profanation of the Sabbath, impudent mockery, cruelty to subjects, and the like." That list may have reflected the moral precepts of society at large more than the Mennonite ethic of nonvengeance and defenselessness. But the document also said that "taking the sword to wage war is forbidden," and it covered some other "Mennonite" concerns such as no taking of oaths.[28]

In any case the new conference and its congregations did try to exercise discipline. The problem was, questions of discipline were more difficult than ever. For the reformers had broken old patterns of authority and introduced a heady mood of freedom.

One of the early acts of the key Skippack congregation and then of the new conference was to censure Abraham Hunsicker. With him they censured a rather strange deacon and nephew of Hunsicker named Abraham Grater. The two had begun to preach open communion. Their doing so posed quite a dilemma. The "new" Mennonites, in the spirit of American denominationalism, had advocated more tolerance toward non-Mennonite Christians. But Mennonites had always used "close" communion to aid discipline. Close communion said clearly who was in good standing and who was not.

Even more troublesome, Hunsicker and Grater wanted to open communion to Odd Fellows (members of the Odd Fellows lodge, not odd as Mennonites!); and the lodge issue was a hot one for "new" Mennonites as for various other denominations of the day. In complicated proceedings during which it also censured the two men's accusers, the new conference voted in 1851 to silence Hunsicker and Grater. Hunsicker went on to form his own quasi-church or churches called the "Christian Society of Montgomery County" and the "Trinity Christian Society." Eventually those bodies joined the Calvinistic Reformed denomination. His Freeland Academy, or Freeland Seminary, evolved into a Reformed-related institution, Ursinus College.[29]

By silencing Hunsicker and Grater the new conference was marking its limits. Several years later it also alienated and censured a minister named Henry Johnson (1806-1879), who had often served as the conference's secretary, was bishop of the historic Skippack congregation, and was Hunsicker's chief critic. This time the formal issue was traditional: the rite of foot washing. Unlike the rest of the "old" Franconia conference, the Skippack congregation had long observed the rite and Johnson wanted it continued. There was also a personal clash between Johnson and a fellow minister, David Bergey. In 1859 the conference ruled that Johnson and some other ministers at Skippack were out of order. In 1861 it expelled him. For more than a century his congregation continued independently with the nickname "Johnson Mennonites." About 1971 it rejoined the Eastern District conference.[30]

The real issue troubling the new conference was that of authority. Its underlying premise was that on important points well-meaning Christians could simply turn to Scripture to settle disagreements, while on lesser ones they could follow the will of the majority.[31] But in practice those ideas were too simplistic. From the outset the new conference turned to another authority to decide what the Bible said: no longer the gathered elders but the written constitution. For instance, as they censured Hunsicker the conferees said they rejected "anything contrary to Scripture or the Constitution," and then cited a verse of Scripture plus a constitutional clause. (Both citations were so unspecific that it took lawyer-like casuistry to apply them.) At a key point during the Johnson censure the conference appealed to the constitution without even mentioning whether foot-washing was taught in the New Testament.[32]

Indeed, in the Johnson case, treatment of Scripture was most odd. By practicing the foot-washing rite Johnson intended to follow a New Testament text quite literally. At first the conference gently declared the matter optional and called for mutual tolerance. But as the case came to a head it said the scriptural statements on foot washing were "to be interpreted in our church as having only a spiritual application." It forbade a literal interpretation![33] By the subterfuge of spiritualizing an awkward passage, the conference got around a simple appeal to Scripture. Yet ten years earlier simple appeal to Scripture had been Oberholtzer's key demand.

The new conference also seemed confused about where its authority stopped and when to leave decisions to congregations. That was especially true in the intertwined debates about open communion and lodges. Of course the open communion question, and a related one regarding whose baptism to accept, also raised another question: the denominationalist one of how to relate to other churches. In 1851 the new conference clearly allowed communion to people baptized as infants. The next year it ruled also that a congregation could allow any denomination's minister to preach so long as Mennonites could consider him evangelical, sound in doctrine, and in good standing with his own church.[34] Without totally abandoning the Mennonite ideal of a close-knit, peoplehood church,[35] the "new" Mennonites sought a place in American denominationalism.

That place was not a revivalistic one. To friends in Germany Oberholtzer wrote of the second birth coming by faith and of knowing "the way of salvation." But his concerns were for catechism, nurture, and "purity of doctrine," not experiential conversion. In that vein he conducted his program to teach children, his *Kinderlehre*. In 1848 and 1861 the conference sponsored more printings of the Elbing catechism.[36]

Meanwhile some "new" Mennonite ministers, particularly William Gehman and William Schelly from the northern edge of the conference district, began to advocate prayer meetings. At an 1853 session (with Daniel Hoch present), the conference approved the innovation. But it did so very cautiously, saying prayer meetings were only optional and to be held only "at proper times and in proper order." Soon it had occasion to apply the "proper order" principle, for stories and rumors cropped up saying that enthusiasts at Gehman's meetings were shouting, leaping, and rolling on the floor.

In 1856 "new" Mennonite leaders met in special session and

said more clearly that the gospel did not require the prayer meetings. Thereafter the conference expelled twenty-four of Gehman's strongest supporters, forbade them from using the Upper Milford meetinghouse, and called Schelly to task for supporting the party. Schelly shared his feelings with Daniel Hoch of Canada, and Hoch eventually hinted that the Oberholtzer people were legalists after all.[37]

At work were three different models of church. For signs of true piety and of being part of God's people the old group insisted on more external signs and submission to traditional, oral authority. The revivalists looked to experiential conversion and fervor. And the "new" Mennonites, neither traditional nor Methodistic, were more like Pennsylvania-German Reformed and Lutherans: staid, nurture-oriented, and Pietistic, but not revivalist. Oberholtzer and his supporters worked for a purer piety through better teaching of orthodox doctrine, through removing outdated encumbrances, through more efficient and modern church government, and through wider sharing with churches which were conservative in a Protestant sense.

THE GENERAL CONFERENCE (GC) OPTION

Soon there was a slightly different model to choose: a progressivism expressed in mission, higher education, and other activism. Both Hoch and Oberholtzer had spent much of their energy negatively, reacting against what they considered the formalism, legalism, and outmoded ways of the "old" church. The new model was more positive. Partly it must have been so because most early leaders were recent immigrants from Europe. As newcomers they had not built up strong reactions against the older communities' controls.

The new model took form as a "General Conference of Mennonites in North America." The conference began in 1860, scarcely larger than a mustard seed.[38]

In 1856 an item appeared in *Das Christliche Volksblatt* proposing that Mennonites join into some sort of union. The *Volksblatt*, produced by John H. Oberholtzer and a joint-stock association, had replaced Oberholtzer's first paper, *Der Religioese Botschafter*. Publishing such papers was itself a form of progressive activism. Also, in 1858 the East Pennsylvania conference took up another topic on which Oberholtzer reported: mission. It said that Oberholtzer as conference chairman should write to European Mennonites for "definite information concerning their missionary teaching and practice." Meanwhile a similar mood was building far away in Lee County, Iowa, in a small congregation of immigrants mainly from the Palatinate and Bavaria in southwestern Germany.[39]

Apart from one or two Amish families the earliest Mennonites in Iowa were those in Lee County. The very first, arriving in 1839, were a Palatine native named John C. Krehbiel (1811-) and his young family. In the 1840s and early 1850s others arrived named Bergthold, Gram, Roth, Schmitt, Risser, Ellenberger, Herstein, Goebel, Deutsch, Ruth, Leisy, Sprunger, Vogt, Hertzler, Lehman, etc., plus more Krehbiels. One Krehbiel was a young man named Christian, later a notable General Conference leader. One Ruth was Susanna, a bright woman who in several years would become Christian's wife. Like some other able women of her day she would contribute immeasurably but privately to Mennonite history, by rearing a family of leaders and by supporting her husband's public career.[40]

By 1849 the immigrant settlers organized a congregation, and soon built a meetinghouse near the village of Franklin. Others who lived closer to nearby West Point began another congregation there and eventually (in 1863) built a meetinghouse. In 1853 the two congregations formed a plan of union and a constitution. The constitution covered matters such as communion and ordination, mandated yearly classes for substantial pre-baptismal instruction, obligated parents to enroll their children at age 14, and said ministers should then decide who was ready for membership. The charter, like John Oberholtzer's, had a mood more of nurture and confirmation than of experiential new birth. And oddly, it did not mention nonresistance or avoiding military service. By 1854 Lee County Mennonites also began a German-language school and called a Bavarian who had studied in Switzerland, Christian Schowalter, to be its teacher.[41]

The Lee County Mennonites were not traditionalists. Back in southwestern Germany, Mennonites were being swept by Pietism on the one hand and secularism on the other. For at least seventy-five years they had been struggling and sometimes disagreeing about how much to change. By mid-nineteenth century quite a few had opened themselves to education, office holding in local government, trained and salaried pastors, and the like. The Iowa settlers had emigrated partly to get away from some of the secularization and from military service.[42] Yet compared to most Mennonites in America they were decidedly progressive. They supported mission, education, and Mennonite union, and they believed generally that change would bring progress. With such ideas, a few Mennonites met in 1860 and planted the mustard seed that would produce the GC church.

In 1859 Berend Carl Roosen, a prominent Mennonite pastor in Hamburg, Germany, replied to the Pennsylvanians' inquiry about mission. He told the Pennsylvanians how to send money to a Mennonite mission agency in Holland; and from then on some did.[43] Also in 1859 those two lonely congregations in Iowa began to reach out. Meeting together, they decided to take up monthly collections for home and foreign missions; send one of their ministers to visit and serve communion to a few Mennonites living at Oskaloosa, Iowa; and form a committee (three Krehbiels and one other) to correspond with other congregations and with Oberholtzer's *Volksblatt* and invite other Mennonites into their union. The *Volksblatt* responded in the mood and language of true progressives. "Brethren," it asked, "what shall we do? shall we remain inactive, or shall we stride forward?"[44]

The East Pennsylvania conference took note also, but with a time-honored pattern of giving encouragement but no money. It recommended that ministers attend voluntarily. Only two did: Oberholtzer (only after someone paid the penniless leader's fare), and one Enos Loux. At West Point they found no other non-Iowans[45]—not even Ephraim Hunsberger, a like-minded man whom they had visited en route. Hunsberger was an eastern Pennsylvanian who had been ordained as bishop by Oberholtzer in 1852 and then had gone west to serve a few progressive Mennonites near Wadsworth in Medina County, Ohio. An activist, he had joined with Daniel Hoch to form a kind of union between their congregations.[46]

In 1861 the General Conference would hold its second session at Wadsworth. Seven years later it would plant its first important institution there, a school it would call Wadsworth Institute. As for Hoch, in 1860 he was still partly overlooking the inherent difference between his revivalism and the more staid and organizational progressivism of the new GC movement. He attended that second meeting at Wadsworth and was elected conference chairman for a term. Yet neither Hunsberger nor Hoch attended that first conference in Iowa in 1860.[47]

The founding event was on May 28 and 29—probably in a German Methodist meetinghouse where the West Point congregation met before it had its own building. Except for Oberholtzer and Loux the only nonlocal person present was a minister named Joseph Schroeder from near Polk City, Iowa. But many local people turned out and a committee of four Iowa farmer-preachers plus Oberholtzer went ahead and drew up a plan of union. (The four were Schroeder, two Jacob Krehbiels, and David Ruth.) With marvelous audacity they named their tiny body a "Union of All Mennonites of North America."[48]

Following the committee's plan the gathered assembly adopted resolutions which said:

1. All Mennonite branches in North America should join in fellowship "regardless of minor differences."

2. They should sever relations only if "a person or church" abandoned "fundamental" Mennonite doctrine "concerning baptism, the oath, etc., (wherein we follow Menno Simon)" based on the gospel as taught by Jesus Christ and his apostles.

3. There had to be "unequivocal Scripture evidence" before passing a judgment of heresy.

4. No excommunication would be valid without "a real transgression or neglect" in violation of Scripture.

5. "Without molestation or hindrance," congregations and districts would have freedom to follow whatever rules they established "for their own government" so long as the rules did not violate "our general confession."

6. There should be no interference if on account of "existing customs or ordinance" a person chose to leave one congregation and unite with another congregation of the conference.[49]

To unite, the group said, was "conformable to 1 Cor. 12: 12-27." With that conviction the optimistic gathering turned to the content of its progressive activism. First, missions, both home and foreign. The group established two mission treasuries, one in Iowa and the other at Oberholtzer's printing firm at Milford Square, Pennsylvania. Second, publication. For that it endorsed and recommended support for "the Publishing House already in existence in our denomination"—that is for the Milford Square enterprise. Third, education. The conference pledged "that an institution for theological training shall be established as soon as it can be accomplished."[50]

Those GC general conference founders did not intend to start a separate branch of Mennonites. Instead, their goal was a rather loose union of all. The new organization was to carry on certain activities for Mennonites in common but not exert centralized control over congregational discipline, at least not over "nonessentials."[51] Yet for some years, few congregations responded.

The second meeting of the conference, at Wadsworth in May of 1861, attracted a wider range of delegates, yet they came from only eight congregations: two in Iowa, one in Illinois, one in Ohio, three in Pennsylvania, and one at Waterloo, Canada. Even a most optimistic history of the conference, published by a son of Christian Krehbiel in 1898, admitted that "this, indeed, was but a small number to inaugurate the movement which should ultimately embrace all Mennonites of America." The third session, at Summerfield, Illinois, in 1863, attracted delegates from several more "new" Mennonite congregations in Pennsylvania and from the Hoch-related congregation near Niagara Falls in Canada in what came to be known as Vineland. But after that there was little change or expansion for a decade and a half—except that the Canadians often sent no one.[52] Perhaps the Canadians were beginning to sense the differences between Hoch's and the GC styles of progressivism and reform.

In the 1880s and '90s some Swiss-speaking congregations joined. At that time the Swiss were sorting themselves and taking different points along a spectrum of traditional to progressive. As they did, the GC option attracted congregations at Berne, Indiana; Fortuna, Missouri; and Wayne County in the eastern and Putnam and Allen counties in the western parts of Ohio. In the 1890s and in the twentieth century various other liberal-minded congregations of Amish or "old" Mennonite background would join. Among all who joined, the Swiss at Berne were so prominent that for a time their town was a center of GC publishing and other activities, especially because of a dynamic young pastor named Samuel (S. F.) Sprunger.

Much more important for the long run was a massive influx of immigrants from the Russian empire in the 1870s. Their joining changed the conference from a fledgling body of reformer-activists and made it an established denomination. It gave the GC church new ethnicity and moved its center of gravity far to the west. In the latter twentieth century the GCs' institutional center is Newton, Kansas; their U.S. membership is 60 percent (total North American membership, 70 percent) from Russian and Prussian Mennonite extraction.[53]

Even as a fledgling movement, however, the new conference got right to work. One task was to send out a *Reiseprediger*—a traveling minister, for which it quickly appointed a Palatine named Daniel Hege. Hege had studied at an academy in Germany and, for three years, at an Evangelical seminary in Missouri. The conference appointed him mainly to be pastor to scattered Mennonites, an activity that in the nineteenth century made up much of what Mennonites called "home mission." Unfortunately, he soon died, at age 36; but before his death he also worked for the cause of union and for another cause dear to progressives, Wadsworth Institute.

The resolution favoring the school had been passed after a

John H. Oberholtzer (1809-1895), mid-century Mennonite church reformer.

Jan Gleysteen collection

strong plea from Hege that Mennonites needed a school to produce ministers more able to explain God's Word in a way to bring people to a "personal living experience," promote Mennonite unity, and be a "means toward the spread of the Gospel." In his travels Hege raised money for the purpose—$5,700 by late 1863, gathered from twenty-four congregations and some individuals.[54]

Wadsworth Institute opened in 1868 and lasted only a decade. In its brief life many currents swept across its campus: from American and European Mennonitism, from the nation's optimism, from a college-building fever that had many denominations in its grip, from progressives at odds with people not quite so progressive, and from financial burdens too heavy for the school's few supporters. However logical eastern Ohio seemed as a central location, the institution surely suffered from not having a large Mennonite community around it.[55] It suffered also from an unfortunate clash within its faculty, especially between the Iowa teacher Christian Schowalter, now at Wadsworth as principal, and a well-trained Mennonite scholar imported from Germany, Carl Justus van der Smissen. That clash was probably due in part to trustees' not making lines of responsibility very clear.[56]

More fundamentally, the school did not appeal to a very wide spectrum of Mennonites. Much about it did not convey a gospel of humility. Christian Krehbiel, preaching at the institute's dedication, made two or three references to humility but spoke generally

Courtesy of Mennonite Library and Archives at Bethel College

Wadsworth Institute, Wadsworth, Ohio.

in tones confident and progressive. He used imagery not of Jesus' manger but of his triumphal, palm-strewn entry into Jerusalem. And instead of referring to the earth as a vale of tears he spoke of "our enlightened world."[57] The institute's building had lines that were simple, rectangular, and quite plain. But it was a high, three-story affair crowned with a columned belfry and a bell which weighed (by one perhaps-exaggerated report) "about eight hundred pounds." Such architecture may have seemed natural to Europeans transplanted to Lee County in Iowa or to Summerfield in Illinois. It may have pleased Oberholtzer-style progressives who felt comfortable in Reformed or Lutheran churches. But it was quite unlike those marvelous symbols of humility, the severely plain, low, towerless meetinghouses of most Mennonites in America in the mid-1860s. Besides (due perhaps to civil war inflation), the cost of the building was much more than expected. The school struggled with a troublesome debt.[58]

There were other unhumble symbols. The European van der Smissen wore an academic robe; and once when a visitor touched it and asked its meaning, the scholar curtly replied that he would not discuss tailoring.[59] Students went home dressed in ways the home folks thought too fashionable, and speaking high German rather than their communities' dialects. An example was young S. F. Sprunger of Berne, Indiana, a future GC church leader who studied at Wadsworth for three years and was graduated in 1871.

According to someone's later memory, in 1870 Sprunger went home for Good Friday services and the people were "totally unprepared for what they saw." He had "a Bible under his arm." But instead of a "homemade coat with stand-up collar" he wore a different coat, "a stiff white collar," a "white shirt with a black stripe," and a silver watch chain. Invited to speak a few words, he "shocked the audience by standing." Also he spoke German instead of Swiss. According to the reminiscence it was "something new to hear a student." "The young of the church enjoyed it. . . . But the old patriarchs of the church thought it was sheer pride."[60]

The school offered studies ranging from biblical history to geometry to rhetoric, music, penmanship, and more. Nevertheless, not as many students enrolled as promoters had hoped. In 1871 there were only 28, and early in 1876 still only 30. In the mid-1870s women were allowed in—apparently more for tuition money than for equality. A disappointment was that the most popular program was a "normal" or teacher-training course, not one designed to produce church leaders. Moreover, in 1876 that class of thirty included only nine Mennonites.

In 1877, despite some changes, enrollment dropped to six students. In 1878 the institution's trustees sold the property even though the $5000 price left a troublesome debt.[61] The school closed. But it was not a total failure. It had brought able young people together from different communities and given some training to persons who would be strong leaders of the GC branch in the next generation. For instance, it trained future pastors such as Sprunger. And it trained early missionaries such as John B. Baer of Pennsylvania on the home field and Samuel (S.S.) Haury of Illinois on the "foreign" one (among American Indians in Oklahoma).

Mennonites had not risen to the colors either of the school or of the new "unity" conference. To optimistic progressives there was no good reason why they did not. After all, the founders had not tried to impose a centralized uniformity. So why did so few Mennonites respond?

Among some scholars a thesis has persisted which says that during much of the nineteenth century Mennonites lived in a time of dark ages. Robert Friedmann divided North American Mennonite history into three periods: a continuation of European patterns until 1800; an awakened and modern period after 1880; but from 1800 to 1880 a "Middle Period . . . of slackening or 'losing the first love.' " Samuel F. Pannabecker, historian of the GC Mennonite branch, wrote that about 1770 a change occurred. European-reared leaders had died and left the church to new shepherds who,

Courtesy of Mennonite Library and Archives at Bethel College

Left: Samuel F. Sprunger (1848-1923), Swiss Mennonite church leader at Berne, Indiana. Above: S. F. and Katharina Sprunger in their old age.

however intelligent, were "simple and unlettered." Being such, the newer leaders were suspicious of change and not very able to "recognize and pass judgment on moral and religious values in a new situation." Therefore, said Pannabecker, "the seventy-five years from 1775 to 1850 may be regarded as the Dark Age in American Mennonite history."[62]

The "dark ages" thesis is a myth—not necessarily meaning "untruth," but rather "a way of understanding." The myth has served reformers, some who have stayed in the "old" Mennonite church and some who have broken with it. But the various scholars, reformers, and apologists who have used it have not agreed on what made those ages dark. Friedmann wrote as if it was a matter of straying from pristine Anabaptism. Pannabecker pointed mainly to a decline in literacy and a lack of progressive outlook. Reformers touched by revivalism, whether inside or outside the "old" church, have spoken of dead form and "formalism," a lack of fervor, and failure to be active for mission and other such causes. However fair or unfair, the charge of dead formalism often comes in such standardized language as to sound almost like a liturgy. Others, especially the Reformed Mennonites and people such as Jacob Stauffer inclined to the "old order," have been sure that deterioration came because of lax discipline and its consequences, secularity and pride. So the dark ages thesis is four or five different theses. Its meaning has depended on the critic's criteria.

Probably, the reasons why so few Mennonites joined the new GC conference are more specific. First, it relates to who the reformers were. They were either (a) unknown recent immigrants with few family connections or other ties into established Mennonite communities, or (b) Oberholtzer or Hoch people who were already controversial.

Second, they experienced shallow support from the large communities east of the Allegheny Mountains. Most well-settled Mennonites particularly of eastern Pennsylvania were not much interested in what happened in the vague, obscure "West." (Even late in the twentieth century, eastern Pennsylvania Mennonites seem to think the trip from Lancaster or Souderton to Indiana or Kansas is much farther than the same trip in the other direction.)[63]

Third, they had quite different definitions of what it meant to be "Mennonite." Hoch, Oberholtzer, and the new GC progressives accepted change. Yet because they held to specific points of Menno Simons' teaching, the Dordrecht confession, etc., they were sure their change was in line with Mennonite tradition. Their definitions were largely those of formal, written theology mostly made in Europe. But many Mennonites used quite a different definition. To be sure, they cited the same points and the same documents. But the meaning they found was the one forged in America beginning about the time of Heinrich Funck and stated best by Christian Burkholder. It was a definition made in America, a definition that looked to humility to replace the Anabaptists' strong emphasis on suffering.

As historian John Ruth has written of the Oberholtzer controversy: it was virtually impossible to capture the traditionalists' understandings in words, for they were "barely articulatable."[64] But their key terms were "Jesus the meek and lowly," humility (or negatively, pride), defenselessness, and the Christian's faithful "walk." And a central conviction was that the world was far from any path of enlightenment and progress. Instead, the world operated from self-aggrandizement, power, and pride. So it lay in darkness, at enmity with God.

Photo courtesy of La Veta Habegger

Christian Krehbiel and sons at home.

Fourth, there were some grounds for suspicion that the progressives might not even be as faithful to specific doctrines as they claimed. Hoch's as well as Oberholtzer's constitution took that softened position, for instance, about suing at law. More importantly, the reformers' new conferences were not absolutely clear that Christians ought not go to war.

In the fall of 1861, as the U.S. civil war was getting under way, the East Pennsylvania conference "considered" "the matter of the present war," but, according to its minutes, "no action was taken." Through 1862 and 1863 it discussed the fact that "defenseless [nonresistant] Christians" were being "sorely pressed." It noted that many members faced with a military draft had declared their conscientious objection, and it considered how to aid war sufferers. Finally in the fall of 1863 some conferees urged that persons not drafted be obliged to help those on whom the draft fell (probably meaning help to pay exemption fees). But on the crucial question of what to do about persons who had taken up arms, the conference merely said that "each congregation should deal with its own such members according to the circumstances." It added vaguely that in doing so they should "avoid offence to our [conference] constitution."[65]

As for the GCs' general conference, its original plan of union of course mentioned keeping "the fundamental doctrines of the denomination; namely those concerning baptism, the oath, etc." Surely those words could include nonresistance. But they were not explicit; and as no less a supporter than Christian Krehbiel later recalled, in the civil war years the conference did not give a clear answer to the question of pacifism.

In 1863 several Canadians attended the general conference

sessions. Fearing that under Canadian law their break with the old church might cost them their military exemption, they asked the new conference to clarify where it stood. Krehbiel later said that although Palatines such as himself had come to America to avoid military service, "it was a delicate question" and "no forthright answer was given." He did not say why it was "delicate." But in 1881 a writer in the GC newspaper *Zur Heimath* recalled that nonresistance had been controversial in the early sessions of the new general conference. There was suspicion, he said, that some Wadsworth teachers did not support it.[66]

Through the decades since those first sessions many Mennonites in the new (GC) branch have supported pacifism vigorously. For instance, in 1894 the Wadsworth-trained S. S. Haury went far beyond his immediate topic (on teaching nonresistance in the Sunday school) to write one of the two or three best treatises on Christian pacifism put forward by Mennonites in nineteenth-century America.

Yet in the 1860s those "progressive" Mennonites hesitated. Their timidity was quite in contrast to what was happening in the old church. For instance the "old" Mennonite Indiana conference, advising against voting, declared forthrightly in 1864 that "we are a nonresistant people and can not . . . hold office, nor take the sword, nor resort to any violent means whatever." Three years later it declared in even stronger terms that its people needed to spread the "truth" of "nonresistant Christianity." Meanwhile in 1863 "old" Mennonite leader John M. Brenneman and emerging leader John F. Funk each published a booklet to reassert Mennonite pacifism. They set forth pacifism and kept it connected to the gospel of humility.[67]

Fifth, among almost all people in the old church there was a profound lack of any feeling of the need to express their understanding of gospel to the world as a truly prophetic message. There was no deliberate effort to make the Word of God compelling. Nor were they particularly eager to meet the world on its own terms well enough to challenge its outlook and its sin or to go forth in mission.

The progressives, although they did not say so exactly, envisioned that a certain amount of secularization or at least keeping in step with a progress-minded society would help them do God's work. In the 1860s there was virtually no leader of the "old" Mennonites, except the still-unproven John F. Funk, who sensed that point at all.

Sixth, the fact that already by the 1860s a few in the old church were beginning to respond very selectively to the progressives' concerns, but in another way: doing so even while continuing to embrace the old humility- and nonresistant-gospel symbols, idioms, and theology. Such people seemed to hope that there might be a synthesis that kept the old but added elements of the new.

In 1864 a relatively well-educated, business-trained, ambitious twenty-eight-year-old John F. Funk began publishing the first lasting "old" Mennonite paper. He produced it in English and German editions he named *Herald of Truth* and *Der Herold der Wahrheit*. Through it he promoted Sunday schools, missions, and other causes, with support from some key middle-aged leaders, most notably John M. Brenneman. In 1881 an appealing, Virginia-reared preacher named John S. Coffman began holding revival meetings in the "old" church.

By century's end "old" and Amish Mennonites had developed a complement of new institutions and programs ranging from Young People's Meetings to a precursor of a college to a few city and rural missions and a mission just opening in India. Meanwhile, in 1898, some "old" and Amish Mennonites began their own version of a general conference which brought their district ones into more formal cooperation and made them into more of a denomination.[68]

By the 1890s the innovators of those changes had largely broken with the older humility-theology consensus. Be that as it may, in the 1860s people such as Funk and John M. Brenneman were moving to revitalize the old church. They moved cautiously but were by no means reactionary. They rejected more thoroughgoing progressives' invitations because they thought they saw a way that would retain more of the old.

Thoroughgoing progressives talked as if what separated Mennonites were only "minor differences," as the 1860 GC plan of union put it, or "nonessentials," as others have often said.[69] Whether the differences were really minor is of course a matter of judgment, not capable of proof. And therein lay the problem. Progressives during and since the 1860s have scarcely seemed to realize that assumptions about what was "minor" and "nonessential" were partisan judgments. The majority of Mennonites heard the call to unity as a demand that they accept the progressives' ideas about what was important and what was not. If John M. Brenneman thought that a coat of a certain cut was a sign of inner pride, or that communing with Lutherans broke down church discipline, was he harping on "nonessentials"?

* * *

Carl Justus van der Smissen (1811-1890), Mennonite educator.

By the end of the 1860s ruptures were appearing in the seamless web which Christian Burkholder and his generation had woven around the principles of humility, non-vengeance, defenselessness, and church discipline. The forces tearing at the web were strong. Much more than most later critics have admitted, those who wove the web had included salvation by God's grace and Jesus' redemptive work, the new birth, and deep inner (not only external) piety. Yet they had not woven it large enough to hold the more triumphal, outgoing, aggressive passages of the New Testament. In a relatively prosperous, expansive, and optimistic America the web strained.

Some reformers, notably John Herr, Musser, and Holdeman, had sought to protect the web by bringing some experiential religion into it even as they tightened bonds of discipline. Others, such as Hoch or William Gehman, tried to break out of the web and weave a new one. In the center of the new one they put revivalism's inner experience. Around that experience they put a somewhat liberalized set of Mennonite practices plus activism in missions and other causes. Still others—at Milford Square, Lee County, Wadsworth, and elsewhere—wove a new web a bit more from nineteenth-century America's denominationalism and progressivism. Into their web they also put liberalized rules plus activism in mission, education, and other causes. But they gave less room to experiential conversion and more to nurture and issues of church organization.

The old fabric was under strain. Different groups were weaving new fabrics, each with a claim to the name "Mennonite." Coincidentally, or maybe not, the Mennonite web began to rend just when the political fabric of the United States also was about to tear, in the U.S. civil war.

CHAPTER 6

POLITICS AND PACIFISM

> Q: If you do not believe in use of force in any case whatever, what then is your view of "worldly government" as God has instituted it?
>
> A: "Government was instituted . . . to punish the bad, and protect the good, and it is a wise regulation in this corrupt world. 'Let every soul be subject to the higher powers' (Rom. 13:1). So we should also pray God that He may give wisdom and understanding to government to make a right use of the power with which He has entrusted it. . . . And when we are then, under God's blessing, protected by government we are in duty bound to be thankful to God and it for such protection, as also to pay 'tribute' to the same, which is its due, and which is serviceable to peace. But as the whole doctrine of Christ leads into a course of self-denial and separation from the world, Christ makes a distinction between the practice of worldly governments and that of His true followers. . . ." Christ said that Gentile kings " 'exercise lordship. . . . But ye shall not be so: . . . Whosoever of you will be the chiefest, shall be servant of all.' . . . Government is not instituted that the true followers of Christ should rule over anyone thereby." To be sure, force was "allowed to 'them of old' "; but to Christians "Christ has . . . forbidden all revenge and defence by force whereby to wage war with our enemies. . . . We are not to 'resist evil.' " Christ abolished revenge and force, "because his kingdom is a kingdom of peace."

So wrote the Mennonite pastor Christian Burkholder in his much published little book of nurture and edification first printed in 1804.[1] His dualistic, two-kingdom analysis was classic Anabaptist-Mennonite doctrine. Probably nobody has ever stated the position more succinctly and clearly.

The Groffdale bishop did not say exactly what the classic doctrine meant in practice. On that question nineteenth-century Mennonites and Amish offered a spectrum of answers. At one end stood a man such as Old Order founder Jacob Stauffer, about 1850. He lamented that some Mennonites served "in worldly offices and strive or campaign for them in order to attain them," even though "Jesus chose His people out of the world and said the world would hate them for His name's sake." Some even served on juries, "to judge worldly disputes and lawsuits, which all belong to the world and not to the defenseless fellowship of Christ." And they campaigned and attended elections—to help elect worldly officials "who have the full power of the sword in their hands and get all their power and force from the common people." Stauffer was sure that all of this was "against the defenseless basis of the gospel" and "against God's holy word, *Ordnung* [order], counsel, and example."[2]

At the spectrum's other end about 1890 was Joseph Taylor, a man with a doctorate in education and experience in interdenominational Christian work in New York City. Taylor was a member of an Eastern District (GC) conference congregation at Springfield, Pennsylvania. In 1896, writing in the GC paper *The Mennonite* (for which he wrote frequently), he declared that for various reasons, not just from Mennonite rearing, he was "opposed to the senseless cry for war which" he was hearing in America. Yet he said that "if our country were in danger from foreign or domestic foes," he would be

> perfectly willing to go to the front and fight. My doctrine of non-resistance doesn't go to the extent of supinely folding one's hands while an enemy is despoiling our institutions and our firesides.[3]

Such words were far from typical. Few Mennonites and Amish came close to Taylor's open support of just war. Most were much nearer to Stauffer's end of the spectrum.

THE TWO-REALM VIEW OF POLITICS

For the great majority of Mennonites and Amish in the U.S. from 1800 to the civil war, Christian Burkholder had stated the essence: Yes, God himself had provided human government, and for good reason. So be thankful to God and give rulers the respect and the money due them. But no, the way of governments was not the way for Christians. Rulers lorded themselves over people; Christians were to be servants. Rulers used force; but for Christians all revenge, all force, and all war were forbidden, simply and categorically.

Apparently Burkholder thought that the contrast between rulers and Christians touched salvation itself. At least he offered some of his political comments in a section called "On Saving Faith and Pure Love to God and Our Neighbor." The contrast was a difference in loyalties. Christ had said, "If my kingdom were of this world, then would my servants fight." And, Burkholder continued, "True followers of Christ confess that they are 'strangers and pilgrims on the earth,' for they 'desire a better country, that is, an heavenly' " one.[4]

For several decades before Burkholder wrote, Americans had spoken and sacrificed much to build a better country. They of course meant a nation which had replaced a tyrannical king with representative self-government, a bill of rights, and an enlightened constitution. But the "better country" of Burkholder's *Address* was a different one, reached by "self-denial and separation from the world." It was a country rid of "all revenge and defense by force"—a "kingdom of peace."[5]

Burkholder had not been swept along by a quarter-century of American talk about liberty. At one point he had his youthful questioner express fear of joining a church which had too many "human laws and rules." "My love of liberty," the fictional youth said, "is very strong." The reply: Turn to God's Word and examine it. "The liberty of which you speak may become an occasion of sin to you. . . . There are many dangers in the freedom you may thus claim."[6] Of course in the immediate sense Burkholder referred to church discipline, not national politics. But he had written his manuscript in 1792. For a person to write as he did when slogans of liberty were still fresh from the American revolution suggests political dissent as well.

The Groffdale pastor (and many nineteenth-century Mennonites who followed) did not cloud their two-realm doctrine with doubts about whether the ethics of that "better country" would work in life on earth. The doctrine made the line between the worldly and the peaceful kingdoms bold and distinct. It offered no perception of overlap, of blurring, of ambiguity, of dilemma. The clarity was a strength because common people could easily grasp such an unambiguous doctrine and use it to avoid being swept along by nationalism, warmaking, and similar idolatries. But it was a weakness because it made the doctrine not only simple but simplistic. It did not speak directly to real dilemmas of trying actually to live in both realms.

Sources for the classic doctrine were the old, cherished Anabaptist and Mennonite writings. On their face, many of them were deeply conservative. Against a backdrop of Münster, Germany, where an Anabaptist faction had led an armed rebellion, Menno Simons had been emphatic that Anabaptists of his sort were not rebels.[7] But while Mennonites and Amish stood for order and tradition they were not gullible about claims governments made for themselves. Beneath the surface simplicity of the two-realm doctrine the mood was subtly resistant. After all, what could be more revolutionary than to reject the idea of a "better country" built on force and to work instead for a "kingdom of peace"?[8] Christian Burkholder's language suggested that Christians honored government not because it was government but only because of God's purposes for it. His advice to pray that it "make a right use" of its power suggested a government held to certain standards, not government a law unto itself. Phrases such as "right use" of power and "serviceable to peace" opened the door for Mennonites to make political judgments about whether government was or was not doing what God had instituted it to do. Government was to "protect the good." In classic Mennonite doctrine that meant first to keep basic order in society. But it meant also to protect the weaponless, revengeless, vulnerable people who were going about building the "kingdom of peace."

Such was the context of Burkholder's conservative advice that Christians should submit to rulers, pay their taxes, and so forth. When government was doing its proper tasks, then submitting and paying taxes was "serviceable to peace." Logically, Burkholder's readers might have inferred that when authorities did *not* protect the good, then Christians no longer owed government their obedience, tribute, and subjection. Burkholder did not put forward such a revolutionary notion nor did many of his readers; but the inference was possible. Indeed the 33-article confession had implied rather clearly that duty to submit to government ended if government did not protect the nonresistant Christians who were building the peaceful kingdom.[9]

Both Menno Simons and the 33-article confession had said forthrightly that the authority of government did not extend to people's "spirits and souls."[10] As a modern would say, it did not extend to religious conscience. Formally, that idea coincided with religious beliefs of Quakers and Baptists and with secular ones of Thomas Jefferson and other national founders. It fit the nation's separation of church and state.

Yet the revolutionary implications in Mennonite and Amish

thought were not those of the American nation. First, Mennonites and Amish were concerned with quality of church, not much with nation. Second, they did not particularly welcome greater democracy as developed by Jeffersonians about 1800 and especially the supporters of Andrew Jackson in the 1820s and 1830s. Such democracy meant egalitarianism and ever-wider participation of (white, male) ordinary citizens in electioneering, voting, and officeholding. Toward it most nineteenth-century Mennonites were skeptical. Third, throughout the century more and more Americans spoke as if their nation were destined to be an especially godly and predominantly Protestant nation, a sort of Protestant "righteous empire."[11] Mennonites and Amish were somewhat open to that notion; but they accepted less of it than seems apparent of people in more popular churches.

So while Mennonites and Amish respected government they were rather skeptical of U.S. political ideas and nationalism.

ACCOMMODATION

In practice from 1800 to the civil war, quite a bit more than in theory, Mennonites and Amish blurred the line between the two realms. Their religious ancestors had done so already in Europe. There they had often agreed to pay special taxes in return for tolerance—even military taxes. Some had done noncombatant military duty. In 1710 a group of Swiss Mennonites, some of whom were about to emigrate to Pennsylvania, said that if necessary they were ready to help "in the building of fortifications, instead of bearing arms." In colonial America Mennonites and Amish had voted and served in some minor, local offices. And especially during the French and Indian and revolutionary wars quite a few had served armies as teamsters or paid special taxes or even hired substitutes to go and fight. So even for military service they had accommodated and blurred the two-realm line.[12]

During the revolution Mennonites and Amish, being pacifists and suspected of being pro-British, widely lost the right to vote. But they soon regained it[13] and in the early nineteenth century many again voted. The Old Order-minded Jacob Stauffer complained that by the 1830s there were "few brethren in the so-called [Mennonite] church who" had not participated in elections or on juries. Many, he said, even deluded themselves into thinking that to vote was a high and solemn duty, lest they lose the privilege.[14]

In 1839 and 1840 some isolated "old" Mennonites in upstate New York urged the Lancaster conference to forbid political participation and do so clearly. In response the Lancaster leaders agreed

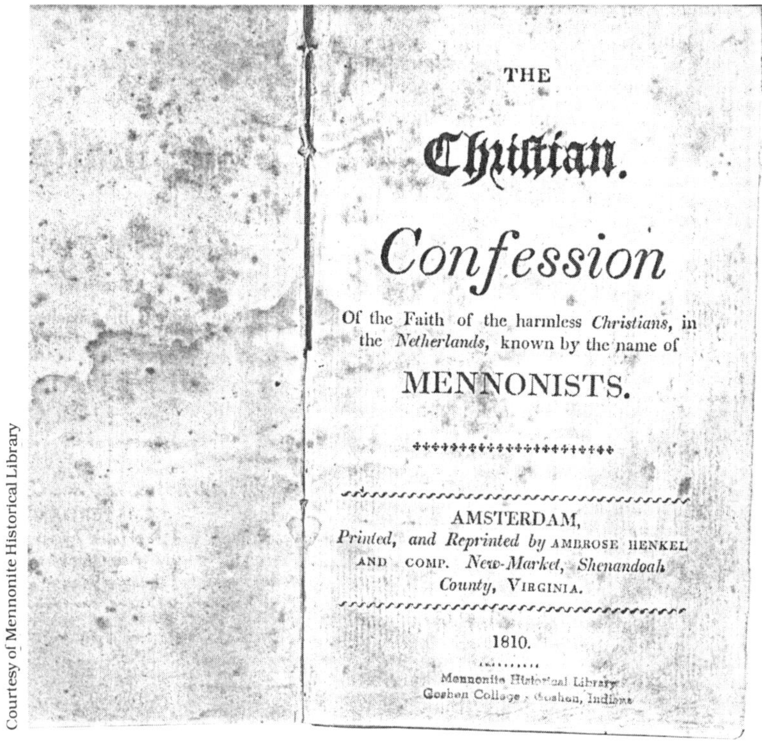
THE

Christian.

Confession

Of the Faith of the harmless *Christians*, in the *Netherlands*, known by the name of

MENNONISTS.

AMSTERDAM,
Printed, and Reprinted by AMBROSE HENKEL AND COMP. *New-Market, Shenandoah County*, VIRGINIA.

1810.

Title page of 1810 printing of Dordrecht confession of faith.

that it "would be better if brethren would refrain"; but they refused to make a flat ruling.[15] Soon thereafter, however, the "old" Mennonite conference in Ohio decided otherwise for its people. (It seems that Mennonites in newly settled areas were more skeptical of political activity than those in old communities such as Lancaster, who were well woven into local community fabric.) The Ohio conference allowed voting for road supervisor, director of the poor, and school director. But it said other voting and jury duty were not suitable for people who rejected military force.[16]

In 1846 David Metzler, a rather Old Order-minded deacon in Mahoning County, Ohio, wrote to a Lancaster conference bishop and explained the Ohio church leaders' position. He said the Ohioans thought that to hire or elect a person to use the oath and wield the sword was just like using and wielding them oneself. Yes,

24 THE CHRISTIAN CONFESSION.

Authority and Magistracy for punishment of the evil, and protection of
the good; and also to govern the
World, Countries, and Cities, and
to keep their subjects in good Order
and Policy; and that therefore we
Tit. 3, 1. may not dispise, revile nor resist
1 *Pet.* 2, them, but that we must acknowledge
17. honour, submit unto and obey them
as the Ministers of God, and be
ready to all good Works, especially
in what is not contrary to the Law,
Will & Command of God; and that
we faithfully must pay them Tribute,
Excise and Taxes, and give what
belongs or is due to them, as the
Matth. Son of God hath taught, and also
22 21. done himself and charged and com-
Ch. 27, manded others to do so. Besides,
27. that we must pray the Lord continually and earnestly for them and
their welfare; that so under their
protection we may dwell, provide
for ourselves, and lead a quiet and
peaceable Life, in all godliness and
honesty; and that it may please the
Lord to require and reward them
1 *Tim.* 2 here, and hereafter in the eternity,
1, 2. all well-doing, liberty and favour
we enjoy here under their laudable
Government.

✦✦✦✦✦✦✦

THE CHRISTIAN CONFESSION. 25

XIV. ARTICLE.

Concerning Revenge.

FOURTEENTHLY. Concern-
ing Revenge and resisting the
Enemies with the Sword, we
believe and profess, that our Lord
Christ, his Disciples and Followers, *Matth.*
have forbidden, and taught against 5, 39.
all vengeance and revenge, and bid- 44.
den and commanded to recompense *Rom.* 12.
no Man evil for evil, and not to 12.
render railing for railing; but to put 1 *Pet.*
the Sword into the sheath, or as hath 3, 9.
been predicted by the Prophets, to *Jes.* 2, 4.
make Plow-shears thereof. By which *Mic.* 4, 3
we understand, that therefore, and *Zach* 9.
according to his Example, Life and 8, 9, 10.
Doctrine, we may not hurt, afflict
or wrong others; but that we ought
to seek the highest Welfare and the
Salvation of others; and that, if ne-
cessity requires it, for the Lord's sake
we must fly from one Country or
Town into another and suffer the
spoiling of our Goods, but not to
make any suffer; and if we are smit-
ten, rather to turn the other check,
than to smite again, or to revenge *Matth.*
ourselves: moreover, that we must 5, 39.
even pray for our Enemies, and

D

Sample spread from 1810 printing of Dordrecht confession of faith.

the forefathers had "approved going to the election." But Metzler argued that while Mennonites voted, politics had only gotten worse. He obviously abhorred the expressions and results of Jacksonian democracy: bombastic speeches; noisy parades; barbecues lubricated with beer, cider, and liquors; and other political theater full of emotion, crowd psychology, hoopla, and huzza. He was not alone.

In 1845 a Mennonite minister near Gettysburg, Pennsylvania, complained that men of his congregation went and helped the world elect its officials. Or at least they went to political rallies to sell "oats, cookies, and beer." Metzler's words were stronger. Politics, he said, had become "an idolatrous Babel business."[17] Together with classic doctrine, Metzler's anti-democratic lament pretty well summed up the Mennonite and Amish case against political involvement. It seems that no well-accepted pre-civil-war Mennonite or Amish leader ever replied to Metzler's kind of thinking with a reasoned religious defense supporting involvement. Many members voted, but without a theology for doing so.

The classic doctrine saw government mostly in negative terms: to restrain evil. Only the most progressive of Mennonites saw political power in positive terms. Such a man was Abraham Hunsicker, the minister who helped John H. Oberholtzer lead his reform and then became too liberal even for the "new" Mennonites. Hunsicker wrote publicly in 1851 that Menno Simons had followed the Christ whose spirit was "charity and benevolence" but had done so in a "gloomy period." Since then "the social, moral and political conditions of man" had "been greatly and wonderfully changed and improved." In the new climate Christians should leave the old ways, take advantage of "the free, mild and liberal spirit of our many good institutions," and "seek ... to ameliorate and improve the condition of man." "Being a progressive creature man must rise gradually." There need be no limits to human improvement "this side of infinity." Among those free institutions Hunsicker must have included government, for he and his family were active in local Whig politics.[18] But the Hunsickers were at the fringe of Mennonitism.

Most Mennonites and Amish were much closer to David Metzler's views than to Hunsicker's. Nevertheless, in limited ways they did take part in community, state, and national politics.

POLITICAL PARTICIPATION THROUGH THE CIVIL WAR

A standard statement is that in political matters Mennonites and other Pennsylvania-German pacifists were a minority within a minority. German-Americans in general were a minority and less politically active than British-Americans. But most voted for the Jeffersonian-Jacksonian Democrats. Mennonites and other German pacifists, a minority within a minority, usually favored the Democrats' opponents. As American political groupings evolved, those opponents were Federalists, then Whigs, then Republicans.[19]

Some Mennonites and Amish did lean Democratic. Historian Delbert Gratz has written that Swiss-speaking Mennonites in Ohio and Indiana forbade officeholding but "took advantage of their right to vote and as a group supported the Democratic party." Christian Reeser, the long-lived Amish minister in Illinois, claimed before he died that he had voted in twenty-one presidential elections. From 1844 (James Polk's election) onward he had always voted Democratic except once.[20]

But apparently Mennonite and Amish Democrats were few.

There were almost none in the big, old communities of eastern and central Pennsylvania where most Mennonite and Amish voting occurred. Late in the 1830s in the large Franconia district a certain Abraham O. Fretz clashed head on against one trend of Jacksonian democracy—a tendency to deny the vote to blacks even while extending it among whites. In 1837 Fretz ran against a Democrat for county commissioner and won by a slim 25 ballots (out of more than 6,500). Democrats determined that blacks had cast at least 39 of the winning votes. Thereupon they went to court and argued that black voting was an invasion of a "sacred right" of whites. A judge agreed and it seems that Fretz soon yielded his office. Probably he had not meant to crusade for blacks' rights. In any case a state convention soon changed Pennsylvania's constitution from saying that "every freeman" could vote to saying "every white freeman" could do so.[21]

Virtually no Franconia Mennonite seems to have leaned Democratic. In 1840 when the Indian-fighting military hero William Henry Harrison was Whig candidate for U.S. president, a couple in the Deep Run congregation named their baby son "Henry Harrison Fretz." During the presidential election of 1856 young John F. Funk, future Mennonite publisher from nearby Hilltown, wrote to the local paper to denounce Democrats. He blamed them for "the accursed demon of slavery," for bloody encounters between pro- and anti-slavery forces in Kansas, and for all other works of "Bogus Democracy." To be sure, in 1856 Funk had not yet declared himself a Christian or joined a Mennonite church. But he did so before 1860, and yet in that year's campaign he still paraded zealously with a Republican "Wide Awake" club. Every man in the club, he noted, was "in full uniform" and carrying a torch. Funk's brother Abraham, or "A. K.," later his partner in Mennonite publishing, was equally or more involved in Republican campaigning. During the civil war he wrote that he was glad to see North and West rally around the American flag. He liked their support of the "rights, the liberties and the independence of a free and self-governed nation."[22]

Such Republicanism was not the political faith only of literate and articulate Mennonites or only of youths. In the fall of 1860, spelling German words almost as badly as occasional English ones, a John O. Clemens in Pennsylvania's Montgomery County assured a friend he was happy: he had been working to help Republican Andrew Curtin be reelected as "gowernihr" of "Penselfania" and Curtin had won. A year later, as the civil war began, the Funk brothers' father, Jacob Funk, Sr., lamented that Bucks County still held Democratic "traters.... But," he observed apparently with relish, "they Must keep vary quiet or Receive a Coat of tar and feathers."[23]

Lancaster area Mennonites were equally or even more Republican. After careful study of early-to-mid-nineteenth-century Lancaster County politics a scholar named Andrew Robertson has concluded that the most heavily Mennonite townships (which were also the wealthiest) voted Federalist, then Whig. Then in the 1850s, as a fast-rising new Republican party absorbed the Whigs, the Mennonite townships switched to the Republicans.[24]

Because of that shift, during the U.S. civil war Mennonite voting influenced national history to a degree it has probably not done before or since. In the 1840s to '60s a sometimes ruthless, sometimes idealistic politician named Thaddeus Stevens was building support, mainly in Lancaster County. He managed to win control of Lancaster County Whiggery and then lead the switch to Republicanism. From that base he went to Washington as a congressman. There, as students of American history well know, he was the main wartime leader of "Radical" Republicans in the House of Representatives. Stevens was "Radical" partly because he had a streak of fiery idealism which refused to compromise on the question of slavery.[25] But he was "Radical" also because his style was arrogant, harsh, acerbic, and vindictive. Yet Robertson's work and other sources show that Mennonites supported Stevens through the very years of war and Reconstruction—and that their support was a key to his continual reelection.[26]

Mennonites claimed to be pacifist, nonresisting, and nonavenging; so honest that oaths were a mockery; and thoroughly humble. How then could they support a man with a style so opposite? Or, as Robertson has put it, "How did the foremost Radical Republican come to receive the overwhelming support of a constituency . . . that has always been noted for its stability, its prosperity, and its conservative politics?"[27]

Regarding Mennonites, Robertson never quite answered the question. The first explanation may be Mennonite wealth; the second, political inertia. Third, Mennonites no doubt liked Stevens because of who opposed him. His opponents were mainly Presbyterian Scotch-Irish, Catholics, his district's few immigrants, and urban workers in Lancaster City.[28] Such groups were all quite alien to the Pennsylvania-German world of Lancaster Mennonites. Fourth, although Mennonites (and almost all Germans) were not crusading abolitionists, neither did they believe in slavery.[29] Fifth, a major explanation must be the doctrine of two realms: Mennonites did not have to assume that a politician for whom they voted should

That "young man from Chicago" John F. Funk, ca. 1860.

Sunday Oct 31st clear and fair for
one day in the week went to 1st Presby
Church sermon by Bz-headed, though
quite intelligent man from Batavia
he preached a tolerable good sermon
afternoon was at home, in the evening
went to hear Rev Mr Barry at the 2nd
Universalist Church (formerly 3rd Presby)
he is tall and quite reverend Looking
a good voice and a good speaker
quite old which makes him the more
solemn & grand his sermon was only a
eulogium on great men &c. to dry alto-
gether for a sermon
Monday Nov 1st Cloudy and same
in the evening, went to hear Senator
Douglass speak in front of Garrett Block
Douglass is good Looking, fine face & plump
a good orator, seems to quite worn
& down with the constant speaking in the
Campaighn (Political) which is now coming to a close this was his last effort

Sample pages from the diary of John F. Funk showing political awareness.

his last solemn appeal upon the Democracy to stand by him and elect him
again, and appeal it was like that
of a dying man without hope of salvation yet make a last, mighty effort to save (if it might be possibly)
himself he abused the Republicans &
Long John their Illustrious Leader as
well as their Candidate Lincoln
he then told them what he had done
how faithful he had Been and then
made the most solemn appeal
for their help. McComas Ex Lieutenant Governor
of Virginia spoke and his was a eulogy
on the Democratic party under Jeffersonian
principles and compared Douglass
to those great men who have lived
in days gone By. then we heard an
Irishman in his wild insensible har-
angue and then O M — then
we went home it rained all the
time and the speaker spoke Bareheaded

operate by ethics they professed for the church.

Finally, once the civil war was under way Stevens worked vigorously to win military exemption for conscientious objectors. But that fact is part of the civil war story.

POLITICAL ATTITUDES AFTER THE CIVIL WAR

War has often forced Mennonites and other pacifists to reconsider their relationship to government. The U.S. civil war may have left Mennonites and Amish with some new hesitation about voting and other political involvement.

The case is not clear. For instance, before the war Amish who immigrated from the 1830s onward and settled in Fulton County in northwestern Ohio had voted quite freely and held township offices. According to local tradition the war stimulated them to stop their officeholding because critics said that if they could participate in politics they should go to war as well. (The critics pointed also to their drinking with neighbors in taverns.) Yet the Fulton County Amish continued to vote and to serve on school boards. Moreover in Pennsylvania just after the war a keen-eyed journalist named Phebe Gibbons wrote that "old" Mennonites voted at elections and served in offices such as school director or road supervisor—although they did not become state assemblymen, and their preachers did not vote. And from the Franconia district in 1867 a minister-son of author Abraham Godshalk advised editor Funk that many Mennonites of his area liked the *Herald of Truth* but did not want articles against voting. According to Godshalk in the old days the fathers had voted and "Religion and Government had been on better footing." Midwestern Mennonites might accept the rule against voting, Godshalk thought, but not those in his area.[30]

Yet a Samuel Godshalk might never have written had the war not intensified the voting issue. In 1866 the "old" Mennonite conference of Ohio ruled once again that members should neither "mingle with the world in going to elections," hold office, nor take "any part in political meetings, political disputes, discussions, or conventions." Its sister conference in Indiana made the connection between nonresistance and non-involvement in politics very explicit. "We are a nonresistant people and cannot, according to our profession, hold office, nor take the sword, nor resort to any violent means whatever," it declared in 1864. Nor should members vote, for "by so doing we would make ourselves liable also even by force to defend and sustain those whom we elect." Anyhow, the conferees suggested, Mennonites were so politically divided that their votes merely canceled each other.[31]

Beneath such statements were two main ideas: separation from the world, and politics' basis in violence. Moreover in the 1860s and '70s John M. Brenneman was exerting strong leadership in Indiana and Ohio. In 1863, in a booklet he wrote to strengthen Mennonites' nonresistance, he advised against politics. "Stand aloof!" he admonished. By no means should Christians take on "party names." How shameful that followers of Christ who were to be "of one mind, one heart, and one soul" quarreled and said, " 'I am a Democrat' " and " 'I am a Republican.' " Writing in wartime, Brenneman thought it surely was beyond "the bounds of a non-resistant Christianity" to "help choose men into office in which it becomes their duty to use deadly weapons."[32]

Thirty years later "old" Mennonite editor Funk advised that if Mennonites acted politically at all they should vote only as individuals, not follow political parties. During the historic 1896 presidential contest between William Jennings Bryan and William McKinley his paper declared with satisfaction that Mennonites were a religious and not a political body. Living godly lives, not filling their heads with politics, they would "get along happily no matter which party wins."[33]

In sum, Funk's paper advised Mennonites either not to vote or else to try (unrealistically) to achieve a politics without party divisions. Further, it implied that on political matters the church had no obligation to find a common mind and offer a united voice.

But Brenneman and Funk were not popes; the Mennonite church had no centralized authority. So different "old" Mennonite and Amish conferences drew different lines. In 1866, even as Mennonite conferences in Indiana and Ohio were trying to stop members from voting, their counterpart in Virginia merely said "we recommend" against political participation—and then added: "but if brethren desire to vote let them do so peaceably and quietly." That ruling held for the rest of the century. The Lancaster and the Southwestern Pennsylvania "old" Mennonite conferences let laymen vote but not ordained ones. The Franconia conference disapproved of electioneering and political mass meetings, and forbade members "to go to elections." But those words may have meant only not to linger there; it is not clear that the conference intended to forbid stopping and voting quietly. While the Lancastrians and the Franconians used the language of forbidding, other "old" and Amish Mennonite conferences used softer language to admonish and disapprove but did not flatly prohibit.[34]

On another matter, initiating lawsuits, "old" and Amish Mennonite conferences usually were adamant. But a Lancaster conference discipline first printed in 1881 left a small opening for a special kind of case. "If a brother is appointed executor" or guardian of an estate and "cannot close the estate without sueing [sic] at law," the discipline said, he could do so. Oddly, the discipline declared further that such a man should stay back from communion until the case was finished. Before again communing the man had to go "before the church" to "ask forbearance" and find out whether anyone were "grieved" by his action. Yet he did not have "to acknowledge an error or transgression."[35] At worst, the ruling may have compromised church discipline and made it perfunctory. At best it provided a bit of flexibility even while keeping members responsible to the church in their economic and legal behavior.

Two other politically related and troublesome matters for "old" and Amish Mennonites were jury duty and officeholding. Once more, rulings varied and allowed some exceptions. Usually the rulings were against jury duty, but some made distinctions between cases. In 1875 the Lancaster body allowed jury service except in capital-punishment trials. In 1881 its exception was criminal cases, language the Ohio body had also used a year earlier. In 1879 the Southwestern Pennsylvania conference preferred that members "try to keep their names out of the Jury Box if possible" and forbade all jury duty in capital-punishment trials.[36]

There were variations also about officeholding. In 1867, in reply to a question of whether being a public-road supervisor violated nonresistant Christianity, the Indiana conference counseled that the answer depended on the wording of a particular state's law. "But," the conference warned, "in all cases great caution is necessary." A Lancaster conference sermon in 1880 said members were to avoid "any civil office, further than supervisor or road master, overseer of the poor, school director, and post master." The printed Lancaster discipline a year later said that even for those offices, members should not electioneer. Most other rulings either forbade all officeholding or allowed the Lancastrians' exceptions.[37]

If pursued further a remark by the "old" Mennonite conference of Ohio at century's end could have been the signal of new Mennonite thought about political involvement, even about the two-realm doctrine. The conference decided that a member might serve as a local public trustee of the poor. After all, the conferees explained, the trusteeship "is an institution that all people need, Christians as well as those who are not Christians."[38] Had Mennonites been more politically inclined the Ohioan's words might have opened a Pandora's box of political involvement. For in effect the phrasing said that the classic line dividing the two realms was not so distinct after all—that there were endeavors which entered both realms. The words anticipated an idea of certain twentieth-century Mennonite scholars such as Guy F. Hershberger and John H. Yoder, who have suggested that in matters such as welfare the two realms might overlap.[39] But in 1898 "old" Mennonites were not ready to explore that idea.

Not all Mennonites were wary of politics. In 1880 as voters elected Republican presidential candidate James A. Garfield, John F. Funk, ordained as minister in 1865, jotted: "Election for President today—did not vote. Our ministers do not as a usual thing vote." However, in Pennsylvania his Mennonite father-in-law and a brother-in-law voted. And in Indiana Anna Landis Funk, wife of Funk's brother and business partner A. K., was thoroughly caught up in the campaign. Was little Wilmer a Garfield man? she asked concerning a two-and-one-half-year-old nephew in Pennsylvania. Her own six-year-old daughter Maud was saying she was for Garfield. Two years later at voting time, Anna Funk reported that "our people are very anxious about this election." On election day, she said, the men were "out voting and the woman on there knees praying."[40]

In the late nineteenth century various district conferences of the large "old" and Amish Mennonite groups drew somewhat different lines against voting. Their variations showed some genuine attempts to be discerning, not simply legalistic. One reason for variety was that the conferences spoke not directly to abstract ethics but to specific cases. The ministers at the conferences were farmers, millers, carpenters, blacksmiths, elementary school teachers, or whatever. That is, they were people involved deeply in their communities' daily affairs. Often they were economic and social leaders as well as pastors. Being practical people they sensed that lines between church and government and between faith and politics were not really as clear as many classic statements suggested. As the Lancaster ruling on lawsuits demonstrated, the lines were not so clear if Mennonites owned property and had estates to settle.

The lines were blurred also because Mennonites and Amish felt themselves to be members not only of their congregations but also of their local communities. The questions the conferences had to decide were not about seeking high offices in state and nation where power was concentrated and obvious. The questions were about helping to provide local schools, roads, poor relief, and mail service. "Old" and Amish Mennonites scarcely thought that taking some responsibility in such local affairs was wielding "power." The political questions with which the conferences wrestled were mainly about how Christians were to thread into the fabrics of local communities, not about power and participation in state and nation.

THREE NEW DEVELOPMENTS

The civil war sometimes strengthened the doubts about the extent to which nonresistant Christians could participate in politics. But from the 1870s onward three developments tended to make Mennonites and Amish in the U.S. more political rather than less: arrival of the Russian (and some Prussian) Mennonites; growing Mennonite and Amish progressivism; and prohibition, that is political efforts to outlaw alcoholic beverages.

Russian Mennonite politics

In the mid-1870s Mennonites arrived from the Russian empire with political experiences quite different from those of Mennonites and Amish already in America. The history of Mennonites in that empire led back to the Netherlands and northern Germany, with ties kept so close that when the Russian Mennonites came to America a few who had stayed in Prussia came also. Culturally and economically, from Anabaptist days onward, those northern regions had generally been more developed than Swiss and upper-Rhine regions whence Mennonites already in America had come. More directly, circumstances in the Russian empire had given Mennonites a great deal of experience developing and operating local institutions, including local governments with elected assemblies in exclusively Mennonite colonies and villages.[41]

Yet there was a paradox. For all their political experience, Russian Mennonites had not lived in a modern nation-state. Russian rulers did not govern a well-formed, well-knit modern nation but rather a loose empire tied together by the czars' autocracy. The "nation" of Russia's Mennonites was Germany—not in the "nation-state" sense of the word but in the older sense of ethnicity. In that sense "nation" meant a people (in German a *Volk*)—a people or *Volk* knit together by common history, language, culture, worldview, and self-understanding. Russian Mennonites clung to their Germanness to the point that historian James Juhnke, analyzing the politics of some who came to America, observed that their self-identity was (first) Christian and (second) German. Only after that was it (third) Mennonite, and then (fourth) their particular Mennonite branch.[42]

The Mennonites of the Russian empire had been quite contemptuous of the empires's native peoples and cultures. Even had there been a modern, integrated Russian nation, the Mennonites would hardly have wanted to be part of it. In fact those who emigrated in the 1870s and 1880s did so because they disliked a series of new laws by which political reformers were trying to bring together and remold the empire's peoples into a modern, integrated nation. The new laws began to remove favorite privileges of Mennonites and others such as complete military exemption and German-language schools. Instead of being part of a modern nation, Mennonites had been more like semi-feudal subjects bound to Russia's monarchs as persons—to czarinas and czars. Or they were like tenants installed to cultivate sections of an empire which the monarchs treated as a huge personal estate. Thus the paradox: Russian Mennonites arrived with local political experience but not experience as citizens of a modern nation.[43]

From 1873 to 1884 about a third of Russia's Mennonites emigrated to North America. About 10,000 settled on the U.S. prairies—mainly in Kansas but also in Nebraska, Dakota Territory, and Minnesota.[44] Whatever its main character the migration was somewhat political. To move was a drastic way to dissent from Russian laws and policy.[45] Moreover, the move involved extensive negotiations with U.S. and Canadian officials of nation, state, or province. And immigrants based their decisions partly on perceptions of the kinds of nations Canada and the U.S. were.[46]

With one part of their mind most immigrants hoped they would be free to remain somewhat aloof from those North American nations. They were seeking not so much the individual freedoms so celebrated in American myths as collective and communal ones: opportunity to establish and maintain semiautonomous German-Mennonite communities and preserve their precious mixture of ethnicity, culture, and faith.

Yet another part of the Russian Mennonite outlook was nation-minded and progressive. Late in 1873 a twenty-four-year-old schoolteacher named David Goerz left the Ukraine and settled at Summerfield, Illinois. Shortly before he did, he expressed both the preserving, separatist mind and the progressive, nation-minded one. At one moment he feared that if Mennonites stayed in Russia they would lose their "independence," "nationality," some "spirituality," and "the free development and fresh blossoming and growth of our people as a 'people of the Lord' (*ein Volk des Herrn*)." At another he lamented the Russian empire's backwardness in contrast to American accomplishments such as building railroads.[47]

Goerz was too intellectual to be typical. Yet most Russian Mennonites who settled in the U.S. quickly adopted some new ways and abandoned the notion of living in communities as closed and separated as in the Russian empire. They accepted some greater degree of integration into American neighborhoods, institutions, and society.[48]

Being of different minds about how much to abandon separatism, Russian Mennonites did not agree about voting. A conservative Krimmer Mennonite Brethren (KMB) group, who for a time established something of an Old World village they called "Gnadenau" near Hillsboro, Kansas, stood adamantly against all voting and officeholding except for school affairs.[49] A larger group, the Mennonite Brethren (MBs), at first leaned hard against political participation but relented before the century closed.

In 1879 in America, MB immigrants established a North American general conference. As they did, they soon took up the question of political participation. Delegates took different positions, but one of them offered a particularly clear statement of the two-realm view. Shortly thereafter the conference resolved that yes, MBs could accept governmental protection; but no, they should neither vote nor hold offices. However, ten years later, in 1888, in a discussion of whether a member should be a delegate to a political convention, conferees did not restate classic doctrine or draw its sharp line. Instead, they posed a classic Christian dilemma. Seeing government more positively, they said they wished to have good government and good officials (good *Obrigkeit*). But they also wanted to keep members from political quarrels. In their dilemma they did not rule on the immediate issue. Five years later another session decided that MBs could hold offices such as notary public but not be policemen.[50]

A greater number of those who arrived from the czars' empire sooner or later joined with the GC Mennonites; and they were not so cautious. Yet even they did not rush into American politics. In 1879 the Kansas conference, soon more or less the core of the GC-affiliated Western District conference, considered whether nonresistant Christians could take part in elections. Different delegates offered a range of arguments for and against. Instead of answering, the delegates asked one of the south German immigrant Krehbiels (Valentin, brother of the better known Christian Krehbiel) to prepare an article for a GC-related paper which David Goerz edited, *Zur Heimath*. In the article Krehbiel reasoned that Christians could participate. Doing so, he said, was a way to witness and be the "salt of the earth." Taking the positive view he also argued that in America good voters made for good government. Finally, he said voting could even be a means for realizing and spreading "evangelical peace principles on this earth." With such words Krehbiel all but ignored classic doctrine and its two-realm dualism. He did admit, however, that no specific Scripture demanded that Christians vote. So he thought the question was one for individual choice. Apparently most Russian Mennonites of the GC branch agreed.[51]

If Krehbiel suggested using politics for peace witness, Mennonites did not rush to do so—at least not those in Kansas, whose political behavior historian James Juhnke has studied closely. Most Mennonites there were Russian immigrants who were rather slow even to become citizens. When they did apply for citizenship their purposes seem to have been mainly local—particularly to set up and control public schools—rather than to become a part of the U.S. nation. They were slow also to vote. In the 1880s and '90s in heavily Mennonite townships, percentages of the population turning out to vote were only about half of what was typical for Kansas. The pattern lasted until mid-twentieth century.[52]

Mennonites in Kansas were slow also to accept public offices. An exception was township posts, which they seem rather erroneously to have looked upon as being like village offices in the old country. After a time in county politics two immigrants, a south German and a Prussian, did eventually serve in the Kansas legislature—but apparently not for the purpose of giving a Mennonite witness. The evidence suggests that as they got deeper into politics they lost interest in their Mennonite faith.[53]

Meanwhile at Jansen, Nebraska, some immigrants from the Russian Mennonite colonies also entered politics; but almost all had left the Mennonite church or had never formally joined. An exception was Peter Jansen, son of immigration leader Cornelius. A zealous and active Republican, Peter Jansen was elected Justice of the Peace about 1880. Thereafter his political involvements deepened until he hoped early in the twentieth century to become a U.S. Senator. At that he did not succeed. Friends did encourage him to run for state governor. But he refused, saying that as a Mennonite he could not take charge of the state militia.[54]

In Kansas the Russian Mennonites quickly produced editors who were quite political. *Zur Heimath*, begun in 1875, edited by David Goerz, and soon serving more or less as the paper for German-speaking GC Mennonites, did not favor a particular party. Yet in its early days it helped immigrants to understand and put faith in America's political system. The years 1885 to 1887 saw the founding of five local German-language newspapers in heavily Mennonite communities: in Marion County, at McPherson, and at Newton. All five were edited by Mennonites, four of them Russian immigrants. Although all claimed to be nonpartisan, four were quite pro-Republican. Two of the Republican-leaning papers were edited by John F. Harms, an immigrant who had worked for a time for John F. Funk in Indiana. Despite official MB caution, Harms was quite political. For instance, he favored a Republican program of high tariffs.[55]

Most Mennonite voters in Kansas also leaned Republican. The state was staunchly Republican when they arrived. Besides, as historian Juhnke has noted, Russian immigrant leaders were introduced to American politics largely by staunchly Republican railroad officials who sold them land. Yet Republicans could not quite take Kansas Mennonites for granted. From 1882 to 1890 Republican shares of votes in heavily Mennonite townships were sometimes 10 or more percentage points behind those in Kansas as a whole.[56]

The 1880s and early '90s were times of strong third-party protests in Kansas, especially by the People's Party, or "Populists." The Populists voiced frustrations many farmers and small business persons felt over disastrous grain prices, widespread farm mortgage foreclosures, and rail-freight and grain-elevator rates that seemed totally unjust. Heavily Mennonite townships cast up to 10 percent of their votes for the protest parties, although it is impossible to say how many of those votes were actually Mennonite ones. The farm depression seems to have hurt Mennonites less than their neighbors. Nevertheless, they suffered, and some took up Populism.[57]

The general movement of Kansas Mennonites was toward the Republicans. They shifted both during peak years of Populism in the early 1890s and as farm prosperity improved later in the decade. By 1898 the heavily Mennonite townships voted 60.8 percent Republican for governor. In 1904 they reached 73.3 percent in a vote to return Republican president Theodore Roosevelt to office. They did so even though Roosevelt advocated a large navy and liked to present himself as a swashbuckling military hero who had led a charge up San Juan Hill in Cuba during the Spanish-American war. According to Juhnke, Kansas Mennonites grew increasingly Republican without ever offering theological reasons for doing so. Juhnke concluded that at the end of the century the Mennonites of Kansas, (1) had never fully got over a "strangers and pilgrims" mentality; (2) voted their economic self-interests; and (3) more and more identified with America and the trends of its politics.[58]

Overall, the immigration from Prussia and the Russian empire brought Mennonites to America who were more ready for political involvement. The immigrants soon produced more editors who were openly political, and probably a higher percentage of voting, than other Mennonites in America had produced in nearly two hundred years.

Mennonite progressivism and politics

A second major influence on Mennonite politics in the 1870s to '90s was an increase in Mennonite progressives. Compared, for instance, to traditional or middle-of-the-road "old" and Amish Mennonite conference leaders, progressives saw far less problem with voting, officeholding, and other political action. Except for some early effort to say exactly what its position was with regard to lawsuits, the "new" Mennonite East Pennsylvania or Eastern District conference kept silent about political involvement. The silence spoke loudly for allowing it. The new GC general conference, after its birth in 1860, did the same. No doubt it was silent partly because it treated the question as one for congregations rather than for the conference.

In general the progressives tended to be those most acculturated into U.S. ways of thinking. Therefore they were least inclined to draw the classic doctrine's sharp line. Among Mennonites near Bluffton in western Ohio in the mid-to-latter decades of the century there was an immigrant Swiss wagon-maker named Johannes Amstutz, nicknamed "Waggner Stutz." A quick learner, he picked up English and enough knowledge of law that his community elected him to be Justice of the Peace. Thereupon his church's ministers reminded him that Christ's kingdom is not of this world. Eventually the congregation excommunicated him. People of the community remembered later that Waggner Stutz had argued that the U.S. was, or claimed to be, a Christian nation. Therefore, he said, to serve in office was to promote Christian order and justice.[59]

Such positive faith that the American political order was an instrument for God's purposes is central to what historians have identified as the nation's "civil religion."[60] Traditional Mennonites also sometimes bordered on civil religion but their version was more likely to be negative and emphasize God's judgment on the nation for its sins. In their view if God had any positive purpose for the nation it was at most to protect faithful Christians in their kingdom work. Progressives were more likely to see the nation as a positive agent to promote God's righteousness, his kingdom, and the reign of peace.

Traditionalists often lacked any vision of mission beyond perfecting the church internally so that it might offer the witness of example. Many progressives hoped to promote the gospel and God's kingdom actively and directly. Their vision often led them into Protestant patterns of building new institutions, from literary societies to missions. In turn, the more Protestant patterns often led Mennonites to new attitudes toward nation. For instance, some Mennonites eagerly attended local or regional interdenominational Sunday school conventions even though the conventions sometimes mixed religion with patriotic oration.[61]

Toward century's end many progressive GC Mennonite congregations formed chapters of the interdenominational youth organization, the Christian Endeavor Society. "*Good citizenship* is one of the great advance movements of the Christian Endeavor society," reported the GC journal *The Mennonite* in 1895. "It is truly a timely topic." The paper's editors were glad that the society produced honest businessmen, honest editors, voters who made "their ballots prayer papers," and duty-loving aldermen, councilmen, mayors, legislators, governors, and citizens. Their list even called for "Christian Endeavor policemen." Such policemen would be honest and would not protect saloons. The editors did not raise questions about Christians being in the police role.[62]

In 1885 a Congregationalist mission secretary named Josiah Strong published a vigorously argued book which he called not *Our Church* but *Our Country*. Historians have since seen the book as a prime expression of civil religion. It forthrightly suggested that God had manifestly destined the Anglo-Saxon peoples and nations to uplift and Christianize the world. Thus it implied that a race and its nations were God's agents as much as was the church. Despite the book's clash with classic Mennonite doctrine, in 1892 the firm of Welty and Sprunger, progressive printers among Swiss Mennonites at Berne, Indiana, published a German translation.

Meanwhile *The Mennonite* often printed language like Strong's. Worthy of Strong himself was a lead article in 1889 by a bright twenty-year-old future editor of *The Mennonite*, Harvey G. Allebach. Using the theme of charity, the young writer thoroughly mixed the idea of Christian charity with what he called the "charity of patriotism." Apparently not bothered by military examples, he asked rhetorically what kind of nation America would be if George Washington "and his band of heroes" had not "exerted their charity of patriotism." Somewhat more in line with Mennonitism he said also that there was a charity which humans had yet to learn: to forgive their enemies.[63]

Other remarks of progressives were less optimistic about patriotism and nation. In the mid-1890s *The Mennonite* stood adamantly against organizations called "Boys' Brigades," which put boys through military-style drills. Soon, it said, the boys would seek outlets for their militarism.[64]

In 1892 the same journal published a borrowed piece that asked: If Columbus had discovered America, who would discover a land of equality, where the measure of a person was not fashion and etiquette, and where white parents did not withdraw their children when a black child was admitted to a school? In his remarkable treatise explaining nonresistance to a German-speaking Mennonite Sunday school convention in Kansas in 1894, the Wadsworth-trained GC missionary Samuel S. Haury made much of how the emperor Constantine's use of military power to spread Christianity had perverted the faith. The base of the Christian church, Haury emphasized, did not lie in any earthly, political regime.[65]

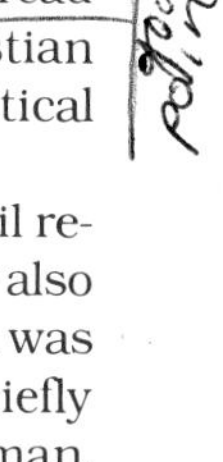

A tendency toward the self-satisfied, positive version of civil religion appeared not only in GC literature but late in the century also within the "old" and Amish Mennonite churches. To be sure, it was not evident among the most mature and careful progressives, chiefly publisher Funk and evangelist and church leader John S. Coffman. Funk's *Herald of Truth* was quite free of civil religion. As for Coffman, a resounding speech he gave in 1896 on "The Spirit of Progress" was a perfect opportunity to espouse a positive civil religion. Coffman spoke optimistically of progress. But except for a brief reference to nations' beginning to use international arbitration instead of war, he referred not to nation but to an invigorated church—a church with new programs for education and mission.[66]

Youthful progressives among the "old" and Amish Mennonites were more likely to confuse nation and Christianity. In 1872 an Amish Mennonite promoter of Sunday schools in Ohio, Jonathan K. Hartzler, observed in the *Herald of Truth* that he was glad to see China and Japan, so full of "idolatry and darkness," now building railroads and sending sons to study in the United States. For they would soon "see that Christian civilization is better." In 1892 and 1893 a young Mennonite preparing to be a medical missionary, Solomon (S. D.) Ebersole, expressed the confusion even more. To advocate city missions he addressed Mennonite Sunday school conventions serving "old" and Amish Mennonite congregations in Indiana and Ohio, conventions which amounted to youth rallies. He spoke stirringly and no doubt for a worthy cause. But at points he mixed church and nation so much that it was unclear what he thought the relation to be among saving individuals, planting churches, and improving the political order.[67]

Those were remarks more or less in passing. Even stronger ones appeared in a *Young People's Paper* published by Funk's press beginning in 1894. The paper's editors, first Menno S. Steiner (a Mennonite) and then Christian K. Hostetler (an Amish Mennonite), both reared in Ohio, were normally among the more careful and sober of younger progressives. Yet in September of 1894 they included an item which presented revolutionary war patriot Patrick Henry as a Christian who had given an hour each day to private devotions; and in 1897 they printed a borrowed article whose author exulted that now "Christian nations control the world." In an 1899 issue the lead article was a glowing portrait of U.S. President William McKinley, even though McKinley had recently led the nation into the jingoistic Spanish-American war.[68] There were more such items.

Thus did some progressives of the "old" and Amish Mennonite churches also blur the classic two-realm distinctions. At times they offered Mennonite youth the slogans, ideas, and saints of civil religion. By no means were such sentiments their whole message. For instance, in 1897 several pieces in the *Young People's Paper* on "Patriotism" did not confuse loyalty to the kingdom of God with loyalty to the American nation. And in the *Herald of Truth* even rather progressive "old" and Amish Mennonite writers kept more of the traditional two-realm outlook.

Many progressives who did not accept all of civil religion absorbed some of its parts. One reason, quite obviously, was that they thought more and more like Americans. Just to be a progressive was to share a major element of American faith, belief in progress. Another reason was that traditionalist Mennonites and Amish had not done well at offering a positive mission for God's people in the world. Progressive Mennonites and Amish were at least thinking about Christians' mission. When they did, some of them tended rightly or wrongly to see the two-realm boundary as a barrier. Sometimes that perception led them to identify with the nation and its civil religion.

Politics of prohibition

In the U.S., a temperance movement began in the late 1700s and grew strong in the 1820s, '30s, and '40s. Revivalists in the movement gave the crusade quite a revivalistic style; and for most of its promoters temperance came to mean not merely moderation but teetotalism—total abstinence from alcoholic beverages. After the civil war, political activists formed a national Prohibition Party in 1869 and a Woman's Christian Temperance Movement in 1874. In 1892, at a peak of success, the Prohibition candidate for U.S. president drew 271,000 votes. Meanwhile some states passed legislation ranging from weak local-option laws to a decision in Kansas in 1880 to make traffic in alcoholic beverages unconstitutional.[69]

Mennonites and Amish did not automatically support prohibition. Through most of the nineteenth century many of them accepted moderate use of tobacco and alcohol. Beloved preachers such as John Geil of the "old" Mennonites or John H. Oberholtzer of the "new" liked their pipes and cigars. Some women smoked pipes—for instance, Katie Troyer Hershberger, who was born in 1859 and as an adult was a member of Amish and "old" Mennonite congregations. As she grew old in the twentieth century she still kept her pipe and joked: "*Noch um essa/ smoke Duvoc/ und dass steht in der Bivel*" (After eating/ smoke tobacco/ and that is in the Bible). Yes, she would laugh, the word "*dass*" ("that") was in the Bible. About the 1870s some of the "old" church's conferences counseled against chewing of tobacco during church because, as John F. Funk explained, "spitting is obnoxious." In 1889 Funk's paper printed a woman's complaint: congregations who opposed smoking gave men five or ten years to quit; but if women dressed too fancily, they had to reform at once.[70]

As for alcohol the position of most Mennonites and Amish through much of the century remained that of Christian Burkholder. "If you find in your youth an inclination for strong drink," he had advised in 1804, "so restrain and deny yourself that it does not become a habit with you. . . . Out of drunkenness grows much evil," with "discord and hatred."[71] In those words the issue was not alcohol itself so much as peace and good order.

Of course gentle teaching such as Burkholder's was one matter and practice another. To prove that the "old" church had deteriorated, reformers pointed to cases of members' drunkenness and bad behavior which followed. At mid-century in Lancaster County, Pennsylvania, the Old Order-minded Jacob Stauffer lamented that several drunken Mennonites had become so noisy that people heard them a mile away. "Is that a light for the world and salt for the earth?" he asked. In the 1870s a cautiously progressive Amish Mennonite congregation in eastern Ohio, Oak Grove, disagreed about whether to let members continue brewing beer. One member promised to quit if the congregation gave him time to close out his business; it did, even though he took seven years. Another refused and left the church. In Russia also, MBs pointed to drunkenness as one evidence that Mennonites needed renewal and reform.[72]

Of course the critics were right: any drunkenness was too much. There were cases of drunkenness and apparently some Mennonite and Amish drunkards. On the other hand the evidence hardly suggests any great number. Moreover, some of the charges surely referred to youths who were not yet members of the church. For instance, even as he denounced bundling and youthful frivolity in general, Iowa bishop Jacob Schwarzendruber lamented that Amish youths ate and drank to excess.[73]

Somewhat less stringently than did the reformers, in the 1870s to '90s the "old" and Amish Mennonite conferences often admonished about drink. They warned less often against individual acts of drinking than against going to saloons with their worldliness and appearance of evil. Some spoke out also against the liquor traffic. Once again they admonished more than legislated—although in 1884 the Indiana Mennonite body said that persons who persisted should be dealt with "as transgressors." The Franconia conference emphasized that parents should try to keep their youths away from excess and from drinking houses especially on the Sabbath.[74]

However, in 1894 the Franconia conference also advised against members' joining temperance societies or taking a temperance pledge. (Temperance promoters often asked for personal pledges not to drink, much as revivalists closed with altar calls.) The church was enough, the Franconia delegates reasoned. Obviously, they did not want temperance societies to displace church loyalty and identity. The same sentiment appeared at quite a different conference, the GC-related Kansas conference (soon the core of the Western District one). What did the conference advise about temperance societies? delegates asked in 1879, as political prohibition was about to win a constitutional victory in their state. Answer: If congregations would follow the command of Christ and work "for proper moderation," members would "have no need to join the temperance society."[75]

One issue, then, was whether to approve semireligious organizations who were not responsible to the church. A second was moderation versus teetotalism. Some Mennonites believed that moderation plus staying away from public drinking houses was enough. Apparently they assumed that if alcohol were surrounded by the controls of home and close-knit neighborhood, it was manageable. A third and major question was: should a church whose theology raised strong doubts about political involvement make an exception in the case of prohibition? Close to that question was the one of civil religion. The temperance movement had grown up with various other reforms ranging from health-food crusades to antislavery. A network of interdenominational Protestant organizations, often more or less revivalistic, supported many of the reforms. Some twentieth-century scholars say that the organizations' leaders aimed for a Protestant kind of civil religion. Clearly they wanted at least to shape the nation and its social order.[76] With their clear two-realm doctrine, Mennonites and Amish had little desire to do that. Should they have?

The most progressive of Amish and Mennonites were likely to say yes. Surely their main motive was to promote more Christian behavior. Another motive, apparently, was to be accepted by other Christians. In 1896, in Kansas, GC leader Christian Krehbiel announced that he now supported temperance and its legislation. His reason? If reported correctly his words were: "Brethren, we have made a name unto ourselves that stinks." So "we must change our attitude, if we want to keep the respect of our English-speaking Christians."[77]

In the 1890s young Mennonite progressives worked with Presbyterians, Methodists, United Brethren, and others to arrange and attend temperance lectures. For instance, two activists who did so in Lancaster County, Pennsylvania, were a certain Isaac Hershey and a Jacob A. Ressler. Within several years Ressler would lead the "old" Mennonites' first team of foreign missionaries (to India).[78] Another forum was those progressive papers, the GCs' *The Mennonite* and the "old" Mennonites' *Young People's Paper*, which printed many temperance pieces. Earlier Funk's *Herald of Truth* had picked up the issue but had done so only slowly. In its first fifteen years (1864-1879) it included only a scattering of temperance articles. Of those it printed, often borrowed from non-Mennonite papers, some were skeptical of teetotalism or of temperance societies. However, beginning about 1880 the paper grew more pro-temperance. Funk probably decided that the "old" and Amish Mennonites were at last ready to face the question. Moreover, in 1879 he added John S. Coffman to his editorial staff and in 1882 made him associate editor. Coffman promoted temperance, lamenting in 1884 that Mennonites were too divided on the issue. He wished they would "blow a trumpet with no uncertain sound"![79]

Many of the *Herald*'s temperance articles were sensible ones about health and the like. A few were lurid and silly horror stories, such as borrowed accounts of men full of alcohol catching fire from spontaneous combustion or from getting too near to flames. (Such

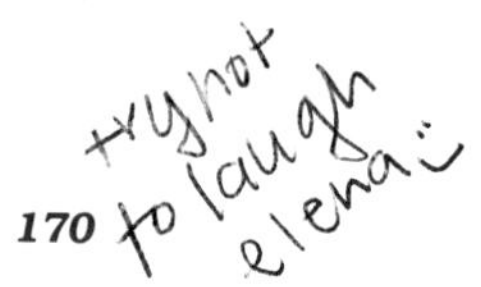

horror tales served also against other evils—for instance, an 1889 piece about a woman burning in a fire lit by sparks from her old husband's pipe and a young girl suffering lockjaw from chewing gum.) By the 1890s the *Herald* was able to print more temperance articles from Mennonite and Amish writers and to borrow fewer from others.[80]

Russian Mennonites also took up the issue. In 1882 John F. Harms was editor of a Funk paper mainly for the Russian immigrants, *Die Mennonitische Rundschau*. As such he extended an editorial welcome to a new German-language temperance society in America and applauded the name of Cornelius Jansen, prominent Russian Mennonite in Nebraska, on the list of founders. Again one motive was acceptance. Harms advised Mennonites not to "set themselves against public opinion in this land" by supporting "the merchants of drink." If Mennonites were the " '*Stille im Lande*' " (quiet in the land) then at least they should not oppose Americans' crusade against drunkenness. People who wanted the privilege of military exemption should not be "rebels against a useful cause."[81]

David Goerz, editing the GC paper *Christlicher Bundesbote*, more or less a rival for Russian Mennonite readership, liked Harms' editorial well enough to reprint it. But he questioned its ending. Who were those "rebels against a useful cause"? he asked in effect. Surely they were not "those Mennonites who hold to 'temperance' in the true biblical sense of the word, without extravagance." What was needed, thought Goerz, was "a godly temperance," not "a human, forced prohibition."[82]

By "forced" editor Goerz obviously meant political prohibition. On that issue "old" and Amish Mennonite conferences were on the whole strangely silent. At the Indiana-Michigan Mennonite conference in 1897 someone posed a question in typical prohibitionist language: What did the conference say about "the liquor traffic as it exists at the present time"? Answer: members should "use all their influence against it" as far as was consistent "with their nonresistant profession." Did that mean to vote? to vote for the Prohibition party? Deftly, the conference did not quite say.[83]

Meanwhile a major event for Mennonite politics developed in 1889. Pennsylvania put the prohibition question to statewide referendum. Of course voting in a referendum was not quite like voting for this or that politician. The *Herald*'s editors made quite clear that they wanted Mennonites to vote. They warmly endorsed prohibition and said it was "a well-known fact" that in Pennsylvania most Mennonites voted if they were eligible. Well, they said, "wherever you take an active part in anything, let it always be on the side of right, on the side of purity." "Help men come nearer to God." "Elevate them to moral purity."[84]

The editors had of course slipped out of two-realm thinking and over into the more American-Protestant idea of positive use of government and its coercion to create a moral society. That idea was even more clear among GC Mennonites in eastern Pennsylvania. In May of 1889, in a burst of rhetoric, the Eastern District conference said that the issue in the Pennsylvania referendum "transcends in magnitude and importance every other question which has ever been submitted to our suffrage." On it hung "the dearest interests for time and eternity of tens of thousands of our fellow citizens." So "the voting members of our church" should take "the side of right and honor" and join "with the Christian people of our State in voting down the curse of the age."[85]

The Lancaster "old" Mennonite conference advised that if any brother could not vote for prohibition, then at least he should not vote against it. A year later the North American conference of the MBs took about the same position but with more caution about partisan politics. Meanwhile even though Kansas politics gave it ample cause to speak, the GC-oriented Kansas conference remained silent about voting for prohibition. In 1883 someone asked what the conference thought of the temperance movement. It answered only that as a Christian body it considered "sobriety and temperance in all things" an "indispensable virtue." No clear political advice. Voting for prohibition in Kansas was hardly more clear. In the state's prohibition referendum in 1880 Mennonites did not vote in exceptional numbers. And in their townships the yes vote was not much higher than in the state as a whole: 57.1 percent compared to 52.3 percent.[86]

At century's end several Kansas Mennonites ran for local office on Prohibition party tickets but without drawing many Mennonite votes. In Indiana meanwhile, editors of the *Herald of Truth* still supported temperance but seemed less and less sure that Mennonites ought to support the cause politically.[87] Mennonites and Amish remained unsure about the politics of prohibition.

AS THE CENTURY CLOSED

Despite their new progressive voices, at the end of the century most Mennonites and Amish still put little faith in government to perform God's positive work. Their caution was in contrast to the prevailing (though by no means universal) outlook of postmillennial American Protestantism. The prevailing Protestantism held that the U.S. nation, its enlightenment, its democracy, its ridding itself of slavery (even if by war), and its education and reform all pointed to God's final reign. Throughout the century many Mennonites and some Amish had entered politics far enough to vote. But they had done so more as persons woven into their local communities than as people caught up in modern nation-building.

After the civil war three changes—new kinds of Mennonites from the Russian empire and Prussia, growing Mennonite progressivism, and prohibition—made Mennonites somewhat more political. An untypical progressive such as Joseph Taylor even endorsed fighting to defend the nation, and readers of *The Mennonite* raised no outcry.[88] Yet on the whole Mennonites had not let themselves get caught up in politics and nationalism.

Most Mennonites and Amish had not shifted their confidence away from faith and congregation and toward politics and government. They kept to personal and church piety, not national. Some individuals may have been openly political but not Mennonites and Amish en masse. In the the final years of the century the classic two-realm outlook still held.

CHAPTER 7

THE DRAFT AND THE CIVIL WAR

"What is the President? But a poor dying mortal like ourselves. . . ."

—John M. Brenneman, 1862[1]

From 1783, when the American revolution ended, to 1861, when the civil war began, draft exemption was no great problem for Mennonites and Amish in the U.S. The nation's founders had resented Britain's standing army and did not make militarism central to their nationalism as some modern revolutionists have done. The U.S. constitution of 1787 expanded the central government's power to make war yet limited its authority to keep a standing army. Of course America was not pacifist. The new nation often sent troops to push back "Indians"; it fought the war of 1812; and it was aggressive against Mexico in the 1840s. Americans objected to a standing central army but not to using force. They wanted force to be in the hands of the people. In 1789 they added the famous U.S. Bill of Rights as amendments to their new constitution. One amendment protected "the right of the people to keep and bear arms." Americans did not reject violence in human affairs; what they despised were (1) despotic central government, and (2) European-style professional armies.[2]

Power in the people's hands included state militias. After the revolution the central government quickly disbanded its Continental Army; but at the state level governments expanded militia laws. Militias typically enrolled male citizens from age 16 or 18 to 60 and mustered them some days each year for exercises and training. Yet the militias did not really flourish. Compulsory duty was not popular among a people preoccupied with individual liberty. By the second third of the century many militia units were hardly more than military clubs. The draft was breaking down.[3]

Valuing individual liberty, the nation's founders were remarkably tolerant if Quakers, Mennonites, Dunkers, and others objected to bearing arms. But they were not nearly so tolerant if conscientious objectors refused to contribute to military effort in any way at all. Lawmakers could not make conscientious objectors be effective soldiers. But they could demand extra taxes, commutation fees, fines, or the furnishing of substitutes. By and large, the nation's pacifists were not poor. They or their relatives and fellow church members had property to tax or confiscate. The idea of most lawmakers was not *exemption*, but *equivalency*.

As the U.S. Bill of Rights was being written the great legal thinker James Madison wanted more absolute language. He proposed to have the U.S. constitution say that "the full and equal rights of conscience [could not be] in any manner, or on any pretext, infringed." And where the document now assures citizens the right to bear arms he wanted to add: "*but no person religiously scrupulous of bearing arms shall be compelled to render military service in person.*" However in its final form the Bill of Rights was not so clear. Modern-day jurists argue whether the constitution makes conscientious objection a right or only a *privilege*. If a privilege, lawmakers may choose to grant it or withhold it.[4]

In the new nation some states granted exemption. Most who had pacifist communities allowed equivalency, at least. Some others said specifically that their legislatures could make exceptions for conscientious objectors. Still others said nothing. Saying nothing at least did not forbid special treatment.[5]

So in the pre-civil war decades Mennonites and Amish felt little pressure to fulfill military duties. In some places the muster laws were enforced so poorly that pacifists enjoyed de facto exemption. In other places they got by with only perfunctory fines or commutation fees. In Virginia a family named Driver kept receipts for fines paid over three decades, 1816-1845, as three Driver sons named Jacob, Daniel, and John declined to muster. In eastern Pennsylvania's Montgomery County in the mid-1840s, Mennonite minister John Gehman noted annual payments of $2, $1, and $1.75 as militia fines or "militia fine and tax" on behalf of "John" (apparently John, Jr., his son in his early 20s). If the payments seemed heavy (which apparently they seldom were) a poor member might receive help from his congregation.[6]

Even during the war years 1812-1815 and 1846-1848 there was little pressure. America fought the war of 1812 and the conflict with Mexico mostly with volunteers. Military records suggest that some Mennonite and Amish sons served; but probably such sons were not yet church members and went by choice. About halfway through the war of 1812 deacon Martin Mellinger of near Lancaster in Pennsylvania told European relatives that some Canadian Mennonites were paying rather heavily for commutation. But in his own region, he said, as yet "none of us has been called to the militia." Nor were pacifists compelled "to furnish any money except the regular taxes." He hinted that Mennonites actually were profiting from the war. Harvests had been good, land values were rising, "and almost everything is bringing a good price." Wheat and rye were selling well, and the price of whiskey was about 20 percent higher than a year earlier. Yet, the good deacon noted, "taxes are being placed on various things." War "is expensive."[7]

The 1812 and Mexican wars seem not to have affected Mennonites and Amish much except to open new lands to which they might migrate. By contrast, a few Quakers landed in jail. The issue was, they rejected equivalency. They not only refused to bear arms but also were adamant against commutation fees and fines. Some of their logic was flawless: that money payments as well as personal service contributed to war. Some of it was more arguable. Resisters used language of the American revolution to insist that their liberty of conscience was inalienable, they had never signed a social contract relinquishing it, therefore they should not have to pay for what was theirs.[8] Such reasoning was arguable because American thinkers had always recognized that individual rights, precious as they were, could never be absolute in organized society. It was risky to defend conscientious objection on the opponents' own ground.

Mennonites by contrast hardly ever put forth such abstract political theory. Instead, they restated their own biblical pacifism. Some modern commentators have held to "dark ages" interpretations which say that, intellectually, Mennonites and Amish were not prepared for the civil war. Late in life John F. Funk wrote that "in as much as there had been no war for a long period of time, the doctrine of non-resistance had almost been forgotten, at least in a sense of it being taught and impressed on the minds of the young men."[9] Such comments are overstatements. Ironically, the young man Funk had himself chosen Mennonitism and nonresistance during the war, intelligently and decisively.

The "dark ages" idea belittles what Mennonites produced. Christian Burkholder's clear words were being printed and reprinted, by 1857 even in English. In their 1837 *Confession of Faith* Peter Burkholder of Virginia and his translator, the song master Joseph Funk, included a chapter reiterating Mennonite nonresistance, again in English. In 1841 in Canada an able bishop named Benjamin Eby published a very readable book on Mennonite history and doctrine. It certainly taught nonresistance, and in 1853 it was republished in Pennsylvania. A manuscript produced on the eve of the civil war by an Amish bishop, David Beiler of Pennsylvania's Lancaster County, was not published until much later but probably circulated hand-to-hand.

Besides such works there were various printings of the Dordrecht Confession, the *Martyrs Mirror*, and other writings. To be sure, most of the publications were not original; but they did not necessarily have to be original to impress Mennonites and Amish. And in fact some were rather original. Christian Burkholder, for instance, went far beyond refusal to bear arms in war; he reinforced Mennonite pacifism with the theology of humility. Peter Burkholder, besides restating the 33-article Peter Twisck confession, included a reflection of his own on Christ's kingdom of peace. In it he said that the kingdom was a matter not only of the future but also of the present church and Christian life. And as his uncle Christian had also done, he connected the forgiving, peaceful, nonresistant ethic to Christ's self-giving on the cross.[10]

Too often the "dark ages" idea rests on tests which hardly fit a folk culture. To say that Mennonite peace thought was "moribund" (one historian's word[11]) is to judge too much by whether pre-civil war Mennonites and Amish expressed themselves in print and other media of modern peace education. Whether or not they produced impressive writings on peace, in their folk life they maintained a remarkably clear self-understanding of being weaponless, non-avenging, and nonresistant. That perception of how to be Christians was woven all through their humility theology and their style. And probably better than most modern peace teaching, it permeated ordinary church life. By applying wrong tests, one can judge too harshly.

THE CHALLENGE OF THE CIVIL WAR

As the civil war began the U.S. government at first tried to raise troops in two ways: by calling up state militias for three-month terms and by offering bounties to attract volunteers into the national army. But in July of 1862 U.S. president Abraham Lincoln signed a law introducing a sterner method: compulsory military service. The law, which still did not quite establish a national draft, put new pressures on states to raise troops. If states did not do it quickly the federal government might assume the task. Later, midway through the war in March of 1863, the central government established the first truly national U.S. military draft.[12]

Pressed by the central government in late 1862 the states in turn stepped up pressure on their citizens, including Mennonites and Amish. "We had been hearing about war for two years but only now feel the draft," wrote an "old" Mennonite preacher in Pennsylvania's Bucks County, Jacob Beidler, in October. Six weeks later a young man named Gross appeared at the Bucks County seat along with many others to seek exemption. "It was a great multitude all day," he told a friend; "I have never seen harder pressing an croding in all the days of my life." Some in the throng had claimed physical disability; others, scruples of conscience.[13]

Response: War-related contributions

Conscientious-objecting Mennonites and Amish responded in various ways. One was to make "voluntary" contributions to causes related indirectly or sometimes rather directly to the war. In November of 1862 preacher John Gehman made a new kind of entry in his accounts: $3.00 paid out "for the sick and wounded soldiers." Thereafter he recorded several more such payments, sometimes for as little as $1.00 or even $.25. Or he gave "*boundy gelt*" (bounty money). That is, he contributed to a fund by which the local community paid lump sums to men who would volunteer. Bounties were a way for communities to try to fill their quotas without having to invoke the draft.[14]

Some communities put heavy pressure on Mennonites to contribute "voluntarily" to such funds. In mid-1861 at Strasburg in Lancaster County pro-Union patriots were soliciting to finance a local unit of cavalry. Some Mennonites, especially Reformed Mennonites, flatly refused to pay. As a result local newspapers got into a battle of words. "These Mennonites are among our richest farmers . . . ," said one; this was a "righteous war" and "these rich but close-fisted farmers must now pay their share." If they did not, then they should not expect sympathy if their "fine farms" were the first to be "overrun" or if someone carried off "their safes or well-filled stocking legs." But, one paper alleged, Strasburg area Mennonites had stubbornly agreed in a special meeting not to contribute money and not to let their young men join military companies.[15]

Not so, declared defenders of Mennonites. The defenders accused solicitors of intimidating. Specifically the solicitors had gone to an aging Mennonite with a tale that rebels had burned Washington and were about to march on Philadelphia and then Lancaster County. The frightened old man had given $100. With precedent in hand the fund-raisers then had told other wealthy Mennonites in the neighborhood that if the old man's conscience let him contribute, theirs should also. So three more Mennonites had each given $100. As for that "special meeting," the defenders insisted (probably correctly) that it had been nothing but an ordinary pre-communion counsel service. The local bishop had indeed said that nonresistant Mennonites could hardly "assist to arm and equip any body of men." But he also had said that if the war brought heavy taxes Mennonites should "pay without a murmur." And he had added that "the wives and children of the soldiers . . . should be cared for; it was our duty and we should be charitable."[16]

As for Mennonites' wealth, one newspaper writer defended it. If Mennonites had wealth, he wrote, at least they had gotten it by honest work. "Heaven knows," he added, "some are poor enough too." And patriotic. Anybody who talked to committees going about the county raising money to provide fighting men with warm clothes and blankets knew that Mennonites were helping to "make the soldiers happy and comfortable." They were as "proud of their country as anybody else" and glad to see the flag defended.[17]

Mennonites themselves remained quite silent in the public dispute. However in October of 1862 "new" Mennonite John H. Oberholtzer, as *Volksblatt* editor, seemed to encourage his people to contribute somehow. He still supported pacifism and challenged readers to resist the " 'war and battle cry' " and remain true to their Savior.[18]

But then he reprinted a story which local newspapers in eastern Pennsylvania were circulating. Two hundred years earlier, the story said, Spain had been about to invade the Netherlands. A Mennonite peasant heard of the danger and appeared at the palace in Amsterdam. If the Dutch government needed money to equip an army, he told officials, Mennonites would help provide it. "Tell me sir," he asked, "how much you need." "750,000 Gulden," the official replied. The man went to the Mennonite congregations and quickly raised the amount. After the war the government tried to return it with interest. But the Mennonites refused. Under Holland's rulers his people had found a home, freedom, and blessing, the peasant said, and if the nation had been defeated they would have lost all. "Your cause was our own."[19]

So ran the story. At the end editor Oberholtzer printed a question that other Pennsylvania papers had asked. In the U.S., nonresisting people had "acquired wealth in abundance." Now the government was in "a death struggle." Would not "our Mennonites, Amish and Dunkers" return a favor to "such a kind mother"?[20]

By and large Mennonites and Amish were trying to draw a fine line—to be "charitable" and yet not pay for actual arms. Quite clearly many of the more traditional ones preferred to be taxed outright rather than solicited, for then their consciences were free: they could simply obey the New Testament injunctions to pay tribute. Many contributed to funds to aid soldiers' families and the like; but the contributions, as the Strasburg case suggested, were not purely voluntary.[21]

Response: Appeals to Republican officials

Since Republicans ruled widely in the North during the civil war, one way to relieve the draft pressures was to appeal to Republican officials. In Ohio, Mennonites and Amish were not at all sure that their state would exempt them. Republicans in Ohio, including officials, were quite afraid that their state was all too full of traitors. That was mainly because parts of it, especially southern Ohio, had many "Copperhead" Democrats. Such people were not really pro-South but nevertheless were quite skeptical of the war, mainly because they saw it as benefiting rich folks and blacks at the expense of poor whites.

In 1863 a certain Jonas Shank wrote from Kalida in western Ohio to a brother in Virginia and more or less agreed. Shank had a son-in-law of non-German, non-"Mennonite" surname who was serving in the Union army but he himself was probably a Mennonite. He was not clearly pro-Democrat. "I am Begining to thing [think] Both parties air to Blame," he wrote; "thoes head men are makeing great fortunes and the poor glass [class] has to face the canons Mouth." Indeed, "I wold Rather see slavery extended all over the creation then to had this curs upon our cuntry." But even "our democrats out hear . . . air not wiling to do anything only gas about it." So Shank simply prayed "that the word of god ma Be speadiley accomplishe and the sword Beaten into plow shears and the spears in to pruning hooks." If only "this eye for eye tooth for tooth" would end! Then people could turn once more to "husbandry commerce and sions [science] and Religon." Thus Shank kept a rather classic Mennonite skepticism about all politics. Yet he tinged his Mennonitism with Copperheadism.[22]

Of course to be anti-Lincoln, anti-Republican, and antiwar was not necessarily to be disloyal to the nation or its government. But Republicans often seemed to think it was. And in Ohio, Mennonites and Amish were not as clearly Republican as in eastern Pennsylvania. For instance, among Swiss Mennonites at Sonnenberg in eastern Ohio's Wayne County there seem to have been enough who were anti-Abraham Lincoln and anti-Republican to make a few who were outspokenly Republican rather unpopular. And in 1862 in neighboring Holmes County, Amish and Mennonites restated their classic position by having their local paper print a part of the old Dordrecht confession. They explained that they did not want to "be accused of being disloyal as has often been the case of late by persons who are unacquainted with our faith and doctrine."[23]

In late August of 1862, as the national government put pressure on the states to furnish troops, someone (likely a local official) wrote to Ohio Governor David Tod and advised him about Holmes County Amish and their convictions. Some Amish, said the writer, were "so wholly non-resistant" that they insisted "they would suffer themselves to be killed rather than take up arms to kill their fellow beings." Moreover, some of them strongly favored the northern (or Union) cause and wanted to see the U.S. government suppress the southern uprising. But, said the correspondent, such statements were not true of all. There also were "a considerable number of" Amish who opposed "the Government and sympathise with the rebellion."[24]

Central and eastern Pennsylvania were different. In Mifflin County, newspaper editors thought Amish could be counted on to vote heavily Republican. Anti-Republicans feared them so much that during an election in 1862 they placed a threat in a newspaper and scattered it on slips of paper on local roads:

> All dutch that took the oath not to bare arms in defence of their country is warned if they vote at this Election their buildings shal be laid in ashes So I Say take warning in time before it be too late
>
> [Signed] *To be Drafted I am*

Apparently nothing much came of the threat. In Pennsylvania, nonresistant people had little to fear. Having voted widely for many years for Whigs and Republicans they had access to key politicians. A story from civil war days in Indiana has the Indiana governor, Oliver P. Morton, implying to two Dunker ministers that if people were not willing to fight they also should not vote.[25] But in Pennsylvania an opposite logic prevailed.

In October of 1862 as the Bucks County minister Jacob Beidler told of new draft pressures, he remarked also that at first Mennonites had done little to respond—partly, he said, because "we were ... too ignorant in this matter." But then "some of our preachers and leaders ... went to our governor," Andrew Curtin. They told Curtin that Mennonites were willing to pay fines; but in a draft, they hoped that their members would "not be compelled to

Columbianna County
~~Allen County~~. Ohio. August the 19th 1862.
A Petition to Mr Abraham Lincoln, President of the united States.
We the undersigned Heartily wish unto our Most Nobel President, Grace.
Mercy, & Peace from God the Father, & of the Lord Jesus Christ.
May the Good Lord abundantly Bless the President, with Wisdom & knowledge from on high, and Enable him to Rule this our Great Nation
with Prudence. We would Humbly Pray the President, not to Consider
us too Burdensome, By Presenting to him this our weak & Humble Petition, theirby Humbly Praying & Beseeching him, to take into Consideration
our Sore Distress. We would herewith inform the President, that their
is a People Scattered & Living, Mostly in the Northern Parts of the
united States; Pennsylvania, virginia, Ohio, Indianna, & Some few in
Illinois, & Iowa, Called Mennonites; who are greatly Distressed at the
Present time on acount of the war. As it is against their Confession

Petition in John M. Brenneman's handwriting to Abraham Lincoln, 1862, asking that Mennonites be exempted from the civil war draft.

go." Beidler was sure Curtin had acted, for now pacifists could go to proper officials, affirm their convictions, and be released from personal service.[26]

Another report says that two Lancaster area Mennonites, preacher Amos Herr and layman John Shank, also went to Curtin, and explained their pacifism from the Bible. The report ends much differently from the Indiana one. "Well," Curtin is supposed to have asked, "what do you people do for us? Do you vote?" "Yes," Herr and Shank responded. All right, said the governor, "we will do something for you." The report adds that an aide then put the age-old question: What if everyone were like the Mennonites? Curtin is supposed to have replied that in that case "there would be no war."[27]

Evidently some Mennonites appealed to Republican officials in person. Others did so in writing.

Response: Petitioning

In August of 1862, as the national draft law required states to recruit quotas of men, Ohio governor David Tod received two appeals from Swiss-speaking Mennonites in his state's Wayne, Allen, and Putnam counties. Both messages told of past Mennonite suffering in Europe for conscientious objection and praised America as a free country. Both expressed loyalty to government and declared willingness to pay taxes. And both urged that Ohio let conscientious objectors pay "a reasonable fine" or commutation fee in lieu of being drafted. Meanwhile in Ohio also, in the same month, bishop John M. Brenneman drafted a historic plea to send higher: to U.S. president Abraham Lincoln.[28]

There is no evidence that Brenneman's petition ever reached the nation's capital; yet it was historic. The idea for it began with Jacob Nold, Jr., the deacon-businessman of Columbiana County, writing to several friends. The year was 1862, draft pressures were mounting, and Nold was worried. Yes, the pastoral Brenneman responded, it did seem "as if our faith was to Be Put to the trial." And "if the Lord intends to Chasten us, we Cannot Escape his hand." But remember how Jesus had spoken a word and calmed the storm. After all, Brenneman asked, "Is not the Lord the Judge of all the Earth?" Then let us "be careful not to put too much confidence in man. Our God is certainly more to be depended on than the President." The president was "but a poor dying mortal like ourselves." Christians should not "lean on a broken reed."[29]

Nold wanted someone to go and speak to Lincoln; but Brenneman let his humility get in the way of such witness. He was, he said, "too weak, & feeble an instrument." Maybe the church should look for some "more experienced Brother." Or perhaps a written petition would serve. Brenneman promised to help write the petition, and soon drafted one.[30] Whether or not the plea reached the government, it is historic. For it was a thorough, precise, and nuanced statement of the dominant Mennonite position on civil war service and on government.

"We, the undersigned," Brenneman began, "heartily wish our most noble President grace, mercy, and peace from god the Father, and of the Lord Jesus Christ." Mennonites hoped the president would consider "our sore distress" and not find "this, our weak and humble petition" too burdensome. The petition explained who Mennonites were and why they could not bear arms. But, Brenneman wrote, the president should "not mistake us to be secessionists or rebels against the government"; we are "entirely free from that guilt." Of the Mennonites the petitioners knew, all favored the Union. They "greatly abhor the present rebellion" and "would certainly be among the last to rebel against so good a government." Indeed, any Mennonite guilty of rebellion should be dealt with accordingly. "We would be far from holding such as brethren in our church."[31]

Brenneman went on to state classic Mennonite positions, simply but clearly. He assured the president that even when persecuted, Mennonites did not allow members "to culumniate, slander or defame" political rulers or resist them with "weapons of war." Instead, considering that vengeance belonged to God, they looked to God for comfort and hoped for heaven. But if government "from Christian principles" allowed "freedom of conscience in all points to believers," then Mennonites "should be the more gratefully submissive and obedient." So, the petition pleaded, they hoped that "our good President" might "favor us . . . and not allow us to be forced or compelled to take up arms."[32]

"By no means" did Mennonites "wish to censure, judge, or condemn other denominations" or Christians whose views were different. But the Canadian government exempted conscientious objectors if they paid an extra tax. And the rebel government of Virginia, after hauling some off in wagons and jailing them, had let them go free upon paying fines and a 2 percent tax on their property. "Now we have the confidence in our President and his officers that they are fully as kind and merciful (and we trust much more so) as they of the South."[33]

Brenneman said he did not want to prescribe policy to the president; but his petition did "humbly pray and beseech him." After all, he wrote, "we are depending creatures": dependent on the

Library of Congress

"Radical" Republican Congressman Thaddeus Stevens (1792-1868) from Lancaster, Pennsylvania.

mercy of God and of officials. Moreover, Mennonites recognized a Christian duty to be "kind-hearted to all the needy and helpless"; so "we . . . promise to be liberal and charitable to . . . [needy] women and children whose husbands and fathers are gone to the army." And if the government would "lay an extra tax upon all Mennonites" who were fit for military duty, "we will not murmur or complain at all." Would the president please issue an order exempting Mennonites if they paid such a tax? Would he issue it to the governor of Ohio? "The Mennonites in Ohio seem to be in the most danger."[34]

It may be unfortunate that John M. Brenneman did not go to Washington and seek audience with Lincoln. Given Lincoln's reflective but common-man temperament, the unassuming but able, pastoral, and biblically oriented Brenneman might have left a deep impression. No doubt it was a case of humility carried so far that it interfered with Mennonites' testifying to what they understood to be Christ's nonresistant gospel.

But as a statement of Mennonite position on government, war, and conscientious objection, the Brenneman petition was classic. Its mood was entirely humble and appreciative, not at all aggressive.

It clarified the difference between conscientious objectors and rebels. It put the case well for respecting government and its authority, yet from a position which kept Christians distinct from them and the nation.

Certain of its points invite a host of theological and practical questions. For instance, were Mennonites carrying submission and subjection further than New Testament writers ever intended? And if they enjoyed the nation's political and economic fruits, could they really be so distinct? Finally, was not readiness to pay a special tax really an offer to contribute to war? Had Brenneman not offered the logic of equivalency?

But in what it glossed over as well as in what it said, the document was a most subtle statement of the Mennonite position. Mennonites did not approach government with eighteenth-century-Enlightenment ideas of asserting rights. Instead, their attitude was one of deference. Only if government put them in an impossible dilemma would they defy it. Even then, they would do so only from the deepest of convictions and with great pain. That is how the Mennonite church approached the U.S. civil war.

PAYING FEES AND HIRING SUBSTITUTES

Almost universally, Mennonites and Amish who sought military exemption were ready to pay extra, compulsory fees. Quakers might object that they ought not to have to pay for exercising their consciences. But Mennonites and Amish were so willing to pay that some congregations helped raise the funds.

What to do about Mennonites and Amish in wartime was a very practical problem. When pushed to their convictions they could be most stubborn and their neighbors knew it. In August of 1862 the correspondent who advised Ohio governor Tod about the Holmes County Amish urged that the state should charge them a fee rather than draft them. The Amish themselves had implied they were willing to pay a fine, he said, without suggesting any limit. In the same week another Holmes County correspondent also advised Tod that it was futile to draft such people. If sent into battle, they "will not fight." It would be better to give them time to find substitutes. "They will pay liberally for substitutes"; and if allowed to hire them, they would probably provide more soldiers than if compelled to go themselves.[35]

In October of 1862 newspapers in Pennsylvania's Bucks County reported that local townships were having trouble raising their quotas with volunteers, especially in German areas. The going price of hiring a substitute was $300 to $500, with some fetching

$700 to $1000. (This, in a day when a year's pay for a working man might be no more than $300.) Meanwhile, in September, Indiana's governor consulted with Lincoln's secretary of war and decided to dismiss conscientious objectors from personal service if each one paid a $200 commutation fee. In October Ohio followed suit. Ohio's governor Tod said that his state would use the money to hire substitutes and to care for the sick and wounded. By the end of the month some 250 conscientious objectors had paid and the fund was up to about $50,000.[36]

The nation's first truly national draft law, the law of 1863, also allowed escape. Under it a drafted man might either hire a substitute or pay $300 for commutation. But those provisions were not only for conscientious objectors; anyone with the means could take advantage of them. While the draft bill was in Congress the "Radical" Republican congressman Thaddeus Stevens from Lancaster had tried to limit the provisions to conscientious objectors but had failed.[37]

Stevens nevertheless, pointed to the law to win favor with Mennonite and other pacifist voters. He assured them that it gave them a way out of military duty, which of course it did. Democrats said loudly that the provisions made the draft a rich man's law: poor working people could not afford to pay $300. So an amendment passed in mid-1864 eliminated the commutation clause for most people. However, Stevens won a fight in Congress to keep it for conscientious objectors. The new arrangement left a Democratic editor in Lancaster quite angry. It was an insult, he wrote, that "wealthy German farmers of Lancaster and other counties, who happen to belong to the Mennonitsh or similar Christian denominations," could still buy exemption.[38]

Despite such objections Lincoln and his government levied four drafts: in summer and autumn, 1863; spring, 1864; autumn, 1864; and spring of 1865.[39]

Not all sons of Mennonites and Amish took advantage of the various commutation or substitute provisions. For instance, if one could qualify it was much cheaper to claim physical disability. Of course not only conscientious objectors did so. In August of 1862 a Republican editor in Pennsylvania's Bucks County scolded that "people who have been healthy all their lives now suffer great affliction, and some who have talked loudly of crushing the rebellion, suddenly find themselves unable to help do the job."[40]

But there were conscientious objectors among the claimants. In September of 1862 a surgeon named McClelland certified that 42-year-old Jacob Liechty of Washington, Iowa, was a "cripple from rheumatism." In August, in eastern Pennsylvania, long lists of men making such claims included many "Mennonite" names. A Philip Swartley listed rheumatism. A Christian Moyer said he had a "deceased" liver (or so wrote a Justice of the Peace named Albright). And an Abraham Kulp was recorded as being a "perfect dwarf" only 4 1/2 feet tall and weighing only 61 pounds. Others won exemption for being a school director or a Mennonite minister or an assistant postmaster. It is seldom possible to tell who among the exempt was actually Mennonite. But the lists are much longer in Bucks County's heavily Mennonite townships than in many townships without Mennonites. An examination of who made their claims by affirmation rather than by oath also suggests many Mennonites.[41]

Another escape, at least a temporary one, was to disappear. Daniel, Christian, Jr., and Noah, three brothers in an Eash family of Howard County in central Indiana, hid for a time. Local lore later said that each evening their father set out a basket of food for them.[42] Other young men went to Canada. Again, the migrants were not only conscientous objectors.

As state drafts got under way in 1862 reports were rife of "skedaddlers" headed across the border. Apparently no one has tried to determine how many skedaddlers were Amish or Mennonite. But, for instance, the family history of later Defenseless Mennonite leader Joseph Ramseyer says his parents entered Canada to escape the draft[43]; and no doubt quite a few other nonresistant people did so also.

Finally, a man might hide by going to a community in the U.S. where he was a stranger, especially to a place with enough volunteers to fill local quotas. In the 1863 letter in which he wrote so frankly to his brother John F. in Chicago about going west for self-interest, A. K. Funk pointed also to the prospect that Pennsylvania might soon charge $200 for exemption. So, the young Funk said, since he wanted to come west anyhow he might " 'hit two birds with one stone.' "[44]

Quite a few men from Amish or Mennonite homes simply went to war—probably most of them not yet baptized, not yet church members. Among Amish, those in Pennsylvania's Somerset County may have been especially ready to enlist. Yet not all went; and a disgruntled neighbor seems to have meant the Amish when he complained that officials were exempting people of certain religions automatically even though they were "the strongest advocates of the war." Were the Amish in Somerset and Garrett counties not consistently pacifist? According to oral tradition, before the war some of them were known to have shot and killed Indians. A prominent Amishman is supposed to have remarked that "killing an Indian was pretty near like killing a person." In civil war time, some of the region's Amish who opposed military service left for Iowa.[45]

As for Mennonites, historian John C. Wenger has written that in Indiana and Michigan "a number of young men from Mennonite families . . . entered the Union Army when drafted." In Ohio's Holmes County young men reared in a Mennonite congregation enlisted even before the draft exerted pressure. In western Pennsylvania Mennonites Mary and Andrew Ziegler commented in 1862 that their son Andrew, Jr., was in the war and wished someone would send him "some good appels to eyte." With their German ears confusing b and p or d and t, they said they did not like his going; "it is a good dele of troupple to us." But "we cand help it."[46]

Near Medina, Ohio, Andrew Ziegler's sister Barbara and her husband John Herr had three sons in the war. "I little thought," wrote the father, "that wee was raising Children to goo to war with the Enemies of our Laws and our rights and liberties." But it was so. Just thinking of the thousands in untimely graves often moved him to tears. As for the mother, she was having "a hard trial [and] wept bitterly Day and night." Years earlier two other sons had died as small children. Now, her husband wrote tenderly, she moaned that it might have been better to have buried the other three sons as children also, "and not have wept more." (Before war's end the oldest son, Benjamin, the only married one, died—probably as a war casualty.)[47]

Quite clearly many young men from Mennonite or Amish homes went to war also from the older communities of eastern Pennsylvania. Records do not make clear how many, since the names of many other people in those communities were the traditionally "Mennonite" or "Amish" ones, often because of Mennonite or Amish roots. Gossip once circulated among Bucks County Mennonites about a young man with the Mennonite-sounding name of Stover (earlier, Stauffer). The rumor said that upon being drafted he ran off to New York, got drunk, and was robbed of "his watch &c."; then, "when he was right side up again he found himself an enlisted Marine in a Man of War." Stover's grandparents and some of his aunts and uncles were indeed Mennonite. However, his parents seem to have joined the Christian church, and he likewise later in life.[48] Yet surely quite a few sons went from Mennonite homes as well. Doing so was far from unthinkable.

In the winter of 1862-1863 John F. Funk, during a visit home from Chicago, worshiped with his boyhood congregation, Line Lexington, in eastern Pennsylvania. The preacher was John Geil, whom Funk described as "straight and erect" with "snow white Locks flowing down over his shoulders." After the sermon the old minister stepped over to a stove to fill and light his pipe. Turning to Funk he asked, "Have they not yet made a soldier of you?"[49]

They had not. Nor did they make a soldier of many another Amish or Mennonite son. Quite a few found ways to buy what they called exemption. From August of 1862 to January of 1863 the Swiss-speaking Mennonites at Sonnenberg in Ohio systematically collected and recorded contributions to the Wayne County Military Committee, which used the cash for everything from paying soldiers to providing them entertainment. Virtually no Mennonites and Amish balked at such equivalency. They might find the fees heavy but they knew their ancestors had suffered worse in Europe. Besides, their sense of community and mutual aid helped. Some drafted men could not pay their fines, observed a Mennonite husband and wife from near Doylestown, Pennsylvania, in 1863. So "we chose 3 brethren as a committee and the drafted brethren who needed help notified this committee, which then examined them as to how much help they would need, for some were needier than others, and then it was brought before the congregation." Did the Bible not say that "if one member suffers all suffer"? Some other Mennonites acted similarly, but not all. A Jacob Kolb from Butler County in western Pennsylvania wished for such an arrangement in his congregation and said he would have contributed, even though he was poor. Instead, he had borrowed $300 to buy exemption for his son. A son-in-law had paid his own fee, even though at first he had grumbled that to earn $300 required so much "torture" that he would never part with the money.[50]

So in the North some young men of Amish and Mennonite families went to war and some did not. Those who held back often escaped by accepting the logic of equivalency and paying for commutation or substitutes. Sometimes they did so with their congregations' aid.

IN THE CONFEDERACY

The Confederate states had virtually no Amish; but Virginia had Mennonites, in its Shenandoah Valley. Unfortunately, the valley was both a path for armies moving north and south and a productive region whose crops the armies were eager to confiscate or destroy. Moreover, the South grew more desperate than the North. Mennonites suffered more in Virginia than in any northern state.

Apparently no Virginia Mennonites or their sons fought willingly for the South's cause. Their theology was firmly against rebellion; and it seems they did not ask whether the real rebels might have been northerners who used the central government against state power. Nor did southern states-rights arguments mean much to a people whose lines of kinship, religious fellowship, and other interests ran northward through the valley into Maryland and Pennsylvania. Finally, they were not slaveholders; the Virginia Mennonite conference forbade slaveowning. The most it permitted was that when neighbors exchanged labor a Mennonite could allow a neighbor's slave to work on his (the Mennonite's) farm. Records of any Mennonites or Amish in North America anywhere ever holding slaves are so meager and indefinite that if there were cases, a handful at most, they were "the exceptions that prove the rule." The rule was simply that Mennonites and Amish were not slaveholders.[51]

Some Mennonites did vote for Virginia's secession from the national Union in 1861; many of those later said they had done so under duress. Others voted against secession. Or (as, for instance, a prominent bishop named Samuel Coffman) they declined to vote at all. The Shenandoah Valley neighbors of the Mennonites were often pro-Union. The Mennonites were probably even more so.[52]

As pressure increased to join or help the Confederate forces, Virginia's Mennonites sometimes cooperated and sometimes resisted. When called to report for military service some men hid. Most men reported; but many of them refused to shoot, sometimes even under threat of court-martial and execution. The situation has spawned many legends, probably in the main true.

Solomon B. Wenger, in later years a lay leader at South English, Iowa, recounted that his 125-pound father had to carry rocks as punishment—until authorities saw they could not break his will and dismissed him. Other legends tell of jailed draftees who, like the New Testament's Paul and Silas, sang hymns and remained true. Or as a Christian Good later told his story, a captain sent him into one battle after another and repeatedly asked him if he had shot. "No, I didn't see anything to shoot at." What about "all those Yankees?" "They're people," Good rejoined; "we don't shoot people."[53]

Some Mennonites worked as cooks or teamsters. By March of 1862 Confederate general Thomas J. ("Stonewall") Jackson decided that it was not efficient to put them and Dunkers and Quakers on front lines. He observed that if they would not shoot, the army had better put them at other jobs so others could fight. Besides, advised Jackson, they had a fine reputation as teamsters; and in that role they might "save many valuable horses and other public property."

At another time Jackson observed that Dunkers and Mennonites generally obeyed their officers but that in battle they refused "to take correct aim." This time he recommended leaving them at home so "that they may produce supplies."[54]

Some Virginia Mennonites hired substitutes. Some won release on various other grounds. Abraham Blosser was a grandson of bishop Peter Burkholder and eventually a strongly anti-Sunday-school publisher with a paper named *Watchful Pilgrim.* In the war he paid $1000 to buy a mail route and be exempted as a postman. Blosser also hid for a time in a mountain cove. Indeed, enough Mennonites and others fled to nearby mountains or to the North that a sort of underground railroad developed. Often Mennonite men and women provided communication, concealment, food, and money. A Margaret Rhodes had a trapdoor in her bedroom floor leading to a chamber where for a time she hid a number of the men. One was Henry Brunk, husband of the plucky Susanna Heatwole Brunk, who later suffered such great hardship on the Kansas frontier.[55]

Several groups trying to hide or head North were captured and jailed by the Confederates. In March of 1862 a group of seventy-four, at least sixteen apparently Mennonite, were captured, marched to Richmond, and kept for about a month in a prison known as Castle Thunder. Meanwhile authorities captured another group of eighteen, mainly Dunkers but including several Mennonites, from whom they took eighteen valuable horses and $6000 in gold and silver. That group (which included Henry Brunk) spent some time in a Harrisonburg jail. Among them were two Mennonite ministers and John Kline, a Dunker elder. Without doubt elder Kline was the strongest leader of the valley's Dunker and Mennonite pacifists. He wrote repeatedly to civilian and military officials on conscientious objectors' behalf.[56]

Perhaps one reason that the imprisoned Mennonites and others were soon released is that in March of 1862 Virginia passed a law which allowed a conscientious objector to escape personal service—if he paid a stiff fee of $500 plus a tax of 2 percent on his property. Perhaps Kline's letters had something to do with the passage of the law. Like Mennonite petitioners in the North, Kline all but asked for the privilege of paying for commutation. In 1861 apparently no Virginia Mennonite made Kline's kind of appeal; but early in 1862 Mennonites joined with Dunkers to request such treatment. Meanwhile the state's Quakers were also active. Whether such appeals carried as much weight as the more pragmatic advice of a Stonewall Jackson, who can say? But Virginia legislators passed the bill.[57]

During the following month (a year before the U.S. government in the North established national conscription) the Confederate government levied a national draft. At first the new law made no special provision for conscientious objectors. But in October of 1862, after various appeals and congressional debates (which included a petition from Dunkers and Mennonites and reading key passages from Peter Burkholder's *Confession*), the law was amended. Now it let conscientious objectors (specifically Quakers, Dunkers, Mennonites, and Nazarenes) hire substitutes or pay $500 each for commutation. In a spirit of mutual aid Mennonites quickly helped gather funds for persons who could not afford what the Virginia and Confederate laws required.[58]

The laws did not end the problems. In 1863 and 1864 the South's needs became critical. If the army could not conscript Mennonite men it could and often did conscript horses, wagons, feed, and food; and sometimes it compelled Mennonite youths to do the hauling. In August of 1863 elder Kline was again arrested and released; ten months later he was murdered near his home. Congregations grew so worried that some of them suspended services or held them in secret.[59]

Further, in 1864 more and more violence came to the valley—often to Mennonite neighborhoods. First the Confederates tried to block the Union army from penetrating southward. Then Union general Philip H. Sheridan decided to pursue a scorched-earth policy. Under war's perverse logic, Union-leaning Mennonites west and southwest of Harrisonburg suffered more from the Union army than they ever had from Confederates.[60]

A respected Mennonite bishop named Lewis J. Heatwole later remembered that in his Dale Enterprise neighborhood "nearly all families . . . spent the night . . . in the open with great fires raging upon every side." A Mennonite refugee named Michael Shank reached Pennsylvania and told of Northern soldiers exceeding their orders and engaging in "pilfering, robbing, and plundering." He said they searched "every room from cellar to garret, breaking open bureau drawers" and "taking whatever suited their fancy." Along the way they took horses and cows and grain and burned "barns, mills, etc."[61] Thereafter some Virginia Mennonites (like many others in the South) faced stark hunger.

Solomon B. Wenger later recounted that his parents kept grain in a room whose door they hid with a cupboard. To get the grain they went to the cellar, drilled a hole up through the floor of the room and let enough run out for eating. Then they plugged the hole until they needed more. When they could, many Mennonite families moved north. Sheridan helped them and other refugees by furnishing teams and wagons to transport pro-Union families part of the way. Bishop Heatwole later estimated that before the turmoil ended a hundred Mennonite families had left—about one family in four.[62]

DISAGREEMENTS AT WAR'S END

Since they were all in the same Mennonite conference, Virginia Mennonites agreed more about how to respond to war and the draft than did Mennonites and Amish as a whole. In March of 1865, as the war neared its end, quite a different conference met at historic Germantown, Pennsylvania, and endorsed the North's cause in language unusual for Mennonites. The conferees noted that a "cruel and causeless war" had been raging, "a rebellion of giant strength." So they resolved that they should give much thanks "and praise to Almighty God" for "the success of our arms on sea and land." The "present war is a struggle between truth and error, right and wrong, freedom and bondage," they continued; and every Christian had a duty to pray for the nation's president and "for our soldiers and seamen, and for the success of our arms." Whoever did not stand up "manfully" behind the government "in the hour of his country's travail" was "recreant to God" and "unworthy the name of an American citizen."[63]

Those Mennonites at Germantown said also that they had "unfaltering confidence" in Abraham Lincoln. They were sure of "the honest purposes of his heart" and of "his fidelity to God." How different was their tone from that of John M. Brenneman!

Several newspapers in eastern Pennsylvania published the resolutions and a copy reached thirty-year-old John F. Funk in Chicago. Funk was just then beginning to be a self-appointed spokesman for "old" Mennonites; and in a letter to his home (Doylestown, Pennsylvania) paper he quickly replied.

To present the resolutions as the outlook of most Mennonites was, Funk said, "entirely erroneous." To be sure, "the great body of the church known as the 'Old Mennonites' believed in being subject to government, paying taxes, etc. But they had always held, and still held, "strictly to the non-resistant doctrine, both in principle and practice." Therefore they believed "that no Christian . . . can advocate war, or under any circumstances take up arms." Certainly such Mennonites believed that no Christian could "rejoice in those terrible victories which cause human blood to flow in streams, and hurry hundreds of thousands, perhaps unprepared, to eternity."

The truly Christian soul would "much more mourn, humble itself before God," and pray and work to achieve God's purposes by other means. Through "kindness" and "the spirit of peace and love," not through war, would come "the final triumphs of truth over error, right over wrong, and freedom over slavery."[64]

Funk guessed that the resolutions at Germantown must have come from a Mennonite branch which had deviated from the peaceful principles of Jesus, Menno Simons, and nonresistant martyrs.[65] Although partisan, he knew whereof he wrote. In fact the sponsors of the resolutions were scarcely Mennonite anymore at all. They were a few congregations—followers of Abraham Hunsicker and others—who had moved far from traditional Mennonite positions. Before many years they would disappear into the Calvinistic Reformed denomination and elsewhere.[66] Nonetheless, in 1865 their resolutions showed how wide was the range of Mennonite and Amish response to the civil war.

In an opposite direction, before the war's end a few Mennonites and Amish also departed from the larger consensus on the question of hiring and sending substitutes.

Most were not so troubled. Christian Krehbiel of Summerfield, Illinois, had to search long and hard for a willing man. At the last minute he found an immigrant German Catholic miner who went for soldier's pay plus $600. "Thus God hears and answers prayer," a Krehbiel daughter later reflected. If God indeed gave the substitute, the substitute nearly gave his life; for he almost died of "camp fever." Later the man returned to Germany and married but was poor and wrote to the Krehbiels for more money. They obliged and finally even persuaded him to return to America where they could help him more. Perhaps they felt a duty to him partly from unease about the whole substitute issue. But they did not say they had done wrong.[67]

The Krehbiels were not the most typical of Mennonites: they were recent immigrants, quite progressive, GC rather than "old" Mennonite, and living near the nation's frontiers. Some members of their congregation at Summerfield were not absolutely pacifist; at least Christian Krehbiel reported later that he had persuaded some of them to withdraw from "an underground organization pledged to defend the nation by the use of arms." And although one reason for the Krehbiels' emigration had been to escape military drafts in Europe, an unmarried brother said he would be the substitute if that were the only way to keep Christian Krehbiel home with his family.[68]

Yet even if the Krehbiels were not entirely typical, a large majority of Mennonites and Amish in both North and South would surely have approved their hiring a substitute. Many Mennonites and Amish hired them—either collectively, by contributing to township or county bounty funds to raise volunteers; or individually and personally.[69]

Yet some objected. If a local newspaper's remarks are accurate, Amish in Mifflin County, Pennsylvania, drew a fine line. The paper said they contributed liberally to a bounty fund but when it came to personal hiring "they deem it as wrong . . . as to go themselves." An Amishman who spoke out clearly as the war was ending was bishop Jacob Schwarzendruber of Iowa. Yes, people in many congregations had hired men to go, he wrote to fellow ministers in May of 1865, but the practice seemed wrong. In the Old Testament the prophet Nathan had held King David responsible for killing Uriah even though David had not done it with his own hand. And the Dordrecht articles made clear that Christians were to "harm no one or cause any trouble, but seek the welfare and salvation of all."[70]

The Iowa bishop did not oppose payments given under compulsion; but he thought voluntary contributions, like the hiring of substitutes, were wrong. He accepted the idea of the $300 commutation fee and said that in moving Congress to provide for it God had treated the Amish well. A commutation fee was a sort of "protection money." Moreover, it fell within Christ's admonition to render to Caesar what was Caesar's. But Schwarzendruber lamented that the Amish, being afraid to suffer loss of goods, had gone another step. Flouting "the example of Jesus and the martyrs," they had contributed voluntarily for war.[71]

Schwarzendruber may have borrowed some ideas from Reformed Mennonite author Daniel Musser. In a booklet Musser published in 1864 at the height of draft pressures, he too distinguished clearly between voluntary contributions or hiring substitutes on the one hand and war taxes and commutation fees on the other. To defend his distinction he went to basic theory in a way that James Madison or any other political and economic theorist in American history could have respected. After all, Musser argued, government had created property; and "all the estate or property we own, we hold only by the tolerance and authority of the powers that be. . . . The money belongs to the kingdom of this world." So the government had every right to ask $300 for commutation. Nor was a war tax different from other taxes. A basic purpose of all government was to defend property by force. That is why the New Testament enjoined Christians to pay government its dues. But personal service and voluntary contributions were another matter. "Cer-

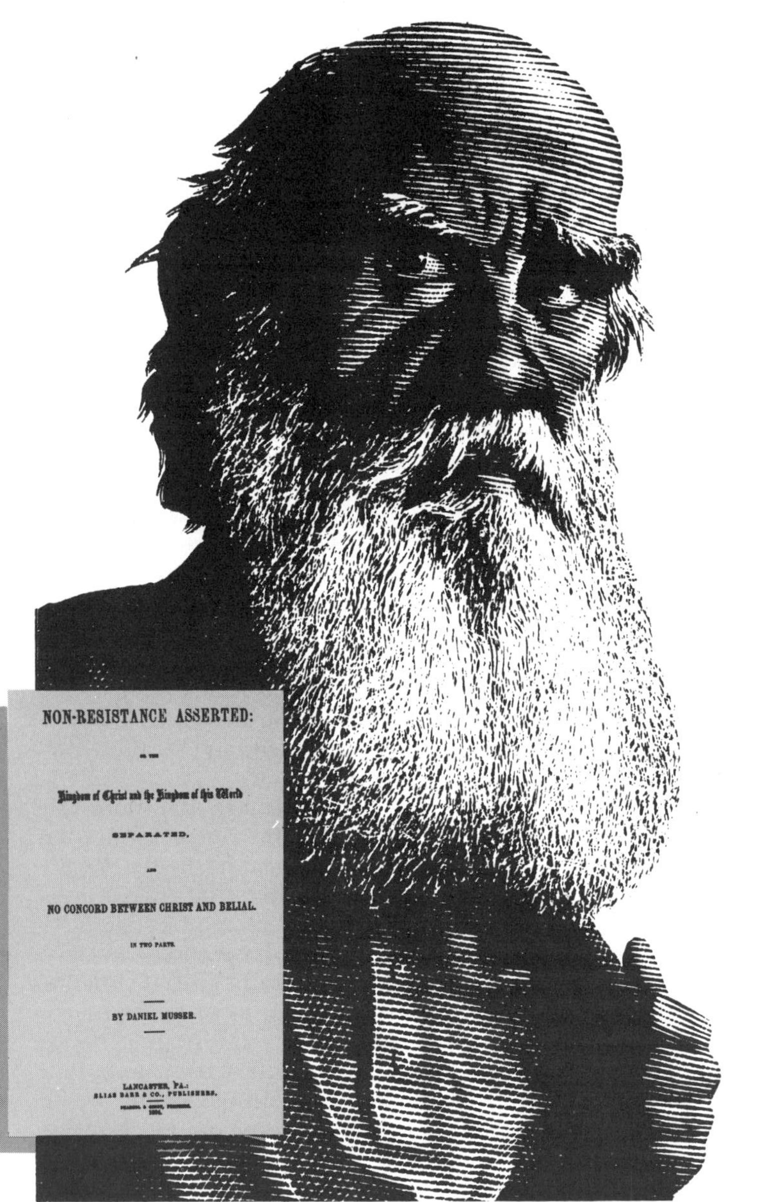

NON-RESISTANCE ASSERTED:

[illegible]

Kingdom of Christ and the Kingdom of this World

SEPARATED,

[illegible]

NO CONCORD BETWEEN CHRIST AND BELIAL.

IN TWO PARTS.

BY DANIEL MUSSER.

LANCASTER, PA.:
ELIAS BARR & CO., PUBLISHERS.

[illegible]

Inset: Courtesy of Mennonite Historical Library; Tolstoy: Jan Gleysteen collection

Inset: Title page of Daniel Musser's *Nonresistance Asserted* (1864) which influenced the Russian pacifist, Leo Tolstoy, above.

tainly" it was "inconsistent in those who profess to be non-resistant, to pay, or arm others, to go and do what they say is wrong for themselves."[72]

NEW STATEMENTS OF NONRESISTANCE

A further way Mennonites responded to the civil war was new writing about nonresistance. Musser made his argument against substitutes and voluntary payments in a booklet which was a clear restatement of the two-realm version of Christian pacifism—the booklet which eventually impressed the Russian pacifist Leo Tolstoy. His tone was highly rational and almost lawyerly.[73] In 1863 John M. Brenneman and John F. Funk also published booklets on nonresistance.[74] They wrote more as if to nurture and exhort.

Funk and Brenneman cooperated; yet they wrote differently from each other. In the 1850s Funk became an adult, got a bit of advanced education at the Hunsickers' Freeland Seminary, and taught school for two years. When he went to Chicago in 1857 to pursue his fortune he was quite a politically minded and secular young man. However, by 1863, with personal encouragement especially from Brenneman, he cast his lot with the Mennonite church and Mennonite publishing.

Against that background Funk wrote his 1863 booklet on nonresistance in a way which might impress bright young people who felt pulled toward the secular outlooks of politics and nationalism. He began not with biblicism but by presenting war as the scourge of nations, and the honoring of military heroes as glorification of blood and gore. Only after such appeal did he switch to more Mennonite-sounding language. As people honored military heroes, he said, they completely forgot to honor "the humble follower of the meek and lowly Jesus." America had been a peaceful nation, blessed by God. But now it was shattered by corruption, resentment, and vengeance. "Blessed are the peacemakers," Funk wrote, in one of many biblical quotations. Christ's kingdom was "not of this world." Rather than fight, Christ's followers should flee—as Menno Simons and other faithful Christians had done throughout history.[75]

Brenneman's booklet seemed aimed at more traditional readers. In any case, it was larger and more pastoral. In it Brenneman did much proof-texting. Yet he also marshaled so many Scriptures and connected them so sensibly that by the time he finished he had shown quite skillfully that the peace theme ran all through the New Testament. (But not through the Old: he accepted the idea of separate "dispensations" with God commanding war in Old Testament times.) All the while he kept his appeal personal. Where

Musser worked with large eschatological concepts of the two opposing realms, Brenneman only implied such abstractions.

The Ohio bishop admonished faithfulness in suffering. Then as a foundation for nonresistance he developed at length the meaning of being a Christian in the biblical sense and not just the cultural. In sum, he argued that to be a Christian meant to be truly reborn and regenerated and to imitate Christ. In effect he made new birth and imitation of Christ one and the same. Thus Brenneman did not separate salvation and ethics. And he rooted both in a thorough and pietistic evangelicalism. Thereafter he cited Scripture after Scripture to show that Christ's followers had no part in war.[76]

As in his petition, Brenneman also advised Mennonites to expel any member who was an antigovernment rebel. And he doubted that a Christian should enter partisan politics.[77] Yet a weakness of both Funk's and Brenneman's pieces was that neither got specific enough to speak to troublesome but practical questions such as the hiring of substitutes. A year later, of course, Musser wrote on the substitute question. Upon reading Musser's argument Brenneman was quite impressed. Counseling with a close friend and thoughtful fellow minister, Peter Nissley of Lancaster County in Pennsylvania, he asked: In the next draft, would Pennsylvania Mennonites hire substitutes? And what about those not hired personally? Near Brenneman's home a Mennonite man had avoided the draft because his township had raised its quota by paying bounties and attracting volunteers. But, Brenneman asked Nissley, "how it can be right & consistent with our profession, for Brethren valintariely to pay bounty mony to hire soldiers to go and kill People." Nonresistant Christians, Brenneman thought, were being "sifted"; and "but few are found Left as pure wheat."[78]

In Funk's paper a few other Mennonites or Amish questioned the hiring of substitutes; and one wrote a long argument also against contributing voluntarily toward bounty funds.[79] But with the end of the civil war the substitute question disappeared before it was resolved. Had the war continued, probably most Mennonites and Amish would have swallowed any qualms and continued as they had been doing. Yet a growing minority might have accepted Musser's kind of logic.

Some might even have developed doubts about paying war taxes and commutation fees. To do so did not necessarily mean to shift from biblicism to Enlightenment reasoning, or from biblical language to that of natural rights and individual liberty. Biblical literalists could have reasoned that rulers who compelled nonresistant people to pay for war were demanding tribute beyond their due. Or they might have said that with money payments (just as with personal service) there was a line beyond which the Christian had to obey God rather than man.

But it is not likely that many Mennonites and Amish would have reasoned in those ways. The simple proof-texting by which most of them interpreted New Testament passages about rulers did not point that way. Nor did their two-realm acceptance of government's dominion over the grubby, unspiritual world of money and taxes. Besides, cultural forces were pulling them toward greater identification with the American nation, not toward greater dissent.

REFLECTIONS

For some Mennonites and Amish the war brought personal tragedy that was real and deep. It did so for quite a few in Virginia. It did so also for persons such as Barbara Ziegler Herr, that mother in Ohio who grieved so much when her three sons became soldiers that she almost wished they had died as children. Yet the Amish and Mennonites fared quite well compared to many people in wartimes. They fared well despite inherent conflict between intense, emotional wartime American nationalism and the stubbornness of Amish and Mennonite conviction.

Unlike Protestants in major denominations the Mennonites and Amish had not put politics and sectionalism above faith to the point of dividing the church into northern and southern branches. Had Mennonites in the South been more numerous, had they lived near the South's centers of power, had fewer of their neighbors been pro-Union, they might have done so; but they did not. And in the nick of time, governments in both sections honored pacifists' consciences to the extent of freeing them from personal service.

Mennonites and Amish might have asked more. They might have demanded that governments honor their consciences as a right rather than only as a privilege gained by humble petition. And, by saying no to paying money which they knew would go for war, they might have insisted on true exemption and rejected equivalency. But they did not. Members who did not like their churches' main consensus generally called for less challenge to American militarism, not more.

Mennonites did not agree among themselves on every point, or the Amish either. Even apart from marginal cases such as that Germantown conference, some families and communities were clearly more pro-Union than others or more willing to let sons go to war.

Nor were "old" Mennonite conferences (not to mention stricter groups such as Reformed or Stauffer Mennonites) ready to do what the East Pennsylvania conference of "new" Mennonites did: let each congregation decide whether or not to discipline members who took up arms.[80]

Certainly many more Amish and Mennonite sons took up arms than was consistent with their parents' tradition. Hence the "dark ages" idea that the churches had left their sons and daughters untaught. But was the civil war generation so much further from the ideal than Mennonites and Amish in the latter twentieth century would be even after reams of modern peace education? If a war were to come at the end of the twentieth century, a war whose purposes seemed as sacrosanct as keeping the nation intact and abolishing slavery, would the religious descendants of civil war era Amish and Mennonites show that they had prepared their sons and daughters better? Moreover, most sons who fought in the civil war surely were not yet church members. And by delaying membership they were exercising what Anabaptists had preached: voluntarism, and baptism only when the person was ready for responsible decision and commitment.

If Mennonites and Amish failed, the failure may have lain elsewhere, not in lack of teaching about peace. Except indirectly, they were not doing what some Quakers and others did: challenging the aggressive militarism that broke out from time to time in America.[81] Perhaps that shortcoming, rather than lack of peace education for their own youth, was the greater fault. When they readily paid their fines and commutation fees, they reasoned that they were simply following the biblical injunctions to render to Caesar what was Caesar's and pay tribute to whom tribute was due. Some modern biblical pacifists will agree. Others will say they interpreted their scriptural texts so narrowly that they gave only part of the Bible's witness. By their accommodation, were they putting a bushel over the "nonresistant gospel" which they professed? Did humility theology keep them from offering a complete witness?

Whatever the answers, the most traditional of Mennonites and Amish did not consider direct and verbal witness to be as important as keeping the church pure or true to its established ways. Partly for that reason, "Old Order" branches took form.

CHAPTER 8

KEEPING THE OLD ORDER

In 1894 Jacob Weaver, a minister in a small and very conservative Mennonite group in Juniata County, Pennsylvania, wrote warmly to a like-minded bishop named Jonas Martin in the Weaverland district of Lancaster County. "A hearty greeting of love to you, wishing you grace, love, and peace from God the heavenly father through Jesus Christ . . . for without Him we can do nothing," the minister began. He was glad that Martin was not one of those Mennonites who said, "This matters not and that not." Christians had to choose whether to walk on the path of the cross or to "make the road wider and change our Christianity to suit the times." It was good to know there were others still "working against the stream of this world." He hoped that he and his congregation might be in fellowship with Martin.[1]

Jonas Martin had just begun an Old Order Mennonite branch. To understand the Old Order outlook, people with modern and progressive outlooks must, at least for the moment, set aside some of their own ingrained assumptions. They must *not* assume:

- That ideas expressed and tested in words are brighter and truer than ideas which take their form in personal and community life.
- That people who accept the ideas of the eighteenth century's so-called Age of Reason are the "enlightened" ones of the world.
- That change is usually good, and usually brings "progress." (The Old Order-minded accepted this change or that—a new tool, perhaps, or rail travel. But they were not progressiv*ists*.[2])
- That the individual is the supreme unit, individual rights the most sacred rights, and human life richest when individuals are most autonomous.
- That the really important human events are those controlled in Washington, New York, Boston, London, Paris, and other centers

Examples of the attire of the more liberal Amish Mennonites in the nineteenth century. Right: Jacob and Magdalena (Shantz) Goldsmith of Henry County, Iowa. Below: Jacob and Barbara (Kurtz) Umble of Lancaster County, Pennsylvania.

Courtesy of the Archives of the Mennonite church

of power—rather than events around hearths or at barn raisings or in meeting at Weaverland or Plain City or Yellow Creek or Kalona.

•That vigor of programs, institutions, activity (including Protestant-style missions) are a test of a Christian group's validity and faithfulness.

•That large organization, organizational unity, and denominational and interdenominational tolerance are better measures of Christian success than is close-knit congregational life.

•That people who imbibe some alcohol or use tobacco have deeply compromised their Christianity.

•Similarly, that people are poor Christians if their sons and daughters wait until adulthood to put off youthful rowdiness and become sober-minded Christians.

•That a structure of rules and explicit expectations (some moral, some mainly just practical for group cohesion) is always legalistic and at odds with the Christian idea of grace.

•That *salvation* refers almost entirely to the individual's original transaction and covenant with God at the time of personal conversion.

•That in church history, words such as *reform* or *renewal* apply only to movements which share the progressivist faith and adopt new methods and new activities; and that leaders who look to the past, or who think faithfulness may come by stricter discipline, are simply reactionary and formalistic.

To set such assumptions aside momentarily does not mean one must romanticize Old Order groups or finally accept the Old Order outlook and critique of modern life. It is only to step outside the prison of mental habits long enough to understand a different view. In the U.S., among Mennonites and Amish, that different view became clear only in the mid-to-latter nineteenth century. Among Mennonites it came to focus first in the 1840s, around Jacob Stauffer of Groffdale in Pennsylvania's Lancaster County. Later it took focus around Jacob Wisler in Elkhart County, Indiana, about 1872; Abraham Martin in Ontario about 1889; and Jonas Martin in Lancaster County in 1893. There was also a less-focused movement in Virginia's Shenandoah Valley about 1900. Among Amish the Old Order view gradually took focus as progressives (best called "Amish Mennonites") and others (who became the "Old Order Amish") began to part ways during a series of *Dienerversammlungen* (ministers meetings) in the 1860s and 1870s. The *Dienerversammlungen* failed to reconcile Amish differences and the Old Order Amish emerged as a decentralized but identifiable group.

JACOB STAUFFER: OLD ORDER LOGIC

Of all Old Order leaders Jacob Stauffer was the most skillful with words. In 1845 he led a group who broke with the Groffdale congregation and the Lancaster "old" Mennonite conference. By 1850 he wrote a quite logical although somewhat repetitious defense, in good German. It was published in 1855, a book of 439 pages, after he died.[3]

The bishops under whom Stauffer served as minister were first an old and venerable one named Peter Eby and then Eby's successor, Christian Herr. Stauffer was unhappy with the way Herr "kept house" and carried out discipline. One case in dispute had to do with a Mennonite couple who had an orphan girl in their home, apparently under contract with the township. They got along with the young woman so badly that the local Justice of Peace heard charges of harsh treatment and they had to pay a settlement of $380.

Another case had to do with Mennonite parents whose daughter married a man not Mennonite. She soon charged that he was mean and even a threat to her life. In a complex set of events the young wife's father and brothers (also Mennonite members) got the help of the local constable, confiscated some of the couple's possessions, and arrested the husband. To make matters worse, when the brothers were en route home with a load of furniture they stopped at an inn, drank too much, and went on their way all too noisily.

In the end the father arranged a peaceful separation between the young wife and her husband. But both cases were troublesome to the church. The first couple agreed that although they tried repeatedly to hold back their anger with the orphan they had failed, and the church had a right to expel them. But when Eby announced the expulsion some members, many of them relatives, complained that the discipline was too harsh.

In the other case the brothers and a few supporters—a half-dozen members in all—were thought guilty; but only the father made a public confession. The question then was what to do. After the father's confession Herr and a visiting bishop retired to the church's counsel chamber (an important institution in Mennonite church discipline) and heard individual members' views. They found a congregation badly divided: some members wanted to let the matter rest; others wanted the half-dozen "set back" from communion and church councils; still others, including Stauffer, wanted to ban (excommunicate) them.[4]

In such cases, Old Order differences with other Mennonites

were not deeply theological: both sides looked back to Menno Simons' writings and other such Mennonite sources, and more or less to humility theology. The differences were practical: how to apply church discipline. The problem of discipline lay deep in Mennonite and Amish understandings. If the true marks of being a Christian lay in practical behavior (rather than in, say, a eucharistic transaction or an experiential conversion); if the group rather than each individual decided what was faithful living; and if answers were to be thrashed out in congregations rather than imposed top-down from hierarchy or synod—then practical disagreement and even schisms were inevitable.

In 1845 at Groffdale the issue finally was an old human dilemma: ideal versus reality. How strictly could a living church be true to its claims? How much allowance should it make for the antics and foibles and sins of real human beings living in real human communities amid complicated networks of neighbors and extended families?

Stauffer saw too much accommodation. And, he asked undemocratically, what did it matter that bishop Herr had two-thirds of the congregation behind him? In the days of Noah or of Abraham and Lot, had the majority been right? "The majority has always been on the broad road."[5] Finally, Stauffer answered those who charged that he and other strict disciplinarians were too harsh and unforgiving. The ban (excommunication) was a way of bringing sinners to repentance and change, he emphasized. Far from being too harsh, it was the highest act of love.[6]

Stauffer and his supporters were sure that across America too many preachers were saying, "*Ach, das macht doch gar nichts aus*" ("Oh, but that's not really important"). And too many Mennonites had a spirit of "*macht nichts*" ("It don't matter"). It was the spirit of the age. So, the disciplinarians asked Herr, which are you going to follow: *Vernunft* (human reason, human insight), or God's Word? Would Herr lead the church to accommodate or would he lead it to a higher and more ideal standard?[7]

Neighboring bishops intervened and, after taking the congregation's counsel, silenced Stauffer from preaching. The charge was that he refused to accept the church's judgment. Stauffer's view was that the church itself had forced a schism. A few months later about fifty members asked him to preach in separate meetings. He obliged, and by March of 1846 an Old Order branch of "Stauffer Mennonites" was fact.[8]

The new church's ministers formed a very specific discipline.[9] Fashionable or decorated clothing such as a certain kind of "double-style or cut-out coat" or "any kind of spotted, colored, pleated, fringed, fluttering" or other "unnecessary thing" were not just outward matters; they were obvious evidence of carnality and pride. So were elaborate hairstyles, furniture, and the like.

Voting, serving on juries, and posting signs threatening trespassers with prosecution meant getting too involved with government and compromising Mennonite pacifism. Nor should members demand collateral for loans to fellow members. As a church, were they not bound and committed to each other already? Neither should members put lightning rods on their buildings: Christians should neither try to frustrate God's mighty expression in lightning and thunder nor put their trust in rods of steel. Nor should a separated people insure their buildings with worldly companies or attend worldly conventions or meetings. And of course they were not to attend singing schools, camp meetings, and other places of disorder.

The reformers recognized that the issues went beyond such rules and prohibitions. A deeper dispute was over passages in Matthew 18 and 1 Corinthians 5. Everyone agreed that the passages gave instructions on how to deal with offenders. Stauffer, seeing rigorous discipline as love, decided that the passages called for practicing "*Meidung*," or shunning. Shunning meant refusal to eat and drink at the same table with a banned person or to buy and sell and have other such dealings. A member in good standing could not even share the marriage bed with a shunned spouse. North Europe Anabaptists, including Menno Simons (as well as Amish founder Jakob Ammann), had taught shunning, and one read of it in the *Martyrs Mirror* and in Mennonites' old Dordrecht and 33-article confessions. So Stauffer meant only to recall the Mennonite church to its own lost, biblical principles.[10]

Stauffer called also for more careful distinction between kinds of sins. Apparently bishops such as Herr were ready to reinstate almost any offender who rose before the church, acknowledged his or her sin, and expressed contrition (sometimes rather perfunctorily). Stauffer distinguished sharply between mere "brother sins" (against a fellow member) and "mortal" sins (against God, bringing spiritual death). He thought the instruction of Matthew 18 to first confront the offender privately applied only to "brother-sins." In that category he apparently included hardly more than the petty frictions and irritations which occur in face-to-face communities such as Groffdale.

Since something like fashionable clothes showed a heart of pride, even attire and such matters were evidence of mortal sin. And mortal sins were not a kind the church had power to forgive, certainly not perfunctorily. For them, it could only excommunicate—not as punishment but to show the seriousness of the sin and how it separated the sinner from God and God's people. Thereafter the church had to wait not for lip service but for signs of deep anguish and true repentance. And the only sign of true repentance was practical righteousness, day-to-day, over a period of time.[11]

In the events of the schism Stauffer thought that the father who helped his daughter separate from her husband had committed a mortal sin. But he believed his own criticism of Herr had been at most a brother-sin which he and Herr could have settled privately. In his view the conference and the congregation had dealt with the serious sin lightly and with the small one heavily.[12]

Finally, the quarrel of Stauffer and his supporters with the Lancaster conference Mennonites went to general attitudes. Mennonites, Stauffer thought, needed a deeper sense of those basic principles, humility and sharp two-kingdom-style separation. They needed less of "*Freiheits-Geist*," that is, the spirit of *liberty*. (He might well have said the *American* spirit of liberty.) And of course they should stop following the majority, be more pious and serious, and talk less of markets and crops and more of salvation. They should quit their *Leichtsinnigkeit*.[13]

Such were the particulars of Stauffer's differences with the Mennonite church of his day and place. On some points—for instance, about lightning rods—his logic was rather silly. If no lightning rods, why a roof? Stauffer paraphrased his opponents. Well, he answered, God told Noah to put a roof on the ark but not lightning rods![14] On other points, for instance, his call for a sharing, mutual-aid church whose members did not demand collateral, the Old Order founder profoundly challenged Mennonites to live up to what they said the Bible taught.

Superficial or profound, Jacob Stauffer said much about the Old Order way of working for church purity and reform.

ORDNUNG

When he classified sins, Stauffer also had a third category: sins against the *Ordnung*—the church's established order.[15] In Old Order perception and thought, hardly any concept is more central than *Ordnung*.

The best-known scholarly analyst of Old Order ways is John A. Hostetler, a sociologist who was reared Old Order Amish. Hostetler has offered many frames for thinking about Old Order life—frames ranging from the idea of the small community to that of a "high-context culture."[16] One frame is to see Old Order groups mainly as folk societies, still guided by oral traditions, the seasons' rhythms, and perceptions of the sacred in daily life. But Hostetler has found the folk-culture idea to be only partly useful. After all, he has written, the Old Order Amish are neither geographically isolated nor primitive or peasant in the traditional sense.[17]

Still another way is to treat Old Order communities as strange islands of traditionalism within Western culture's modernity. But again, they do not quite fit. According to commentator Peter Berger an essential attitude of modern people is nonfatalism: a sense of having choices and some control over their world. Using Berger's definition, a scholar named Marc Olshan has argued that the Old Order Amish (he might have included Old Order Mennonites) are modern. After all, they exercise profound choice and select very carefully what social patterns and change they will tolerate. Indeed, they have accepted technological change. To Sanford C. Yoder, a Mennonite college president in the 1920s and '30s, a fond memory of his boyhood was a day in the 1890s when a railroad flatcar arrived in his Iowa community. It brought a steam engine that his Old Order Amish father had ordered for threshing. Far from simply reacting against new technology, Old Order people have been very discriminating. They have accepted technology if it has fit or even helped their ideals of family, small community, and close-knit congregation. They have rejected what they have perceived as hindrances to those ideals.[18]

One principle which Old Order peoples have preserved is *Gelassenheit*—yieldedness and submission, an attitude derived from Anabaptism and strengthened by Pietism. In a highly interpretive dissertation, scholar Sandra Cronk has offered *Gelassenheit* as the key to Old Order Amish and Old Order Mennonite life, ritual, and outlook. That may be a bit strong. Cronk herself observed that Old Order people have not actually used the word much.[19] It seems that they have been more inclined to use two other words which underlie *Gelassenheit*: *Demut* (that is, humility) and *Ordnung*. Of the two, perhaps *Ordnung* is least understood.

Roughly, the German word *Ordnung* translates as "order." Hence, Old "Order" Amish, Old "Order" Mennonite. Actually the word's meaning is so varied and complex that no English word captures it. Quite legalistically it may mean a body of rules. Progressive Mennonites such as John H. Oberholtzer used the word for *constitution* or *charter*. Or more theologically, they used it to mean the plan or structure of God's salvation, or to indicate how Christians should live after their initial decisions to follow Christ.[20]

But it was the Old Order people who gave *Ordnung* its greatest philosophical, religious, and practical meaning. In *Ordnung* they found what others have found in Roman or eighteenth-century Enlightenment ideas of natural law: a universe with meaning and moral structure, a creation with which humans could harmonize if they would only grasp its pattern and live by its moral design. *Ordnung* assured them that God was far from inscrutable, arbitrary, or essentially judgmental. The God of *Ordnung* was a loving pastor who wanted above all to have his people understand his decrees and observe them—so that they might live in harmony with each other and with his creation.

Old Order leaders were not the kind of theologians and theoreticians who discussed *Ordnung* abstractly. Yet surely their perception of salvation lay close to its harmonizing ideal.[21] They longed for heaven and often spoke Pietistically of the earth as a vale of tears. Yet they worked hard to build earthly communities. And however much they failed, they tried openly to make them communities of harmony which rested not on force but on members' voluntarily grasping and living by the moral structure of God's creation. They believed firmly in salvation by grace, through Christ's shed blood and atonement on the cross. Yet God's grace and cleansing was at least as much to aid Christians to live and harmonize with God's creation and *Ordnung* as it was to bring about that mysterious transaction by which God initially reconciled the individual soul to himself.

In its practical day-to-day meaning, *Ordnung* embraced every part of life. For Old Order peoples the congregation and network of congregations vied with family and extended family as the basic social unit of life and self-identity; and the *Ordnung* provided governance. To an extent it governed by clusters of principles extracted and preserved from past sources. For Old Order-minded Amish some very important documents were *Ordnungsbriefe*—hand copies of letters which had come down through history from ministers meetings in Europe and in America in the late-eighteenth and early-nineteenth centuries. The copies still circulated among ordained leaders.[22] Mennonites had fewer such explicit, written sources of *Ordnung*; but of course for both them and Amish, confessions and catechisms and nurture literature and hymns and *Martyrs Mirror* and Menno Simons' *Foundation-Book* helped the Bible to establish the *Ordnung*.

Yet for Old Order peoples, *Ordnung* was much too subtle to capture in printed words. In the 1870s, to keep the Wisler schism in Indiana from spreading, somebody in the Lancaster conference in

Pennsylvania proposed to negotiate and write out an *Ordnung* for that conference. But David Newcomer, a farmer-deacon in Wisler's new church, advised friends in Lancaster County that he did not think it possible to write one suitable to all sides.

At Yellow Creek Wisler's main progressive opponent was John F. Funk; and Newcomer observed that after all Funk and his side also claimed to follow the old *Ordnung*.[23] No doubt the deacon sensed that in any attempt to put ideas on paper the progressives had greater writing skill and Old Order leaders would be the losers. But even more he may have sensed that words could hardly capture the finer points of *Ordnung*.

As an Old Order Amish bishop has written: in "all its purposes and effects" the "true meaning ... of the nineteenth- and twentieth-century Mennonite and Amish Church Ordnung" is "more than pen and ink can yield." The bishop also observed, among many other points, that "only a person who has learned to love and live a respectful church Ordnung ... can ever appreciate its values." Outsiders often see it as "impractical," "outdated," "bondage," "a law of the Old Testament," etc. But a person living in the church, by its *Ordnung*, "actually has more freedom, more liberty and more privilege than those who are bound to the outside."[24]

Ordnung, said the bishop, is "God's example of the universe—nobody doubts the time of sunrise or sunset, nobody argues the timing of the moon."[25] In other words, not to accept the *Ordnung* and its structure of life is to bring trouble. The trouble comes not because church authority or a judgmental God is arbitrary or capricious. Trouble comes because one is not living in moral harmony with God's creation.

AMISH PIETY: INNER AND OUTER

Among Amish a historic division occurred during the latter half of the nineteenth century. More a gradual sorting-out than a sudden schism, it developed over decades. Most Amish became what may best be labeled "Amish Mennonite." Early in the twentieth century most Amish Mennonites merged into the "old" Mennonite church. Meanwhile a sizable minority of traditionalists became the Old Order Amish. That minority kept the Amish name; thus the "Amish" as known in the twentieth century.

Nineteenth-century Amish in America varied considerably. One reason was a form of church government which gave the final voice to local bishops, ministers, and congregations, not to conferences, synods, or archbishops who might impose uniformity. Another was different streams of immigration and settlement. Still another was that some Amish developed large, rather compact communities. For Amish, this was something new. In Europe they had lived quite scattered, with sprinklings of families here and there, often tied by kinship as much as by congregation. In America some Amish settlements, for instance the one in Pennsylvania's Cambria and Somerset and Maryland's Garrett counties, never became very compact.

But as scholar James Landing has pointed out, others developed a pattern of filling-in. For instance: Wayne and Holmes counties in eastern Ohio beginning in 1808; or parts of LaGrange, Elkhart, Noble, Kosciusko, and Marshall counties in northern Indiana beginning in 1841. In those places the Amish first settled in rather small, scattered groupings, then expanded into spaces between. Thus they moved from low to high density.[26] Along with older communities in the counties of Berks, Chester, Lancaster, and Mifflin in eastern and central Pennsylvania, the high-density communities became strongholds of the Old Order point of view.

Despite differences, until about mid-century the various Amish in North America were in loose fellowship. To deal with common problems and resolve differences in local *Ordnungen* their ministers sometimes met and conferred. They did so notably in 1809, apparently somewhere in Pennsylvania's Lancaster-Berks-Chester County region, and in 1830 and 1837 they did so farther west in Somerset County. Lesser meetings included one in 1826, apparently in Pennsylvania, and others in 1827 and 1831 in eastern Ohio.

At those meetings the mood was generally for stricter admonition and discipline—while recognizing, as the gathered ministers said in 1809 and again in 1837, that the articles should be applied with "Christian discipline and patience." Some matters for concern were the standard ones of dress, hair, and beards; decorated furniture and vehicles; and voting, officeholding, and jury duty. Another subject, of course, was how to induce parents to prevent bundling. And (since Amish communities were closely tied by kinship) another was to forbid marriage of first cousins.[27]

A far-reaching set of issues was how to apply the ban and shunning.[28] Still another was whether or not to hold fellowship with Mennonites and other humble, nonresistant churches. A case that troubled Amish for years began when a young Mennonite named John Burkholder immigrated to Mifflin County, Pennsylvania, and (apparently about 1820) applied for Amish membership. The church there demanded rebaptism. Then he moved to Wayne County, Ohio, and there the Amish honored his Mennonite baptism and took him in. The result was a long and troublesome debate about whether the Mifflin and Wayne County congregations would let each other's ministers preach and otherwise be in fellowship.[29] Of course the real question was how sharply to draw the boundaries which enabled the Amish to be separate and maintain discipline. Such was the stuff of Amish decision and debate.

About mid-century several literate Amishmen put their viewpoints into books addressed to their descendants.[30] Writing from the Old Order perspective was a Lancaster County elder (or bishop) named David Beiler. That writers such as Beiler addressed family rather than congregation says much about the importance of kinship to Amish. Also, it must have been more permissible to assert one's views as a family patriarch than to be assertive with pen and ink in the congregration. Beiler's book, three hundred pages long, was not printed until 1888, some seventeen years after he died. But he wrote it by mid-1857, a manuscript in quite good German which probably circulated among Amish from hand to hand. Beiler used the *Ordnung* idea quite strongly. To say that he made it central would be to exaggerate. His central point was a plea for earnest religion rather than indifference. He wanted little to do with faith in progress. And the earnest religion he called for was to be inner and subjective as well as outer, objective, and governed by *Ordnung*.

Beiler challenged his reader to recognize the divinity and saving work of Jesus, one's own sinfulness (almost but not quite innate depravity), and God's love and grace. He wrote earnestly of the need to repent truly, be born again, and walk a new path. Earnest, practical religion was built around the grace of God the architect of salvation, and around the sacrificed Jesus.[31] Salvation was Beiler's main point, not precisely *Ordnung*. But as the good bishop became practical, *Ordnung* moved very near the center. The new birth would show itself in a reformed life, and that life would show "meekness, humility, patience in adversity," and actual deeds of love for enemies. Persons who believed and took God's promises to heart, Beiler was sure, would "well remain in the *Ordnung* of God and not sin against" it. The humble of heart let themselves be instructed in the *Ordnung* of Jesus Christ, for in their weakness they were always prone to err.[32]

Were the various points of Amish *Ordnung* scriptural? For many of them, such as marriage only within the church, not taking oaths, and nonresistance, Beiler thought the proof was easy. For others he found that scriptural proof came harder, and he was too honest to pretend otherwise.[33] At the time he wrote, some Amish were advocating a change in mode of baptism. (Their main leader was his own younger brother, Solomon Beiler, a bishop in Mifflin County.) The advocates of change would still baptize by pouring rather than by immersion. But they wanted to do it while standing in a stream as Jesus had done in the Jordan River—whereas the traditional way was to hold the rite in the house or barn where the church was meeting. David Beiler conceded that the new mode did not violate Scripture. But he reasoned that Scripture did not demand the change. The change was controversial, and so to keep church unity it is better to keep the old way.[34]

Beiler also admitted that Scripture did not always directly support the ways the Amish exercised excommunication (or the ban, or what Beiler called the "highest call to confession").[35] That troubled him. He feared that to demand what was not clear in Scripture would open the church to all sorts of strange doctrine. But he solved the problem by presenting certain Scriptures as offering types rather than literal command. For instance, Old Testament accounts of banishing people from the community for leprosy and sin instructed the church in how to deal with especially sinful members. With such indirect interpretations Beiler argued that the *Ordnung* was scriptural indeed.[36]

That Beiler had trouble defending the ban was odd, for Mennonites and Amish usually found proof-texts for it quite easily in Matthew, chapter 18, and 1 Corinthians, chapter 5. Oddly also, he did not write of *Meidung*, even though the shunning question was important to the Amish. But if at some points he did not present Amish views typically, overall he offered a well-composed statement of Old Order Amish belief and piety at the time of Old Order beginnings. Those beliefs and understandings began with God's grace and atoning acts, not with works and legalism. Practical piety rested on ideas of *Ordnung*; and behind *Ordnung* lay some careful thought, not mere reaction.

An aging Beiler also showed a deep and conservative sense of social order. In 1862 he penned a memoir with the tone of an old man nostalgic for days long past.[37] He thought that in his youth Amish life had been simpler and better. Plows had been of wood rather than metal, and there had been no "machines to cut sausage meat." The Amish had gone to church barefooted instead of in "fine shoes and boots." Young people had been more ready to stay home to work, getting just enough education to read and write. Now they went "to school every winter for months at a time," traveled "in the world among relatives and acquaintances," and wasted "the precious time of grace in telling jokes and in unprofitable conversation." And parents now winked if their children did not behave according to the *Ordnung*.

Besides, confusion had increased as Amish had established many new congregations, some of them made up of "foreigners . . . with strange manners and customs." Finally, deference had declined: among the Amish of his youth, Beiler said, "much more submission was shown toward the ministers, especially toward the old bishops."

Was it as one scholar has suggested, that the poor old bishop was simply faced with "vast economic and sociological forces" which he could not understand?[38] Perhaps. But who had the better grasp of how social and technological change might alter faith, David Beiler or progressives? Did the David Beilers who chose the Old Order way really think more simplistically than did people who easily assumed that change brought "progress"?

Whatever the answers, Beiler called for deep earnestness about faith. Partly he would have faith be quite subjective and grace-centered, as he drew on both Anabaptist traditions and Pietism. Partly also he wanted it to be objective, expressing itself openly in works and in strict observance of *Ordnung*. Meanwhile he resoundedly rejected progressivism.

MORE *DIENERVERSAMMLUNGEN* AND THAT SORTING OUT

For Americans, 1862 was a discouraging year of war over the fragmenting of the U.S. nation. For Amish leaders it brought the first of the century's most important series of *Dienerversammlungen*, or ministers meetings. Unlike sporadic meetings earlier, until 1878 there would be a meeting every year except 1877. The issues discussed were mostly very Amish questions about ethics, behavior, appearance, style in daily life, and how to exercise discipline.[39] Ministers who attended hoped that the gatherings might bring agreements and keep the Amish from fragmenting. In one sense the Amish leaders succeeded better than did national ones: they did not send young men out to shoot each other. In another sense they did not, for the Amish continued to fragment.

Forces of fragmentation were strong, from causes both external and internal. Externally there was revivalism. For instance, the main issue underlying the "Egly Amish"—how experiential conversion and feelings of salvation fit with traditional Amish tests of readiness for baptism—was discussed at the *Dienerversammlung* of 1863.[40]

And there were vast secular changes: geographic dispersion,

for instance, and new transportation. At the first *Dienerversammlung* in 1862 John Stoltzfus, a deacon from Pennsylvania's Lancaster County, marveled that two men who lived 900 miles apart in Maryland and Illinois had served on the same program.[41]

But probably even more important than external forces were tensions and perhaps deficiencies within Anabaptist-Mennonite and Amish theology and practice. There was that Amish lack of central authority. Also, the gathered ministers were perplexed because their theology made little place for ethical ambiguity or dilemma. And finally, hardly any Amish studied human affairs in ways to give them mental tools to deal with variety in human culture or changes in folkways over time. Some moderately progressive ones solved that problem by treating *Ordnung* as organic and adaptable. But others, the Old Order-minded, saw *Ordnung* more as fixed and essentially constant.

An important matter for the *Dienerversammlung* in 1862 was the controversy about baptism. Through the 1850s, in Mifflin County's "Big Valley" community, a minister named Abram Peachey strongly opposed the change Solomon Beiler wanted. Peachey had strong backing from David Beiler and other Lancastrians. In 1851 the Big Valley Amish invited ordained men from other communities to come and mediate. Such use of visiting mediators was standard practice in such disputes. The visitors strongly advised against stream baptism but said they had no Scripture to forbid it. Thereupon the local congregation neither endorsed the practice nor forbade it. Yet Peachey wanted to stop it, saying that a practice which the Bible did not require might be forbidden if it caused discord.[42] In this case traditionalists such as Peachey and Beiler seem to have rejected a church decision (the decision that, finally, stream baptisms could not be forbidden).

Solomon Beiler, wanting change in baptism, seems generally also to have been uncompromising. He was hardly a "liberal." For instance, as the *Dienerversammlungen* progressed, he joined with those who said a spouse of a shunned person had to join in the shunning—whereas more flexible leaders such as bishop John K. Yoder of the Oak Grove congregation in Wayne County, Ohio, argued against using shunning in ways that disrupted marriages.[43] On the baptism issue Solomon Beiler was more fundamentalist than "liberal." He simply had decided that stream baptism was the more scriptural way and would not yield to arguments either of prudence or of his church's tradition. With both sides sure of their ground, by the early 1860s a division of Mifflin County Amish was under way.[44]

Barn three miles east of Smithville, Ohio, located at the site of an earlier barn in which the first *Dienerversammlung* was held in 1862.

Bericht der

Verhandlungen

der fünften jährlichen Zusammenkunft

— der —

Amischen Mennoniten-Diener und Brüderschaft,

gehalten den

20., 21., 22. und 23. Mai 1866,

am Wohnort von Johannes Struphar, in der Nähe von

Danvers, McLean Co., Illinois.

Gedruckt in der Office des „Herolds der Wahrheit," No. 91 und 93 Randolph-Straße,

Chicago, Illinois.

Courtesy of Mennonite Historical Library

Title page of proceedings of a *Dienerversammlung* held in Danvers, Illinois, in 1866.

From their outset the *Dienerversammlungen* were largely under the careful control of leaders who would allow limited change.[45] It was not a simple case of progressive modernizers wanting larger-scale organization versus conservatives preserving local, small-unit control: for during the 1850s it was conservatives, including David Beiler himself, who had suggested the broad-based meetings. In the end, however, Solomon Beiler worked with Amish leaders in Wayne County to set an actual date and get the first meeting under way. With that beginning the more change-minded ministers gradually won control. At the first meeting, in the spring of 1862, there were seventy-two ministers present. By calculations of historian Paton Yoder, fifty-three of them favored some selected change and only fourteen were adamant against it. After 1865 the truly Old Order-minded virtually stopped attending. No bishops from Pennsylvania's Lancaster and Berks counties ever attended at all—although some ministers and deacons did so until 1868, when their bishops explicitly rejected the conferences.[46] From the outset the meetings were gatherings mainly of leaders who were ready for some change.

Over the decade and a half the gathered ministers discussed many, many issues, ranging from attire to political participation, from lightning rods, insurance, and lodge membership to how to respond when a shunned member joined another nonresistant group.[47] From a non-Amish point of view many of the questions might seem trivial. But often the ministers spoke to fairly important issues. What was the nature of the deacon's office? When should the congregations' leaders be firm and when flexible in applying church discipline, especially shunning? Could Amish tolerate differences? If so, how could they maintain fellowship among congregations? And what should the church do about major new practices—not only stream baptism but others, notably the building of meetinghouses? One way or another almost every question touched large issues of toleration and of congregational versus broader church authority. Many pitted the authority of church tradition against somebody's interpretation of Scripture.

And of course almost every question touched the nature of *Ordnung*. The ministers did not discuss that nature explicitly or theoretically. Yet assumptions about it underlay virtually everything they said. Traditionalists who emerged from the *Dienerversammlungen* era as the Old Order Amish perceived their church's *Ordnung* and even its highly particular rules on matters such as dress or meetinghouses as needing to be quite fixed and uniform for all congregations. Others saw *Ordnung* more as a product of the church's discernment in a given time and place. These could allow some carefully controlled and organic change and contemplate church unity and continued fellowship despite some variety.[48]

The difference came to a head in 1865. The conference met again in Wayne County, Ohio. But just before it did, traditionalists called a *Dienerversammlung* of their own in adjacent Holmes County. There they drew up a new discipline which they then presented to the larger gathering. They implied that church unity was possible only if all the congregations were willing to accept their list of rules and prohibitions. Of course the list was traditional, ranging from not wearing "gayly colored [*scheckich*], striped, or flowered clothing," to restricting the church's counsel meetings to members only. The traditionalists said it was a list which "we consider . . . to be right and good and in accordance with the word of the Lord and our confession of faith." It fit with what "we have been taught and instructed by our forefathers." So they intended "to stay by the same," as they had promised at baptism. They would "give the hand and kiss of fellowship" and "maintain spiritual unity" with "all those who confess the same with us, and work together, and manifest the same by deeds."[49]

No statement could have expressed the Old Order outlook better. It proposed a list of rules but not any centralized organization to impose and enforce them. The emerging Old Order Amish were not modernizers or builders of centralized, rationalized institutions. They wanted uniformity, but not by coercion. The aim was a spiritual unity so strong as to bring agreement on details of practice.

The traditionalists were no doubt unyielding, but the more change-minded leaders hardly came halfway, either: they gave the Holmes County document short shrift by scarcely even discussing it.[50] So after that the Old Order-minded virtually stopped coming; and 1865 may be taken as the year in which the Old Order Amish became a distinct group.[51]

Again, the Old Order group's opponents were not on the whole "liberals." They constantly used *Ordnung* language, and sometimes they ruled strictly, for instance, against musical instruments.[52] But compared to the Old Order-minded, they defended *Ordnung* differently. They were more inclined to allow new scriptural interpretations, for instance on that question of stream baptism. And they constantly pleaded for "patience" with minor variations in discipline and practice.[53] Thus they took a tiny step or two toward what progressive Mennonites and others called making a difference between "essentials" and "non-essentials," and toward what Americans call "tolerance." And they proceeded as if *Ordnung* could be more than a brake; it could be a guide for cautious, organic change.

That series of *Dienerversammlungen* lasted only until 1878 and did not become a permanent Amish Mennonite general conference. However in 1882 and following, Illinois and Missouri Amish led out to form a Western District Amish Mennonite conference; in 1888 others began an Indiana one; and in 1893 still others an Eastern one.[54] These conferences attracted the more-or-less-progressive "Amish Mennonites." A generation later they merged with district conferences of the "old" Mennonite church.

According to Paton Yoder the main work of the 1862-1878 *Dienerversammlungen* was to put out "brush fires." At that task, Yoder concluded, the conferences had some small successes but some rather large failures.[55] Perhaps the largest failure concerned a bishop named Joseph Stuckey and his congregation at North Danvers, Illinois, in the early 1870s. Although Stuckey was a man of wide contacts, several *Dienerversammlungen* concluded that he should discipline the maverick Joseph Joder for his universalist doctrine. Stuckey refused, apparently less concerned about Joder's ideas than with how Joder behaved as an Amish brother. After 1873 many even of the change-minded Amish considered Stuckey and his followers to be out of order. But the Stuckey group continued their church life and took a progressivist path which eventually led their descendants into the General Conference (GC) Mennonite church. Yoder concluded that the *Dienerversammlungen* actually contributed to the Stuckey schism.[56]

Other Amish such as some of those in Butler County, Ohio, went directly into the GC body by affiliating with its Middle District conference.[57] Of course still others, mainly in Ohio, Indiana, and Illinois, followed Henry Egly on the path that led eventually to the Evangelical Mennonite Church.[58]

Apparently the forces for splintering Amish fellowship in the latter-nineteenth century were just too great to be conciliated. Alongside the division in Mifflin County,[59] Pennsylvania, a similar one broke out in eastern Ohio's Wayne and Holmes counties. Some of the quarrels there were disputes around a bishop named Jacob Yoder. In 1862 the Wayne County congregation, Oak Grove, had built its first meetinghouse. Yoder supported stream baptism. He also interpreted the sin of Eve to have been lying, whereas standard Amish dogma emphasized her disobedience. Moreover, he was the bishop who finally fell from office tarnished by a reputation as a horse trader and by having declared bankruptcy.[60]

Eventually in 1889, under another bishop Yoder (John K.), the "Oak Grove" congregation would suddenly let lay people lead out and form a new discipline. Although the new code still forbade such frivolities as mustaches for men and hats for women it allowed members to put off hooks and eyes in favor of buttons and it let men get ordinary barber shop haircuts and go beardless. It also approved "protracted" (revival) meetings and an evangelizing or mission fund. Amish congregationalism was at work.

Oak Grove let evangelists come and preach: Mennonite John S. Coffman; and Coffman's nearest Amish-Mennonite counterpart, Daniel J. Johns of the Clinton Frame congregation in Indiana. Johns began yearly revival-harvests at Oak Grove which brought remarkable numbers of youths into the church. After a visit in 1890 there was a baptismal class of 42 and by May of 1893 the congregation baptized 70 more.[61] In contrast to the Old Order Amish, many congregations in various communities went more or less the way of Oak Grove: they allowed meetinghouses, Sunday schools, cooperation with "old" Mennonites, orderly revival meetings, evangelization, adjustments in attire, and other cautious changes.

Among the late-nineteenth-century Amish varieties, one of the strangest was "sleeping preachers"—several men, most notably a Noah Troyer and a John D. Kauffman—who became famous in the 1870s and '80s for preaching or admonishing while in trances. Near Shelbyville, Illinois, followers of Kauffman's "Spirit-preaching" (as adherents preferred to call it) formed a half-dozen congregations which became a separate church known informally as "sleeping-preacher Amish."[62] It was an era when trance-preachers were appearing among other powerless peoples, especially American Indians, who were displaced and under severe cultural stress. Perhaps the phenomenon among the Amish also had something to do with cultural stress and lack of power.

Far more important was the Old Order Amish response—a whole social system to preserve the old *Ordnung*. It was a dissent from American faith in progress, and a set of choices about modernity. But even more, it was one way of answering ongoing dilemmas in Mennonite and Amish understandings of faith and church.

JACOB WISLER: OLD ORDER MENNONITES IN INDIANA, 1872

Before century's end more groups of Old Order Mennonites emerged, especially about 1872 around bishop Jacob Wisler at Yellow Creek in Indiana's Elkhart County and in 1893 around bishop Jonas Martin at Weaverland in Pennsylvania's Lancaster County. Clearly objecting to progressives' innovations, Wisler and Martin were "reactionary" in the strict meaning of the word. Of course only a person of progressive bias will assume that to react as they did was necessarily to be wrong.

The events at Yellow Creek were momentous. "Old" Mennonite leaders in many communities watched closely, fearing quite correctly that a schism might spread throughout the church. In 1862 the Yellow Creek congregation was in good enough health that in one visit John M. Brenneman baptized forty-six new members. A young John F. Funk felt so drawn to the congregation that in 1867 he moved to nearby Elkhart and affiliated with it.[63]

But by the latter 1860s Yellow Creek Mennonites were plagued by three factions. One wanted revivalistic progressivism. Before Daniel Brenneman became that faction's leader two Yellow Creek ministers with Methodistic inclinations defected to the Evangelical Association.[64] Another faction, trying to walk in the middle, was cautious progressives who had the support of the Indiana "old" Mennonite conference. Of them, John F. Funk, already ordained when he moved to Elkhart, became leader and symbol. At the least the middle group wanted Sunday schools, church publication, and a willingness to consider change.

The third faction was bishop Wisler and his supporters. To them Funk symbolized a lack of the plain, old humility. They complained that the Funks' carriage and house furnishings were ostentatious and that John Funk kept a fashionable coat for certain occasions in addition to his plain one. (Funk implied such rumors were false.[65]) Most of all, the third faction did not want change. In 1869, as troubles boiled, Wisler gave his formula for peace: keep practices as they had been when he had arrived in Indiana from eastern Pennsylvania in 1848. By that he meant primarily no Sunday schools and no protracted (series of) meetings, indeed no evening or "night" meetings at all. Other issues were "bass" singing or singing in parts, singing schools, a new practice at funerals of bringing the body into the meetinghouse (probably for final viewing) during the service, Funk's new *Herald of Truth*, and the use of English in worship (although Wisler was somewhat flexible on the language question).

Sunday schools were the most pressing issue. In 1871 Wisler supporters John and Mary Weaver rhetorically asked Pennsylvania friends: "Is the Sunday School commanded in the Bible?" No, they said, it was at most a human invention, not a gospel matter. But the Bible did command "love, peace and unity" which the Sunday school was destroying. Moreover, the Sunday school had "risen so high that no brother or sister may speak against it." So it was "idolatry."[66]

To a great extent Wisler and his supporters were reacting against Daniel Brenneman and all he stood for, especially on matters such as evening meetings and singing in parts. But they were also out of step with the Indiana conference, which in 1870 explicitly endorsed Sunday schools for congregations who wished to have them.[67]

One of the problems in the whole affair was confusion about authority. In 1867 Wisler voluntarily stopped preaching until the congregation might request him to begin again; yet, with the encouragement of a visiting bishop from Ohio named Isaac Hoffer he resumed preaching. And he did so even though a close vote in the congregation directed him not to. Numerous times committees of bishops and ministers gathered from distant communities to deal with his and Daniel Brenneman's cases, and recommended various degrees of censure or requested conciliatory public statements from one or both of the two men.[68] In one meeting to reinstate Wisler's position as bishop Funk rubbed a raw wound by refusing to let Wisler sit on the symbolic ministers' bench until the vote was actually taken.[69]

Such interpersonal frictions were important. But far deeper were different understandings of *Ordnung*. Wisler and his supporters constantly talked of keeping to the old *Ordnung* or the "old foundations."[70] But as Wisler supporter David Newcomer admitted, Funk and his supporters claimed the same.[71]

The affair was complex. Complaints against Wisler ranged from his not having followed Matthew 18 in carrying out discipline to his having spoken disrespectfully of the new birth.[72] Even the respected John M. Brenneman, not noticeably partisan toward his brother Daniel and normally an effective mediator, seemed powerless to heal the differences more than temporarily.[73]

Meanwhile, in a time when the Yellow Creek congregation met only every other Sunday, as early as 1869 Wisler and his supporters began for a time to meet separately on the off Sundays. Finally in 1871 a committee recommended that Wisler be reduced to ordinary minister. Unhappy with that, early in 1872 the Wisler supporters began again to meet separately. Apparently there were about one hundred of them, with about three hundred Yellow Creek members remaining in the Indiana conference.[74]

Two years later the conference expelled Daniel Brenneman. With help from the Ohio conference it kept trying to win the Wisler group back. But the 1872 division remained final. In 1875 deacon Newcomer told a friend that he and the rest of the Wisler people were enjoying peace and just wanted to be left alone. With a few congregations in Ohio they formed their own conference. In the twentieth century questions about telephones and automobiles further divided that conference also, but that is a later story.[75]

JONAS MARTIN OF WEAVERLAND IN LANCASTER COUNTY, 1893

In 1893 a schism drew away about one-third[76] of the "old" Mennonites in the Lancaster conference district of Weaverland-Groffdale-Bowmansville. It occurred around bishop Jonas Martin and created an Old Order Mennonite body, the Weaverland conference. Martin had been ordained bishop in 1881, at age forty-two, by the district's aging bishop George Weaver, a traditionalist who was more or less Martin's mentor. Lancaster County was not the Midwest, and the issues were somewhat different from those around Wisler. Notably, there was less revivalism. To be sure as Weaver ordained Martin in 1881 there were rumors of his keeping a minister named Benjamin Horning out of the lot because Horning had a "Methodist spirit."[77] But in the Jonas Martin story there was no Daniel Brenneman.

Among Lancaster conference leaders there were some mildly progressive men, especially a bishop named Isaac Eby. And in the membership there were young people anxious to become progressive activists—most notably three Mellinger brothers, John, Jacob, and Ezra; Abram Metzler, Jr.; Christian (C. M.) Brackbill; Jacob (J. A.) Ressler; Isaac Hershey; and other young men and women ready to follow their lead. A year after the schism these organized themselves as the Mennonite Home Mission Advocates.[78]

Unlike the progressives, Martin, for instance, held the older Mennonite attitudes regarding tobacco and wine. Said he: "*Von ma de Taback abschneit kommt die Hochmut in de gmeh*" ("Doing away with tobacco opens the church to pride"). Why? Because tobacco farming, which required intensive manual work, kept youths at home where they would not learn proud ways. Also, Martin thought that wine was all right in moderate amounts. When Pennsylvania's prohibition amendment came up for referendum in 1889 and the Lancaster conference resolved that members at least should not vote against prohibition, people understood that Martin opposed their voting for it. At any rate he fended off pleas from activist young progressives such as C. M. Brackbill who wanted him to give active support to the reform.[79]

Another issue was use of English, especially English singing at church. The matter was troublesome partly because in the 1880s some who wanted English singing had used questionable tactics to promote it. As for English itself, Martin was not adamant against some use of it in church services. For the sake of visitors he himself often made some remarks in English.[80] It was a time when in their letters many Mennonites used English as they wrote of weather, crops, and other mundane news, but used German for pious greetings and closings and for discussing church affairs.[81] As twentieth-century people might say, German was their soul-language.

Therefore many traditionalists were uncomfortable with English in worship. Moreover in Martin's district the preacher most adept in English was a John K. Brubaker, and he seemed deviant in other ways. To more thoroughgoing progressives such as Midwesterners who began a mission in Chicago in 1893, Brubaker could seem like a hopeless conservative, an anti-city reactionary.[82] But, being a veterinarian with money to spend, he took trips to the West and even to Alaska to visit missions. And he installed an organ in his home for a daughter. Even bishop Isaac Eby thought the Brubakers' organ "a great mistake" so long as the Lancaster conference "earnestly testifies against it."[83]

In short, English went hand-in-hand with what passed in the Lancaster conference as progressivism. As one Old Order supporter liked to say, "*Es ist nix letz mit die English Sproch, aver von die Deitsch leit mohl English varre velle, sel is Hochmut*"[84] ("There's nothing wrong with the English language, but when Dutch folks want to be English, that's pride"). No doubt in many cases he was exactly right.

Another cluster of issues grew out of a strange affair. On the night of September 26, 1889, zealous Old Order partisans entered a newly built meetinghouse in eastern Lancaster County, Lichty's, and ripped out a new pulpit. In its place they left only a traditional singers' table. Local newspapers seized on the event to titilate their readers.[85] To some Mennonites it was a dastardly deed and barely forgivable. But to the Old Order-minded it was understandable, even if hardly right. To them a high pulpit was a sure sign that Mennonites wanted to be like the proud, popular churches who set their clergy above and apart from their congregations. It mattered little that building-committee members argued that one of the ministers at Lichty's, John Zimmerman, needed a high stand for his Bible because he had only one arm. The committee was already suspect because earlier it had rejected a building site which an Old Order-minded owner had refused to sell unless he could write a deed forbidding Sunday schools, singing schools, and evening meetings.[86]

The pulpit case was mysterious and troublesome for years. Not until 1908 did a woman confess that her family had done the stealthy deed.[87] Meanwhile, in 1890 bishop Martin excommunicated at least seven pro-pulpit members for speaking too much and too critically. Three or four more pulpit supporters withdrew voluntarily, and the case became a source of charges and countercharges about how Martin was exercising discipline. By the spring of 1892 the Lancaster conference rebuked Martin for being too harsh. But it let eleven pro-pulpit people who had spoken unlovingly confess their error publicly, and be reinstated. A year later the conference again censured Martin for high-handedness. And although it also rebuked some of his critics, it asked him to confess error and forbade him to officiate in upcoming communion ceremonies.[88]

Such was the background of the 1893 schism. In addition, in 1893 the Lancaster conference leveled more formal charges against Martin:

- That contrary to the conference he had opposed a legal charter that one of the congregations, Kauffman, had taken out to help govern its property.
- That he refused to accept a conference decision allowing ordained men to perform marriages for non-members.
- That his attitudes and actions against the Sunday school were not in order.

The separation occurred on Friday, October 6, 1893, during fall sessions of the Lancaster conference. Viewpoints differ on whether the conference expelled Martin or whether he withdrew.[89]

The Kauffman meetinghouse charter

The issue of the Kauffman meetinghouse charter rose after a wealthy politician, public official, and benefactor died in 1886 and left a certain will. The man's parents (but not he) had been Mennonite, so he bequeathed a substantial sum to "Kauffman's," a congregation near Manheim in northwestern Lancaster County. The money was for maintaining the congregation's property, for its poor, and for missions. In order to receive it the congregation took out a legal charter. But that went against the tradition of Mennonites who tried to stay clear of legal arrangements in order to avoid lawsuits and stay separate from coercive government.[90] Bishop Martin and his supporters had opposed the charter. The issues were not petty. To make a congregation a legal entity was to make it formally an institution of society. And to do that was perhaps to compromise Anabaptist and Mennonite understandings of church as the people of God, belonging to another realm. Neither side seems to have articulated that issue clearly. Yet in his nonverbal, folkish way, Jonas Martin must have sensed it.

Marriage of nonmembers

The main question was what to do when unbaptized sons and daughters of Mennonites wanted to marry and have Mennonite ordained men perform the ceremonies. The question had troubled the Lancaster conference for decades. It was the issue around which, in 1890, preacher Amos Herr had given Virginia bishop Samuel Coffman that rare Mennonite argument for compromise.[91] Before he died in 1883 old bishop Weaver had written out a determined statement against such compromise, putting his case in strong language of separation from the world. But in its first printed discipline in 1881 the Lancaster conference had remained silent about performing marriages for nonmembers.[92]

Later, probably in the fall of 1892, the conference must have given explicit permission to do so. But Martin still declined. Temporarily, when such couples came to him he sent them to the more flexible Isaac Eby. But that soon raised a question of what Eby should do if a couple came from Martin's district without first having gone to Martin. Was Eby free to marry them?[93] The marriage ceremony question also was not petty. Not only did it raise that issue of compromise; it also involved issues of how much marriage was a civic as well as a church matter and of Mennonite ministers' acting in a civic role.

Sunday schools

Of all the issues, the Sunday school was the prime one. To the Old Order-minded across the Mennonite church the new form was the main symbol of unwanted change. Apparently no Sunday school opponent either at Yellow Creek or at Weaverland spelled out the reasons, but some articulate Virginians did. The Sunday school, declared a Virginia layman, Israel Rohrer, Sr., in 1894, had originated with "worldly churches." Now "all ungodly people and criminals of our day are boasting of being engaged in the Sunday school work." As for the Mennonite churches the innovation had come precisely because John F. Funk, "without the consent of a conference," had gone "out to that Babel city, Chicago, and started a paper."[94]

Rohrer's words only repeated a bit more sharply what had been said by other anti-Sunday-school Virginians in the 1870s—by a layman (later a preacher) named George Brunk, and especially by

Abraham Blosser, the grandson of bishop Peter Burkholder who was a postman during the civil war and sometime editor of the *Watchful Pilgrim*.

In 1872, with others endorsing him, Brunk sent a long manuscript to John F. Funk replying to Funk's pro-Sunday school logic and complaining that the *Herald of Truth* did not print opposing views. The manuscript asserted a long set of arguments such as that Mennonite Sunday-school promoters used unfair tactics and that the schools allowed women and laymen and non-Mennonites to teach. It continued with objections to Sunday schools' mixing Scriptures with other books, including books from religious groups not opposed to war and bloodshed and lawsuits. And it charged that Sunday schools drew youths away "to Other Societies who have almost a world wide way to heaven." After an exchange between Funk and Brunk, Blosser took up the cause and added many more pages.[95]

Some of the Virginians' arguments were almost purely reactionary: "we object" because the Sunday school "is Somthing [*sic*] New that has crept into our Church"; and "our Forefathers ... would also object." At points the Sunday school opponents seemed to reject innovations as thoughtlessly as some progressives accepted them. But of course, being Mennonite, they couched their points also in the language of humility and separatism: of alarm at following the "proudest and dressiest Classes of our country," and the like.[96]

On the whole, again, the issues were not petty. The Virginians raised questions about following new authorities, such as lay teachers and questionable books. They saw in the Sunday school movement something similar to what twentieth-century Mennonites have feared in radio and television preachers: "parachurches" drawing away members' loyalties and competing with Mennonites' understanding of biblical faith. They seemed to sense that Sunday schools were an expression not only of the popular churches who supported war, ostentation, and other evils, but also of the American nation.

Latter-twentieth-century historian Robert T. Handy, making his case that nineteenth-century Protestant crusaders were fostering a version of national or "civil religion," has included the American Sunday School Union as one of the interdenominational Protestant organizations promoting the civil-religion outlook.[97] The Virginians spoke crudely but they discerned some truth that Sunday schools' supporters overlooked.

On the other hand opponents did not seem to consider that

loyal Mennonites might use the Sunday school to teach separatism, nonconformity, nonresistance, and other Mennonite principles. They seem not to have considered that Sunday schools could become transmitters and defenders of Mennonite faith.

As early as 1863 a Sunday school had begun in a Lancaster conference congregation. And by 1875 or maybe even earlier the conference said formally that Sunday schools might "be allowed" if "maintained according to the rules and order of the church." The first Sunday school in Martin's Weaverland congregation opened in June 1891, with a thirty-six-year-old businessman named Samuel Musselman as superintendent. Later the progressive Musselman would work with Midwesterners to promote Mennonite missions.[98]

Held on Sunday afternoons as was the custom, the Sunday school met in a schoolhouse. Soon the building was too small; so the organizers announced they would use the church's meetinghouse. However, after a few weeks the congregation voted down that arrangement, 154 to 37. Amos B. Hoover, an Old Order Mennonite historian, has suggested that probably the pro-Sunday-school sentiment was much stronger than the vote indicated, since custom and procedure worked against younger members' voting. In any case, the school closed.[99] Meanwhile other issues such as the pulpit controversy remained troublesome.

In the end the tensions may look like a struggle between conference and congregational authority. But inasmuch as the Martin group promptly formed a conference of its own,[100] that struggle was probably not the issue. In October of 1893, pressed by conference to admit error, Martin reportedly replied that he was in harmony with "the old ground and counsel, but not with the new things"—especially not with performing marriages of nonmembers and with Sunday school. So, for seeming "determined to stand against the Conference," his opponents stripped him of his ministry within the "old" Mennonite church and expelled him from both conference and congregation. Those were drastic steps. The conference made them even harsher by allowing the relatively progressive conference leaders Isaac Eby and John K. Brubaker to announce the decision to the Weaverland congregation.[101]

Meanwhile Martin held a service for his supporters in the course of which he baptized twenty-two new members. And he announced that another service would follow at Weaverland on October 22, the off-Sunday in the pattern of every-other-Sunday services.[102] Thereafter, the schism was fact.

The difference between the old church and the new was not clear-cut. The "old" Lancaster conference remained cautious about accepting many of the changes which progressives were demanding.[103] In the new Weaverland conference was a key businessman named John Kurtz, who invented or promoted various new kinds of farm machines and was otherwise innovative. In future years Jonas Martin himself allowed some new machinery, most notably telephones. However, two years before he died in 1927 his conference divided over automobiles.[104] Like Wisler's group the Weaverland conference was troubled by a rather static concept of *Ordnung*. Yet the differences between the Lancaster conference and the Old Order were differences only of degree.

* * *

The divisions seared the lives of earnest and conscientious but otherwise quite ordinary people. Pathos ran deep as friends or family members took different roads. Yet not all of life was church troubles. Deep piety accompanied the pain and so did joy. In April of 1889 Jonas Martin's wife Sarah Witwer Martin died after bearing the couple's twelfth child. Twenty months later at Weaverland in a Sunday morning church service, in the midst of the pulpit and Sunday school disputes, Martin married Annie Wenger. Tradition says that a band later stopped at the Martins to serenade—and that to tease the bishop its members all wore red kerchiefs around their necks. As a successful cattle farmer Jonas Martin almost always wore one in barn and field.[105]

Amid such day-to-day living the Old Order-minded of Lancaster County liked to say, "*Mir vella halta vas vir hen*" ("We want to hold to what we've got").[106] But there was more than reactionism in the Old Order outlook. For persons not too locked into progressivist assumptions to appreciate it, Jacob Stauffer constructed an intelligent and coherent system of Old Order ideas. Among the Amish, relatively literate and thoughtful leaders such as bishop Jacob Schwarzendruber or schoolteacher S. D. Guengerich chose the Old Order side.

Jacob Wisler, Jonas Martin, and the Virginia Sunday school opponents, while surely reactionary, raised serious issues. The Old Order people had a brave vision of living in harmony with creation rather than always pursuing change. Their response was one way to cope with the secularism and civil religions of the U.S. (and Canada). And it was one set of answers to questions and dilemmas that are always present in Anabaptist, Mennonite, and Amish understandings of church and faith.

Jan Gleysteen collection

Catherine the Great.

CHAPTER

9

THE BACKGROUND OF A NEW IMMIGRATION

Could you help raise a fund to aid Mennonites coming from Russia? asked Amishman Johannes Gascho in Ontario of Frederick Swartzendruber, an Amish leader in Iowa, in 1874. The martyrs of old, imitating and obeying Christ, had helped "each other in every way they could." Now Mennonites and Amish in North America should help the Mennonites of Russia—with counsel, prayer, and deeds.[1]

Deeds meant money. For a decade or more the government of Czarist Russia had been trying to change its empire into a more modern nation-state. To do so officials had been carrying out vast reforms. For instance, in the 1860s they had issued far-reaching decrees to free the empire's serfs. Also catching their attention were Mennonites and other foreigners who had lived in the empire for up to a century—with special privileges, and in colonies quite apart from Russia's other peoples. In 1870 the government said it intended to end such privileges. Since one privilege was exemption from military service the announcement caused Mennonites a crisis of conscience. So in the next two decades some 18,000 Mennonites emigrated from the Russian empire to North America.[2] To help, Russian Mennonites assisted each other and North American Mennonites and Amish probably gave and loaned $150,000 or more.[3] The events brought forth the century's most impressive outpouring of Mennonite mutual aid.

In October 1872, David Goerz, a young Mennonite schoolteacher in the Ukrainian port city of Berdyansk, wrote to a friend in America saying that some Russian officials were now suggesting that Mennonites might perform their draft duty in hospital and sanitation work. Already at least one Mennonite had publicly backed the idea, but Goerz was skeptical. Health service might be all right in itself, he reasoned, but it also might lead "to full military

Courtesy of Mennonite Library and Archives at Bethel College

Left: **Paul Tschetter (1842-1919);** ***right:*** **David Goerz (1849-1914); leaders of Hutterite and Mennonite immigration from the Russian empire in the 1870s.**

service." And performing military service would rob Mennonites of "our nationality and the principles of our faith to which our fathers . . . witnessed with their own heart-blood."[4] By "nationality" Goerz meant Mennonite peoplehood, not Russian citizenship. As much or more than in America, Russia's Mennonites were an ethnic group as well as a church. They were German-speakers living in tightly bounded villages and colonies whose economic, political, and social patterns were veritable islands amid Russian culture.

Goerz's correspondent in America was Bernard Warkentin, the man who would eventually be such a successful wheat miller in Kansas. Both young men would soon be key figures in the emigration to America. A few months after rejecting the idea of health service, Goerz told Warkentin he saw a positive attraction in America: the young nation's progressivism. "While the American plows through his endless savannahs & prairies with a steam engine," he wrote, the Russian was bogged in mud. In Russia there were great surveys and great visions but the railways themselves were still only a dream.[5]

Actually in the 1870s progress-minded Mennonites did not have to choose America over Russia. Since about the 1850s Russia's Mennonites had been increasing their wealth, expanding their institutions, and founding daughter colonies.[6] Contrary to Goerz's view, Mennonite progressives could choose quite logically to stay in the Russian empire.

A DIFFERENT HISTORY

The histories of Russia's Mennonites were quite different from the histories of most Mennonites in North America. Most Russian Mennonites had roots not in Switzerland and south Germany but in Anabaptism farther north. Their ancestors had migrated eastward from places such as Flanders and Friesland in the Netherlands to the Danzig area and other regions of what became Prussia.

There were exceptions: Hutterites, who had come from Tirol, Moravia, and Transylvania; and some congregations in Volhynia in "Polish Russia," whose roots were Swiss and south-German Amish.[7] Those people spoke their own Hutterite or Swiss dialects. But most of Russia's Mennonites spoke a Low German dialect, *Plautdietsch*,[8] which had evolved in Prussia and in the Russian empire. In written and other formal expression they had shifted from Dutch to German, and so could communicate with nearly all Mennonites in America and elsewhere. But their every day speech was *Plautdietsch*. No other Mennonites shared it, and it was a strong mark of Russian Mennonite ethnicity. Emigrants would bring both the dialect and the ethnicity to North America.

Mennonites had begun settling in the Russian empire in 1789 in response to an invitation offered to various peoples by a remarkable ruler, Czarina Catherine the Great. Most had gone to southern regions served by the Volga and Dnieper rivers, especially to the Ukraine.[9] There, at first, they lived on a rough frontier and suffered scourges ranging from grasshoppers to robbers to dishonest officials. But they planted two early colonies, naming the first "Chortitza" (often known as the "Old Colony") and the second "Molotschna" (established 1803).[10] Both settlements included numerous villages and eventually both fostered various "daughter" colonies, thereby spreading Mennonites into new areas nearby or quite distant.[11] Molotschna was the more progressive, and by the 1820s it began attracting attention as a flourishing economic island and a new center of Mennonite life.[12]

THE PRIVILEGIUM

The settlers in the Russian empire and their offspring enjoyed a remarkable set of privileges, embodied in a *Privilegium*, or formal set of guarantees from the Russian government. The "*Privilegium*"

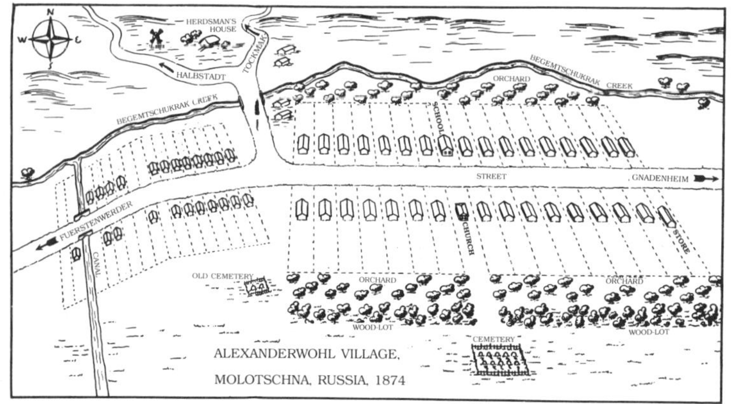

Layout of Alexanderwohl, a typical nineteenth-century Russian Mennonite village.

allowed their communities to become cultural islands and to produce a distinctive kind of Mennonitism. Much of it grew from enticements extended by Catherine in 1763 to all colonists, not only Mennonites. The enticements ranged from travel assistance to manufacturing privileges to religious freedom (except to proselytize other Christians within the realm) to autonomy for local politics to exemption from compulsory military or civilian service.[13]

Other features, such as the right to affirm rather than to swear oaths, the Mennonites negotiated specially. However, the privileges came along with an important restriction: settlers and their descendants could not sell lands granted by the crown—65 desiatins (about 175 acres) of arable land to each family—without official permission.[14] By mid-nineteenth century that restriction became most troublesome, for it prevented the dividing of farms and so produced a large class of Mennonite landless.[15]

PROSPERITY

Despite those landless, by mid-century Russia's Mennonites enjoyed great prosperity. Various privileges aided Mennonites economically. So also, by the 1840s, did a government "Committee of Guardians for the Foreign Colonists," for the committee wanted to make the German communities be showcases for instructing the empire's other peoples.[16] Meanwhile the Mennonites developed new institutions such as agencies to help widows and orphans, better primary schools, and by the 1830s and 1840s a few new secondary schools.[17] Before the emigration to America in the 1870s Russia's Mennonites would accumulate much experience and skill at managing businesses and institutions.

The institutions included political ones. Under the *Privilegium* Mennonites had their own village assemblies, elected mayors (*Schulzen* was the German title), and mayors' assistants. There were also district assemblies and district *Oberschulzen* ("uppermayors," head-mayors). The system had many questionable features. Only landowners could vote. The powers of the *Schulzen* were broad but imprecise and mixed executive and judicial functions. Individuals enjoyed little protection against pressures from their communities.[18] Nor did the Mennonites gain experience with modern nationalism or national politics. Instead, they were in a semi-feudal system, living as a special class of state peasants. As such, they thought in terms of winning favors and protection from the czars as personal patrons, not in terms of constitutional or legal rights. Yet, whatever its flaws, the system allowed them considerable experience in local, representative government.

RELIGIOUS FERMENT

The 1840s, '50s, and '60s brought religious revival. Virtually all the reformers who promoted it were persons under deep influence of German Pietism.

In the analysis of one historian, for Mennonites in the Russian empire the principle of separation from the world had come to mean "not so much the original emphasis of refraining from worldly activities, but more an isolation of the closed colonies"—a separatism which too easily overlooked "evils of Mennonite origin." Such evils, in the eyes of the reformers of the time, ranged from drunkenness to failure to be missionary. Historians have pointed also to loss of Christian equality, callousness toward the landless poor, and development of "a highly stratified society."[19] Without question such indictments carry much truth.

Nonetheless, another truth is that the mainline-Mennonite (eventually dubbed "*Kirchliche*"—meaning "established-church") congregations provided much of the life and nurture from which renewal grew. And critics must recognize also that at the time of the most important renewal, the one which produced the Mennonite Brethren church in 1860, the same movement revitalized many who stayed within the *Kirchliche* congregations.[20]

The first Mennonites in the Russian empire to break away from the main church became known as the *Kleine Gemeinde* (small church)—formed in the Ukraine about 1812 to 1814. Led by a reformer named Klaas Reimer, the *Kleine Gemeinde* raised issues ranging from rejecting smoking and drunkenness, to forbidding musical instruments, to various questions of stricter nonresistance and separation from civil government. Other issues were millenarianism and bad temper by an elder who opposed Reimer.[21] More or less, the new church became an Old Order group for Russian Mennonites somewhat as Jacob Stauffer's church was for Mennonites in Pennsylvania.

A well-written *Kleine Gemeinde* tract of 1833 called Mennonites to stricter discipline, sharper separatism, less involvement in business and politics, and deeper humility and simplicity.[22] As late as 1864 the *Kleine Gemeinde* had probably no more than 300 members. In 1874 all of them moved to North America. Some settled in Manitoba, where their church eventually became the Evangelical Mennonite Church (Canada). Others settled in Nebraska and Kansas and melded into other Mennonite groups.[23]

In the Crimea in 1867, following a revival, a Mennonite congregation led by an elder named Jakob A. Wiebe joined the *Kleine Gemeinde* but remained dissatisfied. In 1869 it went its own way and its people soon were called the "Krimmer [Crimean] Mennonite Brethren." They also emigrated, settling in Marion County, Kansas, where they formed an old-world village and congregation known as Gnadenau (Meadow of Grace). Eventually, in 1960, the "KMB" would merge with the Mennonite Brethren, a larger group.[24]

THE MENNONITE BRETHREN

The main renewal movement created the Mennonite Brethren (MB) church. That movement also had deep roots in European Pietism. As do all such movements, this one originated within a particular set of social, political, economic, and ethnic circumstances as well. Some interpreters have suggested close connection between the MB movement and agitations by the landless. More recent ones are inclined to emphasize that business persons, teachers, and other professionals were prominent among MB founders. Some interpreters detect the outlook of an emerging middle class. For instance, historian James Urry has offered such a perspective, and also, in a helpful way, spelled out a context of various social and political tensions which existed in the Mennonite colonies just prior to MB beginnings. Yet, even more, Urry set the MB movement in a context of Pietism.[25] Since their beginnings MBs have unabashedly fused Mennonitism with continental Pietism or American evangelicalism.

From the 1820s onward new secondary schools at two Molotschna villages, Orloff and Gnadenfeld, became centers of Pietistic activities: Christian-reading groups, support for missions, temperance reform, *Bibelstunden* (Bible study-and-discussion hours), intense small-group fellowship apart from or beyond the fellowship of the established congregation, and other extra-church events. The people involved spoke much of *Brudertum* (brotherliness) and were known more and more as "the brethren." In the 1850s a similar, smaller movement developed at a Chortitza village called Einlage. Meanwhile in 1846 an influential Pietist, a separatist Lutheran, began to preach among Russia's Mennonites especially at Gnadenfeld: *Pfarrer* (Preacher) Eduard Wuest (1818-1859). He spoke especially at mission festivals and fellowshiped with the Gnadenfelders in their conventicles.[26]

Although Wuest died in 1859 before the MB church was quite born, Mennonite Brethren have considered him a founder almost equal to Menno Simons. As an able MB historian in Russia, Peter M. Friesen, wrote early in the twentieth century: "Menno built the house in which we live; but when the house was about to collapse Wuest brought "vital air and warmth, food and drink" and strength to rebuild on "the old plan, the old foundation." And, Friesen added: "If the joyous doctrine of justification is overly predominant in Wuest's Christian teaching, it counterbalances Menno's serious, somewhat melancholy theology. . . ."[27] Thus Friesen defended a certain exuberance in MB worship and experience.

Did the new movement really build on "the old plan, the old foundation"? Not all of Russia's Mennonites thought so. Tensions grew so strong that in late 1859 at Gnadenfeld two laymen named Johann Claassen and Jakob Reimer led ten of the most renewal-minded out of a stormy congregational session. On January 6, 1860, at what was later called a "founders' meeting," the come-outers declared their secession.[28] The seceders became the "Mennonite Brethren" and the old church got the nickname *"Kirchliche* [churchly, or established-church] Mennonites." The reasons and beliefs the seceders gave were:[29]

- Too many Mennonites led decadent, corrupt lives.
- The Mennonites were correct that baptism should occur only on confession of faith; but it should occur also only after genuine new birth.
- (Replying to censure for communing with non-Mennonites): Yes, communion should be only with fellow believers, but mainline Mennonites were letting drunkards, fornicators, and other sinners come to the communion table.

- The foot-washing rite was biblical.
- Preachers could be called in two ways: directly by God or through the body of believers.
- The church should ban "carnal and reprobate sinners" until they repented and confessed.
- The Brethren agreed fully with Menno Simons.

The secession manifesto did not mention classic Mennonite nonresistance or emphasize the church as God's new people with a new ethic. Pietistically, the standards of life in the statement were mainly individual: not being a fornicator, a drunkard, a glutton, or an extortioner. Historian Urry has argued that the movement reflected a growing attitude of individualism in matters of salvation. On the other hand, by itself the secession statement did not show that Pietistic influences were introducing great novelties. The statement did not even specify baptism by immersion, which soon became an MB rule and a clear boundary marker between MB and *Kirchliche*. Moreover, it emphasized the points at issue, not necessarily the full range of the founders' beliefs.

By strong identification with Menno the seceders surely implied nonresistance and living corporately as God's people. One of the founders, Jakob Bekker, later put a biography of Menno Simons at the beginning of a manuscript on MB origins. In general, modern scholars emphasize that whatever their Pietism, MB founders turned to Mennonite sources and criteria when questions arose.[30] The MB founders were deeply influenced by Pietism, but they hoped to stimulate people to be more earnest and less compromising in their Mennonite faith.

Reconciliation with *Kirchliche* critics might have been possible, but the colonies' church and political leaders chose punishment instead. Elders applied the ban and shunning to dissenters in ways that sometimes brought economic hardship. Public officials jailed six or eight men for three or four weeks, whipped at least one, kept an MB elder named Heinrich Huebert in prison for ten months, and ruled harshly that marriages performed by MB ministers were invalid. They registered children born of MB unions as being born out of wedlock.[31]

To explain such reprisals church leaders accused the dissenters of faults ranging from one-sidedness in scriptural interpretation to fanaticism and refusal to be instructed, contempt for church order, and rupturing of families. Fortunately for the Brethren, a few *Kirchliche* elders, especially a prestigious Bernhard Fast at Orloff, refused to be so harsh. Their hesitation and some assistance from well-placed Pietists in St. Petersburg helped win support from government. In 1864 Russian authorities ordered local Mennonite officials to recognize the MB marriages. In 1866 after a dreary sequence of maneuvering, appeals, and counterappeals the MBs won official recognition as a church qualifying for the Mennonite *Privilegium*.[32]

Meanwhile the MBs disputed amply among themselves. They disagreed about offering the biblical kiss of peace across the gender line (a practice discredited when a man and two women who advocated it became sexually involved); about how exuberant to become in worship, with dancing, musical instruments, clapping, and other noise-making; and about mixing with non-MBs, including relatives. After several years of study and debate the new church accepted Baptist arguments on mode of baptism and began to allow only the immersed to take communion.[33] However, in the latter 1860s relations with Baptists caused controversy, as did a related matter, smoking. In need of leaders, MBs accepted help from visiting Baptists from Germany, one of whom used tobacco. Moreover, Baptists were not pacifist. In the end the MBs expelled members who smoked. And they decided that Baptists and Mennonites should have separate congregations.[34]

Pietistic ferment among Mennonites produced other movements, most notably a millenarian one which eventually sent some emigrants to North America by a circuitous route. In 1877 Claas Epp, Jr., a Prussian immigrant in one of the newer Mennonite colonies, published a work which accepted an idea of a prominent German Pietist named Johann Heinrich Jung-Stilling that salvation would come from the East. From 1880 to 1882 Epp and others led a migration eastward into central Asia. In 1884, after various hardships and disagreements, some members decided to join relatives and fellow Mennonites in America. Mennonites in America (Russian and other) extended mutual aid, and persons continued to come until the twentieth century.[35]

As for relations between the MBs and the *Kirchliche*, in time the sorest of the wounds healed, albeit with some scars. In Russia, early in the twentieth century, an "alliance" movement developed, bringing a measure of cooperation between the MBs and the *Kirchliche*. And in North America in 1960, a body of the General Conference (GC) Mennonite church, heir of the *Kirchliche*, admitted that Russia's Mennonites a century earlier had needed reform. The GC body officially apologized for wrongs against those early MBs. Some bad memories and estrangement remain.[36] But even at worst, Mennonites did not burn each other at stakes or raise righteous armies or stockpile bombs to slaughter their opponents.

ETHNIC AND CLASS CONFLICT

Neither did Mennonites resort to such deadly means in ethnic or class conflicts. One problem of their colonies was relations with Russian neighbors, whom they often hired: but scholars have established only glimpses of those relations.[37] Better documented is a class problem within Mennonite ranks: that of the landless.

By mid-century tensions were growing, especially at Molotschna, until the landless finally went over the heads of their own leaders and appealed to Russian officials in St. Petersburg. A few sympathetic landowners and church elders backed their pleas and after a time, in February of 1866, the Russian government changed the rules of land tenure. With that change, Mennonites themselves began working together and developed a comprehensive settlement that allowed farms to be broken up, reserve lands to be distributed, and taxation to purchase still more land from other peoples.[38] Much of the credit must go to Russian officials. Yet another fact was that Mennonites had enough sense of peoplehood to soften their own class struggle.

TO GO OR NOT TO GO

Russia's Mennonites had strong bonds of peoplehood. Those in Polish Russia were less wealthy and their colonies less developed. But most of the emigrants went to America with ample experience settling new lands and managing local institutions.

Helping the emigration were Russia's foreign relations. Having fared badly especially against Great Britain and others in the Crimean War of the mid-1850s, Russia was inclined to ally with Prussia.[39] Prussia had long asserted at least a theoretical right to act as protector of Germans inside the Russian empire. So Prussia's Chancellor Otto von Bismarck won a proviso that for a decade Germans who wished to leave the empire could freely do so.[40] The proviso served Mennonites well. Although Russian officials wanted to dissuade them from leaving, and sometimes seemed to withhold passports or put up other blocks, in the end those who wished were allowed to go.[41]

The outcome of the war also forced Russia to open her Black Sea ports to more international trade, a change which widened Mennonite contacts. A port town named Berdyansk, opening on the Black Sea via the Sea of Azov, thrived until it was a city with foreign consuls in residence. The city had a congregation of Mennonites, quite a few of them born in Prussia and generally quite progressive. Some of them mixed in the small international community.[42] David Goerz studied English with an agent of the British and Foreign Bible Society. Cornelius Jansen, a Prussian and a grain exporter, served as Prussia's consul. The Jansen children learned English by playing with the children of the British consul, and Cornelius Jansen himself also gained some use of that language. In his mid-forties, Jansen was thoroughly pious and devotional as well as a man of worldly affairs; among his friends he counted some British Quakers and Bible Society people as well as the British consul.[43]

In the 1860s Jansen was quick to realize the danger to the *Privilegium* and to turn his face toward North America. In the Russian empire he had never moved inland or put down deep roots.[44] So when he saw the danger to the *Privilegium* he wrote to Mennonite leaders in America and asked about conditions there.[45]

ADVICE AND MUTUAL AID FROM AMERICA

One letter reached Christian Krehbiel, who was himself an immigrant. Among other points Krehbiel replied that in America, unlike in Europe, labor was so scarce that the landowner and his sons would have to work with their own hands. But, Krehbiel assured Jansen, a family who was not too large and had strong sons could get started with $800-$1000, especially if it also had a daughter and did not have to hire a maid. Another letter went to John F. Funk. Funk replied, perhaps a little too easily, that in America there was complete religious freedom even for conscientious objection. Mennonites had to pay those $300 fees during the civil war but with mutual aid the fees were not too heavy. As for another strong Mennonite concern, land, Funk discussed U.S. land East and West and informed Jansen of where Mennonites had settled. Immigrants, he suggested, could live temporarily with Mennonite brothers and sisters already established. Nor would they need to bring much equipment: in America they could buy what they needed.[46]

Also reaching Jansen's hands was a message from one Peter Wiebe, a Prussian who had settled on a 400-acre farm at Rolla in central Missouri. Wiebe offered minute details about his farm and its yield, necessary animals and equipment, probable prices, climate, and risks. As for special privileges, Wiebe said the U.S. treated no one specially; but since its constitution guaranteed freedom of conscience, neither could anyone be forced against conscience to bear arms. Just now, in 1871, in conflict with American "Indians," the U.S. army was getting by with volunteers.[47]

Such were impressions of the United States which filtered back to Russia's Mennonites in 1870 and 1871. Early in 1872 Jansen printed the letters in a pamphlet which he then circulated in the Mennonite colonies. He also included a slightly more cautious message from one Gerhard Wiebe, a Prussian now situated near Cleveland, Ohio. Wiebe had consulted a lawyer about conscientious objection in America and learned that really neither law nor the constitution quite guaranteed it. Yet the lawyer advised that precedent was on the side of honoring it. So in the end Wiebe wrote that no land where Mennonites had ever lived offered better guarantees than did the U.S.[48]

Jansen's pamphlet also offered travel information for persons going to America: news of a mission house where they might stay in New York City, for instance, and the address of John H. Oberholtzer in eastern Pennsylvania. It also included some outdated information on Canada; but on the whole, probably without intent, it pointed mostly to the U.S.[49]

OFFICIAL RESPONSES

In March of 1873 Russian authorities suddenly expelled the Prussian Jansen. The charge: spreading false information and persuading Russian subjects to defect. On May 26, 1873, the Jansen family embarked for North America: Cornelius; his wife, Helena von Riesen Jansen; their three daughters; and three sons, and a sister of Helena Jansen, who for years had lived with them.[50]

Meanwhile Jansen and others had sounded out British authorities concerning Canada. In January of 1872 Leonard Sudermann, Prussian-immigrant pastor and elder of the Berdyansk congregation, inquired via the local British consul, a man named Schrab (or Zorhab). So did some Molotschna leaders. Would Canada exempt Mennonites from military duty as it did Quakers? Sudermann asked. Also, he stated that while Russia's Mennonites were not poor, a move would be costly. Could Canada make land available cheaply and advance some money for settling? Schrab advised his superiors that he knew Mennonites well and that they and other Germans were hardworking and bound to expand Canada's output—but that if not properly courted they might go to the United States.[51]

Meanwhile Canada sent assurance that it would indeed grant anyone properly certified as a Mennonite the same exemptions it gave Quakers. Moreover, it would pay expenses for a Mennonite scout or two to come and inspect its lands. And any immigrant 21 years old or older could claim 160 acres free in Manitoba or other North West Territory. Furthermore, the 160-acre plots could be in large tracts so that the immigrants could form solid communities.[52] With such information Canada was practically inviting Russia's Mennonites to come. But Schrab's British superiors were cautious.

Courtesy of Mennonite Library and Archives at Bethel College

Prussian Cornelius Jansen (1822-1894)

They did not want one of their minor consuls to be caught encouraging his host country's subjects to leave.[53]

About that time a German-born agent of Canada named William Hespeler, traveling in Europe to attract immigrants, heard of Mennonite dissatisfaction and headed for the Ukraine. Unfortunately, he telegraphed his mission too openly to Schrab and thereby alerted Russia's spies and police. Nevertheless, Hespeler traveled for two weeks among the Mennonites and other Germans. As he did, he grew more and more enthused about Mennonites as colonists. Many, he sensed, might leave within a year.[54]

MENNONITE VOICES

Meanwhile much was astir within the Mennonite communities themselves. During December and January of 1870-1871 key leaders met in conference at the church in Molotschna's Alexanderwohl village. There they exchanged ideas and chose delegates to negotiate with the Russian government. Thereafter deputations made trip after trip to St. Petersburg. The first arrived on February 20, 1871, with Leonard Sudermann, the Berdyansk pastor, as its head.[55]

Berdyansk was a center of intellectual resistance to accommodation or compromise with the government's reforms. Jansen and eventually Sudermann penned documents clearly restating the classic Mennonite two-realm doctrine. "Render unto Caesar what is Caesar's" did not mean Christians were to render their sons,

Jansen argued; God had given children to learn his "gospel of peace," not for battle. Later Sudermann penned an even clearer restatement of the classic position. Mennonites had always testified that war and Christianity stand opposed, Sudermann reminded the Berdyansk congregation in 1876. He saw no contradiction between that message and a concern for personal and corporate piety. Now, he urged, was the day of salvation. Come with clothes washed in the blood of the Lamb. Obey God's Word and will.[56]

The delegation Sudermann led in 1871 consisted of two elders, three ministers, and a gifted teacher named Hermann Janzen. No *Oberschulze* or other civic official was in the party. Nor could the main spokesmen speak enough Russian to negotiate in that language. Even Sudermann could not, although he was forty-nine, was quite intellectual, and had lived in the empire about thirty years. Some others spoke Russian, but some only poorly. One official, a count who was Minister of State Domains, sharply rebuked the Mennonites for having lived seventy or more years in the empire without learning its language.[57]

Yet the various officials proposed what they probably considered to be favors. They suggested that even if Mennonite young men might have to carry weapons they would not need to use them; and that they might do health and sanitation work. (In fact, Mennonites had helped care for wounded soldiers in the Crimean War, as well as doing considerable teamster work and the like.) The delegates replied that of course their people would help care for the wounded—but not under military organization. Moreover, they did not want their youths mixing with soldiers. Those statements set positions which hardly changed in the next three years. Later Sudermann explained that the deputies might quickly have won the right to perform service without weapons. But he thought such service "would be giving tacit support to the military."[58]

To back their positions the deputies submitted a statement of their nonresistance. Repeatedly, the document used phrases such as "Prince of Peace," "Kingdom of Peace," "Children of Peace," and "gospel of peace." It said further that if Mennonites had to leave "home and fatherland" in order to be faithful, they had often done so before and would do it again.[59] Of course a skeptic could read such words as hardly more than self-righteous rhetoric to protect Mennonites' privileges and position. The Russian officials likely read it too much that way, underestimating Mennonite willingness to leave.[60]

For a long time, at least, officials largely ignored Mennonite talk of emigration. A year went by while Mennonites waited and listened to rumor. In January of 1872 a new delegation visited St. Petersburg and sensed that the government might concede on the point of actually carrying weapons. Its members also surmised that a spy had attended key Mennonite meetings: officials knew just what had been said. Another delegation six months later learned little more.[61]

A FEVER FOR EMIGRATING

By early 1873 emigration fever was building. Congregations of Mennonites and Hutterites in both Polish Russia and the South had already decided to send deputies to North America.[62] But the Mennonites were far from agreed. All wanted some sort of military exemption but they ranged from many who were quite accommodationist to a few who rejected any personal service to nation or even any formal dealings with the state at all.

In January of 1873 a Pietistic Moravian pastor who served as the Mennonite ear in St. Petersburg called for a new petition, this time in Russian. The pastor counseled that while the statement should still ask for military exemption, it should promise general cooperation in Russia's new reforms. Late that month another Mennonite conference at Alexanderwohl drew up such a statement. For whatever reasons, four elders present refused to sign: Sudermann; Gerhard Wiebe of Bergthal; Isaak Peters of Fürstenau village, Molotschna colony; and Jakob Buller of Alexanderwohl. Bergthalers later drew up their own petition, and before long were laying plans to move en masse to Canada. In February a delegation took the majority's petition to St. Petersburg. But the Mennonites were not speaking with one voice.[63]

Meanwhile in 1872 a kind of unofficial deputation of four young men from wealthy families, including Bernard Warkentin, went to America. Besides making the tourists' rounds to places such as Niagara Falls the four visited John F. Funk at Elkhart, Indiana, and the community at Summerfield, Illinois. One or more of them also visited John H. Oberholtzer in Pennsylvania; Jacob Y. Shantz of near Berlin (present-day Kitchener), Ontario (a man beginning to work very hard to bring Mennonites to Canada); and various sites in the West especially on the plains from Manitoba to Texas.

In Canada, Shantz took Warkentin to Ottawa and the Canadian parliament, the minister of agriculture, the governor of Manitoba, and others, to discuss such subjects as Manitoba's weather and relations between Canada's whites and its Indians and mixed-bloods. In the U.S., agents of railroads who wanted to sell

Provincial Archives of Manitoba

Jacob Y. Shantz (1822-1909), Mennonite businessman and lay leader in Ontario who assisted Russian Mennonite settlement in Manitoba in the 1870s.

land and build communities along their tracks quickly sniffed out the four young men and began to converge on them. Warkentin became the main target, partly no doubt because of his abilities but also because, having received news that his fiance in the Ukraine had died, he decided to stay in North America. As guest of the Canadian government and U.S. railroads Warkentin inspected land from Manitoba to Texas.[64]

Back in the Ukraine, Mennonites were most eager for news of America. Where information was poor, half-baked notions circulated. A dialect verse mockingly asked, *"Doch ober wo ist Amerika?"* ("But where is America?")—and parodied women's gossipy answers. The doggerel suggested not only how poor was information, but also, unconsciously, what it meant to be a woman on the sidelines of a decision greatly affecting one's life:

But where is America?
I've heard say that it must be
Forty miles from the big sea.
Lena thinks, she's sure thereon,
It ain't so far from Oregon.
But Mary says, "I hear say,
That it's in Pennsylvaniay."
And old Liz comes and says, "Ach no,
It lies in old New Mexico."
When Michael tired of all the woe
Of letting women go on so,
He said he knew, and told them, "Nah—
It's just there in America."[65]

Here and there individuals or families began to leave. Bernard Warkentin settled at Summerfield. In May of 1873 David Goerz and his small family arrived there also, apparently with a group of some twenty or twenty-five other families. Other clusters went, for instance, to Yankton, Dakota, or Mountain Lake, Minnesota.[66] Serious emigration was under way.

GENERAL TODLEBEN

Early in 1874 Russian officials, now apparently realizing that many Mennonites might indeed leave, began to take Mennonite concerns more seriously. To stop the hemorrhage they sent a German-speaking army general, Eduard von Todleben (or Todtleben), hero of the Crimean War, to visit the Mennonites. He arrived in April and seems quickly to have decided that although many Mennonites were talking of emigration others were not; so the best strategy was to rally the latter. A German-language paper in St. Petersburg reported just about then that many younger, lay Mennonites were tired of letting church elders and other conservatives make the decisions. In the paper's view the conservatives who refused to accommodate to Russia's reforms were just too stubborn.[67] But in fact, who were more stubborn?—those who resisted Russian nationalism and national service, or those who held tightly to home and soil?

On the matter of military service the affable Todleben seems to have offered little that was new. He may have shifted the discussion a bit by emphasizing health and sanitation service less, and forestry service more. Mennonites liked that emphasis, for in forestry camps their youths would live more isolated, away from soldiers. Yet it took them some years to establish that forestry would be their young men's main work. In the spring of 1874 Todleben's larger contribution was probably a less tangible one: rallying sentiment for staying in Russia. Under the czar "you have fine schools, fine churches, fine houses and gardens," Jakob Wiebe, the KMB elder, later remembered the general saying "in pure German." " 'You have fine schools, fine churches, fine houses and gardens.' " And you " 'can hire Russian laborers at low wages.' " So why go to America? There " 'you will have to dig trees, weed the roots and break the prairie,' " all with your own hands.[68]

ACCOMMODATION

For whatever reasons, about the time of the general's visit the accommodationists rallied. By now not only ministers but Mennonite civic leaders were involved, a fact probably strengthening the accommodationists' hand. In any case a new petition from the Mennonites reduced demands mainly to three: (1) freedom to emigrate in the future if the government ever withdrew the offer of alternative work and drafted Mennonites for military service; (2) Mennonite control of colony schools (albeit with a promise to teach the Russian language); and (3) letting the drafted men not be scattered but instead be put in a few "closed groups" where they could be properly supervised, nurtured, and kept under Mennonite church regulations and discipline.[69]

A year later, on May 14, 1875, the Russian government issued draft regulations for Mennonites and partly met those three demands. In essence the regulations provided exemption from carrying weapons; assignment of Mennonite youths to Marine Department workshops, fire prevention, and forestry; and a provision that "the men in service shall be grouped separately in order to permit the practice of their church services according to their persuasion."[70] Over the next half-dozen years Mennonites and the government worked out details. In 1881 the first forestry camps opened.

Russia now had an alternative service system which from the Mennonite point of view was far more satisfactory than noncombatant service under the military. The system was under civilian and a great deal of church control. In return, Mennonites assumed most of the system's costs.[71]

So much for military service. On the other major question, control of schools, Mennonites won less. After all, Russian reformers were trying to meld their empire's people together into a modern nation-state. They wanted the nation's people to become more Russian in language and culture.

In 1881 the government's Ministry of Education assumed ultimate control with power to set curricula in the colonies' schools, establish teacher qualifications, and appoint Russians rather than ethnic Mennonites as teachers. Soon the ministry decreed that except for religion all subjects were to be taught in Russian. The order was a long step toward Mennonites' russification. Yet in practice the change was not as great as some Mennonites predicted. Until the twentieth century the Russian government still allowed Mennonites much local autonomy in education.[72]

With such compromise (and similar ones concerning local government[73]) the Russian government continued to respect Mennonite wishes. In the 1870s and 1880s the accommodations satisfied enough Mennonites that two-thirds of them stayed

A RELIGIOUS ARGUMENT FOR STAYING

A spokesman for those who remained, writing in 1875, was a certain Johann Epp of Am Trakt, a colony of rather recent immigrants from Prussia. Epp charged that the Mennonites who were emigrating pretended to go for conscience' sake while in fact they spoke mostly of America's "beautiful, fertile and abundant lands and . . . excellent ownership rights and other good institutions." He favored the new system of alternative service, and said that Mennonites should be more ready to cooperate with Russia's law than with the U.S. plan of commutation fees and hiring substitutes. A minister and a student of prophecy, he reasoned further that in the world's last days Russia would be safer than America, for he doubted that Mennonites would fare well under modern representative governments. "*Only in Russia*," a bastion of autocracy, he argued, "can a privileged status be preserved." Russia was not "subject to the raging of the antichrist to the same extent as the other nations of the West"—including America.[74]

So ran one Mennonite's arguments against emigration. Whatever the merits of his other points, he was correct in saying that land was important. And a person such as David Goerz certainly saw America as offering better and more progressive institutions. It has been too easy to say, as historian David Rempel wrote in 1933, that those who emigrated were "the most conservative and uncompromising element among the Mennonites."[75] Those who emigrated generally thought the issue was not merely accommodation, but outright compromise. But who were the more conservative? Were those who held onto farms and villages and class system in Russia's empire really less conservative than the emigrants?

PREPARING TO EMIGRATE: THE 12-MAN DELEGATION

As early as 1871 John F. Funk advised Cornelius Jansen that Russia's Mennonites might do well to send representatives to seek out places for settlement in America, and promised that if any came, America's Mennonites would help them. In 1872 the four youths went; then later, in September, a more official delegation began to form. About November two Mennonites from Polish Russia visited the Ukraine with new reports: officials had ordered their ministers to preach in Russian, and many people were restless to emigrate. A few families were already preparing to leave.[76] Meanwhile Hutterite leaders had been appealing to Russian officials and, like Mennonites, were growing frustrated.[77]

Thus the sentiment for a deputation grew. So did the deputation itself, expanding from an idea of sending two or three to actually sending twelve. During February to April of 1873 the deputies left Europe in several clusters: Heinrich Wiebe and Jakob Peters, representing Bergthal; a wealthy farmer named Cornelius Buhr, going on his own account; Cornelius Toews and David Klassen, for the *Kleine Gemeinde*; Paul and Laurence Tschetter, for the Hutterites; Tobias Unruh for the *Plautdietsch* and Andreas Schrag for the Swiss in Volhynia; elders Jakob Buller and Leonard Sudermann, more or less for the main body of *Kirchliche* Mennonites in the Ukraine; and from Prussia, elder Wilhelm Ewert.[78] In America the twelve joined, and then visited Mennonite leaders to seek advice. Russia's Mennonites and Hutterites were finally getting information on which to act.

CANADA OR THE UNITED STATES?

The deputies pondered not whether to emigrate but where. Obviously the main choices would lie along the eastern edge of

North America's vast semiarid plains, on a line which ran from Manitoba to Kansas, jumped over Indian territory (soon to be Oklahoma), and continued in Texas. Often the question was one of climate: how far north or south? That question was also mixed with others: Canada or the U.S.? Where might Mennonites settle compactly?

The delegates left Europe with options open. About the time they arrived the Canadian government began distributing a pamphlet which Mennonite Jacob Shantz of Ontario had written promoting Manitoba. Shantz defended Manitoba winters, emphasized the peacefulness of Canada's Indians and mixed-bloods, and offered high prospects for rapid economic development. Not least he emphasized that Canada would offer land in large blocks.[79]

Without making the point explicit Shantz was suggesting a contrast to land offerings in the U.S. In the U.S. the government had used land grants to induce railroad companies to build lines through the West, and now railroads owned much of the best available soil. But they owned it in a checkerboard pattern of alternate square miles. The government still held most of the intervening acres. The railroads would work hard to attract the Mennonites but the government would not promise the immigrants the intervening sections. Without those sections the newcomers could hardly transplant the solidly Mennonite communities they had known in the Ukraine.

In June and July the twelve delegates spent several weeks inspecting Manitoba. The Canadian government paid expenses[80] and the ambitious Hespeler acted as guide. There the deputies found plenty of people, from ordinary farmers to Manitoba's governor, who sounded as optimistic as Shantz's pamphlet. The governor held a reception with plenty of cake and wine and talk of land and coal and iron and a railroad soon to come. But, unfortunately for Hespeler and fellow officials, just about everything that could go wrong did go wrong. The party set out with wagons, tents, and provisions on a four-day foray into the countryside to inspect townships being offered, but rains set in and made the trip difficult. A guide made a wrong turn and bogged the party in a swamp. It was already mid-June, and even outside the swamp the delegates doubted that in a year such as the present there would ever be a growing season for crops (although elsewhere in Manitoba they saw better prospects). Mosquitoes swarmed and drilled until an exasperated and swollen Wilhelm Ewert pronounced them the worst plague he had ever seen.[81]

Several delagates who stayed longer than the others in Manitoba found themselves holed up for some hours in a house at a point about twenty-five miles from Winnipeg. A group of angry mixed-bloods (Metis) besieged the dwelling while Hespeler stood guard at the door, revolver in hand. It is not clear whether the cause was Meti drunkenness, as a Winnipeg paper suggested, or an ongoing struggle the Metis and the Canadian government were having for control of Manitoba. Most likely it was both. In any case the situation did not calm down until officials sent troops from Winnipeg and arrested a half dozen of the rebels.[82]

Some of the most conservative delegates, Bergthaler and *Kleine Gemeinde*, were caught in that confrontation, yet went ahead and negotiated for Manitoba land. Through the efforts of Hespeler, Shantz, and others, Canadian officials made an attractive proposal. They offered military exemption, 160 acres free to each male 21 or over plus an option to buy more at $1 per acre, assistance and subsidy for ocean travel, exemption from having to swear oaths, and full freedom of worship. Officials offered also to set aside large tracts (eight townships at the outset) entirely for Mennonites, and to let the Mennonites have entire control of their schools. Land in blocks and control of schools were extremely important to settlers determined to create fully Mennonite communities on the Russian-empire model. Canadian Mennonite historian Frank H. Epp has called the offer "the Canadian Privilegium." Most Bergthal and *Kleine Gemeinde* immigrants accepted it, and most of the early Russian Mennonite immigrants to Canada were of their groups.[83]

But Manitoba left most other delegates "considerably disheartened," in the words of Leonard Sudermann. The deputies had suffered bad luck but they also had seen far too little development or access to transportation and markets. A majority of them and well over half of the Russian Mennonite immigrants of the 1870s and 1880s would choose the U.S.[84]

Since settlers who chose Canada were mainly Bergthaler and *Kleine Gemeinde*, and since they recreated compact communities there, some scholars have generalized that conservative immigrants went to Canada and the more progressive ones went to the U.S.—or, in another version, mid-road people went to the U.S. and the progressive stayed in Russia.[85] The case is not so clear. In the end, delegates who chose the U.S. included Swiss-Volhynian Andreas Schrag and Alexanderwohler Jakob Buller, both rather conservative. And among them were two who were deeply conservative, the *Plautdietsch*-Volhynian Tobias Unruh and the Hutterite Paul Tschetter. Unruh and Tschetter were the sort of men for whom the bustle and buildings of U.S. cities were only signs that "the end of the world must be nigh." In the day of judgment such human effort would become "a heap of stones." A deeply conservative group not represented among the delegates but also choosing the U.S. was elder Jakob A. Wiebe and his fellow KMBs who created the village of Gnadenau in Marion County, Kansas.[86] Enough thoroughly traditionalist leaders and people chose the U.S. to raise serious questions for the thesis of conservatives-to-Canada, progressives-to-the-U.S.

* * *

The Russian experience before the 1870s was unique for Mennonites. In the czars' empire separatism came to mean living in tightly bound communities quite largely under Mennonite political, economic, and cultural control. Perhaps even more than in most times and places the term *Mennonite* came to mean not just a religious group but also an intricate mixture of faith, ethnicity, and culture.

Russia's Mennonites gained much experience in operating local government and institutions. Yet they did not live as citizens integrated into a modern nation. Instead they stayed attached in a semifeudal way to their patrons, the czars, and resisted when modernizing reformers tried to meld them into a Russian nation. Moreover, within their own colonies Mennonites' church-state relations were most odd. Having accepted responsibility for local government they developed small-scale versions of the very kind of church-state union which their Anabaptist ancestors had rejected. Therefore, although quite separated from the world as colonies and ethnic communities, they were not separated from the world as the classic Anabaptist-Mennonite doctrine of two realms would have it.[87] So it is scarcely a wonder that when the question of moving to North America arose in the 1870s, Russia's Mennonites were confused and divided over whether keeping the faith meant to stay or to go. It is hardly strange that they disagreed about what was compromise and what was merely accommodation to change.

Yet in the 1870s and 1880s about one-third of Russia's Mennonites moved to North America. Many hoped that in America they might reproduce their exclusively Mennonite settlements. Some 10,000 of the 18,000 settled in the United States. In the long run the U.S. offered ample economic opportunity and religious and other freedom. But it did not allow the immigrants to reproduce the closed ethnic-and-faith communities they had known in the Russian empire.

CHAPTER 10

FROM RUSSIA TO AMERICA

> The issue is not whether Mennonites have a good or a bad religion; it is that "successful republicanism" requires "a homogeneous unity of the whole body of citizens."
>
> "If there is any portion of the world that can send us a few advocates of peace, in God's name bid them welcome."
>
> —Senators George F. Edmunds of Vermont and Thomas W. Tipton of Nebraska, debating a "Mennonite bill" in the U.S. Senate, 1874.[1]

Before the Prussian Wilhelm Ewert and the eleven delegates from the Russian empire left North America, they inspected lands in Dakota Territory, Minnesota, Nebraska, Kansas, and Texas.[2] In Dakota, Ewert, Sudermann, Buller, and Schrag tried to arrange for a compact settlement some fifty miles west of Fargo, but failed. In Nebraska, both railroad and state officials helped the Mennonites tour land. The delegates found some of it to be quite good, but foresaw a problem: a need for very deep and expensive wells.[3]

Sudermann, Schrag, Ewert, and Buller (plus Shantz) went on to Summerfield, Illinois. There especially, railroad officials and a variety of other agents and promoters descended upon them. Much of the activity was in the house of Christian and Susannah Krehbiel. The husband apparently enjoyed the coming and going; but Susannah Krehbiel later wrote pointedly of having to care for house and babies amid all the commotion of Mennonites and agents negotiating around her table.[4]

Meanwhile the Hutterite Tschetters and Unruh headed east. There, through the influence of the Northern Pacific Railroad, they won an audience with U.S. President Ulysses S. Grant. The question of what to offer the Mennonites was after all a question of nation-building.

THE MENNONITE QUESTION IN POLITICS

The two Tschetters and Unruh met Grant at his summer home near New York City. In substance the president did little more than assure them that the U.S. constitution guaranteed freedom of conscience. The delegates found him "friendly" and "plain" but did not seem greatly awed by his power. Their attitude seems to have been much like John M. Brenneman's concerning Lincoln: "the President" is "but a poor dying mortal like ourselves. . . ." In his diary Paul Tschetter gave the visit with Grant only about as much space as he gave to a dispute with some Moravians who argued for letting women preach.[5]

More intrigued was young Peter Jansen. The Jansens were living temporarily near the Shantzes in Ontario and working for the cause of Mennonite immigration. Early in November, helped by an influential Quaker, Cornelius and Peter Jansen also visited Grant. Peter, accustomed to Russian officials in grand uniforms amid bevies of guards, later remembered that the president's only protector was "a single colored man" without even a sword. The president himself had a "rather worn Prince Albert coat" and remarked that in his youth he had milked twenty cows each morning and evening. To the delight of the twenty-one-year-old Peter he let the Jansens stay during a visit of six Indians escorted by General George A. Custer. Custer visited with the Jansens in German, then took the Indians and Peter to a theater.[6]

Before going to Grant the two Tschetters and Unruh prepared a petition. Already the idea of Russian-style closed communities and cultural islands was eroding. An early draft written by Paul Tschetter in effect asked for the whole Russian *Privilegium*: tracts for solid communities; Mennonite local governments and German schools; freedom from oath-taking, jury duty, office-holding, and compulsory voting; and of course military exemption. The final version kept most of those requests, including the one about schools. But, perhaps on the political advice of a Northern Railroad official, in the end the petitioners did not ask for separated communities with governments of their own. And they stated explicitly that Mennonites intended to be naturalized and become citizens. The suggestion was that they were ready to be part of the nation.[7]

In response, ignoring the precedent of national drafts during the civil war, Grant's Secretary of State Hamilton Fish informed the Northern Pacific Railroad that military duty and commutation as well as schools were matters for *states* to decide. Inconsistently, however, he argued further that if war should come the U.S. Congress could hardly exempt "any particular class of citizens on account of their religious creed or scruples."[8] On the other hand Grant's Interior Secretary, Columbus Delano, suggested in a public report that the government should temporarily hold back some of the alternate sections among railroad land until Mennonites could buy.[9] His wording could have opened the door to others than Mennonites. Perhaps he was in concert with certain speculators; and perhaps Fish was unfriendly because he suspected as much.[10] Whatever lay behind the scenes, in December Grant himself advised Congress that "a large colony" of a "superior class" of Russian citizens wished to immigrate and "would without doubt be of substantial benefit" to the U.S. He recommended that Congress consider setting aside the land.[11]

Meanwhile two prominent American Mennonites petitioned Congress itself. In the fall of 1873 the Mennonites of America had begun setting up committees to aid the immigrants. Most important were a "Mennonite Board of Guardians" centered in Indiana and Illinois and a "Mennonite Executive Aid Committee of Pennsylvania." Late in 1873 John F. Funk of the Guardians board and Amos Herr of the Pennsylvania committee appealed to Congress. Among other points they emphasized Canada's attractive offer. If the immigrants negotiated for railroad land, they asked, might not the government reserve them some of its intervening sections until perhaps 1881? They pointed out that the Russian Mennonite way was to have fifteen or twenty families settle compactly, on one large tract.[12]

In late 1873 and early 1874 Congress took up a bill that embodied the suggestions of Delano, Funk, and Herr. Of course one issue was military exemption; but oddly, the debates scarcely brought that issue to focus. Perhaps as a matter of strategy Funk and Herr had not even mentioned Mennonites' pacifism. At one point a Connecticut senator clearly objected to any settlements of people "exempted from the defense of our common country." His remark invoked a response from Thomas W. Tipton, senator from Nebraska, a state trying hard to attract Mennonites. Did America not have "enough of the fighting element" already? Tipton retorted. "If there is any portion of the world that can send us a few advocates of peace, in God's name" let them come![13]

Nonetheless, Tipton rather confused the issue by implying that although they might not fight, Mennonites would contribute during wartime. Yes, exulted Senator Simon Cameron, a Pennsylvania sponsor of the bill, in the civil war his state's Mennonites had done their duty. They had been thoroughly loyal, paid their taxes, spent up to $1000 per man for substitutes, and served in hospitals.

Indeed, said Cameron, many Mennonite sons had taken up arms. Other remarks on the Senate floor blurred the issues even more.[14] Politicians were again interpreting Mennonites as offering equivalency rather than clear-cut pacifism. In the end perhaps few senators understood how much Mennonites insisted on exemption.

Much clearer in the debate was the issue of letting the immigrants form compact settlements. After all, that question went to the very heart of nationhood: could America be pluralistic, or must it meld all its people into one? Declared another New Englander, Vermont senator George F. Edmunds: it was well enough for the nation to have different political parties, sects, and "social grades"; but they must not be separated by territory. No, they must intermingle, so as to "learn to respect the opinions of others, and harmonize their own with them."[15] But a Minnesota senator named William Windom tried to diffuse the issue. Windom, a stockholder in the Northern Pacific Railroad, had a personal as well as his state's interest in attracting Mennonites. He claimed that the Mennonites did not intend to settle in large blocks. Nor were they all alike, for some were wool-growers and manufacturers, not farmers. But a Wisconsin senator, Matthew H. Carpenter, agreed with Edmunds. What would the nation do, he asked, if a hundred thousand Irish Catholics applied, then another hundred thousand German Protestants, then twenty thousand "French communists"? Would politicians decide whose beliefs were best?[16]

There were other issues: an allusion, for instance, to the impropriety of perhaps letting Mennonites have land in Minnesota which the government was holding in trust for the Sioux Indian tribe; and some debate about how the "Mennonite bill" might open a door to greedy speculators. In reply Windom, Cameron, and other promoters said again and again what desirable farmers Mennonites were. Declared Pennsylvania senator John Scott: "Mennonites, Tunkers, and 'Ahmische' " were among his state's best citizens; no "other class" surpassed them in "thrift, industry, economy, integrity, and good morals."[17]

The defenses failed. In April of 1874 the Senate rejected the bill.[18] In mid-1874 Mennonites began arriving from the Russian empire in large numbers; but they came without a national policy or *privilegium* to attract them.

ATTRACTIONS, TENSIONS, AND THE BEGINNING OF AID

In addition to developments in the Russian empire "pushing" them, there were forces "pulling" the Mennonites to the U.S. These were mainly three: fellow Mennonites happily settled; state governments; and not least, railroads eager to sell land.

Some of Bernard Warkentin's advice seemed to favor the U.S. over Canada. Before the twelve deputies arrived in 1873 he traveled extensively in both countries, even to Colorado, Wyoming, and Texas; and writing back to the Ukraine he made quite clear that he did not care for Manitoba's climate. In fairness to Canada he suggested British Columbia, and later denied a rumor circulating in the Ukraine to the effect that Canada was dominated by Catholics.[19] But Warkentin settled at Summerfield, Illinois, and clearly preferred the United States. Also, key Mennonite leaders in the U.S. wanted the immigrants to consider their country. In 1873 Christian Krehbiel had pointed out advantages of Kansas to delegate Buller. In 1872 and 1873 John F. Funk had traveled with Warkentin and then with the delegates to inspect land, especially in Minnesota and the Dakotas. In November of 1872 Funk had informed *Herald of Truth* readers that Canada would make Russia's Mennonites a "very liberal offer." Why, he asked, could the U.S. not also make "some arrangement of this kind"?[20]

Mennonites in Canada and the U.S. began to offer help. When he came to North America in 1873 the Swiss-Volhynian delegate Andreas Schrag had with him a written petition from his group's ministers and village heads saying that about half of the Swiss-Volhynians were poor. If the U.S. government did not offer enough, would America's Mennonites extend a loan? Whether or not in direct response, some Lancaster area Mennonites soon formed a local committee for "Russian Aid." In September, 1873, Funk published a similar plea from low-German-speaking Volhynians of whom Tobias Unruh was a leader. Readers began to offer plans for organizing aid, and in October Funk elaborated a plan of his own. He proposed that each Mennonite congregation in America should appoint a solicitor. And district conferences should appoint committees to coordinate the work.[21]

Funk further proposed a central committee to channel the money to its greatest need and keep careful records. In October the Indiana conference of "old" Mennonites, meeting at Yellow Creek, formed such a committee: Funk, a certain Isaac Kilmer, and Warkentin.[22] In November the Western conference of the GC Mennonites met at Summerfield, Illinois, and also created a committee: Christian Krehbiel, a Daniel Baer, and again, Warkentin. Soon Funk and Kilmer traveled to Summerfield and the two committees merged.[23]

Thus was born a new inter-Mennonite agency for mutual aid.

Krehbiel became president; David Goerz, secretary; Funk, treasurer; Warkentin, agent; and Kilmer and Baer, additional members. The agency took the name "Mennonite Board of Guardians."

In the spring of 1874 local committees in eastern Pennsylvania cooperated to form the "Mennonite Executive Aid Committee of Pennsylvania." As president they chose Herr, a minister and strong leader; for secretary, John Shenk; treasurers, Gabriel Baer and Herman Godshall; and correspondent and agent, Caspar Hett. Herr, Shenk, and Baer were from Lancaster County. Godshall was from Souder Station in the Franconia and East Pennsylvania conference region. Hett, from Philadelphia, was a deacon in an East Pennsylvania conference congregation; so that committee also was inter-Mennonite.[24]

The whole Russian Mennonite immigration of the 1870s took place in a climate in which Mennonites were not sure how far to trust each other. In the end the frictions were mainly surface ones and did not run as deep as did a genuine spirit of mutual aid. But there were obstacles to confidence, especially the old barrier at the Allegheny Mountains which made eastern and "western" Mennonites suspicious of each other. Funk assured Herr that the Guardians board wished to cooperate with the Pennsylvanians; but board members immediately feared that the Pennsylvania committee would add confusion and rivalry.[25]

On February 27 Warkentin and Jacob Shantz had signed a one-year accord with a steamship line, the "Inman," by which the line agreed to bring Mennonites from Hamburg to New York and send them west over the Erie Railroad. The price was to be $41-$42 per adult (half-fare or less for children), with the transportation companies providing amenities ranging from German-speaking ship stewards to ice water in railroad cars. In return the Guardians board was to "use their entire influence to have all of said Mennonites choose the said Inman Line and Erie Railway as their route."[26]

Inman required that to cover fares the board deposit money in New York. But Hett soon advised that Pennsylvanians did not want to send their money to New York. The Pennsylvania committee had arranged with a firm named Peter Wright and Son to bring Mennonites from Antwerp to Philadelphia. By working with the Wright firm, the Pennsylvania Railroad, and a steamship line named "Red Star," that committee had negotiated prices from Antwerp to points in the U.S. West. Their fares were some $5 or $6 per person below the Inman-Erie fares; and besides, the Red Star Line was owned largely by Quakers. Moreover, bringing the immigrants through

Philadelphia would make it easy to arrange temporary lodging in the large Mennonite communities nearby.[27]

In fact Warkentin as Guardians board agent had earlier negotiated with the Wright firm.[28] Why he and Shantz chose the Inman-Erie arrangement is not clear. Whatever the reasons, easterners were suspicious. Traveling in the East in the summer of 1874 on Guardians board business, David Goerz understood that Cornelius Jansen, whose favorite location was Nebraska, stood "in poor stead in the eyes of the Pennsylvanians." That, he said, was "because they do not understand his agitations." Goerz also understood that they considered Shantz "an agent of the Canadian government" and thought his word was not reliable. Whether the Pennsylvanians had any real basis for their suspicions also remains unclear. According to Goerz, the easterners suspected Warkentin as well. Until Goerz set them straight they feared the young man might be an agent for Kansas.[29]

Adding to the mistrust was the climate at "Castle Garden," port of entry for immigrants arriving at New York. Agents of all sorts swarmed around and elbowed their way forward to do business with the newcomers. One evening in August of 1874 Goerz was ending a hard day of meeting new arrivals for the Guardians board. He expected that the next day elder Buller and a large group of Alexanderwohlers would be in port. Other Mennonites also would be on hand to greet them: several Pennsylvanians, Carl J. van der Smissen of Wadsworth Institute in Ohio, and Cornelius Jansen. "Brother Buller will have to provide himself with some leather," Goerz wrote privately, "if he wants to defend himself somewhat against the many mosquitoes who will all, out of a sincere feeling of obligation, try to see him."[30]

The main villain in Guardians board eyes was not a Mennonite but an agent named Hiller. The man busied himself especially with meeting immigrants who arrived via the Hamburg-American Line quite independently of either the Guardians board or the Pennsylvania committee. His exact interest in Mennonites is obscure.

A year earlier a certain Hiller had courted the twelve-man deputation on behalf of the Northern Pacific Railroad, but there is some evidence of more than one Hiller.[31] Whoever he was, he met some Mennonites at Castle Garden and helped them head west. Warkentin complained that he shunned poor ones. There was also a scandal concerning a brother-in-law and helper of Hiller. According to reports the brother-in-law tried to keep a group from getting off a train in Nebraska by telling them that a cholera epidemic was raging. Supposedly as a result, several children died from living too long in packed and dirty railroad cars. There were other reports that a Hiller intended to sue some Mennonite leaders. Goerz considered the man to be full of "knavish wickedness."[32]

The Hiller case offers background on the choice many made for Kansas. Whether or not Mennonites were fair with Hiller, such bad relations were quite a contrast to very good ones they had with an agent of the Santa Fe Railroad with Kansas land to sell, Carl (C. B.) Schmidt. If the accused Hiller was indeed the Northern Pacific's agent, as he probably was, his task was to sell land in Minnesota and Nebraska. If so, his case explains even more strongly a gradual turn away from Minnesota and Dakota—especially by Buller and a very large group of Alexanderwohlers, who finally chose Kansas. As a delegate Buller had favored the North.[33] But when Buller and his followers arrived, just at the time of the scandal, they hardly seem to have considered Dakota or Minnesota at all. Moreover, most Mennonites who went to Dakota chose government or private land near Yankton rather than railroad land farther north.

One of the first sizable groups of any Russian Mennonites to settle in the U.S. did go to Yankton: some fifteen families from the Crimea who arrived in August of 1873, led by a Daniel Unruh. About the same time another thirteen families went to Mountain Lake, Minnesota. In May of 1874 Andreas Schrag and some ten families of Swiss-Volhynians also settled in the Yankton region, followed in August by some forty Hutterite families.[34] Yet by late summer of 1874 the main scene had shifted south to Kansas. One estimate says that of roughly 1,275 Russian Mennonite and Hutterite families who arrived in 1874, only about 200 settled in Dakota and 15 more in Minnesota (plus 230 in Manitoba). Some 150 stayed in eastern communities (perhaps to go west later) and 80 went to Nebraska. About 600, or nearly half, went to Kansas.[35] No doubt there were various reasons for the shift. For instance, Amos Herr claimed to know of a group who rejected Dakota because it offered no immigrant reception houses—the long, barrack-like temporary shelters railroads or other promoters provided in various places.[36]

Another magnet to Kansas was the key group at Summerfield, Illinois. More and more, the Summerfielders were enamored with that state. By late winter of 1875 a large part of their congregration, including Warkentin, resettled at Halstead. They had learned to trust the Atchison, Topeka, and Santa Fe Railroad ("the Santa Fe"). Mennonites dealt especially with two of its land agents, C. B. Schmidt and Albert (A. E.) Touzalin. During 1873 Touzalin cultivated Krehbiel, Warkentin, and others, offered very liberal terms, and managed to get several of the deputies to inspect Kansas land. Meanwhile he hired Schmidt, a German immigrant, to be his commissioner of immigration. Later, just when Mennonites were arriving in a rush in 1874, Touzalin would shift to the Burlington and Missouri River Railroad to sell its land in Nebraska. Thereafter dealing with the Santa Fe mainly meant dealing with Schmidt. In February and March of 1875 Schmidt visited Mennonite communities in Prussia and the czars' empire to attract more settlers.[37] Mennonites respected both men but especially Schmidt. He spoke German; and he walked deftly between the Mennonites' and his employer's interests.

The Mennonites could drive close bargains. Among the first to tour with Touzalin were two brothers from the Crimea, Peter and Jacob Funk. Christian Krehbiel accompanied them. In Marion County (Kansas) Krehbiel convinced Touzalin to sell the brothers land at $2.50 per acre, although he well knew it was worth the railroad's asking price of $4. His clinching argument was that the Santa Fe had better give the land to the Funks rather than let them and the Mennonites they would influence "go to Nebraska, Minnesota, or elsewhere." Mennonite leaders made the most of such logic. Railroad officials had to decide whether to hold out for highest land price or sell cheaply on the hope that the immigrants would soon build prosperous communities and make business for their trains. Touzalin's later shift to the Burlington road involved exactly that issue.[38]

The bargaining spilled over to questionable ethics. To be sure, in 1873 David Goerz seems quietly to have declined an offer from the Red Star line that he, the Guardians board secretary, also act as the line's agent "on a very liberal scale of commission." And elder Buller declined two sections of free land that the Santa Fe offered him as leader—although in the end he followed a fellow minister's suggestion that he accept and distribute the acreage to Alexanderwohlers' poor.[39]

But Christian Krehbiel was not so careful. He allowed the Santa Fe to sell him land near Halstead for exceptional terms and a very low price ($2.50/acre for good land near the railroad). Later, as Krehbiel was slow actually to move to Kansas, Schmidt reminded him that the transaction had been with "the clear understanding that a man of large influence was to make his home and attractive improvements upon it at once." Nor was David Goerz entirely sensitive. By January of 1875 he consented to edit an immigrant-oriented paper, *Zur Heimath*, which the Guardians board quietly let the Inman line subsidize. (The arrangement ended within a year and the paper shifted to support by subscription.) As for John F. Funk, despite the board's agreement with Inman, he instructed Goerz to tell Europeans of the low rates of the Red Star line.[40]

Courtesy of Mennonite Library and Archives at Bethel College

Caricature of Carl B. Schmidt.

Students of late-nineteenth-century America know that railroad companies were both cause and victims of some of the tawdriest wheeling and dealing in the nation's history. In that setting, on the whole the ethics of the Mennonites look quite honest. Yet mildly questionable deals were all too available, and Mennonites stepped into the ethical haze. That climate no doubt helped Mennonites mistrust each other.

The youthful Warkentin felt the mistrust often. Already before the main immigration was under way he considered resigning as Guardians board agent. He was struggling to build a mill and a house and get established at Halstead. Yet he continued, and worked very hard for the immigrants—traveling to New York, meeting arrivals in the Castle Garden melee, making all sorts of arrangements, and helping newcomers cope with uncertainties.[41] A huge uncertainty was where to look for land; and on that subject Warkentin's interest in Halstead aroused suspicion. But he claimed to be objective. In May of 1874 he remarked how "absolutely necessary" it was to have an "impartial" Mennonite present in New York "at all times." When Andreas Schrag and his group headed for Dakota Warkentin remarked that "I am and must be completely neutral."[42]

Neutral as Warkentin tried to be, in the long run the Guardians board people worked most easily with Schmidt and the Santa Fe who were selling land in Kansas. In March of 1875 Cornelius Jansen, by then a promoter of land in Nebraska, rather openly accused the board of pro-Kansas bias. Board officers and a few other people had just held a conference at Elkhart, Indiana. The conferees (who included Samuel F. Sprunger of the Swiss group at Berne, Indiana, and former Hutterite deputy Paul Tschetter) had decided to work in Kansas with the Santa Fe to settle poor immigrants of Tobias Unruh's group. Jansen had recently seen many more Mennonites go to Kansas than to Nebraska. Morever, he was under stress from a daughter's recent death and other tensions.[43]

Whatever lay behind his complaint, a meeting a few days later at Halstead directed a committee to send him a spirited reply, apparently penned by Wilhelm Ewert. Now living in Kansas, Ewert was the committee's chairman. Moreover, without mentioning Jansen's name he replied further in *Zur Heimath*.[44] His tone might have left some readers feeling, "Methinks thou dost protest too much."

Nevertheless, there seems to be no real evidence that the board or a "Kansas Local Relief Committee" formed by the Halstead gathering acted against the wishes or the interests of the people whom it was supposed to help. Any judgment to the contrary is only that: a judgment.

WHERE TO SETTLE: THE CASE OF THE ALEXANDERWOHLERS

No doubt the greatest strains of the immigration were the kind often lost to the records. Parents watched children die—aboard ships, in railroad cars, in immigrant houses, or wherever. The daughters of Cornelius and Helene von Riesen Jansen felt deep pain at leaving a pleasant existence in Berdyansk, living with strange Mennonites in Ontario, resettling at Mt. Pleasant, Iowa, and living quite apart from any Mennonite congregation.[45] Even families who moved in larger groups felt such pain. For women and no doubt for many men other than leaders the uncertainties and uprooting were often the biggest strains. Leaders faced the additional task of deciding where to settle.

Some opportunities were not in the West. For instance, in March of 1874 the Guardians board received an offer from a Boston philanthropist who had been resettling blacks in the South and now invited Mennonites to an area near Richmond, Virginia. The board apparently paid little attention to this and several other non-Western appeals. Yet not all the immigrants went directly to the prairies. Scholar C. Henry Smith has estimated that in 1874, the prime year of immigration, 150 families remained in the East or the old Midwest.[46]

Some stayed for several years. For instance, in 1877 a few who had stopped in Pennsylvania's Lancaster County but now wanted to move west requested the same favorable rail rates they would have enjoyed had they gone west when the arrived three years earlier. A scattering stayed permanently. In the twentieth century a preacher and a deacon in two of the oldest Amish Mennonite congregations in northern Indiana, Maple Grove and Clinton Frame, were brothers named Andrew and David Yontz (Jantz). In 1874 their parents, low-German-speaking members of Tobias Unruh's group, had brought them from Volhynia at ten and two years old.[47]

Yet for the vast majority the great decision was where to settle in the West. A prime example was that large group of Alexanderwohlers.

Some immigrants were choosing Kansas. On a Saturday in July 1874, an infant daughter of John and Salome Funk died. But the next morning at daybreak two KMB leaders, elder Wiebe and a preacher named Friedrich Sawatsky, knocked at the Funks' door. They and two dozen KMB families had immigrated. Knowing of John Funk and his community they had come by train to Elkhart. Could they have food and shelter? Despite his family's grief Funk went out into Sunday's dawn, opened the Mennonite meetinghouse, and got a grocer to deliver food. Eventually he found an empty house. The KMB party stayed almost a month while its leaders went west to scout land. Then they headed for Marion County, Kansas.[48]

Others, including some forty families of *Kleine Gemeinde* from the Alexanderwohl settlement in the Molotschna, chose Nebraska. A few weeks ahead of the KMBs those forty families arrived at Castle Garden and were met by Peter and Cornelius Jansen. From there they went to Clarence Center, New York, where they stayed for a time among Mennonites, and then they procceded to the Jansen's favorite state. There, in Jefferson and Gage counties, they and the Jansens soon bought land and helped found a large Mennonite community near the town of Beatrice and what later became a village named Jansen. At first the *Kleine Gemeinde* settled very much as in the Ukraine, with homes built along a straight road called "Russian Lane" and clustered to form villages with familiar names such as Rosenfeld, Heubeden, Neuanlag, and Blumenort.[49]

As for most Alexanderwohlers, very early, back in the Ukraine in the fall of 1872, David Goerz had understood that a majority preferred Canada—on grounds it offered better guarantee of military exemption. However in 1873, as their leader Jakob Buller finished his deputation trip, Warkentin understood the Alexanderwohl elder to be firmly in favor of Dakota. Buller had traveled in Texas and Kansas and considered the former too hot. He also seemed adamant against the latter even though Christian Krehbiel argued that Dakota would require more clothing, fuel, and fodder.[50]

Leonard Sudermann (1821-1900) and Marie Sudermann Sudermann.

Courtesy of Mennonite Library and Archives at Bethel College

Yet when they actually immigrated Buller and the Alexangerwohlers did choose Kansas.

By June of 1874 Alexanderwohlers informed the Mennonite committees in America that some 800-900 of them were about to come. They had collected an aid fund of some 12,000 rubles for their poor but still might need some help to get established. On August 27 and September 3 large numbers of Alexanderwohlers arrived at Castle Garden. Buller led one contingent and a teacher and preacher named Dietrich Gaeddert led another.[51] Gaeddert and those with him soon left for Topeka, Kansas, where they camped in an empty factory building as guests of the Santa Fe. En route, during a brief stop at Summerfield, Illinois, local Mennonites relieved the travelers' dreary diet with fruits and other fresh foods. Meanwhile the group with Buller, about 475 persons, headed for Elkhart, Indiana. Mennonites there were just bidding farewell to the KMBs' monthlong stay when a telegram announced that Buller and his people were coming.[52]

This time railroad agents helped the group move on immediately. The nearly 500 persons proceeded to Lincoln, Nebraska. There they accepted hospitality from the Burlington and Missouri River Railroad while a scouting party went looking at Nebraska land with Touzalin. But already they were thinking strongly of Kansas. One person later remembered that Buller's mind was already made up. In any case Alexanderwohl leaders asked the Santa Fe's Schmidt to be with them at Lincoln. To Touzalin's displeasure Schmidt was there.[53]

The barracks of the Burlington route were much too small, so Touzalin and his helpers also used the local fairground. Families bought stoves and began cooking and baking. Young men worked at temporary jobs such as helping butchers who were nearly swamped with the sudden demand for meat. On Sundays the immigrants gathered for worship, at least once in a circus tent. Meanwhile the scouting party went out to inspect land, accompanied by some young men to dig wells. In Franklin and Webster counties their digging did not succeed, so Touzalin took them back eastward to York and Hamilton counties[54]—a location where Mennonite Brethren and others would soon build a Mennonite community around the town of Henderson. From there the party returned to Lincoln.[55]

The fairground at Lincoln quickly became an ampitheater pitting Touzalin and the Burlington against Schmidt and the Santa Fe. But Heinrich (H. R.) Voth, a young man who eventually would be prominent as a GC missionary among American Indians, later remembered that the scouting committee entered the negotiations with a pro-Kansas bias.[56]

Why? A plausible reason is that unlike any other western states up to then, Kansas gave conscientious objectors full military exemption. Very likely Kansas legislators gave it less from principle than to attract Mennonites as settlers—or to please the Santa Fe Railroad. Ever since 1865 the militia law of Kansas had included a provision that each year a conscientious objector might declare himself to be such, pay $30 toward public education, and thereby be freed from duty. In March of 1874 the state's lawmakers had eliminated even the $30 fee.[57] Later through the efforts of Touzalin, Nebraska also exempted conscientious objectors. But it did not begin doing so until 1877.[58] That was three years after the Alexanderwohlers were in Lincoln; so for them, did the exemption law of Kansas make the difference?

Perhaps so, but not clearly. In the spring and summer of 1874 Santa Fe officials had indeed circulated news of the new Kansas law among Mennonites in the Russian empire. Yet *Kleine Gemeinde* and some other religious conservatives chose Nebraska over Kansas. Meanwhile KMB elder Jakob Wiebe scouted for land in Nebraska in 1874 but then chose Kansas. However in a later explanation of his choice, the elder did not mention the exemption law of Kansas but instead wrote of the problem of water and wells in Nebraska. An overall impression left by statements of the Alexanderwohlers or persons who observed them suggests that they too were looking first at land quality, wells, and such matters.[59]

Apparently the Mennonites who settled in the U.S. no longer put much faith in legal guarantees. They seem gradually to have accepted an idea found in letters circulating among Russia's Mennonites as early as 1872 and 1873:[60] that the U.S. nation's constitution, its general climate of religious freedom, and its tolerant record during the civil war offered assurance as good as any specific law. After all, a law could suddenly be repealed. Did not the Russian experience prove that?

Much more alive was the question of land. On the fairgrounds in Lincoln, with Peter Jansen as his interpreter, Touzalin gathered the land-scout committee and the people for final bargaining. His problem was that Schmidt placed himself where he could give the Alexanderwohls a signal that he would match a Touzalin offer.

Before the session ended Touzalin made offers which Warkentin, also present, considered "fantastic." The Burlington would: drill a well and install a windmill and pump on every quarter-section; give the Mennonites enough hay for one winter; build plank surfaces across sandy stretches of market roads; build an immigrant house for 150 to 200 families to occupy temporarily, and deed it to the settlers; furnish lumber in Nebraska at the cheaper Chicago price; sell the land, supposedly worth $3-$4, for $2-$2.50 and easy terms; sell even better land for the same price; and ship in the Mennonites' belongings and for a time such necessities as lumber, grain, and coal without charging freight. In the end Touzalin even said that if the entire group chose Nebraska the land would be free! Schmidt matched every offer except the last. Later he said he could have matched that one also but he guessed he did not need to. He guessed right: most Alexanderwohlers chose Kansas.[61]

Schmidt's victory was not absolute. Some Alexanderwohlers, poorer ones and perhaps others, did choose Nebraska,[62] probably thinking they could acquire more acres there. Thirty-four families bought Burlington land and settled in York and Hamilton counties. The railroad helped them and mutual-aid-minded American Mennonites in Iowa sent some tons of wheat, flour, and apples. Other Alexanderwohlers went to Minnesota, Dakota, or Manitoba.[63]

Still, Schmidt had won. The great majority went to Kansas. After the showdown Schmidt arranged for a train to come on the Burlington tracks and take them to Topeka. There they camped alongside the Gaeddert contingent and some fifty-three families of Swiss-Volhynians led by elder Jakob Stucky. Voth, the missionary, later remembered that in addition to the factory building there was a barrack house so long that he counted 129 family cookstoves visible in one straight line.[64]

Meanwhile the railroad quickly built four new immigrant houses at points in Marion, Harvey, McPherson, and Reno counties, in the state's eastern half where the Mennonites were buying land. Mennonites were mainly choosing land north and northwest of the still-raw town of Newton, which at that time was where the Santa Fe loaded cattle coming off the historic Chisholm trail. There they began to gather hay, dig wells, and build. True to Schmidt's word the railroad shipped in lumber, household goods, stock, horses, and implements, all freight-free.[65]

As spring neared the Alexanderwohlers began moving into their new homes. Mainly they formed two communities whose centers were about twenty miles apart: "Hoffnungsau" (Meadow of Hope), between present-day Buhler and Inman; and a larger settlement simply called "Neualexanderwohl" (New Alexanderwohl), farther east and northeast around present-day Goessel. Meanwhile the Volhynians with Stucky purchased Santa Fe land more or less between the two Alexanderwohl centers.[66] To the east and northeast in Marion County the KMBs established Gnadenau. And in the same county already during the summer of 1874 Wilhelm Ewert had begun to gather some Russians and fellow Prussians and form a congregation.

In 1876 other Prussians would take up land southeast of Newton near Whitewater, begin a congregation named "Emmaus," and call Leonard Sudermann to be their pastor. Other Prussian and Russian Mennonite neighbors settled nearby in scattered groups. In 1876 also, significant numbers of Mennonite Brethren (MBs) began to arrive. They went especially to Hillsboro and vicinity in Marion County, where a few of their number had already settled in 1874. By 1874-1876 a scattering of "old" or Amish Mennonite families from the East or the older Midwest were also establishing scattered farms and small congregations. Kansas was developing quite a Mennonite mosaic.[67]

Within that mosaic the KMBs and the New Alexanderwohlers almost defied the American pattern of individual farmsteads in favor of Russian-style Mennonite villages. At the outset the Gnadenau KMBs did so quite thoroughly. Their layout centered on a long, straight street which dissected three sections. At the middle of its three-mile stretch, houses lined the street to form a village. And at the center of the village were the church and the school. Soon helping to make the settlement remarkably self-sufficent were a store, a blacksmith shop, a mill, a shoemaker, a tailor, and a machinist. Fields lay in long, narrow strips back from the central street and other roads.[68] Such was the layout of the KMBs' Gnadenau.

The New Alexanderwohlers did not reproduce the traditional pattern so thoroughly, yet they too laid out long, narrow fields running back from section lines, and at certain points built houses together in straight rows. Except for Hoffnungsau, other Kansas communities scarcely reproduced the Russian pattern at all.[69]

Gnadenau and New Alexanderwohl rather soon abandoned their layouts. Within twenty-five years the Gnadenau congregation relocated its meetinghouse; apparently the central village was already breaking up in favor of separate, more American-style farms.[70] At New Alexanderwohl, for generations the people retained strong congregational life, Low-German or *Plautdietsch* ethnicity, and a strong sense of community. But gradually their landscape took on the American pattern of farmsteads scattered on quarter-section or other-sized parcels.[71]

The Alexanderwohlers were not entirely typical of Russian Mennonite immigrants. More than many others they moved almost as a whole congregation, were very numerous, and established an aid fund of their own. Yet their story had many typical elements: arrival through Castle Garden; some help from the aid committees; weakening of earlier interest in Canada despite its formal military exemption and free land; more and more interest in Kansas rather than states to the north; avid courting by railroads; settling near other Mennonite groups yet far enough away to make for a rich Mennonite mosaic; and, in the end, abandoning the Russian Mennonite village pattern.

WHY THE VILLAGE PATTERN FAILED

Probably nobody can give proof of why the Russian village pattern withered on U.S. soil. Perhaps one reason lay hidden within the immigrants themselves. In 1873 David Goerz suggested that Mennonites back in the Russian empire were losing their communal spirit of "one for all, & all for one" and living more and more according to the American phrase, "Help yourselves." He implied that such individualism was strongest in those who refused to emigrate;[72] but maybe quite a few who left also were tired of the closeness of village life. Yet surely some strong reasons lay also in America—especially: (1) the U.S. pattern of dividing Western lands into square sections and compact rectangles; and (2) relative safety as frontiers go, since marauders or resentful tribes were already removed or pacified at the times and places Mennonites settled. In the Ukraine, Mennonites had not established close villages only because of their peoplehood and communalism. They had huddled also for security.[73]

MUTUAL AID

Settlers may have lost the village pattern but like American Mennonites and Amish they retained another sort of communalism: mutual aid. They did not turn it into radical sharing, for they neither developed common ownership (which some Hutterites recovered in America) nor established thoroughgoing equality. In Kansas Alexanderwohlers and others put some of their poor on tracts of only 40 acres even though it took about 160 acres to make even a modest farm.[74] Moreover, immigrants and American Mennonite donors often preferred loans over outright gifts.

In the summer and fall of 1873, before the main aid committees were formed, people such as the early Lancaster committee and John M. Brenneman assumed the aid should be given as gifts. Since there were 40,000 to 60,000 Mennonites in America they thought raising enough gift money should be easy. But by October others, for instance a Jacob Leisy of Summerfield, Illinois, were suggesting that to raise money fast enough might require loans. Leisy suggested the loans be interest-free. John F. Funk proposed that congregations might choose: gifts or interest-free loans.[75]

Almost everyone discussing aid assumed that Mennonite aid would come communally from congregations and conferences, not individualistically from a few spectacular philanthropists. As time went on individuals did send money directly to the Guardians board. Yet congregations did likewise. On the receiving end also, aid committees thought in terms of congregation. For instance, they helped poor settlers at Canton, Kansas, to organize as a congregation which might then take responsibility for money extended to its members.[76] Aid to the immigrant Russians was the church working as church, not only as individuals.

As soon as the Guardians board took form early in 1874 it sent circulars to Mennonites in Europe saying that Mennonites in America were ready with three kinds of aid: gifts, loans, and help with travel arrangements. But in the case of passage money the board soon decided it could only lend, not give. Its reason seems to have been pressure for funds: more and larger requests for aid than anticipated, and demands from ship lines for deposits in advance.[77] The committees were accepting money as loans. Women helped: a quick sampling of persons on lists of the Pennsylvania committee suggests that perhaps one lender in nine was a woman. Some loans specified interest, some not.[78] In 1874 a standard pattern of the Pennsylvania committee was an interest-free note for five years. But in August of 1874 a committee in Canada set a standard of 6 percent and eight years for helping Manitoba settlers. And in March of

1875 a conference sponsored by the Guardians board set guidelines of 6 percent and seven years.[79]

The major committees tried to proceed in formal, business-like ways. If Funk had assumed working traditionally through deacons and conferences he had also written in a more modern vein, calling for careful records and accounting. For a time during peak immigration in 1874 and early 1875, committees had a hard time keeping records up-to-date and in order. Time and again in 1876 they tried to assure lenders that notes for loans were forthcoming.[80] Were such modern, systematic means scriptural? An aging Ontario Mennonite minister named David Sherk admitted that they did not seem to fit Jesus' teaching that in almsgiving the left hand should not know what the right was doing. But, Sherk said, where the need was so great, systematic methods seemed "absolutely necessary."[81] It was rare for Mennonites to admit so openly that they sometimes put practical considerations ahead of observing Scripture literally. But, like Sherk, the committees did not take Jesus' words literally either.

On the other hand, even in churchly terms there was a certain logic in loans rather than gifts. After all, most immigrants hoped to finance land and accumulate property. In 1875 the secretary of the Pennsylvania committee, John Shenk, began to ask whether some immigrants were not investing too much of their "ready means" in land. He thought that if they would buy less acreage and settle more compactly, well-to-do settlers could employ fellow immigrants who were poor.[82] The Pennsylvanians for whom Shenk spoke surely overlooked the fact that Russian Mennonites were divided into different, close-knit groups—and that the poor and the well-to-do might not necessarily be part of the same community. They also seem to have judged the western settlements by standards of the East, where rainfall was abundant, agriculture intensive, and trade and small industry woven with rural settlements. But surely they were correct in their central assumption: that meeting human need was one matter and helping newcomers become land-investors was another. The church was not necessarily obligated to give alms for people to accumulate property.

In the winter of 1874-1875 there was a notable shift: fewer calls for passage money, more calls for help in starting up farms. To quite an extent the shift took place with arrival of a group of "helpless Poles." The "helpless Poles" were a large contingent of Tobias Unruh's group of low-German-speaking Volhynians or Polish Russians. Some members of that group fared reasonably well; but the majority faced one trouble after another.[83] And especially one shipload, who arrived at Philadelphia on Christmas Day of 1874, put the aid committees to their greatest tests ever: tests of whether they could cooperate, of how best to use resources, and of whether and how to attach poor people to the land.

From the beginning, the low-German-speaking Volhynians felt beset and afraid. Late in 1873, from Europe, Unruh wrote to Funk with an extended image of his people being sufferers in Egypt. He thought that Mennonites in America had to become the Joshuas to lead them into a land of promise. Similarly, some of Unruh's fellow ministers offered a strange mixture of classic Mennonite two-realm outlook and the idea of America as God's instrument. The children of light, they said, should have nothing to do with the children of darkness. If only the people might be led to "virgin America" they might find a "land of peace" and "shelter under the eagle's wings." There they might keep God's "celebration days and sabbaths and precepts throughout the land without fear."[84]

Such imagery obviously helped unfortunate people at the deepest levels of their existence; but it did not help much with their practical affairs. After Unruh returned and reported from America, emigration fever ran high. But his people had no end of troubles—from having to sell property at extreme sacrifice, to American Mennonites' insisting at first that European Mennonites provide some of the aid the group needed, to many delays and great expense getting passports. In the end the Pennsylvania committee provided help even for travel in Europe and the majority of Unruh's people used the Pennsylvania plan of traveling via Antwerp and Philadelphia.[85] They should have left in time to find quarters in America before the dead of winter. But because of the delays most did not leave Antwerp until late November. Then one ship with 375 of them, the *Abbotsford*, previously a Red Star Line vessel and still booking passages through the Wright firm, had a string of problems. It collided with another vessel in the Antwerp harbor, stopped in London for repairs, left harbor quickly because smallpox broke out aboard, broke down at mid-sea, collided with a relief vessel trying to transfer passengers, and had to be towed back to London. In America, however, the ones who suffered worst were not the passengers of the *Abbotsford*. They were another large contingent, some five hundred persons in ninety families, who arrived at Philadelphia on Christmas Day.[86]

The ninety families suffered because they headed for Kansas in the dead of winter without making clear arrangements for their arrival. At Hutchinson after nightfall on December 31 a Santa Fe train left them off. Before morning the temperature dropped to twelve degrees below zero (Fahrenheit). Warkentin, as Guardians board agent, had gone to St. Louis to meet them but was at his wits' end. "I don't know what to do," the usually resourceful young man pleaded with fellow board members. Schmidt and other Santa Fe officials had refused to house the refugees in Topeka, where Warkentin thought food might be cheaper and some winter work available. The railroad men argued that Hutchinson, though smaller, had empty buildings and people willing to help. But town leaders at Hutchinson wanted the railroad to take the group back to Topeka; so at first they refused to open the buildings.[87]

Warkentin and others managed to put the refugees into those Hutchinson buildings temporarily. They also obtained three tons of flour, installed sixteen or seventeen ovens, and butchered an ox to relieve a diet for five days on the train of only bread. A few days later, hoping to check an outbreak of diarrhea, a railroad official managed to disperse the group to other buildings in Newton and Florence. Nevertheless, through the early weeks and months of 1875 Warkentin and the Guardians board felt taxed to their limits. When word of the refugees' plight reached other communities money flowed in, especially from fellow Mennonites but also from others—even from England, whence a Quaker friend of Cornelius Jansen sent a substantial check. But five hundred people consumed coal, flour, and potatoes by tons, and pork and beans by the hundreds of pounds. Especially at first, Warkentin found himself having to spend money faster than the committees sent it. He was irked especially at the Pennsylvanians.[88]

The "helpless Poles" offered the toughest test ever of whether Mennonites in East and West would cooperate. They had been doing so—more or less.[89] Early in 1874, traveling in the East, Warkentin wrote privately that he, Peter Jansen, and Jacob Shantz were having "rather strange experiences" among Pennsylvania Mennonites. He decided that "the unification of the American Mennonites, which we hope for so much, is still in the far-distant future." After the Pennsylvanians established their own committee, Funk, as Guardians board treasurer, wrote publicly that to have two committees was not ideal. Yet he said the two were in "fullest harmony" and he wished the Pennsylvanians God's blessing. Four months later, in September of 1874, Funk wrote in his *Herald* of help being planned for Unruh's people. He reported that the Pennsylvanians were furnishing about half that aid, and the Guardians board would help with the rest.[90]

That is how the Guardians board and the Pennsylvania committee worked: rather separately, yet sharing the task. The

Christmas arrivals strained that pattern. The night they landed in Hutchinson, Warkentin was thoroughly disgusted that the Pennsylvanians had sent them west "without giving them a cent for the trip." After four begging telegrams and two letters to Pennsylvania in a week without so much as a reply, he was even more exasperated. Soon the Pennsylvanians did send at least $1500, but too late to meet the first crisis.[91]

It is not clear why the Christmas group headed for Kansas so soon. Others of their group from other ships stayed for shorter or longer times in Pennsylvania, Ohio, Indiana, and Illinois.[92] Santa Fe agent Schmidt claimed privately that the Pennsylvanians had promised to take responsibility for sending the ninety families on. However, Funk reported publicly that the Pennyslvanians had arranged to host the families in the East until spring but that the Volhynians themselves had wanted to go on.[93] The truth of the matter is lost. However, since American Mennonites were paying the fares it seems that somehow the Pennsylvanians could have stopped the group. Perhaps some coercion would have been kindness.

As spring came in 1875 the task shifted from quick relief to settling the poor on land. Again Easterners could have taken a larger part. When the Guardians board sponsored that conference in Indiana in March concerning the "helpless Poles" the Pennsylvanians gave assurance that they would support the meeting's decisions but they sent no delegate. Mainly, the conference decided that there should be a new committee in the West. Hence a second conference at Halstead, Kansas, later in March. That conference formed the "Kansas Local Relief Committee."[94]

By then Mennonites at Summerfield were offering to outfit a dozen of the poor families for a start on the land; and some Kansans soon offered the same. Meanwhile the Halstead conference endorsed a suggestion from Wilhelm Ewert to mix benevolence with profit. The main idea was for well-to-do Mennonites to buy undeveloped lands and settle the poor. Besides buying the land the investor would have to finance a simple house; pay the immigrant for building it; furnish oxen, wagon, implements, and seed; and spend approximately $3 per acre for breaking of the virgin sod. For the second year the immigrant would shift from being a hired man to being a renter. His rent would be either cash or a third of the crop. The immigrant would benefit, said Ewert, and as land values rose the philanthropist-investor would also profit.[95]

Ewert and the conferees assumed that the arrangement would appeal to "brethren in the East." But Pennsylvanians scarcely responded. Instead, in the May issue of Funk's *Herald* secretary Shenk published his piece which argued that settlers should not try to get too much land but instead settle more compactly. Requests to the Pennsylvanians for loans already totalled more than $160,000, Shenk argued, a sum far larger than the committee could raise. Besides, more immigrants would be coming. And donors had given their money for travel fares, not for land. To be sure there were Mennonites in the East with money to lend; but their own congregations also had poor people who needed help.[96]

Other commentators thought the poor should scatter much more as laborers throughout established Mennonite communities. The idea was logical but it overlooked immigrants' desire to stay together and reestablish their communities. Moreover, Bernard Warkentin once complained that some Mennonites in the East wanted to keep healthy, able-bodied immigrants while letting the old and weak go West. Apparently other Mennonites invoked the American myth of self-help. A reply came from David Holdeman, minister-uncle of reformer John Holdeman and a man active in assisting the "helpless Poles.' " Holdeman lamented that some people said that after all, previous immigrants had begun with only their two hands and had thrived, so why help these people? Holdeman replied that yes, no nation was kinder than the U.S. toward immigrants. But generosity on Mennonites' part could show the nation their appreciation. Besides, how could a family with five or ten cows object to helping fellow Mennonites who shared one cow between two families?[97]

Few investors responded to Ewert's plan; so the Guardians board and the Kansas committee let the Santa Fe Railroad carry the debt. At Great Bend and nearby Pawnee Rock some poor Mennonites (not all from the Christmas group) settled on government land; but the main effort of the committees was to settle nearly a hundred families near Canton, on railroad land. The prices and terms the railroad offered seem quite generous, although to be sure the land was not the best and it lay rather far back from the tracks.

Once more the railroad shipped in lumber, implements, and other necessities freight-free.[98] With the railroad financing the land the committees were able to spend for other purposes. They gave relief to widows, aged, and others who were especially helpless; and for the able-bodied they financed oxen, implements, seed, cows, etc. They also helped pay for crude houses. At first they wanted the settlers to build with sod, but soon they saw that sod houses took too much labor just when settlers needed to be breaking the soil for spring planting. So the Kansas committee (with others' backing) financed 18′ × 20′ wood shelters requiring about $40 each. Meanwhile, of course, the immigrants worked hard, not only on their farms but sometimes as wage-workers near home or more distantly.[99]

In May of 1876 the Kansas committee disbanded. By then it and the Guardians board and other contributors had helped the Canton congregation with $9000 worth of gifts and more than $2500 in loans. Gradually the Guardians board and the local treasurer, Christian Hirschler, induced borrowers to sign notes for lenders.[100]

COLLECTING—OR NOT COLLECTING—ON THE LOANS

A mutual aid problem perhaps second only to that of the "helpless Poles" came later, in the 1880s: collecting on the notes of borrowers (not only Volhynians) as they came due. By late 1876 the work of the Guardians board was slacking off. Seeing what burden the notes made for borrowers, the board used gift money to pay 25 percent of each note's face value. So it relieved settlers of that much debt. Further, it put aside some money to pay lenders later in cases where deaths or other circumstances prevented some borrowers from meeting obligations.[101] Thus it protected lenders perhaps at the cost of not giving maximum help to the poor. That policy fit the generally conservative character of the aid. On the other hand the decision probably relieved the board from a temptation to coerce people who were slow to repay. In any case, often, collecting was not easy.

In the 1870s to 1890s crop prices were depressed and times were hard for U.S. farmers, especially for debtors in the wheat and cotton belts. In general Mennonites were not the poorest of western plains farmers.[102] But many who had borrowed through the aid committees found their five- or seven-year notes coming due just as land payments were high and crop prices low. Deaths, moves, and other disruptions made further problems. And a fire at Halstead, Kansas, destroyed many records which David Goerz had kept as Guardians board secretary.[103]

Most debtors may have paid quietly and smoothly; but after 1881 as notes came due board treasurer Funk received a rash of inquiries from frustrated lenders.[104] The Pennsylvania committee faced similar problems and decided simply to calculate what percentage of the total amount loaned it had collected, then pay each lender that percentage. As late as 1887 the percentage was only forty-four. "This business has been hanging over 12 years," wrote Shenk to the lenders, "and I have been writing . . . [to borrowers] till my hand trembles." He was "sick and tired of it." In 1915, when the notes were forty years old but farming more prosperous, some people at Canton, Kansas, were still in touch with families in eastern Pennsylvania regarding unpaid balances on their parents' notes.[105]

If American Mennonites in the 1870s had given as freely as Brenneman and others thought they could, instead of seeking repayment, they might have caused less strain to themselves and to relations with the newcomers. As it was, the whole business hardly helped the cause of inter-Mennonite unity, the cause which Warkentin said in 1874 "we hope for so much."[106] Yet, imperfectly, the Mennonites had cooperated more than competed. They had acted together, as a church, to come to the aid of fellow Mennonites. Essentially the Board of Guardians finished its work by 1881. By then it had distributed nearly $40,500: some $23,600 for passages, $11,800 to help the poor Volhynians survive and settle, some $600 for Warkentin's and others' official travel, plus amounts, for instance, for food during train travel in North America. The Pennsylvania committee distributed even more—almost $44,000.[107]

In addition some immigrant groups, notably the Alexanderwohlers, aided their own poor. With a church to back them even the needy "helpless Poles" in Kansas were better off than, say, black ex-slaves who were having to resettle on the land without resources. Mennonites watched out for their individual interests. Yet their sense of peoplehood was strong and their mutual aid genuine.

HARDSHIP AND PROSPERITY

The uprooting and resettling involved much pain and hardship. No doubt some settlers suffered the more because they were left out of decision-making. When KMB elder Jakob Wiebe's people arrived in Kansas he took his family in a wagon to a spot in a field. "Why do you stop?" his wife asked. Because, he said, "We are going to live here." She began to weep.[108] Sometimes whole groups suffered, and not only those "helpless Poles."

Settlers in Dakota, even as far south as Yankton, were not prepared for the region's winters. In 1874-1875 both fuel and food ran short. Moreover, Shenk, Baer, and Godshall of the Pennsylvania committee, visiting to help, found at least two Mennonites, an old grandmother and a young woman, who had been badly burned in prairie fires. Such fires were a plague of the prairies perhaps second only to another: grasshoppers, which bred profusely in the first several years after the breaking of new sod. The locusts came suddenly in great hordes and in a few hours could totally destroy a year's crops. In one case in 1874-1875 they were a backhanded blessing to Mennonite settlers at Henderson, Nebraska. A grasshopper attack induced some non-Mennonite settlers to quit and sell or rent land to the Mennonites cheaply. Then in 1875 a cool spring kept locusts' eggs from hatching well. So the Mennonites enjoyed a good first crop after all. But often the story was opposite. Largely because of grasshoppers it took about three years both at Yankton in Dakota and at Mountain Lake in Minnesota for the first immigrants to harvest enough crops to begin to prosper.[109]

Such troubles were harsh reality, yet finally not the main story. Sooner or later, on the whole, Mennonites prospered. Some (Warkentin of course a prime example) prospered spectacularly. A few did so because they arrived with considerable wealth. On a visit to Mennonites in Prussia in 1875 the Santa Fe's Schmidt estimated that a Penner family near Danzig might come to America with as much as $200,000. The family did come, to Nebraska; and by the mid-1880s one son alone, Gerhard, Jr., a church elder, owned some 125 milk cows which he stabled in two large barns 120 feet long and 30 and 36 feet wide. To process their milk another son, Johannes, built a cheese factory and shipped cheese to markets from Chicago to Denver.[110]

Not every Mennonite venture succeeded. Mennonites brought with them a skill in building an ingenious stove. With a system of flues running through heavy masonry the device used quick-burning prairie grass as fuel but retained and radiated heat for hours. The stove attracted some interest[111] but soon yielded to an American economy which could deliver coal and factory-made iron heaters quite cheaply even to the frontier. Another, more faddish failure was growing silkworms. In the Ukraine Mennonites had experimented with the creatures; then they immigrated just as a flurry of interest swirled through the U.S. South and West. Settlers in Nebraska and Kansas planted mulberry trees to feed the worms. David Goerz, in the *Christlicher Bundesbote*, ran article after article on the silk prices and where to sell. But in the end the American experiments could not compete with worms in Japan. Mennonite cocoons disappeared even faster than Mennonite stoves.[112]

WHEAT

Wheat quickly became the Russian Mennonites' main staple: especially hard winter wheat, of the "Turkey Red" variety. Some folklore about Mennonites' introducing Turkey Red to America will not bear careful scrutiny. In 1941 a Kansas radio broadcast claimed that some Mennonite children had hand-selected seeds to bring from the Ukraine, and had brought exactly 259,862![113] In fact it is doubtful that Mennonites were the first to grow a hard winter variety in the U.S. A railroad historian in an account that may or may not be reliable has said that before Mennonites arrived some French people were growing such wheat in Marion County, Kansas, but having trouble milling it.[114] However, even if Mennonites did not introduce hard winter wheat they did a great deal to popularize its cultivation. Already in the Ukraine they had learned to grow and mill it. In America as early as 1877 Warkentin replaced stone grinders in his mill at Halstead with steel ones suitable for harder grain. In 1885-1886, now operating a larger mill at Newton, he imported several thousand bushels of seed from the Crimea and thereafter experimented with new strains. Mark A. Carleton, an official of the U.S. Department of Agriculture, visited him in 1896 and then visited the Ukraine. After his return he and Warkentin developed a number of hybrids, several of which became standard.[115]

Meanwhile more ordinary Mennonites were expanding production. "The native American stands on the corner and complains," wrote one Western editor, but "day after day, through all the fall and winter, the Mennonites . . . come in with wheat."[116] At least in Kansas, religious Mennonitism and Russian Mennonite ethnicity became thoroughly intertwined with the culture of wheat. They intermingled so much that a century later at the centennial of the Russian Mennonite arrival, a non-Kansan could hardly tell whether the festivities were about an act of faith, a unique ethnicity, or grain.[117]

Sooner or later most of the Russian Mennonite communities grew reasonably prosperous. Mennonites had arrived a half-dozen years earlier "with only a few hundred dollars each," rhapsodized a Newton, Kansas, editor in 1882; now they were "clearing $1,000 to $2,000 annually on wheat alone" and their average worth was "$8,000 to $10,000." No doubt the editor exaggerated, as local boosters do; moreover, he wrote before the worst of wheat-belt depression. But scholars who are more careful agree that gradually, whether in Kansas, Nebraska, Dakota, or Minnesota, Russian Mennonite communities prospered impressively.

Even historian James Juhnke, who uncovered considerable tax delinquency and debt problems among Mennonites in Kansas during the farm depression, concluded overall that the state's Mennonites thrived. He thought that (at least before the worst of the depression) "economic prosperity" was the Mennonite communities' "most impressive characteristic." And he believed that during the depression "an ethic of individual hard work" plus "a sense of mutual responsibility for the welfare of their families and congregation" helped the Mennonites cope better than their neighbors.[118]

VARIETIES OF MENNONITES

If the Russian settlers gave America's breadbasket new varieties of wheat, they also gave its religious and ethnic baskets new varieties of Mennonites.

Except for scattered families such as those Yontzes in northern Indiana, few Russian Mennonites joined the large "old" or Amish Mennonite conferences. One explanation is geography: the strong "old" and Amish conferences were not in regions where land was available. Another, obviously, is extensive cultural difference. Any Russians who stopped temporarily in established "old" and Amish Mennonite communities, as quite a few did, found Mennonites who must have struck them as strange indeed. American Mennonites lived interspersed among non-Mennonite neighbors. They spoke strange dialects, even if Germanic ones, or else English. Some members of the Pennsylvania committee were so poor at writing German that they corresponded in English even with Guardians board secretary Goerz. John F. Funk corresponded in German but already in the old country David Goerz, ever the schoolteacher, found the German in Funk's *Herold der Wahrheit* to be "faulty."[119]

Some warm personal friendships developed, for instance between Leonard Sudermann and John M. Brenneman's friend Peter Nissley in Pennsylvania. But contacts also produced contempt. Visiting in Indiana, Hutterite deputy Paul Tschetter was quite put off by Yellow Creek Mennonites' use of English, Mennonite women who smoked and chewed tobacco, and a "music box" (no doubt an organ) in Daniel Brenneman's home. From a liberal viewpoint Warkentin and Peter Jansen were critical of Mennonites in Pennsylvania. Also, in Iowa Peter and Cornelius Jansen found some Mennonites to be so dirty that Peter refused to eat their food. Contempt soon flowed the other way as well.[120]

Probably most "old" and Amish Mennonites who met any of the Russians did so under bad circumstances. Naturally the ones who stopped with them were often the poorest and least refined. After long weeks on trains and ships they were none too presentable. Susannah Krehbiel later remembered receiving a young man who was thoroughly dirty and loaded with vermin until her husband Christian made him bathe. She herself "cleaned his clothes with everything I could think of and cut his hair." Moreover, even more refined ones must have upset comfortable routines and caused domestic strains.[121]

The authors of a 1905 Mennonite church history, Amish Mennonite Jonas S. Hartzler and "old" Mennonite Daniel Kauffman, allowed that some Russian Mennonites possessed a "fervent piety and zeal" and were clean and honest. But the authors seemed to make those Russians the exceptions, for they suggested that the "manner of living" of many others invited "reproach." Such was the view a full generation after the Russians' coming.[122] It was a stereotyped view, of course; but stereotypes divide.

Also keeping the Russians apart from the "old" Mennonite and Amish churches were developments inside those fellowships at the time the immigrants came. Most American Mennonites and Amish were in no condition to reach out well to new kinds of people—even to new sorts of Mennonites. The Amish were in the final years of the *Dienerversammlungen* and the painful sorting of Old Order and Amish Mennonite. Among "old" Mennonites the Wisler schism was still fresh and the Daniel Brenneman schism was brewing. Leaders across North America feared that their fellowship might disintegrate.[123]

Since those disputes turned heavily on questions of discipline and practice, absorbing the newcomers could only mean more trouble. Getting involved in the quarrels between *Kirchliche* and MB would have devastated a church already dividing over revivalism. Believing in close fellowship, "old" Mennonites and Amish have faced a dilemma: cultivating internal relations often blocks relations with others. In the 1870s and 1880s they attended to their internal relationships at considerable expense to relations with the newcomers.

A few congregations of Russians, especially some led by elders Aaron Wall at Mountain Lake in Minnesota and Isaak Peters of near Henderson in Nebraska,[124] did form a group who fellowshiped closely enough with "old" Mennonites that Funk's *Herald* and the 1905 Hartzler-Kauffman history treated it almost as if it were a German-speaking conference of the "old" Mennonite church. But that tie would come undone in the twentieth century. In the end the conference became a small denomination, known since 1937 as the "Evangelical Mennonite Brethren," or EMBs.[125]

Some Russian immigrants joined another small American Mennonite group: the "Church of God in Christ, Mennonite" (often called "Holdemans" after founder John Holdeman). One strong link

Courtesy of Mennonite Library and Archives at Bethel College

Aaron Wall (1834-1905) and Aganetha Dick Wall.

was the contacts David Holdeman made and the considerable help he gave as he worked with the Kansas Local Relief Committee on behalf of the "helpless Poles" at Canton, Kansas. Tobias Unruh settled in Dakota and soon died; so the Canton group had no strong leader. Then in 1878 John Holdeman visited. By then his church in Ohio was foundering, but at Canton he baptized or rebaptized seventy persons. By 1883 the "Holdeman" congregation there numbered nearly 220 members, with four ministers. Meanwhile in 1879 John Holdeman also visited Manitoba, where he drew some *Kleine Gemeinde* and other Russians into his fellowship. (He had less success among *Kleine Gemeinde* at Jansen, Nebraska.) By the latter 1880s the Holdeman church had many more Russian members than American ones.[126]

So the Holdemans became a unique denomination: predominantly Russian Mennonite in ethnicity but committed to a revivalist-touched yet disciplined and separationist version of American Mennonitism.

GENERAL CONFERENCE MENNONITES' SUCCESS

The American Mennonites who had most success attracting Russian immigrants were those affiliated with the General Conference of Mennonites of North America—the "GCs." That, of course, was the body formed in 1860 at West Point, Iowa.[127] Before the Russians arrived it mainly drew together the "Oberholtzer" or "new" Mennonites in the East and relatively recent immigrants from Switzerland, the Palatinate, and Bavaria who were scattered mostly in New York, Ohio, Indiana, Iowa, and Illinois. The genius of the GC Mennonites lay with program- and institution-building; finding a Mennonite place within American denominationalism; and in general, accepting "progress" and modernity. With their modernizing tone one might have expected them to repel many Russian immigrants, for instance the large Alexanderwohl congregation and the Swiss-Volhynians. After all, a vast majority of the Russians were solid conservatives. They had emigrated to protect their faith, were trying to rebuild their congregations and communities, wanted to remain agrarian, held authority in deep respect, rejected social or political agitation, and maintained strong and paternal families.

By no means did the GCs win all the Russians. The puzzle is that they were able to win so many. They were, after all, a denomination whose history and ethnicity was mainly south German and Swiss. Answers to the puzzle are mainly three:

1. *Congregationalism*

"Old" Mennonites were quite synodical. They accorded bodies of their ministers, their district conferences, considerable authority. Amish conferences were less synodical and more like advisory councils; yet the Amish also aimed always for consensus, consistency, and similarity—no matter how difficult. Even if they had to allow some variations in practice the "old" and the Amish Mennonites had no theory for variety and pluralism.

The GCs succeeded by using their central structures mainly for program while leaving discipline and intensity of fellowship to congregations. So their structures allowed flexibility and variety. "Old" and Amish Mennonites had grasped one horn of a persistent Christian dilemma: the principle that God's people really should present the world with a clear, common, corporate voice and example. The GC Mennonites chose the other horn (the horn on which American denominationalism also hung): the principle of mutual acceptance, tolerance, cooperation, and more Christian freedom. Actually, like any group, the GCs also set limits on freedom and tolerance. For instance, they ruled in 1861 against membership in lodges. But their main strategy was to bring Mennonites together around a core of biblical and Mennonite belief. They emphasized the core, not clear boundaries.[128] That strategy allowed immigrant and American Mennonites to come together with considerable freedom for different traditions.

2. Well-established immigrants as GC leaders

Most notable were the Palatines and Bavarians at Summerfield in Illinois and Halstead in Kansas. But there were also some Krehbiels at Clarence Center, New York, and Cleveland; the budding Swiss-Mennonite GC leader Samuel (S. F.) Sprunger at Berne, Indiana; and others. Most were people who had come to America in the 1830s, 1840s, and 1850s. Although not highly educated, quite a few had good enough command of high German and of European culture to win the respect of the Russian Mennonites, even of an intellectual such as Goerz. By the 1870s they had lived long enough in America to interpret its ways. They had some people of affairs among them, people not held back by a theology of humility. So they were effective arrangers between the new culture and the old.

3. Support of church schools, missions, and other moderately progressive programs

Education was important not only to those Russians who went to Canada. Those who chose the U.S. were more content to work through public schools and teachers' associations instead of completely parochial systems; but they too cared deeply about education. As for missions, in the Russian empire even *Kirchliche* Mennonites had been supporting German or Dutch or English missionaries in far-off places, however aloof they stayed from non-Christian tribes closer home. In America, schools and missions became important forums where the newcomers began cooperating with GC American Mennonites or earlier immigrants, and with each other.[129]

At first schools were the more important. Although a GC-related "Western conference" existed before the immigrants arrived, in time the core of the GCs' Western District conference was a temporary "Kansas conference" which immigrants and the south Germans at Halstead formed. The Kansas conference began in late 1877 to establish and control a Mennonite *Fortbildungsschule*, or preparatory school, to train teachers. The *Fortbildungsschule* opened at Halstead in 1883. In 1886 Mennonite teachers in Kansas also formed a professional organization with a title meaning "German Teachers' Association."[130]

The next year education-minded leaders incorporated a college, Bethel. In a time of wheat-belt depression ten years passed before its doors opened, but in 1893 classes began. Not all congregations gave support; some immigrants thought a full-blown American-style college was too "worldly." At first about the only help

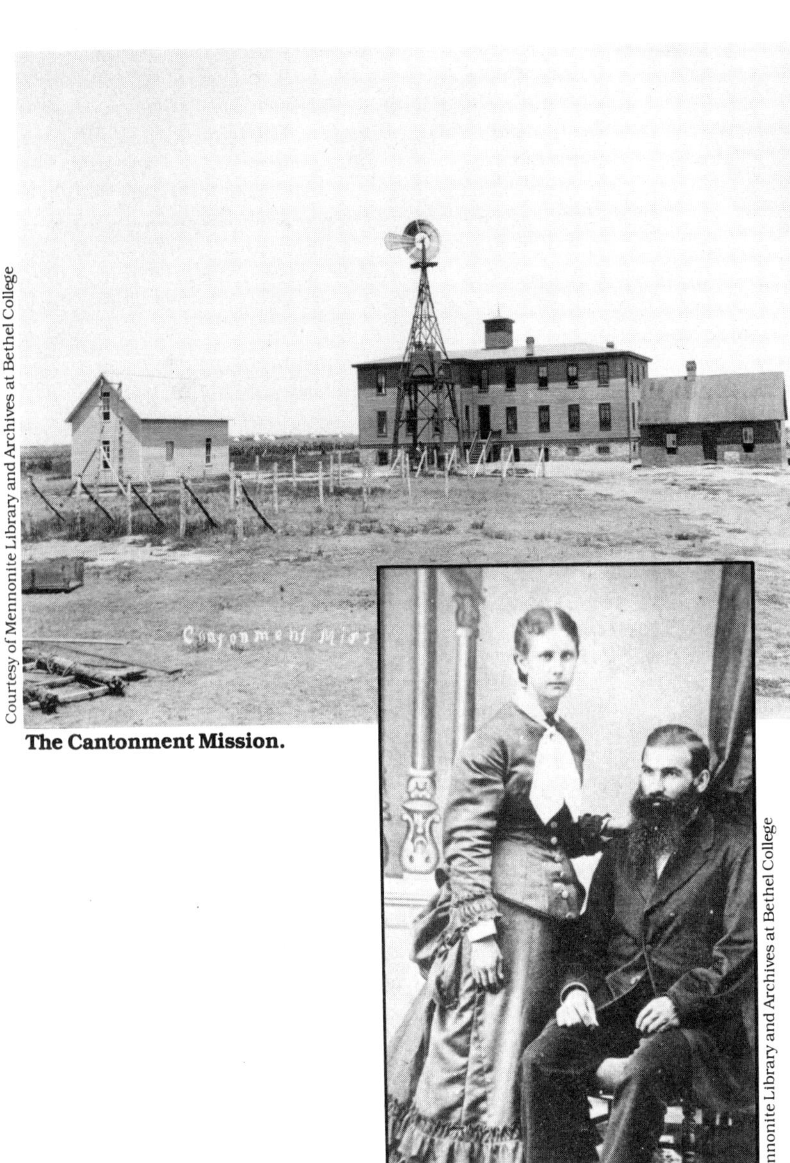

Courtesy of Mennonite Library and Archives at Bethel College

The Cantonment Mission.

Courtesy of Mennonite Library and Archives at Bethel College

Samuel S. Haury (1847-1929) and Susanna Hirschler Haury.

the Kansas conference gave was approval to form a separate corporation to govern the school. Also, as the college opened, the conference removed competition by closing the *Fortbildungsschule*. In 1895 the new institution began reporting to the conference and so became more officially a Mennonite college.[131]

Meanwhile the Kansas conference brought diverse immigrants and immigrant congregations (Palatine-and-Bavarian, Swiss-Volhynian, Prussian, Alexanderwohler, and other) together. Some of those congregations were already joining the central GC body; for instance, New Alexanderwohl did so already in 1876.[132] But education and the Kansas conference were important for tying the newer immigrants to those at Halstead and via them to the GC Mennonite branch.

Out of the Western conference, which actually had reached all the way east to the Niagara area, emerged "Western District," "Middle District," and "Northern District" conferences, all GC-related. The East Pennsylvania body begun around John Oberholtzer's reforms became the "Eastern District" conference. GC Mennonites remained rather divided between Americans in the East and immigrants in the West, as symbolized by two more or less official papers, the German-language *Christlicher Bundesbote* begun in 1882 and published in Kansas, and the English *The Mennonite* begun in 1885 and published in eastern Pennsylvania. Yet the English and the German wings worked together reasonably well. A major activity was to support itinerant ministers (*Reiseprediger*). Mainly, the *Reiseprediger* served scattered Mennonites, but they also began to scout for other mission fields.

From 1880-1881 onward the GC denomination's mission board supported Samuel S. and Susanna Hirschler Haury, Bavarians from Halstead, in opening mission work among the Cheyenne and Arapahoe tribes in Indian Territory, or Oklahoma. Soon the Haurys were assisted by many others including H. R. Voth, the young Alexanderwohler who later remembered those 129 stoves in a line, and Voth's wife, Barbara Baer, daughter of south German immigrants.[133]

The work with Native Americans was a story in itself: the first mission outreach clearly recognized as such among Mennonites in America. The Mennonites worked within an ideology held by benevolent-minded Americans who were sure that to save the Indians they had teach them Christianity and white culture hand-in-hand, make them American, and assimilate them.

The mission also worked closely with the U.S. government. In 1882, after a mission house burned at its first location, Darlington, it accepted $5000 of government funds to rebuild. In the same year, to open a new station, it accepted the buildings of a military stockade the U.S. Army was abandoning at a place called Cantonment. Moreover, in 1884 missionary Haury requested (and got) troops to come and help quell a fracas between Indians and white cowboys after the cowboys had killed a Cheyenne leader in a dispute about horses.[134] The close ties with government were odd for Mennonites with their history of pacifism and church-state separation.

A major activity of the missions was operating schools. To extricate some young Indians from tribal culture—or, as the Mennonites said, to remove them "from the influence of their former associates in the camps"—the Mennonites took them to the *Fortbildungsschule* at Halstead. Later, "with the consent of the government," they took them to a special school which Christian and Susannah Krehbiel, by then living near Halstead, opened on their farm.[135]

Unfortunately, in the first two decades the missionaries had many setbacks. Despite their schools and other efforts they seemed unable to win many Indians to ongoing Christian faith or to plant congregations. They did not even realize much of their optimistic, progressive hope of (in their view) civilizing and uplifting the native. Nevertheless, the work was a start—an attempt by Mennonites to proclaim the Christian gospel beyond their own families. In the twentieth century some congregations have emerged as fruits of the work.[136] And in 1899 the GCs opened a mission in India with generally more impressive results.[137]

A key side effect of mission work was to stimulate even further cooperation between American GCs and the various immigrants from Switzerland, south Germany, Prussia, and the Russian empire. Of all Mennonite branches, the GC was most successful in joining Russian Mennonites with American ones and with earlier immigrants.

THE MENNONITE BRETHREN

MB immigrants scarcely joined hands at all with any American Mennonites. No doubt the major reasons they did not were: (1) strong sectarianism and group feeling left over from recent MB origins and related tensions; (2) closely related, their using signs of inner experience and outward fervor strongly as tests of true faith; and (3) circumstances of their immigration. The second of those reasons came with a somewhat continental-Baptist flavor symbolized in baptism by immersion. Immersion served as a clear boundary marker between MBs and most other Mennonites.

The first reason, group feeling and unhealed wounds from their origins, set the MBs off especially from *Kirchliche* immigrants who became GC. An example was Heinrich Friesen, a Mennonite who had served Russia as a teamster in the Crimean War. In 1879 Friesen and his family emigrated to Kansas, where eventually he was a delegate to the GC Western District conference. He settled near MBs at Hillsboro and Goessel. Sometimes he attended a meeting, particularly a Sunday school convention, at an MB church. Yet he carried painful memories of his trip to America on a ship carrying mostly MBs. In old age Friesen claimed that the MBs had taken the most comfortable places, shoved others aside, and harassed him and his wife with false accusations against two feeble-minded brothers who traveled with the Friesens. Whether or not Friesen's descriptions were fair they expressed the ongoing hurt that existed between MBs and many who became GC.[138]

The second reason, emphasis on inner experience and outward fervor, might have opened the MBs to renewal-minded groups such as Daniel Brenneman's or Daniel Hoch's. But the MBs' Baptist flavor and their insistence on immersion surely did not help; and besides, those groups were scarcely formed when the MBs arrived. More important were the walls between MBs and the "old" and Amish Mennonites. The staid, humility-oriented theology of those groups helped build the walls. By the same token the MB ways of expressing faith and judging the faith of others, plus again their Baptist flavor, also made for estrangement.

As for circumstances of MB immigration, at the outset among the twelve delegates in 1873 there was no MB[139] to establish rapport with American Mennonite leaders. In 1874, when one of the first MB groups was about to leave the Russian empire, Funk asked Goerz whether those people really were Mennonites and whether the Guardians board should support them. Later Funk had close ties with one MB leader, John F. Harms. Harms worked for a time at Elkhart editing the *Mennonitische Rundschau*. Then in 1884 he moved to Kansas and soon became editor of the main MB paper, *Zionsbote*. But he really was not an MB member until after he moved west.[140] Moreover, the Funk-Harms connection was scarcely more than a business arrangement. It did not develop into grassroots ties among "old" Mennonite, Amish Mennonite, and MB churches.

Most MBs arrived a year or more behind the large immigration waves of 1874-1875 when the major committees had been most active. Although those committees probably aided some MBs they apparently did not aid many.[141] Probably the reason was not discrimi-

John F. Harms (1855-1945), Mennonite Brethren editor and church leader.

Next page:
Artist's rendition of one of the earliest Mennonite Brethren meetinghouses in Kansas. Montage of oil and petrified wood by S.L. Loewen.

Courtesy of Mennonite Library and Archives at Bethel College

nation; at least Christian Krehbiel and Bernard Warkentin said clearly to Guardians board colleagues that there should be no such prejudice.[142] More probably the reasons were the facts that: (1) most MBs arrived after the committees had worn down their enthusiasm and resources; and (2) they came in scattered groups, not well organized even among themselves.[143] Since they were poorly organized, they did not have the leadership or structure to be effective in seeking American Mennonites' help.

From 1874 to 1900 enough MBs settled in the U.S. to create about a dozen congregations in Kansas, Nebraska, the Dakotas, and Minnesota. In addition some migrated beyond the Rockies and in 1892 began a fledgling meeting at Dallas, Oregon. California congregations, including a huge one at Reedley in the San Joaquin Valley, came later, in the twentieth century. But in Oklahoma about a dozen MB congregations began by 1900, as immigrants moved onto lands formerly promised to Indians. Moreover, with their emphasis on renewal, warm and heart-felt piety, plus purity of life, the MBs continued to win some fellow Russians.[144]

As in Europe, MBs felt attracted to Baptists. For instance, until the 1890s, when it began to develop foreign missions of its own, the MBs' North American conference sent modest sums and a half-dozen members to work in Baptist foreign missions.[145] Relations with the Baptists were not always smooth. The first North American MB congregation, Ebenfeld, near Hillsboro, Kansas, suffered greatly from schism in the 1870s and 1880s, partly after a visiting Baptist

Photo by Orley Friesen.

evangelist won enough MBs away to begin a Baptist congregation in the town.[146]

In the early 1890s an MB pastor complained that in and around Hastings, Sutton, and Henderson, Nebraska, despite earlier good relations, the Baptists were now accepting excommunicated MBs and planting resentment against faithful ones. After lengthy discussion the MB conference still said its congregations should accept Baptists as MB members if they came with certificates of good standing in their former congregations. But it also said such people could be examined to find where they stood with regard to MB church standards, or the MB *Ordnung*.[147]

In the 1890s also, the MB conference grew increasingly determined to have its own foreign missions rather than furnish personnel and money for Baptist ones. Late in the decade it still sent four missionaries (two couples) to work under a Baptist board, in Cameroon in West Central Africa; but three of the four soon died and the other returned.[148] Meanwhile it had given support to Abraham and Maria Friesen, a couple from the Russian empire working in India under a Baptist board in America. But in 1898 it resolved that it no longer wished to support others' missions. Soon it began a process of transforming the Friesens' work (and that of two MB single women and a second couple sent out from North America) from a Baptist to an MB mission. In the 1890s the MBs also began a mission among Commanche Indians in Indian Territory, or Oklahoma, at a place called Post Oak.[149]

The MBs were gradually changing from being largely a "movement" to being a denomination. As a movement they arrived without a firm sense of history and traditions. As a movement they did not have clear boundaries against other experience-oriented, immersionist, voluntary church groups. Nor did they have a clear church order. If that created confusion, even more resulted from their rather disorganized arrival from different communities with different practices. But in 1878 and 1879 leaders met and founded a North American MB conference. Supporting itinerant ministers and mission was a major purpose, but another was order and discipline. Immediately the leaders and conferees discussed and passed resolutions on a great variety of topics—ranging from whether to let a member marry a non-member (no), to which holidays Christians should celebrate. The conference encouraged congregations to properly organize themselves, examined the duties and rights of its ministers and elders, and in other ways aimed for order and structure. Indeed, the conference record scarcely echoed the original MB exuberance, emphasis on experience, and resentment against established church authority.[150]

Through such change, and in its decisions about relations with Baptists, the MB conference gradually decided that their church should be less Baptist and more clearly Mennonite. In 1892 Abraham Shellenberg, elder at Buhler, Kansas, made an extended statement on the conference floor on the differences between MBs and Baptists. The main points he cited were standard Mennonite ones: foot washing, divorce, oath-taking, and nonresistance. A strong leader, Shellenberg obviously spoke for the conference as a whole. Indeed, regarding nonresistance, in 1890 the conference went even further than most Mennonites and advised against keeping guns even for hunting. And on the whole the conference proceeded with the classic Mennonite two-realm outlook. It also kept the Mennonite assumption that a great variety of questions were proper subjects for church decision and discipline, not only individual choice.[151] Through the years, late-nineteenth-century MB leaders in North America decided that their church was indeed to be Mennonite.

* * *

The approximately 10,000 Mennonite immigrants who arrived in the U.S. from the Russian empire or Prussia in the 1870s and 1880s varied considerably. Enough were deeply conservative to undermine easy generalizations that the conservatives went to Canada.

Mennonite Library and Archives at Bethel College

Pioneer life on the prairie.

The Russian and Prussian Mennonites who chose the U.S. entrusted themselves to that nation's democracy. Few of them were much concerned about nation-building. They were concerned to reestablish their families, their communities, and their churches. Probably some were even skeptical about government without a monarch (or at least without oversight from England).[152] Yet they entrusted much to U.S. democracy: their faith, their German ethnicity, and their forms of community. In turn they contributed to the nation by turning prairie sod into farms, developing hard winter wheat, and expanding food production for America and the world.

More subtly, they gave the nation exactly what their promoters promised: orderly, productive communities of politically loyal citizens. The Russian Mennonites brought a strong sense of obligation to government and society. Even if they saw themselves as living first of all in another realm and could not express that citizenship by taking up arms, they deeply respected government and the nation.[153]

First and last, the immigrants were people of faith. And sooner or later, virtually all Russian Mennonites found one niche or another in the U.S. denominational pattern. Most did so by joining the Mennonite branch already most comfortable with U.S. denominationalism: the GC. Quite a few others—MBs, KMBs, EMBs, even some GC congregations—joined American denominationalism more slowly by gradually identifying with those whom twentieth-century Americans call "evangelicals." A few, notably communal Hutterites and the Old Order-like Holdemans, never adopted the denominationalist outlook. But most Russian Mennonites did.

The Russians added much to American Mennonitism. They brought vision and experience and ability to create institutions such as schools, newspapers, missions, mutual aid institutions, and the like. They kept alive a knowledge of German and thus helped all of America's Mennonites stay in touch with their history. They added great strength to Mennonites' agrarian, conservative bent for private property and land. They reaffirmed the Mennonite class pattern: being property owners but wanting wealth more for immediate family well-being than to accumulate modern, abstract fortunes or to gain high-level power.

The Russians added a depth of pacifism, especially to the GC branch whose commitment to that ancient Mennonite doctrine was eroding.[154] Virtually all the Russians brought a strong German-Mennonite ethnicity. Sometimes that ethnicity may have been confused with faith, yet it also reinforced faith by enhancing rootedness, sense of peoplehood, and the Mennonite stubbornness against going to war. Most of all the Russians and Prussians added choice and variety to Mennonitism in America. In so doing they helped Mennonites live up to a central point of their beliefs: voluntarism.

If the U.S. nation has succeeded in drawing previously sectarian Mennonites into its denominational consensus it has also offered the Mennonites choices and opportunity to develop their faith. The Russian Mennonite experience in America is a case in point.

CHAPTER 11

THE QUICKENING AT CENTURY'S END

If the young people go to church at all, they go not to the Mennonite churches but to others " 'where not everything looks so dead.' "

"Much good is to be accomplished through various institutions, and why are we not at it?"
—Menno S. Steiner, 1890, 1891[1]

"Take this plain doctrine take Mennonite dress put it on a dozen of brethren and the same amount of sisters. Fill them with the Holy Ghost and a heart burning with holy fire for the salvation of souls giving them a fair education just enough so that they can preach, teach, and act intelligently, and send them out in the world to save sinners and I'll assure you that you will have the most powerful army of Christian soldiers to be found anywhere on the face of the earth. . . ."
—George L. Bender, 1894[2]

In the last quarter of the nineteenth century a throbbing new activism pulsed in "old" and Amish Mennonites. "The quiet in the land" became restive. The new mood in these two large branches of Mennonites in America changed them in various ways, some of which they saw and some not. It altered their relation to America's Protestants, to its Protestant-blessed denominationalism, to American society, and to past Mennonite tradition and religious understandings.[3]

About the time of the civil war "old" and Amish Mennonites began slowly to open their windows to new breezes. Early on, a window opened to Sunday schools. Apparently the first ongoing Sunday school among "old" and Amish Mennonites (after a few temporary starts) began in 1863 among Amish at West Liberty,

Ohio. But before that and for a generation thereafter, the Sunday-school minded also participated in "union" (interdenominational) schools or in those of other churches. As a youth John F. Funk attended and taught in a Baptist one.[4] Another window opened quite early to publishing and bookselling. Especially for twenty or twenty-five years after beginning his *Herald of Truth* and *Herold der Wahrheit* in 1864, Funk took articles wholesale from Protestant journals. He also advertised and marketed many Protestant books.

The "old" and Amish Mennonites opened their windows only cautiously and partially. Much like later pastors warning against television preachers, Funk warned in 1893 that too many Mennonites were reading "Talmage, and Moody and Spurgeon and other authors, and newspapers" without knowing the writings of their own church. In 1890 he began to publish Sunday school lesson commentaries so that his people would be less inclined to use interdenominational ones; many, for instance, were buying from David Cook, a freelancing publisher in Chicago.[5] By 1890 many Mennonites surely saw their Sunday schools as protection against others' doctrines rather than as a window to interdenominationalism.

But however cautiously, "old" and Amish Mennonites were breathing Protestant breezes. And given the connections between a generalized Protestant outlook and nineteenth-century civil religion, they breathed American culture as well. *By opening themselves to American Protestantism, Mennonites and Amish Mennonites found a religiously approved way to become more American.*

Revival meetings were another waft of new air, through a window partially opened. "Old" and Amish Mennonites remained cautious about revivalists' series or "protracted" meetings. Often the meetings seemed to bring confusion. In 1888 a minister in a lonely congregation at Bronson, Michigan, wanted an "old" Mennonite preacher to come and head off Dunkers who wished to hold such a series in the Mennonite meetinghouse. Daniel Brenneman had recently held meetings in the community for a month, and another preacher was scheduled to come. Having an "old" Mennonite preacher come would be a good excuse to tell the Dunkers "no."[6]

Meanwhile Funk's *Herald* suggested that camp meetings did more harm than good, because in their wake came sensuality, Sabbath violations, and other excesses. An 1885 *Herald* editorial said further that the methods of modern revivalists produced people who treated religion as "merchandise," picking it up and then lay-

Courtesy of the Archives of the Mennonite Church

The John S. Coffman family. Front row *(left to right)*: John S., Barbara, Elizabeth, Daniel. Back row: Anna Sowers *(hired girl)*, Samuel, Jacob, Fanny, William, Ansel.

ing it aside until the next revival. What Christians really needed was to be "constant, devoted, firm," and "steadfast," and to "adhere to the work, and run the Christian race without flagging."[7]

The *Herald* imagery of work and running bespoke the new activist mood. Funk was not rejecting revivals out of hand. Neither did his paper invoke humility theology against them in the way Christian Burkholder had done in 1804. Yet a part of Burkholder's message remained: the real test of conversion was long-term performance, not immediate experience.[8]

Some scholars have accepted a notion that Funk himself introduced revivalism to the "old" Mennonite church after being influenced in his Chicago years by the man who became the foremost late-nineteenth-century American revivalist, Dwight L. Moody. The evidence of such direct Moody influence is weak. The person who really brought revivalism into the "old" and Amish Mennonite churches was John S. Coffman.[9]

Coffman was born in 1848, son of the prominent bishop Samuel Coffman. He grew up in Virginia, where Mennonites had long used English and intermixed much with people of other denominations. There he gained what in that day passed for higher education in Mennonite circles: a term in a local normal school and a few years as a schoolteacher. The man was gifted: a singing school teacher, a clear thinker and writer, a pleasing speaker. While not ambitious in any grasping sense, Coffman was not, like John M. Brenneman, highly diffident.[10]

In 1879 Funk invited Coffman to move to Elkhart, Indiana, and join the *Herald*'s staff. He did so, and eventually became associate editor. Responding to Funk, Coffman wrote that he needed only a "comfortable living" and wanted to "be of the greatest service in promoting" the glory of God. But in good American fashion he wrote also of self-improvement. The Mennonite church, he said, needed preachers who "excite interest and command attention."[11]

Command attention Coffman did. Within a few years he was the "old" Mennonites' most widely traveled minister and a revivalist. Thoroughly loyal to the Mennonite church and faith, he preached a revivalistic call to conversion yet tried to fuse it with the doctrine and some of the spirit of an older Mennonitism. He was warmhearted and careful. In 1894 a prominent younger evangelist, Menno (M. S.) Steiner, was impatient because bishops in Pennsylvania's Lancaster County did not want youths attending Moody Bible Institute in Chicago and other advanced schools. Writing to Steiner, Coffman referred to the bishops as the "Lancaster Sanhedrin." Yet he quickly added that "those brethren are sincere, and we love them." Indeed, he said, the East's "fearful, conservative disposition" would probably help a new Mennonite school at Elkhart remain sane and healthy.[12]

Ultimately, Coffman helped bring profound change in Mennonite understandings, especially a tendency to divorce Mennonites' teachings about practical Christian living from the idea of salvation.[13] But he and his generation never quite understood that consequence. Coffman meant to undergird and strengthen the Mennonite faith, not change its essence. And for many persons he surely did undergird it—by deepening their Christian commitments, whatever the impact on their theology. His preaching and activism attracted many, many "old" and Amish Mennonite youths of the late-nineteenth and early-twentieth centuries to stay with their churches.

Holding their own youth was probably the activists' main concern. That was true even though they also spoke much, and obviously sincerely, about mission and outreach. The way to hold youth, they thought, was to create more program, more outlet for talent, and a faster tempo.

In 1885 (after preaching in southwestern Pennsylvania where throughout the century the scattered Mennonite and Amish con-

Menno S. Steiner.

gregations had lost many a person to other churches, Coffman lamented that hardly any mortal knew "what I have to feel and suffer." He was seeing "the church losing her young people" through "lack of continued effort." "What can be done to encourage our young people and keep their influence in the church?" the "old" Mennonite conference of southwestern Pennsylvania inquired seven years later. Its answer was activity: Bible classes, Young People's Meetings, and other programs. Ministers should be alert to keep the programs "consistent and evangelical." But youth needed "Gospel work *in* the church so that they may exercise their influence *for* the church."[14]

The gentle Coffman became a spiritual confidant, pastor, and adviser on Christian service to one young person after another whose lives he touched. They were a generation of youths who spoke and thought in English more than German; youths who were open to the optimistic, expansive spirit of an America in which travel had become easy and businesses were expanding. The brightest of these quite often attended normal school in places such as Millersville in Pennsylvania or Ada in Ohio. Many taught school for a time, thereby gaining additional skills in English and as leaders. Here and there one even went to a real college—for instance, M. S. Steiner. In 1889, after three years teaching school, Steiner moved from his home community in western Ohio to Elkhart, began working for Funk, and became one of a cluster of bright youths drawn to Funk and Coffman. In 1891 and 1892 he studied for a year at Oberlin College.[15]

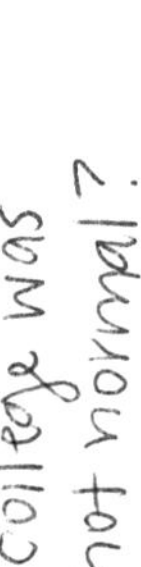

The activists spawned a burst of new programs. In 1882 the congregation at Elkhart began a "Mennonite Evangelizing Committee." At first the fledgling organization mainly sent ministers to scattered Mennonites in North America. By century's end it was evolving into what would soon be an official "old" Mennonite board of missions and charities operating in North America and abroad. For young people, "old" and Amish Mennonites (unlike many GCs) shied away from forming chapters of a popular, interdenominational youth organization called "Christian Endeavor." But some congregations began Young People's Bible Meetings after the Elkhart congregation initiated them in 1887.[16]

By 1894 women began organizing within congregations to support missions, often through sewing circles.[17] (Already in 1881 GC women, mainly at Halstead, Kansas, had begun a *Frauen-Nähvereins*, or Women's Sewing Circle, with Wilhelmina Eisenmayer Warkentin and Helene Riesen Goerz—wives of Bernard Warkentin and David Goerz—as president and secretary.) In 1889 Coffman, Steiner, and others created a Mennonite Book and Tract Society. Mennonite Bible conferences began about 1890 and, like larger Protestant ones whom they imitated, often had prophecy and the subject of premillennialism on their agendas.[18] By 1890 a joint Indiana-and-Virginia committee compiled an English-language songbook which Funk's firm published. The collection brought Mennonites faster tunes than heretofore, and lyrics somewhat more expressive of individual faith and pilgrimage as compared to corporate praise and worship.[19]

In 1894 some Mennonites at Elkhart opened a school for advanced education, called "Elkhart Institute." Within a decade the church would adopt it, move to nearby Goshen, and make it into the "old" Mennonites' first college—Goshen College. In 1896 Steiner and a group mainly of fellow Ohioans opened an orphanage near Orrville, Ohio, and soon began planning an old people's home which they opened in 1901. In 1898 the "old" and Amish Mennonites jointly began a biennial general conference. However, the most populous district conferences, Lancaster and Franconia in eastern Pennsylvania, refused to join.[20]

People who favored the new developments soon referred to the 1880s and 1890s as having brought a Mennonite "awakening" or even "Great Awakening"; and historians have perpetuated the name. However, those were partisan terms—labels which American revivalists had long used to put down their opponents' religion as being formal and dead or at least somnolent and inert. Historians now might do better to call the changes a "Mennonite quickening."[21] Without question there was an increase in tempo.

The events among "old" and Amish Mennonites near century's end were not the first Mennonite quickening. In their own ways the movements led by John H. Oberholtzer, Daniel Hoch, William Gehman, Ephraim Hunsberger, Henry Egly, Joseph Stuckey, Daniel Brenneman, the founders of the General Conference (GC) branch, and their various associates had also been attempts to quicken as well as to reform.

BASIC CHANGE 1: A MORE OUTWARD-LOOKING VISION

The quickening was the cause or expression of a number of profound changes in "old" and Amish Mennonite faith. However much reformers were concerned first for their own youth, a basic change was that "old" and Amish Mennonites began to look beyond themselves. As did the GC, MB, and some smaller Mennonite branches in the same decades, they began to open missions.

Earlier in the century a few "old" Mennonites had that larger vision, especially the more English-speaking and acculturated ones in Virginia. In 1837, adding a translator's statement at the end of Peter Burkholder's *Confession* book, song master Joseph Funk closed with a call to all denominations to forget minor differences and unite "to promote the redemption of Christ, by the spread of his glorious gospel, and the extension of his kingdom from shore to shore." About two decades later bishops Martin Burkholder (son of Peter) and Samuel Coffman (father of the future evangelist) began itinerant preaching among nearby mountain peoples. They met in groves, schoolhouses, or other places, mostly in what soon became West Virginia. By 1890 such preaching began to produce small Mennonite congregations, who sometimes ordained men not ethnically Mennonite to be their leaders.[22]

In 1865 John M. Brenneman confided to his friend Peter Nissley that while other denominations spent millions to preach to the world's heathen, he feared "that we mennonites are too slack in seeking souls." About the same time Brenneman and several others began challenging readers of Funk's *Herald* to consider mission. From near Lancaster, Pennsylvania, a Bavarian immigrant layman named Philip Mosemann suggested that Mennonites in America should send money to European Mennonites' missions. He added that he knew of some in America who already were giving for foreign work, even with their ministers' approval. For the next two-and-one-half decades not many "old" and Amish Mennonites acted on such advice; but some voices continued.[23]

Those voices made clear that the gospel preached in mission should be a pure and truly biblical one. Among other points the doctrines of peace and nonresistance had to be central. In 1865 Brenneman wrote of a Chinese emperor who had complained that " 'wherever the christians go, they make the ground white with the bones of men.' " Yes, Brenneman said, Mennonites should support missionaries but not those who taught that war was a Christian duty. Too few of "the great mass of mankind" knew "anything about the principles of nonresistance," the "old" Mennonite conference of Indiana agreed in 1868; "we should seek to spread the same abroad."[24]

In 1894 the Amish Mennonite leader D. J. Johns built a major mission sermon around the idea of God entrusting to Christians a "ministry of reconciliation." In the course of it he challenged his listeners to "make known everywhere this principle of nonresistance." God himself had demonstrated the principle when, to redeem the world, "He gave His only begotten Son."[25]

Such remarks seemed to suggest that "old" and Amish Mennonites thought their people should take into mission a unique style and message. But in the 1890s, as their missions actually began, the founders mainly imitated Protestant models. In the early 1890s some young Mennonites, especially some living temporarily in Chicago, caught a vision for that city. In 1892 and 1893 one of them gave two notable public messages setting the vision forth. He was Solomon (S. D.) Ebersole, a man from rural Illinois who was in Chicago to study medicine. The settings were what amounted to rallies for activist youths: "old" and Amish Mennonites' first two church-wide Sunday school conventions. One was in 1892 at John's congregation, Clinton Frame, near Goshen, Indiana, and the second occurred a year later at the Zion Mennonite congregation near Bluffton, Ohio. At points Ebersole spoke explicitly as a Mennonite, pointing for instance to the missionary zeal of early Anabaptists. But he admitted privately that he had been out of touch with Mennonite Sunday schools for some years. And he did not explore whether following Anabaptist principles might mean missions different from those of modern Protestants.[26]

Mainly, Ebersole spoke the Protestant missionary movement's language of individualism, missionary philanthropy, and mixing church and nation. His words were not noticeably attuned to the Anabaptists' idea of re-creating the church as God's new people. For instance, he presented Jesus and Paul as individual missionaries, not much as church founders.[27]

At points Ebersole mixed Christian mission with nationalism. A reason for mission, he suggested, was that "our cities rule the nation and as our cities are, so our government will be." Moreover, Chicago's immigrants were "not becoming naturalized, Americanized or Christianized." Using standard phrases of Christian uplift current in his day, Ebersole said further that before the mass of "poor and ignorant" and "unchristian human beings . . . can become true *disciples of God* they must be enlightened and trained, physically, mentally and morally." Missions, he said, were the only means. He proposed a medical department; relief; literature distribution; teaching of sewing, cooking, and other manual skills; presenting "the crucified Savior and speaking of his love and mercy"; and inviting people to Sunday school, preaching, Bible studies, and prayer meetings.[28]

Whatever the strengths and weaknesses in what Ebersole suggested, his proposals followed standard Protestant ideas and mission models. Late in 1893 he, Steiner, and others opened a station on the south edge of Chicago's downtown. It was the "Chicago Home Mission," first formal mission of the "old" and Amish Mennonites. Steiner, at twenty-seven, became its first superintendent. The backbone of its staff was several young women—Lina Zook from the Oak Grove Amish Mennonite congregation in Ohio and others. Women kept some activities going even during a troubled time in 1896 that caused the mission to close formally for some months. In the twentieth century the effort would develop fully into a going concern and would plant a functioning, if not always flourishing, congregation. Meanwhile its program was much as Ebersole had foreseen.[29]

No one should judge harshly the young founders of the Chicago mission for using the ideas and models most available. They were pioneers and experimenters. And they tried to take God's good news beyond Mennonite and Amish families, at a time when most people in their churches had little vision for doing so. Nevertheless, they had not yet found ways to build missions that would embody Mennonites' particular understandings of gospel and of how God wanted his people to live and work in the world.

Later in the 1890s young activists in the Lancaster "old" Mennonite conference in Pennsylvania began a mission that reflected prevailing Protestant and American attitudes differently. Even after Old Order Mennonites departed with Jonas Martin in 1893 the Lancaster "old" Mennonite conference remained very cautious toward activist programs and reforms. Nevertheless, by early 1895, with some careful political footwork so as not to overstep limits set by their bishops, a gathering of some 150 persons created a mission organization. Among a dozen of its main founders were, for instance, John (J. H.) Mellinger, 36, future secretary of a Lancaster conference mission board, and Jacob (J. A.) Ressler, 27, leader in

1899 of the first "old" Mennonite foreign missionary team. The founders named their organization the "Mennonite Sunday School Mission"—a shrewd choice, for after all, the conference had accepted Sunday schools.[30]

As the 1890s progressed, people connected with the organization operated a half-dozen Sunday schools in rural and city areas of their county, gave relief to poor people in a nearby mining community, brought "Fresh Air" children from New York City for stays in the countryside, and stimulated the creation of a women's sewing circle in the Mennonite congregation at the town of Paradise. In 1899 they would open a city mission in Philadelphia somewhat on the Chicago Home Mission model.[31]

Meanwhile in 1898 the activist Lancastrians began another work: an "industrial" mission to teach the work ethic and responsible citizenship in a Lancaster County neighborhood. The neighborhood was on what was called "Welsh Mountain," and its people were black.

Nineteenth-century Mennonite attitudes toward blacks

If measured against prevailing American standards—not against an ideal—nineteenth-century Mennonite and Amish attitudes toward blacks had not on the whole been very harsh. Some individuals were harsh. "Never Let the words black and White be seen in the Herald Eny more," wrote a Virginia minister named Jacob Hildebrand in 1873, objecting to something in Funk's paper. To keep subscribers, "if . . . you are in faver of Malgemation [amalgamation, meaning integration] that is Nigger Equality you had better ceep it to yourself." But such outbursts were few, at least on paper. Most Mennonites and Amish lived quite apart from blacks. They might have occasional contact with a black beggar or appreciate a black camp meeting preacher.[32] But mainly they lived as if blacks and their problems were irrelevant to their own lives.

The quickening brought some change. Its periodicals were capable of some awful slurs. In 1897, denouncing an excess of religious emotionalism, a Michigan layman named John O. Smith wrote that if shouting really was evidence of having gotten glory, "then our colored people have the most of it, and weak-minded women, too." Funk's *Herald* published those words.[33] More typically, however, the activists' writings alluded on occasion to blacks' plight in language common among benevolent and uplift-minded white Protestants and Quakers of the day.

An exchange in the *Herald* in 1889 pretty well summed up late-nineteenth-century Mennonites' public attitudes. Abram B.

Kolb, son-in-law of Funk and a member of his editorial staff, ran an article criticizing the South's lynching and other atrocities against Negroes. His choice aroused some Virginia Mennonites to protest that not all Southerners were alike and that whites had done much to educate and uplift blacks. With that reply, associate editor Coffman published a note conceding some of his fellow Virginians' points but reminding them that they could hardly speak for the deep South. Most of all, said Coffman, the *Herald* had wanted to say that before God Negroes and whites were alike.[34] Such, generally, was the racial outlook of articulate Mennonites in the quickening period: not hateful, but not looking at life through blacks' eyes, either. The tiff in the *Herald* was between whites—all of whom thought they were kindly and benevolent.

Perhaps race was less to the point than was Mennonites' ethnicity. In 1892 a deacon in Illinois, Abram Burkhart, urged *Herald* readers to support missions and spread a gospel without war and bloodshed. But then he added with obvious sarcasm: "We must . . . bear in mind that the Mennonite church has been strictly a white man's church. The idea of a negro or a chinaman being a Mennonite, such an innovation would certainly make trouble, we being so dignified (?)."[35]

If Lancaster Mennonites lived on one side of an ethnic barrier, the barrier was all the higher because of class. In general the Lancastrians were well established economically,[36] and not very ready to see life through the eyes of the black or the poor. So their strategy on Welsh Mountain was the philanthropic one of uplift. They started an "industrial" mission aimed at teaching cleanliness, work ethic, management, and social responsibility to a group who had a reputation, deserved or not, for begging, stealing, and dissolute living. Their means were many and various, from beginning a school to giving families pigs to raise to starting a shirt factory.

What of soul-saving and church-planting and accepting blacks as Christian brothers and sisters? Oddly, in light of Anabaptist and Mennonite concern for church, the Lancaster activists at first bypassed that question. "The Welsh Mountain Mission is an industrial rather than a religious institution," a mission report would say in 1906. Later, in 1917, another generation began baptizing blacks and accepting them as fellow Mennonites. But the founders at Welsh Mountain let an African Methodist and a black Presbyterian minister, especially the latter, do the work of trying to bring blacks into congregations.[37] It was as if they had taken Burkhart's remark about Negroes and Chinamen and Mennonites at face value. Thus they avoided the question of whether, locally and specifically, God's people should be a people of different races.

The Welsh Mountain mission was rural and close to home. Nevertheless, the Lancastrians operated from prevailing attitudes of benevolent-minded Protestants and other Americans, not particularly from insights of their own faith.

India: Separate missions, not inter-Mennonite

Meanwhile some Mennonites of the Lancaster area and elsewhere looked all the way to India. In 1898 Lizzie K. Brubaker of Lititz, Pennsylvania, wrote to Elkhart saying that activists in her vicinity had sent four offerings totaling more than $180 to one Alice Yoder. Yoder, a Mennonite (or former one) from the Lititz area, was in India under the Christian and Missionary Alliance.[38]

The fact was, by that time Mennonites across North America were looking for channels to help India missions. Capturing their attention in the 1890s was Indian—especially Indian orphans'—suffering in the wake of a severe famine. By about 1896 the famine had reached crisis proportions, and throughout North America many church people and others were publicizing and dramatizing the plight. Mennonites had already been working with Protestant organizations to aid suffering Armenians. Now they sent relief to India through an agency set up at Elkhart called the "Home and Foreign Relief Commission" (HFRC).[39]

For three or four years the HFRC was more or less inter-Mennonite, a fact which in turn raised hopes that Mennonite groups might cooperate to start a mission in India. For a time in 1897 it had as a transportation agent John A. Sprunger—a maverick and entrepreneurial GC Mennonite from Berne, Indiana, whose own free-lance projects (publishing, an orphanage, a deaconess home, and much more) were the epitome of quickening activism.[40]

As its agent to India the HFRC sent George Lambert, an erstwhile Mennonite Brethren in Christ (MBC) preacher who had just joined the "old" Mennonites. After traveling and viewing the India famine firsthand, Lambert published a sensational book about it which Funk's press and a GC-related firm at Berne, Welty and Sprunger, published in simultaneous editions. To complete the inter-Mennonite pattern, in 1898 the HFRC appointed David Goerz as vice-president and a Russian immigrant GC elder, Heinrich H. Regier of Mountain Lake, Minnesota, as a member. And from the grass roots, relief contributions came from a wide variety of Mennonites, ranging from Old Order Amish to Russian Alexanderwohlers.[41]

Such cooperation for relief raised hopes—especially among GC leaders, always unity-minded—that Mennonites might simply move from joint relief to a joint India mission. But the move was not to be. On August 10, 1898, there was a conference at Elkhart specifically to consider such a plan. But already in mid-June Funk's *Herald* served notice of the meeting's failure by in effect disavowing the idea. Also, Funk had privately informed the GC mission board secretary, Andrew B. Shelly (1834-1913), that the idea was not likely to succeed. Shelly was disappointed. And the gathering at Elkhart decided that "under existing circumstances" the "attempt to organize a united mission work" was premature. It was "not deemed advisable at this time."[42]

In truth not even all progressive or quickened Mennonites cared much for inter-Mennonite cooperation, certainly not in mission. In GC circles Shelly knew he had to proceed cautiously. And among "old" Mennonites a rising young evangelist and church leader was Daniel (D. H.) Bender. He was a brother of George (G. L.) Bender, a key person in Funk's circle who had done much to get the HFRC started. Yet in May of 1898 D. H. Bender wrote privately that he could not understand why the HFRC was "combining with the Berne people. . . ." He thought "they should either keep in the bounds of our church or keep it out of the columns of our church papers." The fact was, he and other rising new leaders, notably Daniel Kauffman, cared more for another controversial project: bringing "old" and Amish Mennonites together in a combined general conference. Before the end of 1898 they succeeded; and their move for unity helped create the atmosphere in which, by 1920, almost all Amish Mennonite district conferences merged into "old" Mennonite ones. In 1898 D. H. Bender was afraid that consorting with GC Mennonites at Berne might "hurt the Gen. Conf. cause."[43]

Cooperation between GC and "old" Mennonites in mission failed no doubt for several reasons. (1) An effect of the quickening was to harden Mennonite divisions by creating more denominational institutions and thereby more institutional interests to protect. (2) The quickening did not obliterate the fundamental reasons for "old" and GC Mennonite separation in the first place. Rising new leaders of the "old" church such as D. H. Bender, and especially Daniel Kauffman, were no more convinced than their grandparents that only trivia and nonessentials divided "old" Mennonites from GCs. And (3), very fundamentally, Kauffman and his generation shrewdly perceived that the quickening had moved the "old" and Amish Mennonite churches to a new phase. In that phase they wanted to stop fellow members from riding off in all directions (as the quickening had encouraged) and get them on one road. To do that they wanted stronger church authority, doctrines, and institutions. The time had come to consolidate and rationalize what the quickening had created.[44]

In 1899 a team comprising J. A. Ressler, medical-missionary William A. Page, and Alice Thut Page arrived in India to open the first "old" Mennonite foreign mission.[45] The MB, GC, and "old" Mennonite branches were all beginning missions in India, but separately.

Nonetheless, "old" and Amish Mennonites had learned to look outward and think of God's message for people of the world, not only for their own inner circles.

BASIC CHANGE 2: MORE PROTESTANT, MORE AMERICAN KINDS OF STRUCTURES

The "old" and Amish Mennonite quickening altered more than tempo. Students of history know that in the late-nineteenth century Americans were rapidly changing their society in the direction of more formal organizations, some of them quite large-scale. Entrepreneurs created business corporations such as Standard Oil and International Harvester while others built complex universities, government bureaucracies, modernized military commands, "Charity Organization Societies," and "institutional church" programs.

Such was the context in which M. S. Steiner, in 1891, twenty-five and attending Oberlin College, challenged Mennonites to see that there were institutions to build, and to be "at it." He argued that in Bible times before Christ the building of temple and synagogue had been evidence of religious prosperity. In his time Jesus had taught in them, not only in open fields. Now, it was Mennonites' time. They should establish a publishing house, truly under church control, to help spread the "peace doctrine" of Christ. They should plant "mission stations ... in the dark regions of the earth." They should begin Bible institutes to train teachers, missionaries, and evangelists, and spread "the doctrines and teachings of Christ ... far and wide." The list went on. "Why are we not at it?"[46]

Sometimes activists admitted that such institutions could be dangerous: structure might become cumbersome, or leaders might act as if they were owners. But as the 1890s closed, quickened Mennonites were busy acting is if they hoped to meet Steiner's challenge.[47]

Creating new institutions was heady stuff. It also tended to shift emphasis from congregational life to an idea that church consisted of agencies and programs. Sometimes the programs seemed more concerned with doing than with quality of being, more with goals than with relationships.

In light of traditional Anabaptist and Mennonite emphasis on church as congregations of God's new people, quickened Mennonites might conceivably have tried harder to keep their activism centered in the congregations. For example, instead of a Protestant pattern of sending a few missionaries out and then treating them as special saints, heroic and different, they might have worked more to stimulate established congregations to do as those Virginians had done: proclaim God's good news invitingly to non-ethnic-Mennonite neighbors. In new places they might have been less satisfied to establish "mission stations" and more determined to plant congregations. But the Protestant models were available and convenient. Moreover, by and large, those who cared most for traditionally Mennonite understandings of faith were not acting.

New authorities and infrastructures: laymen and youth

The new programs created alternative patterns and structures of authority. With their separate histories Mennonites already differed considerably on how much power lay with congregations versus how much with ordained men or conferences. Moreover, Mennonites did not have professional clergies. Since traditionalists treated religious and secular life as hardly separate, their ministers were often leaders both in church affairs and in economic and other matters. About the only formal office for lay people was that of church trustee. Seldom were there parallel or competing hierarchies. Apart from congregations about the only structures were district conferences. But quickened Mennonites' new programs and institutions created all sorts of parallel structures with new ladders to leadership, new offices, and new systems of status and authority.

The new structures were "church-related" in the sense that their founders established them to serve the churches and strengthen church life. Yet accountability to congregation, conference, or denomination was unclear. So new authorities more or less competed with old. Many activists in the Lancaster conference "are beginning to think for themselves and are throwing away the idea that as the bishops says [*sic*] so it must be," G. L. Bender told Steiner in 1893. "The high priests are losing power fast," said an activist approvingly in 1899, referring to authority patterns in eastern Pennsylvania.[48]

To an extent the change was in the direction of individualism and individual initiative. In 1891 in his call for church institutions Steiner suggested a plan by which individuals could buy stock and thus help create a "church" publishing house. Later as Steiner was deciding about becoming head of the Chicago mission a young activist named Edward J. Berkey assured him that "the church surely will support you"—but "if not, individuals *will*."[49] The quickening chipped away at Mennonite communalism and gave religious approval to accepting some of modern Western society's ways of acting.

The activists themselves sometimes felt the blows of parallel and competing authorities. "You *will persist* in hammering away at me about [entering] the Ministry and missionary work," one of the bright youths working for Funk at Elkhart, Christian (C. K.) Hostetler, responded vigorously to Steiner in 1892. ". . . But to do the work of an evangelist *without being called to* it by my brethren: the church"—"without being ordained, simply consulting my own tastes, or inclinations or *convictions*"—" 'Ay, there's the rub.' " Keep the work "in the order of the church," evangelist Coffman warned Steiner concerning the Chicago mission. But in fact the mission was a creature of the new Sunday school conventions and of a youthful, self-appointed "City Mission Committee," not clearly of the church. That fact partly explains its temporary closing in 1896. Of course in a way its confusion was as much due to older authorities' inaction as it was to the young activists' moving ahead.[50]

Various conferences finally approved the Sunday school conventions and the Chicago mission, but only with qualifications. "A S.S. Conference may be held to advantage if properly conducted," resolved the Indiana Amish Mennonite body in April of 1894, but "should not be left too much in the hands of the younger members. . . ." "Mission work in the cities and elsewhere is heartily approved," and the Chicago mission deserved support and prayer, the conference said further—provided that workers "teach and practice the doctrines of the Holy Scriptures as" understood by the congregations. Other conferences west of the Alleghenies responded much the same.[51]

Women

As new programs and structures gave greater scope to lay people and especially youth, women took up new roles.[52] Yet in the end their positions in church life were not as "improved" as they might seem.

In broader nineteenth-century American culture, a side effect of revivalism and religious reform had often been to modernize churches in certain ways, including some change in women's roles. When they drew accusations of having let women lead public prayers, Daniel Brenneman's revivals were not the first to raise such controversy. Long before, Anabaptists, Quakers, and American revivalists had allowed women new activities. In the 1830s some followers of America's foremost revivalist, Charles G. Finney, had created exactly the kind of controversy that Brenneman would create. Reforms and revivals often allowed women new expression and opportunities to lead, even if not always with full recognition.[53]

In muted ways the various Mennonite quickenings did the same. A Sunday school might easily have more women teachers than men. Women gave a few of the addresses at the new Sunday school conventions and wrote a few of the articles in the new church papers. In its first year, 1864, Funk's *Herald of Truth* had five articles by women using one percent of the paper's space. In 1884 the percentage was 3.8; in 1904, 11.6. (The statistics do not count anonymous pieces and obituaries, many surely written by women.) The fractions were far below women's share of Mennonite membership. Moreover, except for some missionary pieces, women seldom wrote conference reports, editorials, or other items reflecting prestige and power.[54] Yet the quickening opened some doors, at least a bit.

There were also new organizations of women—sewing circles and others. In the GC branch women's missionary societies appeared, the first apparently in 1867 in the very cradle of the GC conference, the Zion congregation at Donnellson, Iowa.[55] Also among the GCs an idea of a special order of deaconesses took root. Beginning apparently in 1887 the free-lancing John A. Sprunger established training schools or homes for deaconesses at Berne, Indiana, and in Chicago, Toledo, and Cleveland. Apparently in the West no deaconess was ordained before 1900; but as early as 1890 David Goerz suggested doing so. His idea began taking root, especially in connection with a hospital, Bethesda, which Alexanderwohlers opened at Goessel, Kansas, in 1898. Among MBs, in 1897 and 1898, their general conference used the term *deaconess* for women workers at a school they were opening for Native Americans in Oklahoma.[56]

"Old" and Amish Mennonites did not recognize women's contributions so formally, yet they let women exert some new leadership. Most remarkable was the case of the mission in Philadelphia. In the late 1890s when activists wanted to open that mission they could not find an ordained male to take the lead. Fi-

Courtesy of Lancaster Mennonite Historical Society

Amanda Musselman.

nally in June of 1899 they opened a program organized around a Sunday school, although with other activities also, much as in Chicago.

Formally, the school's superintendent was one Joseph Bechtel, a lay businessman from a rural Franconia conference community, now living in the city. But the mission's full-time workers were Mary Denlinger and Amanda Musselman. Denlinger, 31, had grown up in Pennsylvania's Lancaster County then moved to Missouri. At age 23 she had made her Christian commitment under the preaching of John S. Coffman, and later she had worked in the Chicago mission. Musselman, 29, from a different community in Lancaster County, had been baptized at 27 and also had worked briefly at Chicago. In the new Philadelphia work, by the fourth Sunday, the two women found themselves conducting Sunday services without a male worker present. However, Denlinger reported that "we had a blessed day all through." She added a plea to pray for Bro. Bechtel, for "he has no experience in this work, and feels his weakness."[57]

Nevertheless, despite such innovation, it is not clear that the quickening's progressivism and influence toward modernity were improving Mennonite women's position overall.

The older Mennonitism had taught humility and submissiveness for both genders, not only for women. It did not treat those qualities as "feminine" or as women's special adornments. Submission and humility were keys to practical living and character for all Christians. Moreover, in older Amish and Mennonite practice—at least in America, whether or not among Russian Mennonites—a sense of companionship between husband and wife spilled over into church roles. Modernity had not yet put home and family life into one sphere, and work and church life into others. As long as congregations rather than institutions and programs remained central, church life was highly relational, like families. Perhaps because of such patterns, pre-quickened Mennonites and Amish ministers and bishops, even in letters written about church affairs, very often signed their wives' names with their own and wrote long greetings and closings addressed couple-to-couple.[58] Unself-consciously, they let their wives share church leadership in ways that male leaders of progressive, quickening programs did not. Modernity sharpened and divided roles. The older Mennonitism blurred them and treated wives more as companions in their husbands' work.

The "old" and Amish Mennonite quickening seems also to have brought more of a double standard between genders, at least for attire. Some leaders took notice and tried to resist. In 1877 the Kansas-Nebraska Mennonite conference said that since the sisters were to dress simply and modestly the brethren should do the same—"so that we may all 'be of the same mind one toward another.'" In 1891 its counterpart in Indiana agreed, saying "it would be unjust to ask 'the sisters only to dress plain' and let 'the brethren . . . conform to the customs and fashions of the world.'" No less a quickened leader than M. S. Steiner shared the concern. "We boys dress as we please," he observed to G. L. Bender in 1892, "but as soon as the girls try to gain the same privilege, we think them off and quelch [*sic*] them under." As for Bender, in 1893 he and some of the other young men at Elkhart began to wear the collarless "plain" coat precisely because they saw young women adopting plain dress.[59]

Maybe the quickening did not really sharpen the double standard; maybe it only made people discuss it more. More likely, however, it sharpened it. For instance, the disciplines Amish people used in the early nineteenth century, reaffirmed by Old Order-minded Amish in 1865, admonished about beards, neckerchiefs, false shirt-bosoms, and other matters pertaining to men as avidly as they laid out regulations for women. But in that notable example of Amish Mennonite quickening, the Oak Grove congregation in Ohio, the new discipline introduced in 1889 seems quite clearly to have left fewer restrictions for men than for women. In addition to being generally modest, women were still to wear the prayer veiling during worship and even daughters not yet baptized were not to wear hats and other symbols of "pride." Men were to be modest also, and the discipline recommended that married ones wear beards as before. But it did not insist on beards and it allowed ordinary haircuts and headgear. Some other, undesignated restrictions may still

Nathaniel B. Grubb.

have applied. But the discipline relaxed rules for men more than for women.[60]

Consciously or unconsciously, in 1897 Jonathan K. Zook (1831-1913), a 66-year-old Amish Mennonite layman in Missouri, practically used "higher criticism" to answer persons who objected that women in missions and elsewhere were no longer keeping silent in church as the biblical writer Paul had taught (1 Cor. 14:34-35). Present-day Christians did not have to take those words literally, Zook suggested, because they "doubtless originated from custom and social standing of the sexes among the heathen at that time." However, by the 1890s "old" and Amish Mennonites had opened their churches ever more to Protestantism and its quarrels; and rather than following Zook their writers were likely to attack higher criticism.[61] So the quickened often referred to Paul's words in 1 Corinthians 11:3 and 14:35 which seemed clear and straightforward if read literally. Using those verses they were about as eager as traditionalists to insist that in God's order women were subordinate to men.

Such reading was not quite as strong among GC as among "old" and Amish Mennonites. At a GC youth convention in Ohio in 1897 a male speaker argued for allowing Christian Endeavor chapters to have "lady leaders." And already in 1889 Philadelphia pastor Nathaniel (N. B.) Grubb wanted to let women be Sunday school superintendents, saying that the church ought to recognize their talents more. A bit earlier Grubb had designated twelve of his congregation's women to be "Assistant Pastors" for pastoral visiting. In 1891 he told a conference of Eastern District ministers that they ought to let women preach.[62] But even among GCs Grubb was at one end of a scale, not typical.

In 1888 *The Mennonite* editor Andrew B. Shelly had told fellow "new" Mennonite ministers that there was plenty of teaching for women to do in Sunday schools, missions, and elsewhere; they did not have to violate Paul's commandment against preaching. After Grubb's remarks of 1891 a conference reporter noted that eastern GC fellow ministers might tolerate women's preaching but not really favor it.[63]

As for "old" Mennonites, in a basic outline published in 1891 as *Fundamental Bible References* evangelist Coffman classed the prayer covering as a "secondary" rather than a "principal" ordinance. Yet in standard "old" Mennonite fashion he cited 1 Corinthians 11:2 to say that "this custom" together with that of long hair "shows the spiritual relation . . . of the believing woman to her husband," who was her head. Nor were quickened women themselves inclined to challenge such direct readings. Later, in the early twentieth century, a dispute would develop over the existence and governance of a "Mennonite Women's Missionary Society." It was a dispute between top "old" Mennonite church leaders and able women officers of the society, not least of whom was Clara Eby Steiner, widow of M. S. Steiner. But even those women conceded that in its outer relations their organization should be subordinate to the church and to male church leaders.[64]

The quickenings opened Mennonites somewhat more to larger American culture; and concerning women its main publications showed it. On the one hand such progressive journals as *The Mennonite* and the *Young People's Paper* sometimes expressed the aspirations of the women's movement of the day. For instance, in 1894 an early issue of the *Young People's Paper* published an item borrowed from a non-Mennonite source which argued that in courtship women should have equal rights with men.[65]

On the other hand, the papers ran many articles which, like much public discussion in nineteenth-century America, emphasized a special set of roles for women. They were roles which would not lead to the kinds of power and status which were usually the measures of success. Women were to be special keepers and nurturers of home, family, and children; were to be submissive; were to be especially pure, and guard society's morals; and were to reinforce all those virtues by being special examples of piety. Mennonite papers of course never said that men had any less obligation than women to be pure and pious; on those points they recognized no double standard. But article after article upheld the idea of women as primarily keepers of home and family. More than exploring biblical teachings about relations between the sexes, the papers' references to women generally reflected American culture's "ideal of true womanhood."[66]

The quickenings opened new opportunities and avenues for women, yet continued an ideal of women being subordinate to men. Meanwhile they opened Mennonites to more modern patterns. In the modern spirit of specialization, in some ways those patterns sharpened the differences in gender roles. And they assumed a society organized more and more around goals instead of companionship and relationships. So in some ways the quickenings put women in what some may consider to have been less fair and less attractive roles.

BASIC CHANGE 3: SEPARATION OF SALVATION FROM CHRISTIAN PRACTICE

The quickenings changed Mennonites' understanding of the Christian message in subtle and deep ways. Among the most profound was change in the very concept of salvation.

From Anabaptist days onward Mennonites had not generally made the strong distinction Protestants generally made between grace and works.[67] Pre-quickened Mennonites and Amish in America certainly believed in salvation by grace. But grace did not mean only God's generosity in forgiving the penitent sinner; it also included his help for the humble and nonresistant attitudes and the righteous living which brought God's blessing. Pre-quickened Mennonites and Amish included atonement and justification in their understanding of salvation; but they did not connect grace only with them. Instead they understood grace to be as broad as all God's acts through history, his creating his church, and his establishing his kingdom of peace. They included all that the Protestant reformers had included. But unlike a tendency among Protestants, they did not narrow salvation down to one forensic process or "plan" or transaction.[68] The German word *Gottselig* (literally, "blessed of God") or *Seligmachung* ("salvation" in the sense of "to make blessed") captured pre-quickened Mennonite and Amish perceptions in a way that the English word *saved* often does not.

Nevertheless, in 1884, with the "old" and Amish Mennonite quickening still in an early stage, Funk's *Herald* found English words to express something of the older idea. What, an editorial asked, was the "old" Mennonites' central message? The answer: "that there is salvation in none other name save in the name of Jesus, and that his blood alone can cleanse from all sin." But the answer did not stop there. Without a break the *Herald* explained that the message also was "that by repentance, faith in Christ and a willingness to obey the word of God in all things we become converted and true children of God." Salvation came also "by obedience." Through obedience and consecration "we can live a life acceptable to God . . . . Without obedience and self denial we can *never* be saved."[69]

That statement was a step along a path of change[70] but still did not make the sharp separation of grace and works many Protestants have made. It had ample room for atonement yet refused to separate salvation from practical Christian living. After all, if obedience had nothing to do with salvation—nothing to do with God's answer to human sin and lostness—then why did he ask it? Was he capricious? Was he vain? No, the God of the pre-quickened was not arbitrary or power hungry. As the concept of *Ordnung* implied, he wanted his children to obey because his precepts offered them the only way to live in harmony with creation and each other and be *Gottselig*—blessed of God. But now among quickened "old" and Amish Mennonites a more Protestant and revivalist concept of salvation took root. The change was not complete and sudden.[71] Nevertheless, salvation was coming to mean more the forensic process of initial forgiveness, justification, and atonement. "Plan of salvation" became a favorite phrase.[72]

It was not that quickened "old" and Amish Mennonite leaders were abandoning belief in Mennonite doctrines such as nonresistance and nonconformity or making them "nonessentials," as happened sooner or later in some smaller and even more "quickened" Mennonite groups. About 1894 evangelist Coffman published a small, tractlike booklet entitled *Christianity Teaches Peace*. Or in 1898 during the Spanish-American war he remarked in his diary that current news "only helps to strengthen my views against all war & violence." Steiner responded to the same war with a sermon in which he denounced "the war method of humanitarianism" and exhorted Christians to see the war as opening new opportunities "for the messengers of the gospel of the Prince of Peace."[73]

What did happen was that leaders such as Coffman and Steiner increasingly put conversion and redemption into one category and Mennonites' deep convictions about nonresistance and other points of practical Christian living into another. For conversion or redemption they spoke of "salvation" or "plan of salvation." For matters such as nonresistance, nonconformity, and not taking oaths they used another category, and a negative-sounding one at that: "restrictions." Coffman did so at least as early as 1891 in his

Fundamental Bible References. "These restrictions are for your good; they keep you in safety—save you from many a temptation," said G. L. Bender in an 1894 address urging young people to keep dressing plainly. Others such as Steiner could talk about gospel of peace or Jesus kingdom of peace but not relate those words clearly to their evangelistic message of salvation.[74]

At times Coffman could be very eloquent about the world's needing to learn peace, as, for instance, in his famous 1896 address, "The Spirit of Progress." But he never clearly related such statements to his revivals or to his formulas of "plan of salvation" and "restrictions." Even his 1894 tract *Christianity Teaches Peace* offered no solution. To be sure, it connected the goal of peace among nations with a need for personal, individual commitment to peace. But it did not clearly present peace as part of God's offer of grace and salvation. Indeed, it was not particularly Mennonite in tone, or original. In all honesty, Coffman noted in closing that his statement was "Arranged from Friends' [Quakers'] literature."[75]

Most telling of all in the separation of "plan of salvation" from "restrictions" were basic doctrinal books by Daniel Kauffman. They were especially crucial because they were powerful documents in the quickening's next phase, that of consolidation, and therefore tended to freeze the separation into "old" Mennonite theology.

In 1898 Kauffman published a brief *Manual of Bible Doctrines.* During the next three decades he became by all odds the most influential of "old" Mennonite leaders; and in 1914 and 1928 expanded versions of the manual appeared, with more authors, published more or less as official church dogma. How the books treated the "gospel of peace" idea was uncanny. The 1898 *Manual* separated "plan of salvation" from nonresistance and put the latter under the "restrictions" heading—yet had a rather substantial segment on the "Gospel of Peace." The 1914 book also separated "Plan of Salvation" from teachings on nonresistance, nonconformity, etc., with those teachings in a section entitled "CHRISTIAN PRINCIPLES (Duties and Restrictions)." But it had no "Gospel of Peace" section. It treated nonresistance as the only position in harmony with the gospel—not as part of gospel itself.[76]

The 1928 book again used the word "restrictions" in its heading, albeit with an explanation that only to "the worldly-minded" did teachings such as nonresistance and nonconformity seem to be restraints; "the child of God recognizes them as cherished rules of life." In one line the 1928 book pointed out that New Testament Christians had preached " 'the Gospel of Peace' (Rom. 10:15)." But it did not relate those "cherished rules of life" to the basic idea of salvation, or put the preaching of peace at the heart of the gospel message.[77]

Evangelist Coffman died in 1899, at age fifty. Had he lived longer he might have found a way to put his revivalistic message and his deep concerns for peace and other practical points of Christian living together into more of a whole. But probably not; historian J. Denny Weaver has found that of the main "old" Mennonite thinkers from Christian Burkholder to Daniel Kauffman, John S. Coffman was most consistent in separating ethics from salvation.[78]

The "old" and Amish Mennonites' quickening was a time of opening windows and bringing in new ideas and new programs, not a time of putting together. Its generation infused new movement and energy into religious life and faith, added broader and more outward-looking vision especially for missions, and without question attracted many youths into the churches who otherwise would have been lost to them. But it did not bring its new understandings together into a whole.

BASIC CHANGE 4: FROM HUMILITY TO AGGRESSIVE ACTION

If the idea of salvation changed profoundly, that of humility nearly got lost. Not completely: the older Mennonitism was deeply imbedded in folk attitudes and folkways. These did not suddenly disappear just because articulate new leaders changed the code words from "humility" to "active work." Yet humility lost its central place in the ideal for Mennonite personality and for practical Christian faith.

"Old" and Amish Mennonite activists really wanted to fuse the new and the old; so they still spoke of humility and plainness. Daniel Kauffman worried in 1896 that other churches were drawing Mennonites away from "the plain, peaceable, and self-denying principles of the Bible." In 1898 a listener commended Steiner for preaching the truth of "the meek and lowly lamb of God, who brought this new kingdom of peace and love from high Heaven here upon earth to reign in [his followers'] hearts." G. L. Bender, in his 1894 address, rebuked young activists for getting the notion that plain clothes were "merely custom and a dead formalism"—or the idea that "in order to go out into the world to do active service for the Master" one had to put plainness aside. Gaudy dress, he said, did not reveal a meek and quiet spirit.[79]

Thus new leaders upheld plainness. But now the principle was plainness more than humility. The spirit was different from that in John M. Brenneman's *Pride and Humility* booklet. Bender said in

1894 that plain attire was a "delicate subject. . . . One dare hardly say anything about it without being classed as a cranky, narrow-minded formalist." The main point of the listener who commended Steiner was really to rebuke a preacher (surely meaning Steiner) who used the older language but nevertheless came into the pulpit with hair combed and beard trimmed just so, and with "starched shirt bosoms and shiny collars that glare over the house as the speaker turns."[80]

The problem was, wrote an anonymous minister after the 1892 Sunday school conference, as young people became better educated they seemed to have "a kind of exalted, dominating spirit and a tendency to drift from" the order of the church, especially in dress. The minister quickly added that some uneducated persons had the same spirit, and that he believed "more education is certainly needed in our church." But he hoped that "it can be had and used in an humble, unassuming way." The minister was sensing more than only a generation gap: he was feeling the loss of the humility ethos and its replacement by another.[81]

The same minister wrote also that "we need progressive work." For the newly quickened, no idea or slogan was more central than that of "work"—"progressive work," "direct work," "active work," "aggressive work." Said a speaker at a conference of eastern GC ministers in 1890: "in my ideal congregation all is life and activity. There are no drones." Every person should be working like "the busy bee." Among "old" and Amish Mennonites a steady drumbeat about work grew so monotonous that in 1898 A. B. Kolb finally warned editorially in the *Herald* against it. According to him the "modern system of Christianity" had become "all work—one continued earnest, active, hurrying, rushing, hustling, pushing world of active work." Youth, Kolb counseled, needed also to learn how to hold quiet communion with God.[82]

The slogans of work implied a self-assertion quite foreign to the older ethos of humility. An activist editorial in the *Herald* of 1885 scolded ministers who constantly said that they were weak, unworthy, and lacking in ability. In 1893 Steiner preached on "The Manliness of God." That same year, G. L. Bender rejoiced privately that Eastern activists thought that he, Steiner, and other friends were "just the stuff." The next year one of those Eastern activists, Isaac Hershey, confided to Steiner that as a lad he had never understood "why Mennonite boys were nobody . . . in the family of Christ"—"nor can I yet." Among activists, humility might still be a Christian virtue; but the mark of the truly faithful had become aggressive activity.[83]

The ideal for the Christian personality had changed.[84] To an M. S. Steiner, the change merely restored balance. The Mennonite church was doing all its "pruning on the humility branch," he jotted in his diary in 1895, "instead of symmetrically as the Lord would do it."[85] Balance or no, the new mood took more from the "Onward Christian Soldiers" spirit of aggressive nineteenth-century Anglo-American Protestantism than it did from Christian Burkholder's call to kneel at Jesus' humble manger. It encouraged Mennonites and Amish to move outward in mission. It also brought them closer to the spirit of the America ready to fight the Spanish-American war and gain an empire.

KEY TO ABBREVIATIONS

CB — *Christlicher Bundesbote*, General Conference Mennonite German-language paper, begun 1882

EPMHL — Eastern Pennsylvania Mennonite Historical Library and Archives of the Franconia and Eastern District conferences, at Harleysville, Pa.

HT — *Herald of Truth*, semi-official "old" Mennonite paper published by John F. Funk beginning 1864

LMHS — Lancaster Mennonite Historical Society, the library and archives of the Lancaster Mennonite Conference, at Lancaster, Pa.

AMC — Archives of the Mennonite Church, official depository of the "old" Mennonite church, at Goshen (Ind.) College

ME — *Mennonite Encyclopedia*

MHB — *Mennonite Historical Bulletin*, published by the AMC

MHL — Mennonite Historical Library, Goshen (Ind.) College

ML — *Mennonite Life*, published at Bethel College, North Newton, Kan.

MLA — Mennonite Library and Archives, a General Conference Mennonite Church research collection at Bethel College, North Newton, Kan.

MRJ — *Mennonite Research Journal*, formerly the research publication of LMHS

MQR — *The Mennonite Quarterly Review*, major journal of Anabaptist and Mennonite studies, published at Goshen (Ind.) College

MSHL — Menno Simons Historical Library, Eastern Mennonite University, Harrisonburg, Va.

TM — *The Mennonite*, English-language journal of the General Conference Mennonite Church, begun 1885

YPP — *Young People's Paper*, youth magazine begun in 1894 by John F. Funk's press principally for "old" and Amish Mennonite young people

ZH — *Zur Heimath*, paper published 1875-1881 first by the Mennonite Board of Guardians for immigrants principally from the Russian empire; one of the papers merged to form the *CB*

NOTES

CHAPTER 1

1. Martin Mellinger to Bro.-in-Law (John Weber), and Bro.-in-law and Sister, Feb 26, 1816, Mar 3, 1825, trans. by Noah Good in *MRJ*, 11 (Jul 1970), 31, and 13 (Jul 1972), 27, 35, or in Bender (1931: B2-7), 51, 61.

2. Bender (1931: B2-7), 41.

3. A good place to start re Anabaptists is early chapters and esp. ch. 8 (by John H. Yoder) of Dyck (1981: C1-1). Re diff. in emph. *see* e.g., Davis (1974: C2-45), *passim*, esp. 73, 130ff., 137ff., 141, 143, 157, and ch. 4.

4. *See esp.* a 17th-century Dutch Mennonite book of martyr accounts: van Braght (1982: C1-22).

5. *See esp.* MacMaster (1985: C1-10), chs. 2-4.

6. Ibid., ch. 6.

7. Dyck (1981: C1-1), chs. 3-7, 9, esp. pp. 123-24, 152; MacMaster (1985: C1-10), ch. 2.

8. *ME*, I, 98-99, 219-22; Dyck (1981: C1-1), 148-49; Hostetler (1980: C2-99), 40-46; Gascho (1937: C2-70); *see also* Schelbert (1985: C2-170-2).

9. MacMaster (1985: C1-10), 69-72, 86, 125-26.

10. E.g., Yoder (1961: C2-261), 40, 95-117, 366-370. Frantz (1976: C2-63) wrote of confessional, ecumenical, and sectarian; he did not bring the story forward to the time of the United Brethren, etc.

11. MacMaster (1985: C1-10), chs. 5-7. Re sharing of pulpits, and neighborly relations, see Muhlenberg (1942-1958: B2-61), I, 215, 317-18, 352; II, 343-44, 347-48, 354; III, 377-78, 403, 477, 481, 545, 662.

12. Quot. in Sutter (1976: C2-210), 46-47. Bits of evidence are, for instance, Brunk (1959: C2-30), I, 28; *see also* Hershey (1958: C2-95), 31-32, 43-45, and *passim*; Ruth (1976: C2-168), 36; Landis (1968: C2-124), 13, 19, 21; Miyakawa (1964: C2-142), 53. *See also* Gingerich (1970: C2-76), a helpful but hardly definitive study, *esp.* 26.

13. MacMaster (1976: C2-135).

14. Shetler (1963: C2-188), 98-101; Mook (1955: C2-143), 4-7.

15. Shetler (1963: C2-188), 98.

16. Hayes (1947: C2-91), 12; Renno (C2-163), 1-5.

17. Shetler (1963: C2-188), 178.

18. Yoder (1941: C2-263), 159-63.

19. Ibid., 165-66.

20. Ibid., 167-68.

21. Ibid., 168-69; Studer (1965: C2-206), 177-79; Harvey (1928: C2-89), 8-9.

22. Epp (1974: C1-2), 54-70, *esp.* 55; Eby (1895: C2-56), 19-20.

23. Stoltzfus (1969: C2-203), 44-45; Swope (1962: C2-218).

24. Swope (1962: C2-214), 3.

25. Stoltzfus (1969: C2-203), 72-73, 43; Miller (1977: C2-139), 1-7; Schlabach (1978: C2-171), 1-2; Swope (1967: C2-213); Swope (1967: C2-219), 1-2; Gingerich (1939: C2-78), 44.

26. Gratz (1953: C2-81), 128-33, and *passim*; Lehman (1969: C2-129), ch. 1-3; Lehman (1962: C2-130), 16-17.

27. Gratz (1953: C2-81), 130, 137-38, 132.

28. Swope (1964: C2-215), 20, 28; Paul Henkel, journal of a trip to Ohio, 1806—as described and quot. to me in letter from Richard K. MacMaster.

29. Shetler (1963: C2-188), 106, 52-58; Springs Mennonite Church (1978: C2-195), 2-3.

30. Shetler (1963: C2-188), 313-17.

31. Frantz (1976: C2-63); Sutter (1976: C2-210); Schlabach (1979: C2-174), 410-15.

32. Sutter (1976: C2-210), 41-47; Schlabach (1979: C2-174), 410-15; MacMaster (1985: C1-10), 206, 192-93, 199, 211ff. Boehm accounts in (1823: C2-20), and in Spayth (1851: C2-192), 28-31. The Boehm account in Spayth's book suggests his crisis conversion was soon after his ordination in 1756; his son Henry, in Boehm (1875: B2-8), 12, set the date at 1761; a more recent author suggested sometime 1758-61—*see* Gibble (1951: C2-73), 13.

33. MacMaster (1985: C1-10), 130, 215-19, 227; Sutter (1976: C2-210), 45-47; Newcomer (1834: B2-64), 1-18; Hough (1941: B2-45).

34. E.g., Adam Miller, *Hostetler: Or, the Mennonite Boy Converted* (New York, 1848), 40, 51, 67-79, 95-96.

35. Boehm quot. in (1823: C2-20), 212; Sutter (1976: C2-210), 43; doc. apparently not extant, trans. in Funk (1878: C2-68), 43.

36. For U.B. origins and early history *see* sources cited n. 32 and 33, plus: Berger (1897: C2-17); Drury (1924: C2-51). Re Mennonites and Amish ministers and a congregation becoming U.B., *see esp.* Newcomer (1834: B2-64), *passim*; and Gibble (1951: C2-73), 37-59, 64-65. Huber (1858: B2-46), 9-13, 17-34, 53-54, 179-80, 111, and *passim*.

37. Arndt (1866: B2-1), esp. book 2, ch. 11.

38. Davis (1974: C2-45), 73, 130ff., 137ff., 141, 143, 157, and ch. 4.

39. Funk (1915: B2-24), 269-71; MacMaster (1985: C1-10), 177-79; Ruth (1984: C1-15), 121-22, 125-26, 136-37.

40. Schlabach (1979: C2-174), 411-15; Liechty (1980: C1-9).

41. MacMaster (1985: C1-10), ch. 10.

42. Burkholder (1857: B1-4).

43. Friedmann (1949: C1-3), 238; Burkholder (1857: B1-4), preface.

44. For a rather unfavorable view of Burkholder because of his Pietism, *see* Friedmann (1949: C1-3), 238ff.

45. Burkholder (1857: B1-4), *passim, esp.* 185-89, 194, 219; quot. from 221, 188.

46. Ibid., 188, 221.

47. Ibid., 214-17, 241, 239, 246-48.

48. Ibid., 212.

49. Ibid., 224.

50. A most interesting work in light of my contrasting Mennonite humility with the American mood is Saum (1980: C1-16).

CHAPTER 2

1. Saloma Overholt to Sam Gross, date unclear (apparently about 1885), coll. 180, (A1-3).

2. Schelbert (1968: C2-170); Pannabecker (1947: C2-154), 65-70; Gratz (1953: C2-81), chs. 6-7, quot. from 129. Some further sources on the Bernese immigrants and their communities are: Lehman (1969: C2-129); Lehman (1962: C2-130), 16-18; Amstutz (1978: C2-2); Gratz (1960: C2-82), 165-67; Sprunger (1938: C2-196).

3. Comment by my research assistant Joseph C. Liechty from sources mentioned n. 2.

4. Amstutz (1978: C2-2), 14ff.; on patterns and motives of German immigration *see* Moltmann (1985: C2-142-2).

5. A. K. Funk to his brother, Jan 29, 1863, box 2, (A1-2).

6. John F. Funk diary, 1857-1865, *passim*, and esp. Mar 7, 1858; *see also* 111 and 113 of "Account of J. F. Funk's Trip to Illinois in 1857"; box 1, (A1-2).

7. Jacob Funk to John F. Funk, Apr 28, 1861, box 6, and Mar 19, 1860, box 5; John F. Funk to father, May 23, 1861, box 129; (A1-2).

8. Harry Rexrode to "Friend Hartman," May 10, 1866; Rexrode to "Dear Brother in the Lord," Jul 10, 1865; (A2-5).

9. Gingerich (1939: C2-78), 255, citing a work of a Schwarzendruber grandson, J. F. Swarzendruber. (Being myself a Swartzendruber descendant, I have heard this also in my family's lore.)

10. John M. Brenneman to Peter Nissley, Mar 10, 1865, (A2-30).

11. *HT*, 10 (Jun 1873), 109.

12. Ibid.

13. *HT*, 30 (Mar 1, 1893), 77; for a bit more on this discussion as it took place among "old" Mennonites and Amish Mennonites, *see* Schlabach (1980: C2-172), 40-41, 254.

14. Various collections of 19th-century Amish and Mennonite corresp., esp. in AMC.

15. *See*, e.g., Penner (1976: C2-156), esp. 93-102.

16. Indian-U.S. relations were of course too complex to characterize only as violent. Yet the fact of

violence permeates even a sober account such as Billington (1974: C2-19)—*see esp.* chs. 15-17, 21, 30, and pp. 395-400, 625-29. *See also* Washburn (1975: C2-235), esp. chs. 8-12. For the subtler forms of violence *see esp.*: Sheehan (1974: C2-187); two books by Prucha, (1962: C2-162) and (1975: C2-161); and Miner and Unrau (1978: C2-124-2). For further study, Prucha has published several excellent bibliographies.

17. Unsigned letter fragment, surely by Frederick Hage, May 15, 1835 (quot. is from typed trans. with the fragment), (A2-27). Its internal evidence conforms closely to facts on Hage in a Hagey genealogy ed. by King Albert Hagey and Wm. Anderson Hagey (1951), 523.

18. For such connections among relatives and friends in Ontario, Eastern Pennsylvania, Ohio, and elsewhere, *see*, e.g. (A1-3), (A2-15), (A2-38).

19. Yoder (1941: C2-263), 174.

20. As cited n. 17.

21. Hostetler (1980: C2-99), 99.

22. Borntreger (1907: C2-21), 5-12; Wenger (1957: C2-243), 5.

23. Samuel Mast to Father, 28 May 1865, (A2-27).

24. Bender (1972: C2-16), 71-72.

25. Ibid., 81.

26. Ibid., 72-74.

27. Ibid., 75-77.

28. I have read numerous 19th-century Mennonite and Amish wills in collections in AMC and elsewhere; Bender (1972: C2-16) 79, 80.

29. Bender (1972: C2-16), 80.

30. Ibid., 80-81.

31. Miller (1971: C2-141).

32. *See* n. 2.

33. Smith (1983: C2-193), 58-61, 39-51, 531-59.

34. Gingerich (1939: C2-78), 67-75; Neufeld (1953: C2-147), 170-73, 48-49, 51-55.

35. Gingerich (1939: C2-78), 46, 53, 59, 113-17, 48, 118-19.

36. Erb (1974: C2-60), 45-57, 71-73, 92-93, 37-38.

37. Ibid., 159-71, 221-22.

38. *ME*, III, 235, 237.

39. Cosco (C2-38), 1-13.

40. Ibid., 5, 9, 17-18; Smith (1983: C2-193), 74.

41. Cosco (C2-38), 19, 53.

42. Ibid., 74, 76.

43. Gingerich (1939: C2-78), 69.

44. Swope (1965: C2-217), 6-7.

45. *MQR*, 30 (Jan 1956): C. F. Brüsewitz, "The Mennonites of Balk, Friesland," 19-31; Marie Yoder, "The Balk Dutch Settlement near Goshen, Indiana, 1853-1889," 32-43. Marie Yoder, comp., "History of the Salem Mennonite Church near New Paris, Indiana" (mimeographed, 1955), 1-15.

46. *TM*, 4 (Jan 1889), 53. On failed settlements and congregations *see*, e.g.: Umble (1944-1946: C2-228); Umble (1949: C2-229)—a paper covering Amish as well as Mennonite; chs. on scattered members and extinct churches in Erb (1974: C2-60); Gingerich (1939: C2-78), 333-41; and Yoder (1962: C2-268).

47. Erb (C2-58), 16-35; for Cooprider's U.B. membership *see* Erb (1974: C2-60), 255.

48. Unsigned letter to mother and brother (surely Sarah Gross Lapp to Anna Gross and Wm. Gross), Jan 2, 1878, coll. 163, (A1-3).

49. Harriet Lapp Burkholder statement to author, Feb 1986.

50. Saloma Overholt to Sam Gross, date unclear (apparently ca. 1885), coll. 180; "Miss Saloma" to Samuel Gross, Feb 8, 1885, coll. 180; Samuel and Sarah Lapp to Anna Gross, Oct 19, 1888, coll. 163; (A1-3).

51. The generalization about their greater literacy is impressionistic. Some examples would be the Krehbiels; among the Amish, probably the most literate was immigrant Geo. Jutzi—*see* (1853: B2-51). *See also* manuscripts by Jacob Schwarzendruber, (A1-8).

52. Concerning Amish, *see*, e.g., Pannabecker (1968: C2-153), 11. Concerning Mennonites, consider the role of Lee County, Iowa, Mennonites in forming the General Conference of Mennonites in North America in 1860: *see* Pannabecker (1975: C1-11), ch. 3.

53. Umble (1949: C2-229), 125-26.

54. Daniel Lapp to Wm. Gross, 12 Feb 1895, coll. 160; letter fragment, probably written by Samuel or Sarah Gross in Feb 1895, coll. 164; S. G. Lapp to uncle (surely Wm. Gross), Mar 4, 1895, coll. 164; (A1-3).

55. Wm. and Sarah Hendricks to friends (probably Jacob and Catarina Nold), Apr 24, 1859, f. 1; Wm. Hendricks to Jacob and Catarina Nold), Jun 17, 1861, f. 3; box 9, (A2-31).

56. Mother to "daughter" (daughter-in-law, although clearly for both son and daughter-in-law John and Hulda Landis), Feb 27, 1878; Mother to "son", Dec 16, 1878; coll. 216, (A2-24). For family data *see* Conrad Geil-Jacob Geil genealogy ed. by Jos. H. Wenger (1914), 159-63 (name incorrectly spelled "Landes").

57. *Passim*, coll. 216, (A2-24).

58. Mary Landis letter of Jun 16, 1878; Mother to daughter (daughter-in-law Hulda Landis), Feb 27, 1878; coll. 216, (A2-24). Geil genealogy (n. 56), 160.

59. Lemon (1972: C2-131), 3-6.

60. Apter (1965: C2-4), 61. For more on Mennonites and modernity, *see* Schlabach (1979: C2-174).

61. Columbiana Co., Ohio, Treasurer tax receipts of Jacob Nold, Jr., and Jacob Nold (the Jr. evidently dropped when bishop Jacob Nold, Sr., died in 1834), f. 12, box 7, (A2-31).

62. Swope (1960: C2-211), 2; Stoltzfus (1969: C2-203), 46; Atkins and Keewle to Jacob Nold, Feb 3, 1853, f. 1, box 7, (A2-31).

63. Swope (1960: C2-211), 2.

64. *ME*, I, 36-40 (36-37 for Anabaptists and alcohol); Burkholder (1857: B1-4), 209. For more on changing attitudes toward temperance in the "old" Mennonite church, *see* bibliography of Clemens (1976: C2-36).

65. (B1-15), 1866, pp. 10-11.

66. Columbiana Co. and Mahoning Co., Ohio, Treasurers tax receipts of Jacob Nold, f. 12, box 7, (A2-31).

67. Re Jacob Nold's economic affairs in his last two decades of life *see*: his will and accompanying court doc., f. 13; listing of property, f. 14; Jacob Nold account book from the 1850s, f. 16; Internal Revenue Service and other documents in f. 27; box 7, (A2-31).

68. Landis as quoted in Musser (1873: B1-11), 254.

69. Beiler (1888: B1-1), 26, 46-7, 121; Beiler (1948: B2-4), 102; Stauffer (1855: B1-14, *Eine Chronik*), *passim*, and *esp.* 140, 137, 86, 138; Stauffer (1855: B1-14, *Glaubens-Grund*), *passim*, and *esp.* 321-23, 273, 279. Holdeman had come under some influence of an ex-Mennonite who had become a revivalistic Church of God (Winebrenner) preacher: *see* Swope (1963: C2-216), 4. Hiebert (1973: C2-97), 58, 171, 256-57, 380, 177. For unfavorable contemporary remarks on Holdeman from an "old" Mennonite *see* Funk (1878: C2-68), 198-203. Holdeman (1876: B2-41), 182, 228; Holdeman (1863: B2-42), 166, 95-96, 156-57.

70. Holdeman (1876: B2-41), 228, 267; Ohio conf. report in *HT*, 3 (June 1866), 50, 56; for a dispute whether to allow 10% interest—the going rate, or "rule" of "the world"—*see* John S. Good apparently to John M. Brenneman, (A2-14). Ind.-Mich. conference (B2-48), Oct 8, 1874, p. 22; Western A.M. conference (B2-92), May 28-31, 1891, p. 12; Church of God in Christ, Mennonite, "Conference Reports, 1868-1887" (1879), as quoted in Hiebert (1973; C2-97), 473.

71. Re origins of the E. Pa. conf. and of Hoch's movement, *see* ch. 4.

72. Sect. VII, Art. 4 of Oberholtzer (1972:B1-12), 396, both text and n. 19. [The second session of the E. Pa. conf. ruled that one who went to law without first consulting the heads of the congregation would be excommunicated; the context seems to be for conflicts between members, and it is unclear just in what cases the rule was supposed to apply—see minute at May 4, 1848, in (B2-21), 15. Later John H. Oberholtzer said, "Our conference was not opposed to go to law in a just cause. Every man determines whether his cause is just for himself, but it may be considered by the church. If cause is unjust, the person is liable to expulsion"; *see* (1972:B2-77), 424] Hoch (1850:B2-37). 23.

73. Christian Herr, etc., "Den Lancaster Brüder ihre Einsichten über die neue Ordnung," trans. in (1972: B1-13), 360-65; quot. from 365.

74. *See esp.* Wyllie (1954: C2-260); also Cawelti (1965: C2-34).

75. *TM*, e.g., 13: (Aug 1897) 86; quot. is from (Jul 1897), 79. *YPP*, 1: e.g. (Jul 7, 1894), 107; quot. from (Jun 9, 1894), 93.

76. Menn. Breth. Church (B1-10, 3rd source), 1883, p. 16.

77. Lehman (1978: C2-126), 61-63. C. Z. Yoder, "Reminiscences of Our Forefathers," photocopy of ms. of Jun 1923 (apparently for Smiley reunion); journal and account book (of John Smiley, from internal evidence); box 2, (A2-39).

78. For biographical material on John K. Yoder esp. as bishop (although not his economic life), *see*: *ME*, IV, 1006-07; Lehman (1978: C2-126), 51-59, and *passim*, esp. ch. 4 (the book also has some material on Smiley and much on C. Z. Yoder). Account book of John K. Yoder, 1846-1872, box 2, (A2-39).

79. Account book (n. 78).

80. Lehman (1978: C2-126), 101 and *passim*; *ME*, IV, 1005-06; *Goshen College Announces a Memorial and Tribute, to the Life, Work and Influence of Christian Zook ("C. Z.") Yoder, Smithville, Ohio* (brochure at time of naming a dormitory, 1960?).

81. Lehman (1978: C2-126), 47-49.

82. Ruth (1976: C2-168), 31-109.

83. Schultz (1938: C2-185), 68-69.

84. Schrag (1960: C2-183), and (1960: C2-182).

85. Schrag (1960: C2-182), 64-65.

86. Haury (1981: C2-90), 191. B. Warkentin to "dear Friend" (surely Peter Jansen), Jul 29, 1897, f. 16, (A1-4).

87. Ruth (1976: C2-168), 50, 53, 99, 100, 71, 57-63ff. For the Mennonitism of Michael Bergey *see* Bergey genealogy ed. by David Hendricks Bergey (1925), 131-32.

88. Personal tour with Paul Lederach at Scottdale, Pa., Nov 16, 1983; Harvey (1928: C2-89), *passim*; Shetler (1963: C2-188), 32-33, 179.

89. Pennypacker (1918: C2-157), 16-23.

90. Quot. in Correll (1946: B1-6), 196.

91. Hostetler (1964: C2-102), 282-83.

92. *See* Weber (B2-89).

93. Frances W. Gregory and Irene D. Neu, "The American Industrial Elite in the 1870's," in Wm. Miller, ed., *Men in Business: Essays in the History of Entrepreneurship* (Cambridge, 1952), 199. For more, *see* note in same book, 286.

94. For instance, a guide to study of Germans in America by an accomplished historian of immigration and ethnicism, Carl Wittke, offers material on social and cultural and political contributions but almost nothing on outstanding economic ones. Studies of Pennsylvania Germans suggest economic contribution as farmers but no strong roles as leaders in modern corporate finance, commerce, or industry. *See*: Wittke (1967: C2-255); Wood (1942: C2-259); Rosenberger (1966: C2-167); Cochran (1978: C2-37), 62, 105, 165, 137, 140.

CHAPTER 3

1. Rosina Gerber in *MHB*, 16 (Apr 1955), 4.

2. Musser (1873: B1-11), 252, 240; Herr (1890: B2-35), 108, 114.

3. Stauffer (1855: B1-14, *Eine Chronik*), 6, 86, 139-40, 184, 372-75; Beiler (1888: B1-1), 30-31, 208, 299; Beiler (1948: B2-4), 102; Holdeman (1876: B2-41), 298; John Holdeman, *Christian Nurture of Children* (written 1878; Newton, Kans., 1924), 6-7.

4. Stauffer (1855: B1-14, *Eine Chronik*), 372-75.

5. Eastern District conf. (B2-21; May 3, 1849), 10.

6. *TM*, 8 (Dec 1892), 24.

7. *See*, e.g., *TM*, 7 (Jun 1892), 67.

8. Umble (1963: C2-227), 3-4.

9. *TM*, 4 (Sep 1889), 188.

10. Foster Rhea Dulles, *A History of Recreation: America Learns to Play*, 2nd. ed. (New York, 1965), 223-25.

11. *YPP*, 1 (Sept 15, 1894), 152.

12. *See*, e.g., *CB*, 1 (Oct 1, 1882), 148, and *TM*: 4 (Oct 1888), 7; 4 (Sep 1889), 188.

13. Umble (1941: C2-229), 40.

14. *TM*, 13 (Oct 1897), 2.

15. *TM*, 10 (Jun 1895), 69.

16. Ind.-Mich. conf. (B2-48), Oct 14, 1897, p. 66.

17. John M. Brenneman, "Christians Ought Not Laugh Aloud," in Brenneman (1876: B2-11), 242-43; *see also*, e.g., *HT*, 12 (June 1875), 83-84.

18. Remarks heard during my years at a Mennonite college. To understand Brenneman, *see* Liechty (1980: C1-9), 5-31.

19. *HT*, 4 (Aug 1867), 123.

20. Joseph Funk to John and Mary Kieffer, Sep 14, 1839, (A2-11); Brunk (1959: C2-30), I, 107-08.

21. Brunk (1959: C2-30), I, 138, 108, 125.

22. (A2-11), *passim*.

23. Brunk (1959: C2-30), I, 139-40.

24. Schrag (1967: C2-180), 160.

25. Ind.-Mich. conf. (B2-48), 1875, p. 24.

26. John Gehman expense records at Jun 17, 1837 (p. 24); Jun 15, 28, 1861 (p. 48); (A2-13). Pannabecker (1975: C1-11), 68.

27. Krahn (1951: C2-117), 18; Paul W. Wohlgemuth, ch. 15 in Toews (1975: C1-19), 239-40; MJ diary, Jul 5, Sep 26, 1874, box 1, (A1-4).

28. *See*: Wesley Berg, "The Development of Choral Singing among the Mennonites of Russia to 1875," *MQR*, 55 (Apr 1981), 131-42; John B. Toews, ed. and trans., "Harmony Amid Disharmony: A Diary Portrait of Mennonite Singing in Russia During the 1860s," *ML*, 40 (Dec 1985), 4-7.

29. Wohlgemuth (n. 27), 253.

30. Emaline Myers to Salome Kratz, Aug 23, 1859, box 127, (A2-12).

31. Henry M. Kratz to John F. Landis, Feb 17, 1867, coll. 205, reel 3, (A2-24).

32. *HT*, 20 (Apr 1, 1883), 104.

33. Joseph Funk to John and Mary Kieffer, Feb 20, 1840, Feb 9, 1841, and *passim*, (A2-11).

34. Chase (1966: C2-35), 200-02.

35. Ibid., 27-28, 124, 134, 137-38, 183.

36. Funk: (1816: B2-27), (1832: B2-28); Wayland (1911: C2-236), 7-11; *ME*, II, 423; Brunk (1959: C2-30), I, 114-15; Hostetler (1947: C2-101), 817; Burkholder (1837: B1-5); Funck (1851: B2-23).

37. Hostetler (1947: C2-101), 817.

38. Letters of Funk to John and Mary Kieffer, 1837-1848, *passim*, (A2-11). I did not find Funk mentioning singing school activity until a letter of Jun 22, 1845; *see also* Nov 23, 1845, Jul 3, 1846, Mar 26, 1847.

39. Wayland (1911: C2-236), 10; Brunk (1959: C2-30), I, 123-24; quot. is words of Brunk.

40. Funk as quoted in Hostetler (1947: C2-101), 817-18.

41. Virginia conf. (B2-86), Sep 1860, p. 3; Stauffer (1855: B1-14, *Glaubens-Grund*), 316, 319-20.

42. Aug 15, 19, Sep 19, Oct 12, 1844; Jan 1, 18, Apr 19, Sep 20, 1846; (A2-20).

43. May 4, 1882; 1880-1900, *passim*; (A2-9).

44. Franconia conference (A2-9), *passim*—singing-school ruling at May 4, 1882.

45. *HT*, 35 (Apr 1, 1898), 99.

46. *See*, e.g., Aug 30, Sep 2, 1844, (A2-20); Annie (Kratz) to sister (Salome) Funk, June 2, 1879, (A2-12).

47. Aug 15, 19, 1844, (A2-20); Mollie Kratz to cousin (Salome Funk), Aug 17, 1864, Aug 24, 1874, (A2-12).

48. Catharine Brenneman to Christian, Moses, and Susanna Brenneman, Sep 20, 1868, f. 2, box 1, (A2-3).

49. Maria C. Hershy to sister (Salome Funk), Oct. 27, 1878, (A2-12).

50. Emiline Nold to niece (Salome Funk), Feb 29, 1864, (A2-12).

51. Anna to brother (John Landis) and family, Nov 10, 1880, coll. 203, (A2-24).

52. James L. Morris journal quoted in Stoltzfus (1958: C2-202), 74.

53. Amstutz (1978: C2-2), 61; Musser (1873: B1-11), 239; Susan Ressler to Moses Brenneman, Oct 19, 1867, box 1, (A2-3); Schwarzendruber (1977: B2-69), 3-4, or same language in his "Conference Epistle of 1865," in Bender (1946: B2-5), 228. Original and typed transcript versions of Jacob Schwarzendruber materials are in (A1-8); *see esp.* f. 3, box 1, for transcripts.

54. Emaline Meyers to Salome Kratz, Dec 9, 1857, box 127, (A2-12); Sep 23, Oct 8, 1844, (A2-20); *YPP*, 1 (Jul 21, 1894), 113.

55. "The Use of Good Education" (unsigned ms. presumably by Guengerich), f. 2, box 8, (A2-16); Catharine Brenneman to Christian, Moses, and Susanna Brenneman, Sep 20, 1868, f. 2, box 1, (A2-3); "Speak School Account, Hereford, [18]53," *MHB*, 36 (Apr 1975), 4-6; John F. Funk diary, 1858, *passim*, *esp.* Mar 6 and 19, Apr 10, Jun 7, Aug 30, box 1, (A1-2).

56. Martha Funk to Sallie, May 19, 1878, (A2-12).

57. C. P. Eitzen in (1943:C2-18), 24; *Statuten für den Mennonitischen Lehrerverein von Kansas* (organization's constitution in tiny tractlike form), MLA and MHL; Haury (1981: C2-90), 107-09.

58. Grieser and Beck (1960: C2-84), 95; Henry M. Kratz to John F. Landis, Feb 17, 1867, coll. 205, (A2-24); and *esp.* letters of Salome Kratz Funk, (A2-12), *passim*, e.g.: Henry (Kratz) to sister, Feb 19, 1868, or Salome Funk to sister, Dec 17, 1872.

59. Annie Kratz letters to sister (Salome Kratz Funk), 1864-1886, *passim*, quot. from Dec 20, 1878; for the same use of women in a putting-out pattern in Ohio, see Emiline Nold to niece (Salome Funk), Feb 29, 1864; (A2-12).

60. Smith (1983: C2-193), 88-89.

61. Letter fragment from Juniata NE with no signature (surely from Anna Lapp Hill) to "Dear cousin Mary," Aug 22, 1879, coll. 163, reel 2, (A1-3).

62. Stauffer (1855: B1-14, *Glaubens-Grund*), 411-20; Musser (1873: B1-11), 391-412, *esp.* 398-99.

63. Prieb (C2-160), 14-15.

64. Friesen (1978: C1-4), ch. 18, *esp.* 271-72.

65. Hiebert (1973: C2-97), 58-61; Holdeman (1863: B2-42), 79-83; Holdeman (1876: B2-41), 184ff.

66. *ME*, I, 470-71; Schwarzendruber, in Bender (1946: B2-5), 228 n. 11. Two sources, not impressive as scholarly works but with some facts and perspective are: Stiles (1934: C2-198) and Smith (1961: C2-190). Quot. from Bender (1934: B1-2), 95.

67. Bender (1934: B1-2), 95.

68. Schwarzendruber, in Bender (1946: B2-5), 228; *see also* (1977: B2-69) (Schwarzendruber writings of Aug 1863), 2, 4-5. (B1-15), 1865, p. 5.

69. *ME*, I, 470-71; *see also* Smith (1961: C2-190).

70. Schwarzendruber, in Bender (1946: B2-5), 229.

71. 1857 entries as transcribed in handwriting of Elizabeth Horsch Bender, f. 1, (A2-40); [Leonard Sudermann], "Regarding the Organization of the Zion Church ..." (typed doc. in f. 31, at margin no. 53 [A2-37]).

72. *Primary Question Book*..., 1880 ed., 32; *Intermediate Question Book*..., 41-42; *Bible Class Question Book*..., 1881 ed., 110; Lancaster conf. (B2-58).

73. Gingerich (1939: C2-78), 73, 229-30; Western District A. M. conf. (B2-92), May 29-31, 1890, p. 10; Gratz (1953: C2-81), 176.

74. Ohio conf., May 11, 1867, as reported in *HT* 4 (Jun 1867), 89; "An Old Document from the Lancaster Conference," 4 (typed trans. apparently by Elizabeth Horsch Bender, with a German original, ca. 1880), (A2-7); Lancaster conf. (1881: B2-59); Ind.-Mich. conf. (B2-48), Oct 7, 1875, p. 24.

75. Eastern District conf. (B2-21), May 3, 1850, p. 14; Kans.-Neb. conf. (B2-52), Oct 7, 1892, p. 44.

76. Umble (1941: B2-81), 95, 108, the latter page being part of Umble's trans. of Unzicker; Bender (1937: B2-6), 163, 166, the latter page being part of Bender's transcription of the discipline; Nafziger (1930: B2-63), 143.

77. Cosco (C2-38), 58-59. Although apparently based on oral history, the essence of Cosco's account seems plausible; for more, *see* Gingerich (1939: C2-78), 229-36.

78. Elizabeth Horsch Bender, trans. and ed., "Mennonite Courtship, 1864-65," *MHB*, 35 (Oct 1974), 4-5—printing B. Beachy to Guengerich, Sep 3, 1864, and Guengerich to Joel Beachy, Feb 11, 1865. *GH*, 21 (Jan 31, 1929), 927-28.

79. F. 18, box 1, (A2-23), *passim*; Lehman (1969: C2-129), 176; Friesen (1974: B2-22), 28-29; Annie (Kratz) to sister (Salome Funk), Sep 28, 1872, (A2-12).

80. Letter fragment from "bro. Joe" to John, certainly Joseph Landis to John Landis, from internal evidence early 1872, coll. 214, (A2-24).

81. Joseph Wenger, *History of the Descendants of J. Conrad Geil* ... (Elgin, Ill., 1914), 160; Oberholtzer (1972: B1-12), 396.

82. Miyakawa (1964: C2-142), 54, 60-61.

83. Gratz (1953: C2-81), 175-76; "The Discipline of 1837," in Bender (1934: B1-2), 94.

84. *See*, e.g.: Ind.-Mich. conf. (B2-48), Oct 13, 1865, p. 10, and 1868, p. 4. *HT*: 17 (Jan 1880), 92; 18 (Jan 1881), 4-5; 31 (Jun 1894), 173; 34 (Jun 15, 1897), 186. Menn. Breth. Church (B1-10), 3rd source, 1889, p. 89. *CB*, 1 (May 15, Jun 15, 1882), 76, 93; a scan of the *Bundesbote* showed no significant discussion of the question; a scan of a typed translation of Western District conf. minutes, 1882-1887 (B2-93), showed preoccupation with the issues suggested but not attention to the intermarriage question; Haury (1981: C2-90) does not have an index entry on marriage or intermarriage (however, neither does it for lodges or secret societies, clearly an important issue); Pannabecker (1975: C1-11), 43, 48, 73, 112, seems to suggest that the question arose but was not one on which GCs cared to draw a line.

85. *See* Kern (1983: C2-109). For a succinct and gentle-spirited defense of the exclusivist Reformed Mennonite position, *see esp.* Musser (1873: B1-11), 68-73.

86. Burkholder (1857: B1-4), 244-46.

87. "The Discipline of 1837," in Bender (1934: B1-2), 94.

88. Burkholder (1837: B1-5), 430; Virginia conf. (B2-86), 1874, p. 13; Ind.-Mich. conf. (B2-48), Oct 13, 1865, p. 10; Ind.-Mich. Amish Menn. conf., in Ind.-Mich. conf. (B2-48), Jun 2, 1892, p. 151.

89. Annie (Kratz) to sister (Salome Funk), Mar 21, 1875, (A2-12); the reference to Perkasie was surely to what is now Blooming Glen Mennonite Church—*see* Wenger (1937: C2-244), 23 n. 101.

90. *See*, e.g.: Virginia conf. (B2-86), 1869, p. 10, and 1886, p. 27; Kans.-Neb. conf. (B2-52), Apr 6-7, 1888, p. 16; Ind.-Mich. conf. (B2-48), 1895, p. 162, and 1900, p. 73.

91. Amos Herr to Samuel Kaufman (surely Va. bishop Samuel Coffman), Feb 1890, f. 1, box 11, (A1-1).

92. Ibid.

93. Ibid.

94. Umble (1929: C2-226), 13-14; Ind.-Mich. conf. (B2-48), Oct 12, 1867, p. 12; *HT*, 5 (Jun 1868), 169; Southwestern Pa. conf. (B2-74), Oct 19-20, 1883, p. 20; Menn. Breth. Church (B1-10), 3rd source, Nov 12, 1883, p. 16.

95. *HT*: 4 (Nov 1867), 169; 5 (Feb 1868), 26-28.

96. *See HT*: 4 (Sep 1867), 139; 5 (Jan, Apr, Jun 1868), 9, 10-11, 58, 89, 91-92, 106; Umble (1929: C2-226), 13-20; Lehman (1974: C2-128), 61.

97. *HT*, 5 (Jun 1868), 106.

98. Ind.-Mich. conf. (B2-48), Oct 7, 1875, p. 23; Oct 13, 1887, p. 36.

99. Eastern District conf. (B2-21): Oct 1889, and 1890-1894, *passim*. *TM*, 5 (Dec 1889), 41.

100. For docs. that convey the strong sense of family and include a very typical will, *see* Henry Bower (1836-1909), "Record Book" and "Families and Relations Book . . ." (unpublished, 1895, handwritten in English); at EPMHL.

101. Letter fragment from "bro. Joe" (Joseph Landis) to John (Landis), evidently from spring 1872, coll. 215, (A2-24); letter fragment to "Cousin Mary," Aug 22, 1879, evidently from Anna Lapp Hill, coll. 163, reel 2, (A1-3); Levi A. Ressler to Moses Brenneman, Apr 26. 1868, f. 26, box 1, (A2-3); David Goerz to Bernard Warkentin, Oct 25, Nov 27, 1872, (A1-10).

CHAPTER 4

1. Burkholder (1857: B1-4).

2. For a good, quick intro. to historic continental capital-P Pietism, *see* Stoeffler (1976: C2-200-1). Stoeffler's books are also very basic [(1971: C2-200-2), (1973: C2-199), (1976: C2-200-3)], as is Brown (1978: C2-28).

3. *See* MacMaster (1985: C1-10), ch. 6.

4. Friedmann (1949: C1-3), *esp.* 4, 85-88, and chs. 2, 10; *see also* Friedmann (1950: C2-66). For expanding this paragraph, *see* my 1983:C2-173. For a discussion other than Friedmann's on Anabaptism vis-à-vis Pietism, albeit not a very developed one, *see* Crous (1957:C2-42). *See also:* Durnbaugh: (1959:C2-52) and (1959:C2-53), and Dyck (1973:C2-54). O'Malley (1973:C2-151) is also helpful for points of connection of Anabaptism and Pietism, e.g., in terms such as *Gelassenheit* and *Nachfolge*: *see esp.* 117, 134-35, 156-7. An old source positing continuity Anabaptism to Pietism is Ritschl's classic (1880:C2-165); *see* I, 6-7.

5. *See* Burkholder (1837: B1-5), 7-28, 263-64; makes identification with Waldensians much stronger than with Anabaptists; has quite a polygenesis view of Anabaptists. *See also* Holdeman (1876: B2-41), 27-69.

6. Wenger (1937: C2-244), 323; Friedmann (1949: C1-3), 162-63, 143, 146.

7. Friedmann (1949: C1-3), 189-93.

8. Ibid., 217, 155, 24, 204; Kadelbach (1971: C2-106), 47; Wenger (1937: C2-244), 316; Bender (1932: C2-13), 156.

9. J. H. Oberholtzer apparently to Daniel Hoch, Mar 1, 1856, f. 14, box 1, (A2-7), refers to plans to publish a work by Arnold. Friedmann in *ME*, I, 165, declared that Oberholtzer reprinted Arnold's *Theologia Experimentalis . . .* in 1855.

10. Friedmann (1949: C1-3), 24; Kadelbach (1971: C2-106), 47.

11. Yoder (1969: C2-262), p. 4 of intro. and plate 54.

12. *See* Schlabach (1983: C2-173).

13. MacMaster (1985: C1-10), 169-70; Kadelbach (1971: C2-106), 74, 80-82, 96; Martin Moellinger to Johannes Weber, Feb 29, 1821, published in Bender (1931: B2-7).

14. Kadelbach (1971: C2-106), 69-74, 96.

15. Ibid., 82-96; "Vorrede," in (1804: B2-84); Yoder (1961: C2-266), 27-28.

16. Kadelbach (1971: C2-106), 91-95, 152-55.

17. Ibid., 168-69, 172.

18. Lizzie Brubaker to Jacob and Mary Mensch, Oct 21, 1877, (A1-7).

19. Warkentin to Goerz, Jul 25, 1868, (A1-10).

20. *See*, e.g., (A1-7), or (A1-3); unfinished, unsigned letter fragment, evidently Gross to Coffman, 1899, coll. 119, reel 2, (A1-3). The Pietistic language of some of Gross's correspondents shades off into the idiom of the late-nineteenth-century Mennonite quickening.

21. Sources cited n. 2 and n. 4.

22. Brown (1962: C2-29), 10-11, 31. Instead of asking for a more realistic version of Anabaptism Brown suggested comparison with the Pietism of Spener and Francke. Actually Mennonites had little direct contact with that original Pietism; a better comparison might be with the radical Pietists Jacob Arndt and Gottfried Arnold, Gerhard Tersteegen's sermons and writings, the products of Wúrttemberg Pietists, etc.

23. *See esp.* Handy (1984: C1-5); *also* Miller (1965: C2-141-2), 6, 7, 11, 14, 47. Such writings have stimulated other authors, e.g., Goen (1985: C2-79-2).

24. For Anabaptist v. Protestant views of justification, atonement, and regeneration, *see*, e.g., Friedmann (1950: C2-66), Wenger (1950: C2-242), Bender (1961: C2-15), Augsburger (1962: C2-5), and Weaver (1985: C2-236-2). For some key discussions of the Anabaptists' way of using the Bible, *see* articles in *MQR*, 40 (Apr 1966); and Yoder (1967: C2-264-1).

25. *See esp.* Weaver (1987: C1-22-2). Re the word "salvation," I am not a linguist, but esp. the German *Seligkeit* or *Gottseligkeit*—literally "blessing of God"—often trans. as "salvation," seems to have a rich connotation of total well-being, not just a transaction rescuing one from damnation.

26. Burkholder (1857: B1-4), 222-24, 195-96.

27. Ibid., 211.

28. Ibid., 189, 224.

29. Henrich Martin to Benjamin Weber, Apr 30, 1819, f., box 6, (A2-38).

30. (1874: B2-13), 44, 49.

31. Godshalk (1838: B1-8), 50-59.

32. Burkholder (1837: B1-5), entire, and 383-405, 295-313.

33. Ibid., 7-28, 263-64.

34. Ibid., 266-79, 339-40, 314-16, 296-97.

35. Southwestern Pa. conf. (B2-74), Oct 20-21, 1882.

36. Kans.-Neb. conf. (B2-52), Oct 6-7, 1898, p. 88; Ind.-Mich. conf. (B2-48), Oct 14, 1864.

37. For typical evidence see: Virginia conf. (B2-86), Sep 28-29, 1877, p. 16; Brenneman (1867: B1-3), 7-8; Ruth (1976: C2-168), 40, 75; Eastern District conf. (B2-21), May 2, 1850, p. 13 (N. B. Grubb trans.).

38. (A2-34); King (C2-110), 9.

39. Brenneman (1867: B1-3); Liechty (1980: C1-9), 13.

40. Brenneman (1867: B1-3), 7-8, 20-21.

41. Ibid., 7-10, 13.

42. Ibid., 8, 5, 6, 15-18, and *passim*.

43. Ibid., 7-9, 18-19.

44. Ibid., 19-21.

45. Ibid., 17.

46. Brenneman (1973: B2-10). I owe the main ideas of this paragraph largely to Joseph C. Liechty, through personal contacts and his "Humility" article (1980: C1-9), *esp.* 16-17.

47. Burkholder (1857: B1-4), 226-27; Brenneman (1867: B1-3), 12, 15.

48. *HT*, 5 (Jul 1868), 106. For more, *see* ch. 3 at n. 94ff.

49. Liechty (1980: C1-9), 17-18; Epp (1974: C1-2), 137.

50. *See*, e.g., Jacob B. and Mary Mensch to John S. Kurtz, undated fragment apparently from 1880s (1972: B1-13), 331, 375.

51. For a different interpretation of "manifest destiny," Heitala (1985: C2-91-2).

52. *See* Schlabach (1983: C2-173), 226-27.

53. Musser (1873:B1-11).240, 249, 252, 257, 285, 296, 299, 331-34; Eschelman (1969:C2-62), 12. Whether Francis Herr was expelled or voluntarily withdrew remains unclear; Musser said "expulsion" on p. 299, "withdrew" on 300. Funk (1878:C2-68), 28; Herr (1890:B2-36), 16. Funk insisted on the "old" Mennonite version of the horse story even after a reasoned argument by Daniel Musser against it, pp. 298-300.

54. Musser (1873: B1-11), 296; Herr (1890: B2-36), 4-6, 9.

55. *See* Brown (1978: C2-28), 54; Stoeffler (1973: C2-199), ch. 5; also, Stoffer (1981: C2-201), is especially relevant to Mennonite history.

56. Van Braght (1982:C1-22), 21-26, 44-60 (pagination of most English-language printings).

57. Musser (1873: B1-11), 179; Herr (1890: B2-35), 429; L. S., "Reformed Mennonites," *The Weekly Messenger of the German Reformed Church* (Feb 11, 1846), 1-2; Kern (1983: C2-109).

58. *ME*, I, 200-01, 219-23; II, 69-70.

59. Much confusion with the term "fundamentalism" comes from unclarity whether reference is to a generic quality or to capital-F "Fundamentalism," the historic movement within North American Protestantism beginning about 1910.

60. For all or most of Musser's writing, *see* 1878 ed. of (1873: B1-11).

61. Funk (1878: C2-68), 176; Musser (1873: B1-11), 390-91, 401, 255, 180, and *passim*.

62. Musser (1864: B2-62); Tolstoy (1951: B2-78), 25, 27-30; *see also* Wenger (1964: C2-248).

63. *ME*, IV, 268-69; *Mennonite Yearbook* . . . (1976), 119.

64. Swope: (1963: C2-216) and (1962: C2-212); Hiebert (1973: C2-97), 58, 171, 172. Evidence of influence from Funk to Holdeman is circumstantial; Holdeman might have taken the name "Church of God in Christ" more or less from Reformed Mennonite writings, as they rather often used the phrase "Church of Christ."

65. Holdeman (1863: B2-42), 5, 79-81; Holdeman (1876: B2-41), 128-30.

66. Herr (1890: B2-35), 142-53, and *passim*; Holdeman (1863: B2-42), 89, 153; Holdeman (1890: B2-43), 7-13.

67. Hiebert (1973: C2-97), 190, 212-14.

68. Ibid.

69. Holdeman (1863: B2-42), 142, 144, and *passim*; Holdeman (1876: B2-41), 110-11.

70. Holdeman (1863: B2-42), 137-40, 156-67, 97-98, and *passim*.

71. Hiebert (1973: C2-97), 188, 190, 212-14.

72. Ibid., 220, 22 ; *Mennonite Yearbook* . . . (1985), 181.

73. For basic histories, *see* Storms (1958: C2-204) and Nussbaum (1976: C2-149). Wenger (1961: C2-247), 379-84, offers an excellent quick account of MBC origins.

74. Cross (1950: C2-41).

75. Daniel Hoch, in Hoch, Bauman, and Oberholtzer (1854: B2-40); Hoch (1870: B2-38), and (1868: B2-39); Daniel and Jacob Hoch to David Scherk, Mar 28, 1869, f. 14, box 1, (A2-7). Two hymns apparently by Hoch, printed as broadsides, copies in MHL: "Der Binde- und Lösungs-Schlüssel im Herzen" (1855); and "Welche sich vor dem Reise scheuen. . . ."

76. For the personal-clash idea *see* Wenger (1959: C2-245), *esp.* 113-15; Wenger (1961: C2-247), 366-78; and perhaps also Wenger (1960: B2-91), 48-56, incl. footnotes. For failure-of-conflict-resolution framework: Epp (1974: C1-2), 137.

77. Hoch, in Hoch, Bauman, and Oberholtzer (1854: B2-40), 36-37; Hoch (1868: B2-39), re event of Aug 18, 1849; and Hoch (1870: B2-38), 13-14. Eby's strategy apparently was to seek a working conciliation more than decide guilt and innocence: *see* sources just mentioned, *esp.* Samuel Bauman, in Hoch, Bauman, and Oberholtzer (1854: B2-40), 21-22; and Hoch (1870: B2-38), 13-14.

78. Hoch (1870: B2-38), 12, 10; Hoch (1850: B2-37), 12; on use of Scripture, the various sources by Hoch and associates cited in this section.

79. The Methodism charge and the reply run all through the sources by Hoch and associates herein cited; *see esp.* Bauman, in Hoch, Bauman, and Oberholtzer (1854: B2-40). Re citing Menno, *see* Hoch, in Hoch, Bauman, and Oberholtzer (1854: B2-40), 50, and Bauman, in the same source, 89; also High (1870: B2-38), 13. Re Mennonite doctrines, see Hoch (1850: B2-37), 23, 19, etc.

80. High (1870: B2-38), 10; Cross (1950: C2-41), ch. 10.

81. For rumors of disorder *see* Hoch, in Hoch, Bauman, and Oberholtzer (1854: B2-40), 31-32. Daniel Brenneman was charged with violating 1 Cor. 14:35, i.e., allowing women to speak; *see* Storms (1958: C2-204), 43-44. For women's new roles in revivals *see*, e.g., Cross (1950: C2-41), 177-78.

82. Hoch, in Hoch, Bauman, and Oberholtzer (1954: B2-40), 58, 31-32, 46; Bauman, in same source, *passim*.

83. Hoch, in *ibid.*, 50; quot., 46; more such language: Bauman, in same source, *passim*, and Hoch (1870: B2-38), 15.

84. Wenger (1959: C2-245), 129-30.

85. Wenger (1960: B2-91), 50-55; Storms (1958: C2-204), 43-50.

86. Storms (1958: C2-204), 68.

87. *See*, e.g., MJ diary at Jan 23, 25, 1874, (A1-4).

88. Wenger (1959: C2-245), 112-13.

89. Brenneman, quot. in Wenger (1961: C2-247), 382.

90. *HT*: 16 (Nov 1879), 215; 26 (Sep 1, 1889), 265; *see also* (Sep 18, 1881), 155-56. Storms (1958: C2-204), 68.

91. Storms (1958: C2-204), 68.

92. Nussbaum (1976: C2-149), 2, 61.

93. Diller (1951: C2-47), 31; Smith (1983: C2-193), 111, 58-59, 70; Nussbaum (1976: C2-149), 61.

94. Nussbaum (1976: C2-149), 2.

95. *See* ch. 8. at n. 25-26ff.

96. Nussbaum (1976: C2-149), 4-9, 42-45.

97. Diller (1951: C2-47), 34, 38-39; Nussbaum (1976: C2-149), 12-14, 40.

98. Nussbaum (1976: C2-149), 42-43; Kauffman and Harder (1975: C2-107), 133-34.

CHAPTER 5

1. Hunsicker to Herr, Jan 29, 1848; Herr to Hunsicker, Apr 17, 1848; in (1972: B1-13), 333 and 345, 347.

2. *See esp.* Daniel Hoch, in Hoch, Bauman, and Oberholtzer (1854:B2-40).

3. For a detailed account of the Oberholtzer affair touching a myriad of secular and religious factors, *see* Ruth (1984: C1-15), chs. 6-10, *passim*; *see also* Hostetler (1977), ch. 2-6, *esp.* 4. For argument emphasizing internal tensions rather than secular forces, *see* Harder (1963: C2-85). Harder's argument may rest on a false dichotomy, if Oberholtzer drew on secular ideas to deal with internal disequilibria.

4. A strong thesis that Mennonites' cultural peculiarities prevented mission success runs through Kaufman (1931: C2-108). In writing my *Gospel Versus Gospel* I did not find the evidence convincing; *see* (1980: C2-172), esp. 155-56. Of course a group is not prepared for mission if it is so preoccupied with internal affairs that it cannot deal with the culture to which it wishes to communicate.

5. Ruth (1984: C1-15), 212-13. *ME*, IV, 13; I, 529. Pannabecker (1975: C1-11), 17; East Pa. conf. (1972: B2-20), 408.

6. Isaac F. Meyer in (1972: B2-77), 427; Wenger (1937: C2-244), 353-54; Ruth (1984: C1-15), 232, 239, 246-47, 260, 271-72, 278.

7. For the best primary sources on the Oberholtzer affair, *see* (1972: B1-13); that Oberholtzer's submission and humility was more and more the issue rather than the coat itself seems obvious from such sources; *see esp.* Meyer statement in (1972: B2-77), 425, 427.

8. Ruth (1984: C1-15), 237-38, 254-57; Oberholtzer and Meyer statements in (1972: B2-77), 414-16, 418, 421, 423-24, 425, 427.

9. Ruth (1984: C1-15), 231.

10. (1972: B1-13): Abraham Grater to Henry Nice, Apr 26, 1848, p. 355; Nice to Grater, 1848, p. 361; p. 368 n. 63; pp. 366-69, incl. n. 63, for Franconia conf. minute of May 1848. Oberholtzer, in (1972: B2-77), 418; East Pa. conf. (1972: B2-20), 407. Ruth (1984: C1-15), 271-72.

11. Ruth (1984: C1-15), 266, 272; Wm. S. Gottshall, as quot. in (1972: B1-13), 368 n. 63.

12. Oberholtzer (1972: B1-12), 390, 396, 393-94; on the lawsuit issue *see also* Oberholtzer, in (1972: B2-77), 424. Because so much of the dispute was oral, we have no systematic critique of the constitution by Franconians. But Lancaster conference authorities left written views: doc., Aug 29, 1847, trans. and in (1972: B1-13), 360-65; re salary, 363. Wenger (1937: C2-244), 356. Before actually adopting its constitution the new conf. added language clarifying: exemption from rebaptism was for persons already baptized "upon confession of faith"—*see* conf. minutes of Oct 28, 1847 (B2-21). That conformed to traditional practice at least of the Lancaster conf.; *see* Lancaster doc. just cited.

13. Ruth (1984: C1-15), 270; East Pa. conf. (1972: B2-20), 408; *see* Wenger (1937: B2-244), 356; Eastern District conf. (B2-21), Oct 28, 1847.

14. Ruth (1984: C1-15), 243.

15. Ibid., 237-38, 254-57, 234, 291-92, 212, 282.

16. Ibid., 270; *see*, e.g., Tyler (1962: C2-225), 259-64.

17. Oberholtzer (1972: B2-65), 401, 403; *see* Ruth (1984: C1-15), 241-42; Oberholtzer (1972: B1-12), 388.

18. Ruth (1984: C1-15), 280; *see also* Funk's delightful remarks on Geil, diary, Jan 11, 1863 (on pp. for Nov 29-Dec 1, 1862), box 2, (A1-2); and Funk (1897: B2-25).

19. Ruth (1984: C1-15), ch. 6-10, *passim, esp.* 239-42; note remarks, p. 242, on humility. Oberholtzer (1972: B2-65), 403.

20. Ruth (1984: C1-15), 247.

21. Generalization based on primary sources cited herein and on secondary sources, *esp.* Ruth (1984: C1-15), ch. 6-10.

22. Hunsicker (1851: B2-47), 15; Ruth (1984: C1-15), 270, 274. Ruth has contrasted the "old" and "new" factions' outlooks at length, in his chs. 6-10; *see esp.* 201-03, 212-20, 233, 239, 255, 260, 271-72, 278-83.

23. For modernization vis-à-vis Mennonite history up to Oberholtzer's time, *see* Schlabach (1979: C2-174); its note 1 lists some outstanding authors and works on the modernization process. *See esp.* Weber (1968: B2-88), *passim*, e.g., 61-70.

24. Oberholtzer (1972: B1-12), 391-92, 396; East Pa. conf. (1972: B2-20), 408.

25. Abraham Hunsicker to Christian Herr, Jan 29, 1848, (1972: B1-13), 335; Oberholtzer, in (1972: B2-77), 415-16, 418; Oberholtzer (1972: B1-12), 392.

26. Meyer and Oberholtzer, in (1972: B2-77), 425, 423; Ruth (1984: C1-15), 243-44.

27. Oberholtzer (1972:B2-65), 402; John H. Oberholtzer to editor, *Der Waffenlos Wächter*, 7 (Jan & Feb 1877), 2.

28. Oberholtzer (1972: B1-12), 394-95.

29. Eastern District conf. (B2-21), May 1 and 28, 1851; Ruth (1984: C1-15), 212, 270, 292-97, 307; Hunsicker (1851: B2-47); Grater (1854: B2-30); Wenger (1937: C2-244), 361; *ME*, II, 389.

30. Ruth (1984: C1-15), 297, 303; Wenger (1937: C2-244), 381, 34; Eastern District conf. (B2-21), May 1859, May 1861. *The General Conference Mennonite Church . . . : Handbook of Information*: (1970-71), 8; (1971-72), 8.

31. Oberholtzer (1972: B1-12), 392; Oberholtzer, in (1972: B2-77), 416, 422-23.

32. Eastern District conf. (B2-21), May 1, 1851, May 1859, Oct 1859.

33. Ibid., May 1853, Oct 1857, May 1858.

34. Ibid., Oct 1851, May 1852.

35. Ibid., Oct 28, 1847, May 1, 1851.

36. Oberholtzer (1972: B2-65), 402-03; Eastern District conf. (B2-21), May 1848, Oct 1861.

37. Eastern District conf. (B2-21), May 1853, Oct 1856, Oct 1857; Ruth (1984: C1-15), 302; Wenger (1937: C2-244), 370. Wm. and Anna Schelly to Daniel and Markata Heigh (i.e., Hoch or High), Oct 12, 1857; Hoch's charge, inferred from A. Eby to Hoch, Nov 26, 1872, and undated (early 1873?); f. 1/14, (A2-7).

38. For basic histories of the General Conf. church, from a General Conf. (GC) perspective, *see*: Pannabecker (1975: C1-11); Krehbiel (1898/1938: C2-119).

39. *Volksblatt*, quot. in Krehbiel (1898: C2-119), 20-21; Ruth (1984: C1-15), 300, 304; Eastern District conf. (B2-21), Oct 1858; Gingerich (1939: C2-78), ch. 7.

40. Gingerich (1939: C2-78), 46, 67, 70, 76-78. *See esp.*: Krehbiel (1961: B2-56); and Susanna Krehbiel, "Autobiography," 1911, (A2-22).

41. Gingerich (1939: C2-78), 70-71, 81; plan of union trans. and printed in Krehbiel (1898: C2-119), 56-57; Pannabecker (1975: C1-11), 43; *ME*, IV, 479.

42. Friedmann (1949: C1-3), ch. 5 and *passim, esp.* 65-66, 95-96. Three Goshen College baccalaureate seminar papers (copies in MHL): John D. Roth, "The Double-Edged Sword: Pietism and the South-German Mennonite Religious Dynamic, 1800-1850" (1981); Mervin Horst, "Peter Weber, a Mennonite Minister with the Spirit of Pietism" (1984); Joseph Springer, "Lorentz Friedenreich" (1980). Pannabecker (1975: C1-11), 40-43.

43. *ME*, IV, 357; Krehbiel (1898: C2-119), 28-29.

44. General Conf. church (B2-29); Krehbiel (1898: C2-119), 31-32; *Volksblatt* quot. in Ruth (1984: C1-15), 314.

45. Eastern District conf. (B2-21), May 1860; Ruth (1984: C1-15), 314-15.

46. Ruth (1984: C1-15), 315; *ME*, II, 844; Krehbiel (1898: C2-119), 50-51, 18-19.

47. Krehbiel (1898: C2-119), 79, 142ff., 82, 116, 49-51; General Conf. church (B2-29), 1861, p. 7.

48. General Conf. church (B2-29), 1860; Gingerich (1939: C2-78), 84; Krehbiel (1898: C2-119), 52, 49, 53, 55-57.

49. General Conf. church (B2-29), 1860; trans. in Krehbiel (1898: C2-119), 56-57, and in Pannabecker (1975: C1-11), 47-48.

50. General Conf. church (B2-29), 1860, pp. 5-6; Krehbiel (1898: C2-119), 56, 59-60.

51. Pannabecker (1975: C1-11), 48-49.

52. General Conf. church (B2-29): 1861, p. 14; 1863, p. 19. Krehbiel (1898: C2-119), 80, 116; Pannabecker (1975: C1-11), 51-52.

53. Pannabecker (1975: C1-11), chs. 4-5.

54. Krehbiel (1898: C2-119), 84, 414-16, 93-113.

55. Ibid., 121, 123-24.

56. Ibid., 160-61, and 1875 school committee report, quot. 228-33; Krehbiel (1961: B2-56), 63; General Conf. church (B2-29), 1875, pp. 47-50.

57. Christian Krehbiel, "The First Sermon in the College at Wadsworth: Delivered at the Dedication, 1866," f. 18, (A2-21).

58. Krehbiel (1898: C2-119), 125-28; *Wadsworth Enterprise*, Oct 12, 1866, quot. in Rachel Kreider, "A Mennonite College Through Town Eyes," *ML* (Jun 1977), 8.

59. Krehbiel (1961: B2-56), 65.

60. Lehman (1969: C2-129), 98; Sprunger (1938: C2-196), 26.

61. Hartzler (1925: C2-88), 132-34; Krehbiel (1888: C2-119), 145, 194, 236, 237, 254; re debt, *see*, e.g., General Conf. church (1888: B2-29), 1882, 87.

62. Friedmann (1949: C1-3), 224; Pannabecker (1975: C1-11), 14.

63. My observation from living in eastern Pa., 1976-77; colleagues from that region have agreed.

64. Ruth (1984: C1-15), 239.

65. Eastern District conf. (1888: B2-29), Oct 1861, Oct 1862, May and Oct 1863. (A linguist, Marion Wenger, checked and retranslated the relevant passages.)

66. Krehbiel (1961: B2-56), 67; *ZH*, 7 (Feb 7-Oct 7, 1881), *esp.* 125.

67. Haury (1894: B2-34); Ind.-Mich. conf. (B2-48): 1864, p. 8; 1867, p. 12. Brenneman (1863: B2-9); Funk (1863: B2-26).

68. *See* ch. 11. Re Brenneman's support of Funk's publishing, *see*: Brenneman to Funk, Jul 28, Oct 17, Nov 26, 1863, box 6, (A1-2); Peter Nissley to Brenneman, Dec 20, 1888, (A2-2).

69. 1860 plan of union, trans. and quot. in Krehbiel (1898: C2-119), 56-57; Pannabecker (1975: C1-11), 49.

CHAPTER 6

1. Burkholder (1857: B1-4), 251-52, 243-44.

2. Stauffer (1855: B1-14, *Eine Chronik*), 86-89.

3. *TM*, 1885-1900, *passim*, *esp.* 2 (Aug 1887), 171; 3 (Sep 1888), 182-83; 7 (Aug 1892), 84; 11 (Oct 1895), 1; 10 (Aug 1895), 84; 11 (Sep 1896), 92-93; quot. 11 (Feb 1896), 37.

4. Burkholder (1857: B1-4), 213-14.

5. Ibid., 251, 243-44.

6. Ibid., 226-27.

7. Simons (1956: B2-73), 555. For key Anabaptist sources on the two-realm doctrine, *see* same, *esp.* 117-20, 190-226, 549-57; and also: doc. trans. by J. C. Wenger, in Wenger (1945: B2-90), 249-51; Dordrecht Confession, articles XIII and XIV, printed, e.g., in van Braght (1982: C1-22), 38-44, and in Wenger (1937: C2-244), Appendix XII, and summarized by Wenger in *ME*, II, 92-93; [Pieter Jansz Twisck], 33-article confession printed in van Braght (1982: C1-22), 373-410, *esp.* article XXVII, 402-03 (*see also ME*, I, 681); same Twisck confession rev. and trans. in Burkholder (1837: B1-5), 31-262.

8. *See esp.* writings of John H. Yoder, *esp.* (1972:C2-264-3) and (1977:C2-264-2).

9. Twisck confession in van Braght (1982: C1-22), 402.

10. Ibid.; Simons (1956: B2-73), *esp.* 197, 204.

11. On this Protestant "righteous empire" idea, *see esp.*: Marty (1970: C2-136); Miller (1965: C2-141-2), 6, 7, 11, 14, 47; Handy (1984: C1-5); Wilson (1979: C2-254); Stout (1974: C2-205); Goen (1985: C2-79-2), esp. p. 11 and ch. 1; James F. McClear, "The Republic and the Millennium," and Lois W. Banner, "Religious Benevolence as Social Control: A Critique of an Interpretation," in Mulder and Wilson (1978: C2-145), 181-98, 218-35.

12. Dyck (1981: C1-1), 123; Eby (1940: C2-55), 90; MacMaster (1985: C1-10), 56-57, 230-35, 247, 236-38, 254-59, 265-67; Schlabach (1979: C2-174), 404-05.

13. MacMaster (1985: C1-10), 264, 279.

14. Stauffer (1855: B1-14, *Eine Chronik*), 137, 131, 88.

15. Samuel Martin, etc., to Jacob Hostetter, Jun 30, 1839; Benj. Eby to Jacob Hostetter, Jan 10, 1848, and attached doc. of May 5, 1840, (A2-19).

16. Doc. dated ca. 1843-1845 and quot. in Stoltzfus (1969: C2-203), 67.

17. Cronk (1977: C2-39), 193, 200. David Metzler to Jacob Hostetter and Christian Herr, Sep 2, 1846; Abraham Roth to Jacob Hostetter, Oct 15, 1845; (A2-19).

18. Hunsicker (1851: B2-47), 8-15; Ruth (1984: C1-15), 236-39, 254-58, 291-96.

19. Dorpalen (1939: C2-49), 235. *See also*: Dorpalen (1942: C2-48), 55-76; Ralph Wood, "Journalism among the Pennsylvania Germans," in Wood (1942: C2-259), 134; Luebke (1969: C2-133), 65-66, 87-91 149-50; Wandel (1979: C2-234), 84; Albert B. Faust, *The German Element in the United States: With Special Reference to Its Political, Moral, Social, and Educational Influence* (Boston and New York, 1909), II, 146; Wittke (1939: C2-256), 245-46.

20. Gratz (1953: C2-81), 182; Cosco (C2-38), 55-56, 73.

21. Ruth (1984: C1-15), 219.

22. Ibid., 237; John F. Funk, letter to editor, Oct 3, 1856, reprinted in *MHB*, 34 (Apr 1973), 2-3. Funk diary, Aug 30, 1860, box 1; A. K. Funk to John F. Funk, Oct 15, 1862, May 20, 1861, box 6; (A1-2).

23. John O. Clemens to Tobias and Magdalena Kolb, Oct 21, 1860, f. 17, box 1, (A2-7); Jacob Funk to John F. Funk, Jun 11, 1861, box 6, (A1-2).

24. Robertson (1980: C2-166), 79-80, 84-85, 87, 96-99, 76, 64n.

25. Ibid., *passim*, *esp.* 49-50. On Stevens' character *see also*: Brodie (1959: C2-26); Current (1942: C2-44); Samuel McCall, *Thaddeus Stevens* (Boston and New York, 1909); Williams (1941: C2-253).

26. Robertson (1980: C2-166), 49-50; Lehman (1984: C2-125), *esp.* 11-12; *see esp.* primary sources quot. at length in Lehman (1982: C1-8), esp., 363-72, also 1-3, 26A-26B, 77-78, 95-96C, 126-128, 149, 203, 245-50, 287, 346, 361.

27. Robertson (1980: C2-166), 50.

28. Ibid., *passim*, *esp.* 82, 84, 876.

29. *See* ch. 7 at n. 49-50.

30. Grieser and Beck (1960: C2-84), 56; Gibbons (1872: C2-74), 13 (or 15 in 1874 ed.); Wenger (1937: C2-244), 265; S. Godshalk to John F. Funk, Mar 15, 1867, f. 9, box 6, (A1-2).

31. *HT*, 3 (Jun 1866), 50; Ind.-Mich. conf. (B2-48), Oct 14, 1864, p. 8.

32. Brenneman (1863: B2-9), 55-56.

33. *HT*, 3 (Nov 1866), 88.

34. Virginia conf. (B2-86): Aug 31, 1866, p. 8; Oct 15-16, 1915, pp. 111-12. Weaver (1931: C2-237), 355. Lancaster conf. (1881: B2-59). Southwestern Pa. conf. (B2-74): Sep 19, 1879, p. 13; Oct 20-21, 1882, pp. 17-18. Jacob Mensch, private record of Franconia conf. proceedings (May 5, 1892), reel 1, (A1-7). Mensch clearly recorded the conf. as saying it was forbidden to go to elections ("*Eṣ ist auch verboten . . . um an die wahl zu gehen*"), yet I raise question about the conference's intent because: Franconia Mennonites had a tradition of voting; these are not officially checked minutes; and colloquially, "to go to election" could have referred not to the act of voting but to attendance at the rally surrounding voting. For examples of softer language *see*: Ind.-Mich. conf. (B2-48), Oct 12, 1876, pp. 25-26; and Ohio conf. minutes in *HT*, 17(Jul 1880), 129.

35. Lancaster conf. (1881: B2-59), 2.

36. My survey of 19th-century "old" Mennonite and Amish Mennonite conf. statements, using Erb (1951: C2-59); Lancaster conf. (1875) quot. in Weaver (1931: C2-237), 350; Lancaster conf. (1881: B2-59), 3; *HT*, 17 (Jul 1880), 129; Southwestern Pa. conf. (B2-74), Sep 19, 1879, p. 13.

37. Ind.-Mich. conf. (B2-48), Oct 12, 1867, p. 12; Benj. Herr sermon quot. in Weaver (1931: C2-237), 353-54; Lancaster conf. (1881: B2-59), 3; my survey as in n. 36.

38. *HT*, 35 (Jul 1, 1898), 198.

39. E.g.: Guy F. Hershberger, *War, Peace, and Nonresistance* (Scottdale, Pa., 1953), 162-63; John H. Yoder, *Christian Witness to the State* (Newton, Kans., 1964), 61-72.

40. John F. Funk diary, Nov 2, 1880, box 3, (A1-2). Anna to brother (John) and family, Nov 10, 1880, Nov 7, Nov 1882, coll. 203, reel 3, (A2-24).

41. *See* ch. 9.

42. Juhnke (1975: C2-105), 25.

43. *See* ch. 9, *esp.* at n. 16-19.

44. *See* ch. 10, *esp.* at n. 32-40, 45-67.

45. John B. Toews, "Nonresistance Re-examined: Why Did Mennonites Leave Russia in 1874?" *ML*, 29 (special midyear issue, 1974), 9-10.

46. *See* ch. 9 at n. 46-54, 64, 74-86; and ch. 10 at n. 1, 5-20, 57-60.

47. David Goerz to Bernard Warkentin, Oct 22ff., 1872, Jan 15, 1873, (A1-10).

48. *See* ch. 10 at n. 1, 7, 15-16, 68-73.

49. Juhnke (1975: C2-105), 24, 39; for intro. to Gnadenau, *see* Pantle (1947: C2-155).

50. Toews (1975: C1-19), chs. 3-4. Menn. Breth. church (B1-10), first source, 3-4; second source, 1879, p. 3.

51. Western District conf. (B2-93), 3rd conf., Oct 27, 1879, pp. 2, 11; Juhnke (1975: C2-105), 37, *see also* 18-21, and sources there cited.

52. Juhnke (1975: C2-105), ch. 3, and p. 5.

53. Ibid., 35-36, 52, 80-81.

54. Miller (1953: C2-140); Jansen (1921: B2-50), 54-63.

55. Juhnke (1975: C2-105), 44-48.

56. Ibid., 41-42, and ch. 4, *passim.*

57. *See esp.* Nugent (1963: C2-148); Juhnke (1975: C2-105), 43, 48-50.

58. Juhnke (1975: C2-105), 51, 50, 53, 31, 54.

59. Amstutz (1978: C2-2), 12-13.

60. For intro. to literature of civil religion, *see* Smith (1971: C2-191). Items cited above, n. 11, are very relevant, *esp.* Handy.

61. *See*, e.g., John Landis to brothers, mother, sister, Feb 8, 1862, coll. 214, reel 3, (A2-24).

62. *TM*, 10 (Jan, Mar 1895), 31, 47.

63. Strong (1885: B2-75); *see*, e.g., Paul Toews, "The City," and "The Imperialism of Righteousness," chs. 6 and 11 in White and Hopkins (1976: C2-249). *TM*, 5: (Aug 1890), 161; (Apr 1890), 98. Wenger (1937: C2-244), 376; Ruth (1984: C1-15), 411; Allebach, in *TM*, 5 (Nov 1889), 17-19.

64. *TM*: 9 (Aug 1895), 84; 10 (Apr 1895), 55; etc.

65. *TM*, 8 (Nov 1892), 9; Haury (1894: B2-34).

66. Coffman (1896: B2-18).

67. *HT*: 9 (Feb 1872), 23; 30 (Dec 1, 1892), 370-72; 31 (Dec 15, 1893), 370-71.

68. *YPP*: 1 (Sep 29, 1894), 154-55; 4 (Jul 3, 1897), 108-09; 6 (Feb 1899), 1.

69. *The Dictionary of American History* (1976 ed.), V, 429-30.

70. Re Geil: John F. Funk diary, Jan 22, 1863 (but on pages marked Nov 29-Dec 1, 1862), box 2, (A1-2). Re Oberholtzer: Ruth (1984: C1-15), 398-99. Paton Yoder, "Katie, Amishwoman," *MHB*, 42 (Apr 1981), 1-3; *HT*, 10 (Aug 1873), 137; Tschetter (1873: B2-80), 124-25; *HT*, 26 (Nov 15, 1889), 375.

71. Burkholder (1857: B1-4), 209.

72. Stauffer (1855: B1-14, *Eine Chronik*), 184; Musser (1873: B1-11), 284-85; Lehman (1978: C2-126), 73-76; Toews (1975: C1-19), 24-25.

73. *See*, e.g.: Stauffer (1855: B1-14, *Eine Chronik*), 184; *HT*, 26 (May 1, 1889), 129; Hiebert (1973: C2-97), 190, 203, 212-15. Bender (1946: B2-5), 228.

74. Survey (n. 36); Ind.-Mich. conf. (B2-48), 1884, p. 34; Jacob Mensch, private minutes of Franconia conf., May 6, 1880, May 4, 1882, May 3, 1894, Mar 2, and Oct 3, 1895, reel 1, (A1-7).

75. Jacob Mensch, private minutes of Franconia conf., May 3, 1894, reel 1, (A1-7); Western District conf. (1892: B2-93), 1879, 33.

76. *See esp.*: Tyler (1962: C2-225); Smith (1967: C2-192); Handy (1984: C1-5), *esp.* ch. 2; Marty (1970: C2-136), *esp.* chs. 9, 19; and other sources at n. 11.

77. Krehbiel as quot. in [J(ohn). W. Kliewer], *Memoirs of J. W. Kliewer: or, from Herdboy to College President* (N. Newton, Kan., 1943), 61. Probably Kliewer was referring to the gen. conf. of 1896; it was at Alexanderwohl at the time the context suggests.

78. Isaac Hershey to Menno S. Steiner, Nov 24, 1894, (A1-9); J. A. Ressler diary, Feb 1, 1894 and 1893-1894 *passim*, (A2-33).

79. Clemens (1976: C2-36), 4-8—citing *HT*: 3 (Mar 1866), 18; 5 (May 1868), 76; 4 (May 1867), 67-68; 8 (Jun 1871), 86; 8 (Jul 1871), 104; 9 (Aug 1872), 117-18; 15 (Nov 1878), 195-96; 10 (Mar 1873), 56; 20 (Aug 1873), 135; and 16 (Mar 1879), 48. Clemens attributed Funk's change almost entirely to Coffman's coming—*see* his p. 8—but I suspect that the more general explanation may be equally important.

80. *HT*: *passim*; 24 (Oct 1, 1887), 297; 26 (Oct 15, 1889), 317. Clemens (1976: C2-36), 10—citing *HT*, 20 (Jun 15, 1883), 188—and 14.

81. *Rundschau* piece reprinted in "Mässigkeit oder Prohibition?" *CB*, 1 (Nov 1, 1882), 166.

82. *CB* 1 (Nov 1, 1882), 166.

83. Survey (n. 36); Ind.-Mich. conf. (B2-48), Oct 14, 1897, p. 65.

84. *HT*, 26 (Apr 1, 1889), 105.

85. Eastern District conf. (B2-21), May 7, 1889; also in *TM*, 4 (Jun 1889), 137.

86. *HT*, 26 (May 1, 1889), 137; Menn. Breth. church (B1-10), third source, 1890, p. 107. Western District conf. (B2-93): 1881, p. 7; 1883, p. 37. Juhnke (1975: C2-105), 43.

87. Juhnke (1975: C2-105), 44. Clemens (1976: C2-36), 16.

88. *TM*, 11 (Feb 1896), 37. Taylor's words brought no protest in subsequent issues of *The Mennonite*.

CHAPTER 7

1. John M. Brenneman to Jacob Nold, Aug 21, 1862, f. 5, box 7, (A2-31); printed in *MHB* 34 (Oct 1973), 3.

2. Apparently there is no really careful study of all military service laws in early-19th-century U.S., esp. not of state militia laws—nor of Mennonite responses. The generalization of little problem or pressure comes largely from lack of evidence of any. The best secondary source is Brock (1968: C2-25), 389-404. Although very excellent, Brock's book understandably makes little use of archival materials; and its treatment of state provisions is quite general. So there are wide gaps in important specific knowledge. *See* DeBenedetti (1980: C2-46), 19-20. *See also*: Kremer (1974: C2-120); U.S. Constitution, Art. I, Sec. 8; Freeman (1944: C2-64), 59ff., *esp.* notes on 62; Friedman (1982: C2-65), *esp.* 261; Carleton (1982: C2-33), 74.

3. O'Sullivan and Meckler (1974: C2-152), 28-39, *esp.* 29, 36-37; Carleton (1982: C2-33), 69-76; Brock (1968: C2-25), 335; Freeman (1944: C2-64), 70.

4. Madison remarks, doc. in Schlissel (1968: C2-176), 47 (italics mine); Freeman (1944: C2-64), 75-81.

5. Brock (1968: C2-25), 352, 347, 390; Bowman (1944: C2-23), 111-12.

6. Brock (1968: C2-25), 390, 393-94; docs., 1815-1845, (A2-6); (A2-13), Aug 29, 1842, Aug 25, 1843, Aug 1, 1844, i.e. pp. 32-34.

7. Lewis J. Heatwole, *Mennonite Handbook of Information* (Scottdale, Pa., 1925), 85; Martin Mellinger to brother-in-law and sister, Nov 9, 1813, in Bender (1931: B2-7), 47-48.

8. Brock (1968: C2-25), ch. 8, *passim*; critique of Quaker arguments is mine.

9. For "dark ages" thesis, *see*, e.g., Brock (1968: C2-25), 391; and *esp.* Hershberger (1944: C2-94). Strong, more general use of the thesis is in Pannabecker (1975: C1-11), *esp.* 14-16. Quot. from Brock, 399 n. 20, taken from p. 66 of John F. Funk notebook 7, box 52, (A1-2), from internal evidence written after 1927.

10. Burkholder (1857: B1-4), 203-08, 211-17; Burkholder (1837: B1-5), 218-25, 295-312; Eby (1841: C2-55); Beiler (1888: B1-1), ch. 4; *ME*, II, 93, and I, 529.

11. Brock (1968: C2-25), 391.

12. Murdock (1967: C2-146), 4-7.

13. Beidler (or Beitler) to Jacob Nold, Oct 26, 1862, trans. by Elizabeth Horsch Bender, original and partial trans. in f. 4, box 9, (A2-31); Wm. and Samuel Gross to Henry and Magdalena Detweiler (from internal evidence written by Wm.), Sep 14, 1862, coll. 148, reel 2, (A1-3).

14. Nov 30, 1861; Oct 22, 1862; Sep 4, 1863; Feb 25, Mar 4, Mar 19, Apr 2, Sep 9, and Sep 23, 1864; Mar 8, 13, and 18, 1865; i.e., pp. 49-51; (A2-13).

15. Lehman (1982: C1-8). Pp. 19A-19K treat the dispute at length, quoting from newspapers involved: Lancaster *Daily Evening Express* (Jun 19, 29; Jul 2, 17; 1861); *Lancaster Intelligencer* (Jun 25, 1861); and *Lancaster Examiner and Herald* (Jul 17, 24; Aug 7, 14; 1861).

16. Lehman (1982: C1-8), 19E-19G and 19A-19K, *passim*.

17. Ibid.

18. Ibid., 62-63, trans., quot., and using *Das Christliche Volksblatt* (Oct 1, 1862).

19. Ibid., as in n. 18.

20. Ibid., as in n. 18.

21. Ibid., 35C-35E, 80, 96G-96H, 100G, 100T, 277; (A2-13), as cited n. 14; petition copied into (A2-10).

22. *See*, e.g., Klement (1960: C2-112); Gray (1942: C2-83). Jonas Shank to "Dar Brother [illegible] M. Shank, Mar 1, 1863, (A2-25).

23. Lehman (1969: C2-129), 93-94. Reprint from (Holmes Co., O.) *Farmer*, 1862 (further date unknown), in *The* (Sugar Creek, O.) *Budget*, Aug 29, 1917, also printed in Luthy (1977: B2-60-1); excerpted and treated also in Lehman (1982: C1-8), 35R.

24. Lehman (1982: C1-8), 35P-35Q, quot. letter fragment (end and writer's name lost), Aug 11, 1862, orig. in Library/Archives Div., Ohio Historical Soc., Columbus, Ohio.

25. Lehman (1982: C1-8), 100D-100E, quot. *Lewistown Gazette* (Nov 5, 1862); *HT*, 34 (Jan 1897), 6.

26. Beidler to Nold, Oct 26, 1862 (n. 13).

27. *GH*, 5 (Mar 10, 1912), 429.

28. Petitions quoted and discussed in Lehman (1982: C1-8), 35L-35W. John M. Brenneman to Jacob Nold, Aug 19 and 21, 1862 (two letters), and petition draft in Brenneman handwriting, Aug 19, 1862, respectively f. 3, 5, and 4, box 7, (A2-31); for petition and Aug 21 letter, *MHB*, 34 (Oct 1973), 2-3.

29. Brenneman-Nold material cited n. 28; for flavor, I keep Brenneman's spelling and capitalization, quoting from his letters; but I correct them in his petition, so as not to interfere with the ideas.

30. Letters cited n. 28.

31. Brenneman petition (n. 28).

32. Ibid.

33. Ibid.

34. Ibid.

35. Lehman (1982: C1-8), 35P-35R, quot. Aug 11, 1862, fragment cited n. 22; and D. P. Leadbetter to Tod, Aug 16, 1862, same loc. as fragment.

36. Lehman (1982: C1-8), 73, 35P, 106-07; Murdock (1967: C2-146), 9.

37. Murdock (1967: C2-146), *esp.* 7-15; Lehman (1982: C1-8), 126-37.

38. Murdock (1967: C2-146), *esp.* 7-15, and ch. 4. Lehman (1982: C1-8), 287; *Lancaster Intelligencer* (Jul 28, 1864), quot. p. 362.

39. Murdock (1967: C2-146), *esp.* 7-15.

40. (Doylestown, Pa.) *Bucks County Intelligencer* (Aug 19, 1862), quot. in Lehman (1982: C1-8), 45.

41. Certificate, Sep 4, 1862, (A2-26); Lehman (1982: C1-8), 41-45, 243A-43B.

42. Troyer (1916: C2-224), 60.

43. Murdock (1967: C2-146), 53; Lehman (1982: C1-8), 38, 103, 326 [Lehman erred re Philip Fretz; *see* A. J. Fretz, *A Genealogical Record of the Descendants of Henry Stauffer* . . . (Harleysville, Pa., 1899), 112-14; Diller (1951: C2-47), 38.

44. A. K. Funk to brother, Jan 29, 1863, f. 3, box 6, (A1-2).

45. Lehman (1982: C1-8), 100J, citing Yoder (1959: C2-267); Gingerich (1939: C2-78), 130; I. M. Hay to the district's Army Provost-Marshal Capt. Geo. Eyster, Mar 17, 1865, quot. in Lehman (1982: C1-8), 314-15; Lehman (1982: C1-8), 100J-100Q, citing Yoder (1959: C2-267)—Yoder in turn citing oral interviews; Gingerich (1939: C2-78), 130.

46. Wenger (1961: C2-247), 23; Lehman (1980: C2-127), 61-62. Zieglers to John Yoter and Jacob Yoter and wife, Dec 1862, f. 9, box 7.

47. J. and B. Herr to Jacob and Catherine Nold, 1864? f. 8, box 9; (A2-31). Theodore W. Herr, comp., *Genealogical Record of the Reverend Hans Herr* . . . (Lancaster, Pa., 1908; reprint, 1980), 17, 63.

48. Jacob Funk to brother, Oct 19, 1863, box 6, (A1-2); Fretz, *Genealogical Record of . . . Henry Stauffer* . . . (n. 39), 19, 54-55, 73, 90, 93, 98, 99.

49. Lehman (1982: C1-8), 75, 79, 89, 187, 213; John F. Funk diary, Jan 11, 1863, box 2, (A1-2).

50. Lehman (1969: C2-129), 91-93; Lehman (1982: C1-8), *passim*, *esp.* 106, 112, 115, 197, 200-01, 285; Brock (1968: C2-25), ch. 19; Hershberger (1944: C2-94). Johannes and Catarina Gross to Jacob Nold, Nov 1, 1863, f. 5, box 9; Jacob Kolb to Nold, Aug 28, 1865, f. 6, box 9; both with trans. by Elizabeth Horsch Bender; (A2-31). *See also* doc. printed in *MHB*, 34 (Oct 1973), 4.

51. Virginia conf. (B2-86), 2, 6. *See* MacMaster (1985: C1-10), 31, 100-01, 130, 219-20, 284. James O. Lehman told me on Apr 16, 1977, that wills give evidence that about 1820 some Mennonites in Maryland took over bankrupt plantations with slaves and had to keep the slaves until a certain age. Frank H. Epp, in (1974: C1-2), 79, suggested that a black taken to Canada by Mennonite Abraham Erb might have been a slave; but Epp admitted having no proof. Some sources that assert Mennonite slaveholding probably confuse it with indentured servitude—e.g., Henry S. Landes, "History of Franconia Township," clipping at EPMHL; John L. Ruth has told me that Alan Keyser of Harleysville, Pa., checked the records and found such error. On the other hand, Christian Mast, *Annals of the Conestoga Valley in Lancaster, Berks, and Chester Counties, Pennsylvania* (Scottdale, Pa., 1942),

484ff., tells of blacks in those counties with the "Mennonite" names of Lapp, Shirk, and Springer, suggesting they might have taken names from Mennonite masters; he also tells of a Cyrus Jacobs owning a slave about 1810. Such are the tiny bits of evidence, extremely meager, quite indefinite, and, at most, "the exceptions that prove the rule." The rule clearly was that even though Mennonites did not crusade against slavery, they all but universally rejected it.

52. *See* Horst (1967: C1-6), 17-18, 26-27.

53. Ibid., 28-31, P. S. Hartman quot., 32-33; Morgan (C2-144), 3; Hartman (1929: B2-33).

54. Jackson to S. B. French, Mar 21, 1862, (1880: B2-87), Series I, Vol. XII, Pt. III, 835, quot. in Horst (1967: C1-6), 34; Jackson, quot. in Zigler (1908: C2-269), 98.

55. Horst (1967: C1-6), 39, 40-50, 112, 119; Blosser, in Cassel (1888: B2-12), 136ff; Brunk (1959: C2-30), I, 159-61. Re Susanna Heatwole Brunk Cooprider with references to Harry Brunk, *see* ch. 2 at n. 47, or Erb (C2-58).

56. Horst (1967: C1-6), 50-61, 65-70, 74, 91; Zigler (1908: C2-269).

57. Horst (1967: C1-6), 70.

58. Brunk (1959: C2-30), I, 159, 163; Horst (1967: C1-6), 75-82, incl. quot. from the law.

59. Horst (1967: C1-6), 89-95.

60. Ibid., 96-103.

61. Heatwole, Shank, quot. in *ibid.*, 102-03.

62. Morgan (C2-144), 4; Horst (1967: C1-6), 104-09; Stoltzfus (1969: C2-203), 400; for primary sources on suffering in and flight from Virginia *see*, e.g., *HT* 1 (Nov, Dec 1864), 73, 76, 81-83.

63. *See* n. 64.

64. Lehman (1982: C1-85), 346-56, reproduces the resolutions and Funk's response in full with excellent analysis of circumstances; good but shorter treatment is in Ruth (1984: C1-15), 337-39; resolutions and Funk's reply are reprinted in "Patriotism and the Mennonites," *MHB*, 40 (Apr 1979), 5-6.

65. *See* n. 64.

66. Lehman and Ruth items, n. 64.

67. Krehbiel (1961: B2-56), 43-44; Katie Krehbiel reminiscences, trans. and abr. English version, f. 33, (A2-21); Krehbiel (A2-22), 24-25.

68. Krehbiel (1961: B2-56), 44; Krehbiel (A2-22), 24.

69. Lehman (1982: C1-8), *passim, esp.* 35R, 96C, 100N, 100W, 100(9), 100(16), 107, 114, 214, 285, 336; Horst (1967: C1-6), 34, 39-40, 112.

70. Lehman (1982: C1-8), 100G; 100D, quot. *Lewistown Gazette* (Sep 10, 1862). Jacob Schwarzendruber, letter of May 23, 1865, reproduced in Bender (1946: B2-5), 223-25; original in (A1-8).

71. Schwarzendruber letter cited n. 70.

72. Musser (1864: B2-62), 474-78, 457-58 [pagination is that of 2nd ed. of (1873: B1-11)].

73. Ibid.; for Tolstoy's response, *see* ch. 4 at n. 62.

74. Funk (1863: B2-26); Brenneman (1863: B2-9).

75. *See* John M. Brenneman letters to John F. Funk, *passim*, Jun-Nov 1863, box 6, (A1-2); Funk (1863: B2-26), 2-15.

76. Brenneman (1863: B2-9), 7-41; for how Brenneman connected salvation and ethics, *see* Weaver (1987: C1-22-2), 21-25.

77. Ibid., 54-55.

78. John M. Brenneman to Peter Nissley, Aug 17 and Nov 9, 1864, (A2-30).

79. See *HT*: 2 (Jan 1865), 6-7; 2 (Mar 1865), 21; 3 (Sep 1866), 73; 2 (Mar 1865), 21.

80. *See* ch. 5, at n. 65-67.

81. Brock (1968: C2-25), ch. 8.

CHAPTER 8

1. Jacob Weaver and wife to Jonas Martin and wife and brothers and sisters (in the faith), in Hoover (1982: B1-9), 511-12.

2. Some other Christians in America dissented notably from progressivism, e.g., anti-mission Baptists and most notably premillennialists; however, probably few dissented as thoroughly and holistically as did the Old Order Mennonites and Amish.

3. Stauffer (1855: B1-14; *Eine Chronik*); *ME*, IV, 620; notes on transcription of Jacob and Lydia Stauffer to Abraham Brubaker and wife, Jan 8, 1853, EPMHL.

4. Stauffer (1855: B1-14; *Eine Chronik*), 143-44, 169-89, 196; re Eby, *see* Holdeman (1876: B2-41), 104-07.

5. Stauffer (1855: B1-14; *Eine Chronik*), 186-96, 203-04. 207.

6. Ibid., 50-51, 144, 190, 193.

7. Stauffer (1855: B1-14; *Glaubens-Grund*), 269-70, 376; Stauffer (1855: B1-14; *Eine Chronik*), 189.

8. Stauffer (1855: B1-14; *Eine Chronik*), 199-233.

9. Ibid., 86-88; Stauffer (1855: B1-14; *Glaubens-Grund*), *see esp.* 299-301, 321-24, 304-15, 273-79, 316-20, and 325-72 *passim.*

10. Stauffer (1855: B1-14; *Eine Chronik*), 151-66; Stauffer (1855: B1-14; *Noch ein Bekenntniss*).

11. Stauffer (1855: B1-14; *Eine Chronik*), 50-61, 190-93. (For a reply to Stauffer *esp.* re brother-sin v. mortal-sin, *see* trans. of Abraham Martin doc. with Eli M. Shirk to Harold S. Bender, Mar 22, 1952, MHL.)

12. Stauffer (1855: B1-14; *Eine Chronik*), 236; Jacob Stauffer and Jacob Weber to Christian Herr, Mar 29, 1846, in same, 227-29.

13. Stauffer (1855: B1-14; *Eine Chronik*), 260, 204, 136, 6, and *passim*; on *Leichtsinnigkeit, see* ch. 3 of present book.

14. Stauffer (1855: B1-14; *Glaubens-Grund*), 314-15.

15. Stauffer (1855: B1-14; *Eine Chronik*), 192.

16. Hostetler (1980: C2-99), ch. 1 and pp. 76-77.

17. Ibid., 17.

18. Olshan (1981: C2-150)—Berger definition quot. p. 299. Yoder (1962: C2-268), 415. For some literature to define modernity *see* Schlabach (1979: C2-174), 398, n. 1.

19. Cronk (1977: C2-39), *passim* and 19; *see also* Cronk (1981: C2-40).

20. Oberholtzer (1972: B1-12). *CB*, 1: (Aug 15, 1882), 124; (Jul 1, 1882), 100; *see also*, e.g., (Aug 1, 1882), 114-15, (Oct 15, 1882), 156, and (Jun 15, 1882), 89.

21. I am using the word *salvation* more broadly than often done in Protestant theology—i.e., nearer the idea of redemption in a section, "*Gemeinde* as Redemptive Community" in Hostetler (1980: C2-99), 77; *see also* Cronk: (1977: C2-39) and (1981: C2-40).

22. Hostetler (1980: C2-99), 84. For old disciplines *see*: Nafziger (1930: B2-63); Bender: (1934: B1-2) and (1937: B2-6). For ministers' manuals *see*: Umble: (1941: B2-82), (1941: B2-81), and (1941: B2-83). Mss. of many of the foregoing are in (A1-8). *See also*: Miller: (1959: B2-60) and (1966: B2-14).

23. Lancaster conf. (1881: B2-59). David and Esther Newcomer to John and Catherine Gross, Jan 8, 1878, coll. 72, (A2-15).

24. JFB (B2-2).

25. Ibid., 382.

26. Landing (1970: C2-123).

27. Bender (1934: B1-2), 90-91, 93; Miller (1959: B2-60), 133-136; *ME*, II, 57.

28. Bender (1934: B1-2), 92, 94; Miller (1959: B2-60), 135.

29. Miller (1959: B2-60), 134-41; Mast (1954: C2-137), 1.

30. Jutzi (1853: B2-51); Beiler (1888: B1-1).

31. Beiler (1888: B1-1), 7-8, 22-23, 51-52, 228-29, 236-37, 298, and *passim.*

32. Ibid., 93-95, 172-178.

33. Ibid., chs. 3-5, and pp. 165-66.

34. Ibid., 32-47, 70-72.

35. Ibid., 165-66. Beiler's term was "höchste Bekenntnis." Literal meaning is "highest confession" or more loosely "ultimate acknowledgement." In context Beiler seems to mean the highest or most drastic call to acknowledge one's sin, which fits etymology of the German root word *bekennen*—[*see* Friedrich Kluge, *Etymologisches Wörterbuch der Deutschen Sprache* (19th ed. Berlin, 1963), 63.

36. Beiler (1888: B1-1), 166-79.

37. Beiler (1948: B2-4), 102, 101, 103.

38. John Umble, intro. to ibid., 94-95.

39. For sources *see* esp.: (B1-15); Yoder (1983: C1-23); Gingerich (1980: C2-75); and Lehman (1978: C2-126), 79-91.

40. (B1-15), 1863, pp. 29, 135-136; Nussbaum (1976: C2-149), 2.

41. Yoder (1983: C1-23), 2-3, 9.

42. Zook (1880: B2-95), trans. in Hostetler (1964: C2-102).

43. Yoder (1983: C1-23), 25-26.

44. Ibid., 24, 52-54.

45. Ibid., 5-13, 15; Gingerich (1980: C2-75), 13-16.

46. Yoder (1983: C1-23), 4-13, 15, 52.

47. (B1-15), 1862-1878, *passim*; Gingerich (1980: C2-75), 1.

48. Yoder (1983: C1-23), 21-32; Gingerich (1980: C2-75), 10-12.

49. Yoder (1983: C1-23), 48-49; Gingerich (1980: C2-75), 15-16; doc. from Holmes County, Ohio, Jun 1, 1865, in Bender (1934: B1-2), 96-97.

50. Yoder (1983: C1-23), 50-51.

51. Gingerich (1980: C2-75), 10, 15; Lehman (1978: C2-126), 85.

52. Gingerich (1980: C2-75), 10-12; (B1-15), 1863, pp. 42-43.

53. Gingerich (1980: C2-75), 10-12, 18-24; Yoder (1983: C1-23), 21-28.

54. *ME*, IV, 932; III, 29; II, 130. Wenger (1961: C2-247), 37; Stoltzfus (1969: C2-203), 158.

55. Yoder (1983: C1-23), 40ff.; 60.

56. Ibid., 35-36. For history of the Stuckey group, *see esp.* Pannabecker (1968: C2-153).

57. Pannabecker (1975: C1-11), 68-69.

58. *See* ch. 4 at n. 92-98.

59. Re Mifflin County schism *see*: Zook (1880: B2-95); Yoder (1973: C2-265), 21-22; and Renno (1973: C2-163), 5ff., 8ff., 12-13.

60. Lehman (1978: C2-126), 64-73, 45-47; 142; Treyer (1898: B2-79), 2 (of trans.).

61. Lehman (1978: C2-126), 107-11, 115-17; doc. printed, 110-11.

62. *See esp.*: Melvin Gingerich, "Sleeping Preachers," *MHB*, 32 (Jan 1971), 4-5; Troyer sermons in (1879: B2-71) and (1880: B2-70); Levi D. Miller, "Another Sleeping Preacher," *MHB*, 31 (Apr 1970), 5-6, reprinting *HT* (Jan 15, 1882), 23; Hostetler (1916: B2-44). *ME*, III, 156; IV, 543-44.

63. John F. Funk diary, Oct 9-13, 1862, box 1, (A1-2); Wenger (1959: C2-245), 112. In later accounts Funk put the number of baptisms at 48, probably erroneously; *see* Funk "Sermon," f. 3, box 50, (A1-2); and John F. Funk, "An Address by John F. Funk," *MHB*, 14 (Apr 1953), 3. Joseph C. Liechty has noted that Brenneman's sermon on that occasion may have stimulated Funk to reconsider nonresistance, since in Funk's diary jottings on his visit and on nonresistance are in proximity; copy of Jos. Liechty note in my files, no. 75.5(1862)Ill.

64. Wenger (1959: C2-245), 112-13.

65. John F. Funk unsent letter to Josiah Clemmer, Feb 21, 1878, printed as "Another John F. Funk Letter: On the Wisler Schism," *MHB*, 33 (Jan 1972), 4. For the version Funk sent, *see* Funk to Clemmer, Mar 12, 1878, printed as "On the Wisler Schism: A John F. Funk Letter," *MHB*, 32 (Jan 1971), 7-8; or same in Hoover (1982: B1-9), 933-34.

66. Wenger (1959: C2-245), 121, 125; David and Esther Newcomer to John and Catherine Gross, Jan 8, 1878, May 6, 1875, coll. 72, (A2-15); Daniel Brenneman to C. Henry Smith, ca. 1905, printed in Wenger (1960: B2-91), 49; John and Mary Weaver to Samuel and Anna Weber, Dec 5, 1871, in Hoover (1982: B1-9), 921.

67. Wenger (1959: C2-245), 126-27.

68. Ibid., 117 and *passim*.

69. Ibid., 121.

70. For old *Ordnung* language, *see*, e.g., Newcomer corr. in n. 66.

71. Ibid., Jan 8, 1878.

72. Wenger (1959: C2-245), 116; for primary sources *see* John F. Funk corr., June 23, 1867, and ms. in box 6, (A1-2).

73. For examples of John M. Brenneman's attitudes, *see esp.*: his various letters to John F. Funk, box 6, (A1-2); and two to Samuel Coffman, Feb 8, 1870, Apr 13, 1870, f. 1, box 11, (A1-1); Feb 8 one is also in Hoover (1982: B1-9), 912-16.

74. Wenger (1959: C2-245), 121, 130; doc. in same, 128-29; Wenger (1961: C2-247), 24.

75. David and Esther Newcomer to John and Catherine Gross, May 6, 1875, coll. 72, (A2-15); Wenger (1959: C2-245), 222-36.

76. Weaver (1931: C2-237), 387.

77. Hoover (1982: B1-9), 414.

78. Schlabach (1980: C2-172), 68-73.

79. Hoover (1982: B1-9), 33, 509; Christian M. Brackbill to Jonas Martin, Jun 13, 1885, in same, 73-74; *see also* pp. 504, 635.

80. Hoover (1982: B1-9), 28.

81. On how letters shifted to German for church affairs, *see*, e.g., Newcomers to Grosses (n. 66).

82. Schlabach (1980: C2-172), 61-62.

83. Hoover (1982:B1-9), 461; Isaac Eby to Jonas Martin, Apr. 25, 1892, in same, 153.

84. Lizzie Nolt, quot. her father, in *ibid.*, 593-94.

85. J. C. Wenger, "Anecdotes from Mennonite History: A Tragic Error in Discipline," *Mennonite Reporter*, 8 (May 15, 1978), 823; and in Hoover (1982: B1-9), 823; newspaper items in Hoover, 785-89.

86. Hoover (1982: B1-9), 591-92, 606-07.

87. Wenger, "Anecdotes" (n. 85).

88. Newspaper items, docs., and ed. comments in Hoover (1982: B1-9), 786-89, 793-95; *see also* Wenger (1968: C2-241), 22ff.

89. Wenger (1968: C2-241), 26.

90. Hoover (1982: B1-9), 781-82; "David Kauffman (1770-1846)," *MRJ*, 9 (Jul 1968), 27, 33; the sources only imply that Kauffman's parents were Mennonite.

91. Amos Herr to Samuel Kaufman (surely Va. bishop Samuel Coffman), Feb 1890, f. 1, box 11, (A1-1); *see* ch. 3 at n. 89-94.

92. Hoover (1982: B1-9), 622, 624; doc. in same, 625-30; Lancaster conf. (1881: B2-59).

93. Isaac Eby to Jonas Martin, Nov 10, 1892, in Hoover (1982: B1-9), 155.

94. Israel Rohrer, Sr., quot. in Graber (1979: C2-80), 178.

95. "Exposition on Sunday schools . . ." and related docs. (A2-8); Harry A. Brunk used these to treat the Va. Sunday school controversy in his (1959: C2-30), I, ch. 10. *See also* Bender (1940: C2-14), revised as ch. 10 in Wenger (1966: C2-246).

96. "Exposition on Sunday schools" (A2-8).

97. Handy (1984: C1-5), 39, 230-31.

98. Weaver (1931: C2-237), 279, 385; *HT*, 12 (Jun 1875), 87; newspaper items in Hoover (1982: B1-9). Schlabach (1980:C2-172), 77, 93, 128.

99. Hoover (1982: B1-9), 789-92. 789-92.

100. Weaver (1931: C2-237), 387-88.

101. Docs. and newspaper items in Hoover (1982: B1-9), 796-803.

102. Newspaper item in *ibid.*, 805; Wenger (1968: C2-241), 30.

103. Schlabach (1980: C2-172), 68-74.

104. Hoover (1982: B1-9), 288, 29-30; James R. Martin, "A Brief Biographical Sketch of Jonas H. Martin," in same, 21; *ME*, II, 813.

105. Martin, "Brief . . . Sketch" (n. 104), 19, 21; newspaper items and ed. comments in Hoover (1982: B1-9), 24, 787-88, 25.

106. Martin, "Brief . . . Sketch" (n. 104), 19.

CHAPTER 9

1. Johannes Gascho to Friedrich Schwartzendruber (Frederick Swartzendruber), Jan 22, 1874, typed transcript in box 2, f. 17, (A1-8).

2. The standard figures in the literature put the total "Russian" immigration into all North America, 1873-1883, at 18,000 with about 10,000 coming to the U.S. *See*, e.g., Cornelius Krahn in Krahn (1949: C1-7), 8; and Epp (1974: C1-2), 200. Historian David Haury of the MLA, involved in identifying Mennonite names on ship lists, has informed me (by letter of Feb 12, 1986) that *in Kansas alone* by 1882, including Mennonites of Swiss and south German origin, there may have been as many as 12,000 Mennonites. Surely there were not enough non-Russians in Kansas to account for the discrepancy. Identifying people as Mennonites by their surnames can be quite imprecise, and until Haury has made his case more clearly I accept the traditional numbers.

3. Liebbrandt (1932/1933: C2-132), Jan: 33.

4. Goerz to Warkentin, Oct 1, 1872 (A1-10).

5. Goerz to Warkentin, Jan 15, 1873 (A1-10).

6. Rempel (1973/1974: C1-14), Jan: 18-20, 27-28, 30ff., 37ff. *See also* Toews (1981: C2-223), entire article, *esp.* 296-329. Rempel (1933: C1-13), ch. 14; Urry (1978: C1-21), *passim*, e.g., 431, 451ff., 585, 654, 714ff.; Urry (1984: C2-232-2), *passim*, esp., 11-13, 17, 19-22.

7. Rempel (1933: C1-13), 3/1-9; Hostetler (1974: C2-100), map, p. 9. *See esp.* Schrag (1956: C2-181).

8. Rempel (1973/1974: C1-14), Oct: 261-62. For history and analysis of the dialect, good beginning sources are: Buchheit (1978: C2-32); and Urry (1978: C1-21), 382-92.

9. Rempel (1933: C1-13), 1/19, 3/10-3/11, 1/2-1/3, 1/22, 1/9. For a full discussion of effort to attract immigrants *see* Bartlett (1979: C2-11); for a summary, *see* Stumpp (1973: C2-207), 24-29.

10. *See* Rempel (1969: C1-12), 12; *see also* Kroeker (1981: C2-121), chs. 1-3. Rempel (1933: C1-13), 1/1, 1/14, 1/23-24, 4/1, 4/7, 4/5; Rempel (1973/1974: C1-14), Oct: 296-97, 273. For more on settlers' difficulties, *see* Koch (1977: C2-115), *esp.* 1-51; Urry (1978: C1-21), parts II and III. *See also* a work based on an old ms., Hattie Plum Williams, *The Czar's Germans*, ed. by Emma S. Haynes, Phillip B. Legler, and Gerda S. Walker (Lincoln, Nebr., 1975).

11. Rempel (1933: C1-13), map following 1/28; *ME* IV, 382-3, 764; Dyck (1981: C1-1), 168, 174.

12. *ME*, III, 732, 734; Rempel (1973/1974: C1-14), Jan: 24.

13. For the official Eng.-language version of Catherine's Jul 22, 1763, manifesto, *see* Bartlett (1979: C2-11), Appendix 1; another trans. is in Stumpp (1973: C2-207), 15-18. Both sources print other public docs. of the immigration. German versions of the manifesto appear in: Epp (1889: C2-57), n. on pp. 3-9; and Rempel (1933: C1-13), Appendix I.

14. "Charter of Privileges Granted [by Czar Paul I] to the Mennonites on September 8, 1800," Appendix II in Rempel (1933: C1-13); *see also* his p. x.

15. Rempel (1933: C1-13), ch. 5, and p. 9/6 and *passim*; Rempel (1973/1974: C1-14), Oct: 270, Jan: 5-8.

16. Rempel (1933: C1-13), chs. 7-8, *esp.* 7/1, 7/5ff., 7/12-13, 8/1-6, also, 1/5, 2/2-7; Rempel (1973/1974: C1-14), Jan: 8-9, 16-17, 19, 24-29. *ME*, IV, 870-71. For intro. to the *Waisenamte* see: Jacob Peters, "The Sommerfelder Waisenamt: Origins, Development, and Dissolution," *ML*, 35 (Dec 1980), 8-14. Liebbrandt (1932/1933: C2-132), Oct: 206-07. Friesen (1978: C1-4), 191, 193-96, 199; Toews (1981: C2-223), 320.

17. Rempel (1933: C1-13), chs. 7-8, and p. 14/10; Rempel (1973/1974: C1-14), Jan: 24-29. *ME*, IV, 859, 870-71; II, 155, 686. Peters, "Sommerfelder Waisenamt" (n. 16); Braun (1929: C2-24), 170-74; Toews (1975: C1-19), 18; Toews (1979: C2-221), 142, and *passim*; Friesen (1978: C1-4), 193-94, 770-72, and ch. 38 (a long chapter printing many primary sources on Mennonite education in the Russian empire).

18. Rempel (1973/1974: C1-14), Jan: 10ff., gives a whole, succinct description of the colonies' governments; Jan: 14. Rempel (1933: C1-13), 6/1-3, 6/5, 9/6. Rempel attributed Mennonite prosperity to this political system rather than to special economic favors—*see* his (1973/1974: C1-14), Jan: 10-15.

19. Toews (1951: C2-220), 205. *See*, e.g.: Wiebe (1924: C2-252), 1-9; Toews (1975: C1-19), 22-32, 36—p. 36 offering at least a paragraph of explicit qualification; Toews (1951: C2-220), *esp.* 151-65, 204-10; Toews (1979: C2-221), *esp.* 138-41.

20. For a source making the indictment but also showing piety in the old church, *see* Friesen (1974: B2-22), 1-46, *passim*, *esp.* 22-23. Urry (1978: C1-21), 584-85. *See also*: Friesen (1978: C1-4), 96-105, 154-55, 203; Pannabecker (1975: C1-11), 87-91; Epp (1974: C1-2), 171-76; *ME*, III, 196; Krahn (1951: C2-117), 18. Some writers seem to imply that renewal of Mennonitism depended entirely on infusions from non-Mennonite Pietism—a tendency I think overdone in Toews (1979: C2-221).

21. For some primary docs. and excellent maps regarding *Kleine Gemeinde*, see Plett (1982: B2-66). Urry (1978: C1-21), 157-71; Krahn (1951: C2-117), 18; Abraham Friesen as paraphrased in Bartel (1975: C2-10), 8; Friesen (1978: C1-4), 128, 130, incl. excerpt from Klaas Reimer autobiography.

22. Balzer (1948: B2-3). Toews (1979: C2-221), 139-40. Re *Kleine Gemeinde* as Old Order group: James Urry has used the phrase "closed order" for the outlooks of the *Kleine Gemeinde* and other traditionalists or "maintainers" among Russia's Mennonites. Similarities certainly are intriguing; *see* Urry (1978: C1-21), *passim*, *esp.* 157-70, 306-09. Historian John B. Toews (U. of Calgary) has written that the *Kleine Gemeinde* "objected to the growing secularism in the Mennonite world and by . . . withdrawal sought to remind the larger community of the older stricter norms"—also that their focus was "on definable Christian standards." Such language, and Balzer's own, suggests similarity to Old Order groups in America; *see* Toews (1982: C2-222), 21, 22.

23. Krahn (1951: C2-117), 18-19; *ME*, III, 198, 196. See *ML* 6 (Jul 1951) issue on the Meade, Kansas, community; also, Bartel (1975: C2-10); Urry (1978: C1-21), 678-80.

24. Toews (1975: C1-19), 177, 192. On Gnadenau, *see*: Pantle (1947: C2-155); and *esp.* Wiebe (1924: C2-252) and Jakob A. Wiebe's own account (1947: B2-94). For a history of the KMB *see* Plett (1985: C2-159).

25. Re connecting MBs and landless, *see* Krahn (1935: C2-117-2), 172-73; Rempel (1973/1974: C1-14), Jan, p. 26; Toews (1975: C1-19), 51-52; Toews (1951: C2-220), 205-06; Peter J. Klassen, "The Historiography of the Birth of the Mennonite Brethren," in Friesen (C2-66-2), 118-120. For the middle-class interpretation, *see esp* Urry (1978: C1-21), 556-57, 569-70, 576, 583-84; for background of tensions, *see* same, 401-78; for excellent, extensive discussion of Pietism's entering "Russian" Mennonitism and the implications, as well as of MB beginnings, *see* same, 479-586. For quick intro.

re Pietistic Lutheran and Baptist influences in MB origin, *see* Adrian (1964: C2-1). *See also* John B. Toews, "The Russian Origin of Mennonite Brethren," in Toews (1977: C2-223-1), 78-107.

26. Toews (1975: C1-19), 27-31, 36.

27. Ibid., 31. Friesen (1978: C1-4), 211-13, quot. 211, 213; for more re Wuest, *see esp.* 205-27.

28. For a biography of Claassen *see ME*, I, 612-13; for Reimer *see ME*, IV, 277-78. Toews (1975:C1-19), 33-34.

29. Doc. trans. in Toews (1975: C1-19), 34-35.

30. Toews (1975: C1-19), 55; Urry (C1-21), 481-82, 484-86, 578-79, 584, 585; C. J. Dyck, "1525 Revisited? A Comparison of Anabaptist and Mennonite Brethren Origins," in Toews (1977: C2-228-1), 69, 56; Bekker (1973: B2-4-2), 1-3.

31. Toews (1975: C1-19), 38-40, 45-47, 49; Friesen (1978: C1-4), 243, 320, 322, 324, 326, 258.

32. Toews (1975: C1-19), 41, 38, 42-50; Friesen (1978: C1-4), chs. 15, 17, 21, 23.

33. Friesen (1978: C1-4), chs. 16, 18, 22, 25; Toews (1975: C1-19), 55-61.

34. Toews (1975: C1-19), 53, 72-73. For quick intro. re MB relations with Baptists, perhaps understating Baptist influence, *see* Peters (1959: C2-158). For more, *see* Henrich Epp, ed., *Verschiedenheiten zwischen den Vereinigten Mennoniten-Brudergemeinden und den Baptisten Gemeinden sowie den alten Mennoniten Gemeinden* (Odessa: L. Ritsche, 1908); Abram J. Klassen, "The Roots and Development of Mennonite Brethren Theology to 1914" (M.A. Thesis, Wheaton College, 1966); Albert J. Wardin, "Baptist Influences on Mennonite Brethren with an Emphasis on the Practice of Immersion," *Direction*, 8 (1979); and Urry (C1-21), 574-76.

35. Belk (1976: C2-12), *passim*, *esp.* 62, 82, 87, 177-80, 188-89; Urry (1978: C1-21), 687-713; *ME*, II, 234. There was also a group of Mennonite "Templars": *see* Toews (1982: C2-222), 23-25; and Urry (1978: C1-21), 587-608.

36. Friesen (1978: C1-4), 645-57; doc. in Toews (1975: C1-19), 50. 260. *See*, e.g., J. B. Toews (Fresno, Calif.), "Mennonite Brethren in the Larger Mennonite World," *MQR*, 57 (Jul 1983), 258-60.

37. Rempel (1973/1974: C1-14), Oct: 264. Urry (1984: C2-232-2), 22-24.

38. Rempel (1973/1974: C1-14), Jan: 6-7, 24-28. Rempel (1933: C1-136), 5/3-4, 9/2-3, 9/8-9, 9/12, 9/14; Urry (1978: C1-21), 431-40, 609-45. Rempel has written meticulously about the problem of the landless in the two sources just cited; *see esp.* (1933: C1-13), chs. 5 and 9, and (1973/1974: C1-14), Oct: 270, and Jan: 5-8, 24-33.

39. *See*, e.g., Stephen Graham, *Tsar of Freedom: The Life and Reign of Alexander II* (New Haven, 1935), chs. 8-9; and Nicholas V. Riasanovsky, *A History of Russia* (4th. ed. New York and Oxford, 1984), 385-86.

40. Schrag (1956: C2-181), 125, using a Master's thesis by Helen Shipley as source.

41. Goerz to Warkentin, Jan 15, 1872, (A1-10); Unruh (1973: C2-231), 98-99; Urry (1978: C1-21), 670. Works cit. n. 39.

42. Friesen (1974: B2-22), 8. Sudermann (A2-36), 1-2. Re handling grain, and Cornelius Jansen's exporting, *see* Jansen (1921: B2-50), 16, 18, 23-24—*also* 25, 19. On the effects of the war, *see* Urry (1978: C1-21), 417-30; on the Berdyansk congregation, *see* same, 444-47, 662-65.

43. Goerz to Warkentin, Oct 22, 1872, f. 13, MS-68-1 (A1-10); Jansen (1921: B2-50), 25, 16, 18, 23-24, 28. Helena Jansen, handwritten schoolgirl theme entitled "My Story," f. 12; Thos. Harvey to Cornelius Jansen, 1st-month 13, 1868; f. 13; (A1-4). For the Quakers' impressions from an 1867 trip to the Mennonite colonies *see* Thomas Harvey and Isaac Robson, *An die in den Vereinigten Staaten aus Süd-Russland eingewanderten sogenannten Mennoniten* (8-p. pamphlet printed by John F. Funk's press. Elkhart, Ind., 1879—copies in MHL, MLA, and my possession). Clipping from the (London, Eng.) *Friend* from shortly after Jansen's death on Dec 14, 1894, at fs. 18-20 (A1-4). For background of Quaker and Bible Society connections, *see* Urry (1978: C1-21), 210-15.

44. Jansen (1921: B2-50), 16, 25, 18. Diaries of Margarete and Anna Jansen, 1873-1875, *passim*; Helena Jansen, handwritten theme, "Memories," f. 12; (A1-4). Harvey to Jansen (n. 43); talk by Cornelius Jansen to Mt. Pleasant, Iowa, Conversational Club, serialized in *The* (Mt. Pleasant) *Free Press* (typed copy in MLA), at Jan 6, 13, 20, 27, 1876; clipping cit. n. 43; Urry (1978: C1-21), 444-47, 662-65.

45. Krehbiel (1961: B2-56), 71; *see also* Schnell (1950: C2-179).

46. Chr. Krehbul (Krehbiel) to C. Janzen (Jansen), Dec 24, 1870, 8-12; John F. Funk to C. Janzen (Jansen), Apr 8, May 5, 1871, 5-8, 12-14; in Jansen (1872: B2-49).

47. Krehbiel to Jansen (n. 46), 10-11; Peter Wiebe to J. v. Reisen, May 20 and Jun 18, 1871, in Jansen (1872: B2-49), 15-18, 26, 22-23.

48. Jansen (1872: B2-49); Gerhard Wiebe to Joh. Wiebe of near Danzig, Sep 12, 1871, Sep 22, 1872 (*sic*; from internal evidence 1871), same source, 31-32.

49. Jansen (1872: B2-49), 3, 35, 48-54, and *passim*.

50. Jansen, Club talk (n. 44), at Jan 20, 27, 1876; Helena Jansen, handwritten theme, "Our Leaving Russia, and the Reason, Why!" f. 12, (A1-4); Jansen (1921: B2-50), 30.

51. Liebbrandt (1932/1933: C2-132), Oct: 210-11 (includes trans. of Sudermann statement). Sudermann (A2-36), 3; doc. trans. in Correll (1937: B2-19), 211.

52. Liebbrandt (1932/1933: C2-132), Oct: 212-13. Docs., Feb 3, May 11, 1872, Apr 26, Jun 9, 1872, in Correll (1937: B2-19), 211-13, 217-19, 222-23.

53. Liebbrandt (1932/1933: C2-132), Oct: 217-19. Docs., Aug 18, Nov 7, Apr 3, 1872, in Correll (1937: B2-19), 224-26, 273, 215-16.

54. Liebbrandt (1932/1933: C2-132), Oct: 213-16, 219. Docs., Jun 1, Aug 18, 1872, Mar 1, 1873, Aug 28, Oct 21, 1872, in Correll (1937: B2-19), 220-21, 227, 226, 271-72, 279.

55. *ME*, III, 733; Krahn (1973: C2-116), 5; for details of the trips *see* Sudermann (1943: C2-208), 23-46.

56. Urry (1978: C1-21), 662-65; Jansen's English paraphrase, in Club talk (n. 44), at Jan 20, 1876; Sudermann (A2-35), 4, 9-10, 12.

57. Toews (1979: C2-221), 144; Sudermann (1943: C2-208), 25; Smith (1927: C2-189), 45; Elmer Suderman, intro. to Sudermann (1974: B2-76), iii; Urry (1978: C1-21), 660-62.

58. Sudermann (1943: C2-208), 26-27, 24; re Crimean War teamster work, *see*, e.g.: Friesen (1974: B2-22), ch. 4; Urry (1978: C1-21), 417-23. *See also*: Epp (1889: C2-57); Sudermann (1974: B2-76), 1.

59. Doc. trans. in Sudermann (1943: C2-208), 28-29.

60. Although Urry was generally sympathetic to Russian officials, he agreed with this conclusion; *see* (1978: C1-21), 660, 669, 673-75.

61. Sudermann (1974: B2-76), 3; Sudermann (1943: C2-208), 30-33; Krahn (1973: C2-116), 7.

62. Sudermann (1943: C2-208), 32; Krahn (1973: C2-116), 7.

63. Sudermann (1943: C2-208), 31-35; docs. trans. in same, 28-29, 33; Schroeder (1973: C2-184), 26, 30; *ME*, IV, 153; Krahn (1973: C2-116), 7.

64. Warkentin to Goerz, Jun, Jul 11, Sep 17, Sep 29, Nov 10, Aug 18, Dec 27, 1872, and Jan 8 and Mar 3, 1873, (A1-10). Krehbiel (1961: B2-56), 72-74; *see also* Gustav Hoeffler doc. (welcoming Warkentin to Texas), Mar 1873, f. 1, (A1-5).

65. Free trans. of German verse in Liebbrandt (1932/1933: C2-132), Oct: 209.

66. Goerz to Warkentin, Dec 12, 1872, Jan 15, 1873; Warkentin to Goerz, Mar 3, May 15, 1873; (A1-10). Unruh (1972: C2-232-1), 21-22; Schultz (1938: C2-185), 39.

67. Liebbrandt (1932/1933: C2-132), Oct: 26-27; *St. Petersburg Zeitung*, May 8, 1874, paraphrased in same, Jan: 26.

68. Wiebe (1949: B2-94), 99; Sudermann (1943: C2-208), 37-42. For a positive interpretation of Todleben's role, *see* Urry (1978: C1-21), 670-77.

69. Friesen (1978: C1-4), 596; doc. in same, 595-96; Urry (1978: C1-21), 672-73, *see also* 682-85.

70. Doc. in Sudermann (1943: C2-208), 36-37.

71. Sudermann (1943: C2-208), 37-43.

72. Braun (1929: C2-24), 176-81. Braun thought the changes generally benefited Mennonites. John B. Toews of the U. of Calgary in (1979: C2-221), 148-56, and in (1982: C2-222), ch. 3, indicated some selective broadening of intellect, yet within quite parochial limits. Writers less inclined to see intellectualism as good in itself might find even less benefit in the changes. James Urry has objected to the term "russification," preferring to distinguish between nation-building and cultural absorption; *see* (1978: C1-21), 654.

73. Rempel (1933: C1-13), 9/23-26. Rempel (1973/1974: C1-146), Jan: 15.

74. Intro. and doc. in Gross (1974: B2-31), 460-61, 465-66, 468, 470, 475, and *passim*.

75. Rempel (1933: C1-13), 9/27. A rather similar view is in Urry (1978: C1-21), 684-85, except that Urry avoided the word "conservative."

76. Funk to Janzen, May 5, 1872, in Jansen (1872: B2-49), 13; sources cit. n. 64; Goerz to Warkentin, Nov 27, Oct 1 and 25, 1872, (A1-10).

77. Goerz to Warkentin, Nov 27, Oct 1 and 25, 1872, (A1-10).

78. Epp (1974: C1-2), 189; Schnell (1950: C2-179), 206-07.

79. Shantz (1873: B2-72); Epp (1974- C1-2), 188-89.

80. Elmer Suderman, intro. to Sudermann (1974: B2-76), v.

81. Many sources allude to the deputation trip and its reports. For main primary sources, *see*: Sudermann (1974: B2-76); Unruh (1949: B2-85); Tschetter (1931: B2-80); Buller letters (A2-4); and letter of Wilhelm Ewert to his family, Jun 29, 1873, typed copy, box 68, (A1-2), also published as H. H. Ewert, ed., "Abschrift eines Briefes den Wm. Ewert als Deputierter der westpreussischen Gemeinden

im Jahre 1873 an seine Familie geschrieben hat," *Der Mitarbeiter*, 22 (Oct 1929). *See also* John F. Funk's descriptions in various issues of the *Herald of Truth* [cited in notes of Schnell (1950: C2-179)].

82. Klippenstein (1974: C2-114), 482-87, incl. its n. 31; account from Winnipeg *Manitoban* printed in same. Driedger (1972: C2-50), 291-94; Sudermann (1974: B2-76), 23.

83. Buller letters (A2-4), fragment attached to Jun 6 letter, probably written Jun 24, 1873; Epp (1974: C1-2), 192, 198.

84. Sudermann (1974: B2-76), 16; sources n. 81, *passim*.

85. *See*, for instance: Epp (1974: C1-2), 195; and Toews (1975: C1-19), 80. Samuel Floyd Pannabecker invoked the idea in his (1975: C1-11), 94, but he qualified it strongly. Cornelius Krahn, in Krahn (1949: C1-7), 8.

86. Tschetter (1931: B2-80), 198; Unruh (1949: B2-85), Jul 28, 1873 entry; Wiebe (1949: B2-94); for more, *see* Wiebe (1967: C2-250).

87. For ample discussion of the dilemmas of this arrangement, *see* Urry (1978: C1-21), *passim*.

CHAPTER 10

1. Congressional debates as reprinted in Correll (1946: B1-6), 185, 219.

2. Sudermann (1974: B2-76), 24-30; Unruh (1949: B2-85), at Jun 23-Jul 17 1873; Tschetter (1931: B2-80), 207-12; Buller letters (A2-4), Jul 16, 1873; Krehbiel (1961: B2-56), 77-78.

3. Wilhelm Ewert, Leonard Sudermann, Jacob Buller, and Andreas Schrag to Fred. Billings, Aug 20, 1873; G. W. Cass and Frederick Billings to same, Tobias Unruh, and Paul and Lorenz Tschetter, Aug 28, 1873; both in English and German versions, copies extant in f. 5, box 68, (A1-2). For more re Northern Pacific Railroad effort, *see* Liebbrandt (1933: C2-132), 10-15. Krehbiel (1961: B2-56), 76-78.

4. Krehbiel (1961:B2-56), 76-78; Sudermann (1974:B2-76), 31-32; Buller letters (A2-4), July 26 1873; Susanna Krehbiel autobiography (A2-22), 36-37.

5. Tschetter (1931: B2-80), 217, 215; Unruh (1949: B2-85), at Aug 8, 1873; John M. Brenneman to Jacob Nold, Aug 21, 1862, printed in *MHB*, 34 (Oct 1973), 3.

6. Jansen (1921: B2-50), 30-36. Helena Jansen, school theme, "My Story," f. 12; MJ diary (trans. and typed), Nov 17, 18, 1873, f. 4 (orig. in f. 1); box 1, (A1-4).

7. For the Tschetter-Unruh petition, *see* Correll (1935: B1-7). Re the petition, the bill that followed, and congressional debates *see*: Correll (1946: B1-6); Esau (1961: C2-61); Harder (1949: C2-86); Smith (1927:C2-189), ch. 4. Tschetter draft as trans. in Tschetter (1931:B2-80), n. 42, pp. 210-14 final draft, Aug 8, 1873, in Correll (1935: B1-7), 146-47.

8. Hamilton Fish to M. L. (*sic*) Hiller, Sep 5, 1873, in Correll (1935: B1-7), 148-49.

9. Sec. of Interior report in Correll (1935: B1-7), 149-50.

10. Harder (1947: C2-86), 58.

11. Grant message in Correll (1935: B1-7), 150.

12. Petition from "Some of the Emigrants from Russia and Prussia, called Mennonites" (to the U.S. Congress), in Correll (1946: B1-6), 179.

13. Correll (1946: B1-6), *passim*, quot. 192, 219; petition (n. 12).

14. Correll (1946:B1-6), 219, 192-194, 198-200, 211, 217; Esau (1961:C2-61), 12.

15. Correll (1946: B1-6), 185-86.

16. Esau (1961: C2-61), 6; Correll (1946: B1-6), 185, 190, 210.

17. Correll (1946: B1-6), 204, 183, 188, 200-01, 206, 215, 220, 185, 209, 217-18, and *passim*, quot. 196.

18. Correll (1946: B1-6), 221.

19. Warkentin to Goerz, Jul 11, Sep 29, Aug 18, 1872, and Mar 3, Jan 8, 1873, (A1-10).

20. Warkentin to Goerz, Jan 6, 1874, (A1-10). *HT*, 9: (Nov 1872), 168—incl. quot.; (Dec 1872), 185. Schnell (1950: C2-179), 202-03.

21. Docs. in *HT*, 10: (Jul 1873), 120; (Sep 1873), 151, 153; (Oct 1873), 167. Re Swiss-speaking Volhynians, *see* Schrag (1956: C2-181). Schnell (1950: C2-179), 210-11.

22. Schnell (1950: C2-179), 210-11; *HT*, 10 (Nov 1873), 185.

23. Haury (1981: C2-90), 23-24; Schnell (1950: C2-179), 212; *HT*, 11 (Feb 1874), 19.

24. Gabriel Baer to B. Warkentin, Apr 17, 1874, f. 3, box 68, (A1-2); Ex. Aid Comm. printed circular, May 15, 1874, f. 17, (A2-37); Schnell (1950: C2-179), 215. Sources, even primary ones, disagree re roles of committee members; I take those in the printed circular as most official. Ruth (1984: C1-15), 354.

25. Schnell (1950: C2-179), 214. Warkentin note on Baer to Warkentin (n. 24); Casper Hett to unnamed correspondent, Apr 18, 1874; f. 3, box 68, (A1-2).

26. Handwritten doc., marked "confidential," Feb 27, 1874, f. 19, box 68, (A1-2); Unruh (1962: C1-20), 55; Schnell (1950: C2-179), 213, 215.

27 Hett letter (n. 25); circular (n. 24).

28. Warkentin to Goerz, 16 Feb 1874, (A1-10).

29. David Goerz to Chr. Krehbiel, Aug 22, 1874, trans. in f. 24 (orig. in 7), (A1-5).

30. Goerz to Krehbiel, Aug 25, 1873, f. 11, (A1-10).

31. Warkentin to Goerz, Jul 20, 29, 1874, (A1-10). The main problems in identifying this Hiller with the Northern Pacific's Hiller are: the present sources do not mention his Northern Pacific or Minnesota-Dakota connections; and sources use different initials with the name Hiller. *See*: Warkentin to Krehbiel, Aug 30, 1874, f. 24 (orig. in 7), (A1-5), and to Goerz, Aug 30, 1874, (A1-10); Correll (1935: B1-7), 148; Ewert *et al.* letter (n. 3). But the man's anger with former delegates suggests he might have been the Northern Pacific's Hiller, now frustrated at losing them.

32. Warkentin to Goerz, Jul 20, 29 1874, (A1-10); Goerz to Krehbiel, Aug 31 and 22, 1874, f. 24 (A1-5).

33. Warkentin to Goerz, Aug 13, 1873, (A1-10).

34. Unruh (1972: C2-232-1), 21-23; Schultz (1938: C2-185), 39; J. J. Balzer in (1938: C2-27), 26; Warkentin to Goerz, May 18, 1874, (A1-10); Hostetler (1974: C2-100), 115.

35. Estimate by C. Henry Smith, cited in Unruh (1972: C2-232-1), 23.

36. Amos Herr, cited in Unruh (1972: C2-232-1), 24.

37. Krehbiel (1961: B2-56), 73ff., 78ff.; Unruh (1962: C1-10), 58-59; Schmidt (C2-177), VII/2; Schmidt (B2-68), 13; C. B. Schmidt to A. S. Johnson, Mar 23, 1875, copy in MLA, orig. in Atchison, Topeka, and Sante Fe Railroad papers, Kansas State Historical Society, Topeka, Kans.

38. Krehbiel (1961: B2-56), 75-76. Unruh (1962: C1-20), 61.

39. Chas. Rosenberg to David Goerz, Dec 26, 1873, f. 1, (A1-5); Peter U. Schmidt, "The Beginning of the Hochfeld Village and the Alexanderwohl Church," *ML*, 36 (Mar 1981), 7, n. 11 of p. 8.

40. Materials in fs. 2-5, (A2-21), *esp.*: A. E. Touzalin to Krehbiel, Feb 16, 1874, f. 2; A. S. Johnson to Krehbiel, Jun 5, 1875, f. 3; C. B. Schmidt to Krehbiel, Mar 8, 1876, f. 4; and various land-purchase docs. in f. 5. Krehbiel did recognize the conflict-of-interest issue in: Krehbiel to Goerz, Aug 22, 1874, f. 24, (A1-5). Krehbiel (1961: B2-56), 88-89; Krehbiel defended the *Zur Heimath* arrangement without dealing with conflict of interest. Schnell (1950: C2-179), 215-17; John F. Funk to "brother in the Lord" (David Goerz), Apr 23, 1874, f. 3, (A1-5).

41. Warkentin to Goerz, Apr 22 and *passim*, 1874, (A1-10).

42. Warkentin to Goerz, Jul 29, May 17 and 18, 1874, (A1-10).

43. *ZH*, 1 (Apr 1875), 19-20; Unruh (1962: C1-20), 91-106; Margarete and Anna Jansen diaries, f. 4, box 1, (A1-4), *passim*, *esp.* Anna's at Mar 4, 10, 1875.

44. *ZH*, 1 (May 1875), 28-30; trans. of letter to Cornelius Janzen (*sic*), Mar 22, 1875, evidently by the Ewert committee at the Mar 22-23, 1875, conference in Kansas, f. C-4, box 68-1, (A1-10).

45. Helena Jansen school themes, Margarete and Anna Jansen diaries, *passim*, fs. 12 and 4, box 1, (A1-4).

46. Chas. Stevens (?) to John F. Funk, Mar 10, 1874, f. 17, (A2-37); *ZH*, 1 (Apr 1875), 19; Ewert committee letter (n. 44); John Hertzler to David Goerz, May 28, Jun 21, 1875, f. 12, (A1-5); *HT*, 12 (Jan 1875), 10; Smith (192: C2-189), 107.

47. John Shenk to Goerz, Feb 17, 1877, f. 17, (A1-5); Wenger (1961: C2-247), 348-49.

48. John F. Funk, quot. in "An Interview [by Charles Rittenhouse] with John F. Funk," *MHB*, 45 (Oct 1984), 4; doc., draft of obituary of Salome Funk in John F. Funk's handwriting, box 116, (A1-2); Warkentin to Goerz, Jul 20, 1874, (A1-10); *HT*, 11 (Aug 1874), 136; Wiebe (1949: B2-94), 99.

49. Warkentin to Goerz, Jul 20, 29, 1874, (A1-10); Unruh (1962: C1-20), 76-80; Bartel (1975: C2-10), 9-10. *See also* Paul Miller, "The Story of Jansen, Nebraska," *ML*, 9 (Oct 1954), 173-75, and much fuller account in Miller (1953: C2-140).

50. Goerz to Warkentin, Oct 25, 1872; Warkentin to Goerz, Aug 13, 1873; (A1-10). Buller letters (A2-4), Jul 26, 1873; Krehbiel (1961: B2-56), 78.

51. Jakob Buller, Heinrich Richert, and Heinrich Görtz to David Görz, Jun 1874, f. 5, (A1-5); Warkentin to Goerz, 1874, *passim*, (A1-10). For more on the Alexanderwohlers' own mutual aid fund *see* Melvin Gingerich, "The Alexanderwohl 'Schnurbuch,' " *ML*, 1 (Jan 1946), 45-47. Reports of the numbers who actually came differ greatly. Banman (1926: C2-7), 32; Unruh (1962: C1-20), 91, 95; *HT*, 11 (Oct 1974), 168; "An Interview" (n. 48); Goerz to Krehbiel, f. 24, (A1-5). *See also* Gaeddert (1974: C2-69).

52. Wedel (1974: C2-238), 171; Krehbiel (1961: B2-56), 91; Banman (1926: C2-7), 32; "An Interview" (n. 48), 4; obituary doc. (n. 48).

53. "An Interview" (n. 48), 4; Unruh (1962: C1-20), 94ff.; Banman (1926: C2-7), 32; H[einrich]. R. Voth, in Wedel (1974: C2-238), 174.

54. Sources' (*see* n. 51) numbers as to how many Alexanderwohlers really were in Lincoln are most inconsistent. Unruh (1962: C1-20), 92, 95-97, 101-02; Voth account in Wedel (1974: C2-238), 175, 174.

55. *See* Voth (1975: C2-233), and Hiebert (1979: C2-96).

56. Unruh (1962: C1-20), 97ff.; Banman (1926: C2-7), 32; Voth account in Wedel (1974: C2-238), 175.

57. *The Laws of the State of Kansas* . . .: (1865), ch. 49; (1874), ch. 85. Schmidt later implied that when he was in the Ukraine he promised such a law, and the next year the Kansas legislature passed it. Actually the law was passed in 1874, his trip was in 1875; *see* Schmidt (B2-68), 21-22.

58. Unruh (1962: C1-20), 68.

59. Noble Prentis, "The Mennonites in Kansas," in Krahn (1949: C1-7), 14; Wiebe (1949: B2-94), 99; sources n. 51.

60. *See* ch. 9 at n. 46-49, citing letters in Jansen (1872: B2-49), 6, 22, 31-32; and Warkentin to Goerz, Dec 27, 1872, (A1-10).

61. I crib shamelessly from Unruh (1962: C1-20), 91-106, but have also checked sources extensively (and found some of Unruh's statistics and dates questionable). Voth account in Wedel (1974: C2-238), 175-76; Warkentin to Goerz, Sep 19, 1874, (A1-10).

62. Unruh (1962: C1-20), 101.

63. Ibid., 101ff., 112.

64. Ibid., 100-02; Voth account in Wedel (1974: C2-238), 176-77.

65. Gaeddert (1974: C2-69), 20-22. Re Swiss-Volhynian settlers in Kansas, *see* Haury (1981: C2-90), 42; and Schrag (1956: C2-181). Schrag (1960: C2-183).

66. Gaeddert (1974: C2-69), 8, 23, 25; Haury (1981: C2-90), 37-42, 30-34; Wiebe (1949: B2-94); Wiebe (1967:C2-250), chs. 10-11. Haury (1981:C2-90), 30-34.

67. Toews (1975: C1-19), 133; Erb (1974: C2-60), 221-22, 250, 232-33, 324.

68. Wiebe (1967: C2-250), ch. 11 and center illustrations; remarks and tour by Wesley Prieb, Tabor College, Hillsboro, Kans., to author, summer 1981.

69. Gaeddert (1974: C2-69), 22-23; Prieb (n. 68).

70. Wiebe (1967: C2-250), 12, and center illustration.

71. Prieb (n. 68). For a study of a Russian-style village transplant and its gradual change to the American pattern, *see* Miller (1953:C2-140).

72. Goerz to Warkentin, Jan 15, 1873, (A1-10). For a modern scholar's agreement with Goerz's implication, *see* Urry (1978: C1-21), *passim*, esp. 685.

73. Prieb (n. 68); Rempel (1933: C1-13), IV/6-8; Rempel (1973/1974: C1-14), Jan: 47, 48; Oct: 293, 297.

74. Schmidt, "Beginning of Hochfield Village" (n. 39), 7, 8; *HT*, 12 (Aug 1875), 137.

75. *HT*, 10: (Sep 1873), 151, 155; (Oct 1873), 166, 167.

76. Menn. Bd. of Guard. financial reports in *HT*, 11-13 (1874-1876), *passim*. *HT*, 12 (Dec 1875), 202.

77. *HT*, 11 (Feb 1874), 18, 19.

78. *HT*: 11 (Jun, Jul, Sep, Oct, Nov 1874), 110, 127, 158, 174, 190; 12 (Feb, Mar, Apr, Jul 1875), 30, 46, 62, 126; 13 (Apr 1876), 78. Menn. Exec. Aid Comm. of Pa. records, (A2-29). Some records indicate interest, some do not. E.g., in box 68, (A1-2): ledger of Feb 2, 1874 and note payable to John Gehman, f. 13; a record of a payment made by Tobias Dirks, Aug 25, 1882, and signed by Pa. comm. treas. H. K. Godshall, f. 14. A standard Pa. committee form said payable "five years after date . . . without interest": *see* reproduction in *MRJ*, 15 (Apr 1974), 23. Also not showing interest: Pa. committee records in (A2-17); records re loans still unpaid on Jan 4 and Feb 2, 1915, f. SA-II-282, MLA.

79. Pa. comm. form (n. 78); Jacob Shantz to David Goerz, Aug 11, 1874, f. 24, (A1-5); *ZH*, 1 (Apr 1875), 20.

80. *HT*, 10 (Sep, Oct 1873), 153, 167. E.g., Warkentin as Board of Guard. agent and Christian Hirschler as treas. of Kans. Local Relief Comm. were suspected of mishandling funds, though vindicated by their committees—see *ZH*, 1 (Apr 1875), 23; *HT*, 12 (Dec 1875), 203. *HT*, 13 (Apr, Jun, Jul 1876), 72, 104, 122.

81. *HT*, 11 (Mar 1874), 51.

82. *HT*, 12 (May 1875), 74-75.

83. *See* Unruh (1973: C2-231); re some faring well, 107-27. Since many of the group joined the "Holdemans," *see also* Hiebert (1973: C2-97)—re their immigration, *esp.* ch. 4.

84. Tobias Unruh to John F. Funk, Nov 13, 1873 (*see also* Oct 8, 1874); Peter Becker, Benjamin Becker, and Peter Riechert to Funk, Jan 10, 1874; f. 1, box 68, (A1-2).

85. Unruh (1949: B2-85), Aug 1874; Unruh (1973: C2-231), 83, 96-98; *HT*, 11 (Feb 1874), 18-19; John Shenk to Jacob Mosser (Moser), Apr 21, 1875, in *MRJ*, 15 (Apr 1974), 23. For English-language versions of circulars by which "American" Mennonites offered aid, *see*: *HT*, 11 (Feb 1874), 18-19; copy of Pa. comm. one, May 15, 1874, f. 17, (A2-37).

86. Doc., May 6, 1874, f. 4, (A1-5); Unruh (1973: C2-231), 107-12, 98-99, 115, 121, 123, 119-120; Unruh (1949: B2-85), Nov 23, 1874-Jan 14, 1875; re *Abbotsford*—Kathryn B. Braig (Mariners' Museum, Newport News, Va. 23606) to author, Feb 10, 1986, with attached copies of museum records; *HT*, 12 (Feb 1875), 25.

87. Unruh (1973: C2-231), 116; Warkentin to Bd. of Guard., Dec 31, 1874, (A1-10).

88. Warkentin to Goerz or Bd. of Guard., Jan 2, 7, 10, 26, 1875, (A1-10). *HT*, 12: (Feb, Mar, Apr, May, Jun, Jul 1875), 25, 46, 62, 72, 94, 110. Records in f. 13; Isaac Robson to Funk, third month 10, 1874, f. 1; box 68, (A1-2).

89. Warkentin to Christian Krehbiel, Feb 20, 1875, (A1-10); Schnell (1950: C2-179), 214, 216; Amos Herr to David Goerz, May 10, 1874, f. 4, (A1-5).

90. Warkentin to Christian Krehbiel, Feb 20, 1874, (A1-10); *HT*, 11 (May, Sep 1874), 88, 152.

91. Warkentin to Bd. of Guard., Dec 31, 1874, Jan 7 and 10, 1875, (A1-10); *HT*, 12 (Feb 1875), 25; records in f. 13, box 68, (A1-2).

92. Ruth (1984: C1-15), 356-58; Unruh (1973: C2-231), 113-24; Wenger (1961: C2-247), 348; Warkentin to Goerz, Nov 20, 1874, (A1-10).

93. Warkentin to Bd. of Guard., Jan 7, 1875, (A1-10); A. S. Johnson to Christian Krehbiel, Jan 18, 1875, f. 11, (A1-5); *HT*, 12 (Feb 1875), 25.

94. *HT*, 12 (Feb 1875), 25; *ZH*, 1 (Apr 1875), 19, 23-25.

95. Warkentin to Goerz, Feb 15, 1875, (A1-10); *ZH*, 1 (Apr 1875), 23-25.

96. *ZH*, 1 (Apr 1875), 25; *HT*, 12 (May 1875), 74.

97. *HT*, 12 (Feb, May 1875), 25-26, 94; Warkentin to Bd. of Guard., Jan 7, 1875, (A1-10); *HT*, 12 (Aug 1875), 137.

98. Warkentin to Goerz, Jan 26, 1975, (A1-10); Unruh (1973: C2-231), 111; *ZH*, 1 (Apr 1875), 24. *HT*: 12 (May, Jun 1875), 72, 88; 12-13 (1875-1876), *passim*. The railroad allowed 11 years for repayment; this was its maximum—*see* its land dept. letterhead, e.g., A. S. Johnson to Christian Krehbiel, Jun 5, 1875, f. 3, (A2-21).

99. *HT*, 12-13 (1875-1876), *passim*, esp.: 12 (Aug, Dec 1875), 137-38, 202; 13 (Jan, Mar, Apr, May, Jun, Jul 1876), 11, 41-42, 72, 89, 104, 120. A. S. Johnson to Krehbiel, Jan 20, 1875, f. 22, (A1-5).

100. *HT*, 13 (Jul, Jun, Apr 1876), 121-22, 104, 72.

101. *HT*: 13 (Dec 1876), 198; 14 (Jan 1877), 9. For further (though not entirely clear) explanation, *see* Schnell (1950: C2-179), 225-26.

102. Juhnke (1975: C2-105), 48-52.

103. Schnell (1950: C2-179), 226.

104. Ibid. Letters in fs. 6, 8, box 8; fs. 1-10, box 9; fs. 1-9, box 10; (A1-2). *See also*: printed form, Nov 4, 1884, Funk message to "Lieber Bruder," f. 13; J. F. Harms to Menn. Publ. Co., Nov 4, 1895, f. 1; box 68, (A1-2).

105. Printed form hand-addressed John Shenk to David Hershey, Jan 26, 1877, (A2-17); docs., Jan 4 and Feb 2, 1915, addressed to B. P. Buller, f. SA-II-282, MLA.

106. Warkentin to Christian Krehbiel, Feb 20, 1874, (A1-10).

107. Schnell (1950: C2-179), 227-28; records, fs. 14-15, box 68, (A1-2).

108. Wiebe (1949: B2-94), 100.

109. Gering (1924: C2-72), 32-47; *HT*, 11 (Dec 1874), 201-02. Gingerich (1960: C2-79), 143-44; Wiebe (1949: B2-94), 101; Haury (1981: C2-90), 65; *CB*, 1 (Jul 15, 1882), 110; *HT*, 12 (Mar 1875), 45; Schultz (1938: C2-185), 65-66; Epp (1974: C1-2), 216; Warkentin to Goerz, May 30, 1876, (A1-10). Re Henderson: Unruh (1962: C1-20), 103, 113; J. J. Friesen, "Remaking a Community: Henderson, Nebraska," *ML*, 5 (Oct 1950), 10-12. See also Annette Atkins, *Harvest of Grief: Grasshopper Plagues and Public Assistance in Minnesota, 1873-1878* (St. Paul, 1984).

110. Re Warkentin's success, *see* ch. 2 at n. 85-87. C. B. Schmidt to A. S. Johnson, Mar 23, 1875, copy furnished to author by John Schmidt of MLA; Schmidt (1933: C2-178), 51, 58, 53-55; Jansen (1921: B2-50), 46-47; Unruh (1962: C1-20), 87; *ME*, I, 256.

111. *See esp.* reprinted in *ML*, 4 (Oct 1949): J. D. Butler, "The Mennonite Stove," 16-17; C. L.

Bernays, 39. *And see* Noble Prentis, "A Day with the Mennonites," reprints in Krahn (1949: C1-7), 22; *HT*, 13 (Jan 1876), 10.

112. Rempel (1973/1974: C1-14), 21; *CB*, 1, (Apr 15, May 15, Jun 1, Jul 1, Sep 1, Nov 1, 1882), 61, 77-78, 85, 101, 133, 165; Miller (1963: C2-140), 78-79.

113. Convers. with Cornelius Krahn, Jun 20, 1981, at Newton, Kans.; script of Jul 6, 1941, program of Kansas State Network of Mutual Broadcasting System, f. 15, box 68-1, (A1-10); Schmidt (C2-177), IX/1.

114. James Marshall, *Santa Fe: The Railroad that Built an Empire* (New York, 1945?), 86—questionable because of apparent error re C.B. Schmidt's role in obtaining Kansas' militia exemption law.

115. *See* ch. 2 at n. 85-87. Schmidt (C2-177), IX/2-3; Krahn, in Krahn (1949: C1-7), 11-12.

116. Quot. by Krahn in Krahn (1949: C1-7), 11.

117. This was my reaction as I visited Kansas in 1974 and Mennonite museums there since. *See also* a non-Kansan's script for a centennial play: Urie A. Bender, "Tomorrow Has Roots: A Centennial Drama" (1974), copy in MHL.

118. Editor quot. in Juhnke (1975: C2-105), 53, also 45, 48-49, 53; Miller (1953: C2-140), 75-143; Unruh (1972: C2-232-1), 29-36; Schultz (1938: C2-185), 67-72.

119. Letters in fs. 3, 4, and 5, (A1-5); Goerz to Warkentin, Nov 27, 1872, (A1-10).

120. "Ein Brief aus Russland," Leonard Sudermann to Peter Nissley, Nov 18, 1873, box 68, (A1-2); Tschetter (1931: B2-80), 123, 125, 127. (Tschetter said women chewed tobacco, but another source challenged that—*see* p. 218 of diary.) 121. Warkentin to Christian Krehbiel, Feb 20, 1874, (A1-10); MJ diary, May 14, 1874, f. 4, box 1, (A1-4).

121. Susanna Krehbiel autobiography (A2-22), 41-42.

122. Hartzler and Kauffman (1905: C2-87), 314.

123. For the Wisler, Brenneman, and *Dienerversammlungen* stories, *see* ch. 8 and ch. 4 at n. 73-74, 84-91.

124. *HT*, 13 (Dec 1876), 196-97; John J. Friesen, in (1950: C2-186), 20-27; H. J. Fast, J. J. Balzer, and A. A. Penner, in (1943: C2-18), 11-23. *ME*, II, 550; IV, 153. (1939: C2-98).

125. *See* e.g., *HT*, 21 (Mar 1, 1884), 73. Hartzler and Kauffman (1905:C2-87), 314-15.

126. *HT*: 12 (May, Aug, Dec 1875), 74, 137, 203; 13 (Jan, Apr, May, Aug 1876), 11, 74, 89, 137. Hiebert (1973: C2-97), 63, 113, 116, 119, 140-43, 146, 66, 218, 222.

127. *See* ch. 4 at n. 38ff.

128. Pannabecker (1975: C1-11), 52; doc., quot. in same, 47-48.

129. Friesen (1978:C1-4), 659-60. [Some writers have said erroneously that to settle in the Russian empire Mennonites gave up all right to do mission work within the empire; in fact, the law forbade proselyting only other Christians; *see* Kroeker (1981:C2-121), 25-26.] Haury (1981:C2-90), 76.

130. Haury (1981: C2-90), 75, 81-85, 88-89, 107ff., 94-100.

131. Ibid.

132. Ibid., 81; Pannabecker (1975: C1-11), 103-04.

133. Pannabecker (1975: C1-11), 346, 202-03. *ME*, I, 212; II, 680, 747; IV, 155. Juhnke (1979: C2-104), 5.

134. On American ideology, *see*, e.g., Fritz (1963: C2-67); for Mennonite missionaries' concurring, e.g., *TM*, 4 (May 1889), 122-23. Juhnke (1977: C2-103). *ME*, II, 746-47, 680; IV, 155. Barrett (1983: C2-8), 16-17, 28, 23-24, 26. Mission reports in *TM*, 1-16 (1885-1900), *passim*; Juhnke (1979: C2-104), 12, 10, 13; Re Haury's calling out troops, Juhnke (1977: C2-103), 24-25, and Barrett (1983: C2-8), 21.

135. *TM*, 3 (Jan 1888), 53.

136. Juhnke (1979: C2-104), 13; Pannabecker (1975: C1-11), 303, 306; Barrett (1983: C2-8), 19, 23-28; Juhnke (1977: C2-103), 18-19, 2-3.

137. Juhnke (1979: C2-104), ch. 2, *esp.* 28, 32, 35-36, 41, 43.

138. Friesen (1974: B2-22), 12ff., 65-66, 71-73, 61. Speaking at a "Mennonite Experience in America" conference, Goshen College, Goshen, Ind., Aug 3, 1981, GC-reared historian James Juhnke emphasized that as he grew up, mid-twentieth century, much of his self-identity was being "not-MB"; news of a relative joining the MBs seemed like news of a death.

139. Epp (1974: C1-2), 189.

140. John F. Funk to David Goerz: Mar 1, 1874, f. 4; 25 (no month) 1874, f. 1, (A1-5). Harms (1943: B2-32), 4; *ME*, II, 665.

141. John F. Funk to David Goerz, Mar 1, 1874, f. 4, f. 1, (A1-5). Christian Krehbiel to David Goerz, Aug 25, 27, 1874; Bernard Warkentin to Krehbiel, Aug 30, 1874; f. 24, (A1-5). Toews (1975: C1-19),

133, 190. Toews did not write of "American" Mennonite committees aid to MBs; I take his silence as further indication the aid was not extensive.

142. Christian Krehbiel to David Goerz, Aug 25, 27, 1874; Bernard Warkentin to Krehbiel, Aug 30, 1874; f. 24, (A1-5).

143. Toews (1975: C1-19), 132.

144. Ibid., 472-74, 148, 146, 154, 134; Epp (1974: C1-2), 283-96; Mr. and Mrs. (*sic*) Herman J. Neufeld, "The History of Menn. Breth. Church of Buhler, Kansas" (Tabor College [Hillsboro, Kan.] term paper, 1949), 5.

145. Menn. Breth. church (B1-10). These minutes, *passim, esp.* 2nd source, 1882, p. 17; 3rd source, 1884, p. 25, and 1896, pp. 186-89. Friesen, in (1950: C2-186), 19; *ME*, IV, 908; Toews (1975: C1-19), 114.

146. Toews (1975: C1-19), 133-34.

147. Menn. Breth. church (B1-10), 3rd source: 1892, pp. 141-43; 1893, pp. 144-45.

148. Ibid., 3rd source: 1884, p. 25; 1892, p. 143; 1889, p. 87; 1896, pp. 186-89; 1898, p. 208. Toews (1975: C1-19), 401, 410-11; Friesen, in (1950: C2-186), 19.

149. Menn. Breth. church (B1-10), 3rd source: on the Friesens, 1890-1899, *passim, esp.* 1898, pp. 207-08; 1899, pp. 215-16; 1892, p. 145; 1894, p. 165; 1895, p. 175. *ME*, II, 404; IV, 33. Abraham Friesen statement in Friesen (1978: C1-4), 675-82; Toews (1975: C1-19), 401; Mrs. H. T. Esau (*sic*), *First 60 Years of M. B. Missions* (Hillsboro, Kan., 1954), 29.

150. Menn. Breth. church (B1-10), *passim, esp.* 2nd source, 1879, pp. 7, 18, and 3rd source: 1889, p. 89; 1895, p. 176; 1890, p. 106; 1887, p. 56; 1888, pp. 61-63.

151. Ibid., 3rd source: 1892, p. 142; 1890, p. 106. Re two-realm view, *see* the conf. decisions re business and politics: This book, ch. 2 at n. 76; ch. 6 at n. 50.

152. *See* David Goerz to Bernard Warkentin, Nov 12, 1872; Warkentin to Goerz, Dec 27, 1872, Jan 8, 1873; (A1-10).

153. *See* Juhnke (1975: C2-105), 54-62, 74-76, 82, 89-90, 109-116.

154. *See* ch. 5 at n. 65-67.

CHAPTER 11

1. *HT*: 27 (Nov 1, 1890), 323; 28 (Dec 1, 1891), 358.

2. Geo. L. Bender to Menno S. Steiner, unclear date (Jul 14, 1894?). (A1-9).

3. For my own fuller statements re "old" and Amish Menn. quickening, *see* my: (1977: C1-18); (1978: C1-17); (1980: C2-172), ch. 1-3; (1975: C2-175). For a recent, different interpretive framework *see* Hostetler (1977: C2-98-8) and (1986: C2-98-4).

4. Gates (1964: C2-71), 26; John F. Funk diary, May 8, 1853, (A1-2).

5. *HT*, 30: (Nov 1, 1893), 340; 27 (Jan 15, Mar 1, 1890), 20-21, 72.

6. Harvey Friesner to John F. Funk, Nov 21, 1888, box 12, (A1-2); Wenger (1961: C2-247), 133-34.

7. *HT*: 19 (Sep 1881), 155-56; 22 (Mar 15, 1885), 88-89. For a general intepretation of the encounter with revivalism, *see* Hostetler (1977:C2-98-8), ch. 5.

8. *See* Weaver (1987:C1-22-2).

9. *See*, e.g.: Harold S. Bender's articles on Funk and on revivals in *ME*, II, 422; IV, 309. Wenger (1966: C2-246), 91. It is true that Funk's *Herald* sometimes quoted or reprinted Moody favorably, or cited him as a model—e.g., *HT*, 33 (Jul 1, 1896), 203. But the evidence for deep personal influence of Moody on Funk seems to consist solely of a statement Funk himself made when 92: see *An Address by John F. Funk on the Occasion of the Ninety-Second Anniversary of His Birth, at the Mennonite Church, Elkhart, Ind., April 6, 1927* (tractlike doc.; copy in MHL). By 1927 nearly seven decades had passed since Funk's Chicago years, Moody was so famous as to be legend, and Funk was old. Time, fame, and age can of course distort the most sincere memory. Moreover, interestingly, in a similar doc., *Sermon Preached by John F. Funk at the Mennonite Church, Elkhart Ind., Sunday, April 5, 1925, Celebrating His Ninetieth Birthday, April 6, 1925*, Funk did not mention the Moody influence. More definitive is evidence (or lack of it) from the Chicago years themselves, or more near them. Funk's diary of that time reveals no such influence—*see* John F. Funk diary, 1857-1867, *passim*, (A1-2). And in 1876, in a personal account of visiting a Moody revival in Chicago, Funk's tone was that of a cool observer, not of warm nostalgia for a friend and mentor—see *HT*, 13 (Dec 1876), 201-03. In 1876 Funk may of course have been afraid to show open endorsement of Moody lest he hurt his paper; yet there is no solid reason for believing he hid his true position. As for a statement in the Bender *ME* articles that Funk and Daniel Brenneman conducted the first revivals in the "old" Mennonite church (at Masontown, western Pa., 1872), *see* Bowman (1972: C2-22), who argued that the first were a series by Coffman at Bowne, Michigan, in 1881.

10. *ME*, I, 633-34; Sutter (1974: C2-209).

11. John S. Coffman to John F. Funk, Mar 10 and 13, 1879, box 8, (A1-2).

12. Sutter (1974: C2-209), 11-13; Wenger (1966: C2-246), 111; John S. Coffman to Menno S. Steiner, Jul 11, 1894, (A1-9).

13. Weaver (1987: C1-22-2), esp. pp. 31-33.

14. Shetler (1963: C2-188), chs. 1-8, *passim*; John S. Coffman to John F. Funk, Nov 23, 1885, box 9, (A1-2); *HT*, 29 (Dec 1, 1892), 359.

15. John S. Coffman corresp., *passim*, (A1-1); *ME*, IV, 626-27.

16. Schlabach (1980: C2-172), 38-40, 65, 88-92; for evang. committee's early work, *see* Marion G. Bontrager, "The Birth of Evangelism in the Mennonite Church and the Traveling Evangelist West of the Mississippi River 1864-1865" (Goshen College baccalaureate thesis, 1959), copy in MHL; *ME*, IV, 1008-09.

17. Gingerich (1963: C2-77), 113-14.

18. *CB*, 1 (Feb 1, 1882), 21; Women's Missionary Assoc. (1935: C2-258), 22. *ME*: III, 594; I, 328-29, 558. *See* Coffman (1898: B2-17); Kraus (1958: C2-118), 71-110; Sandeen (1970: C2-169), ch. 6.

19. *ME*, II, 881; *Hymns and Tunes for Public and Private Worship and Sunday Schools* (Elkhart, Ind., 1890); Yoder (1961: C2-266), 64-71.

20. *ME*, II, 186, 546-47. John S. Umble, *Goshen College, 1894-1954* (Goshen, Ind.: Goshen College, 1955) 1-25. *ME*, IV, 86, 87; III, 633. Re gen. conf. origin *see esp.*: *ME*, III, 622; (1921: B2-67), 28-53; and *HT*: 31 (Oct 15, 1894), 315-16; 33 (May 15, 1896), 147-48; 34 (May 15, 1897), 155; 34 (Dec 15, 1897), 371-72; 35 (May 15, 1898), 152-53; 35 (Aug 1, 1898), 225, 226-27; 35 (Dec 1, 1898), 363-64; 36 (Feb 1, 1899), 35; 36 (Feb 15, 1899), 51-52; 37 (Jul 1, 1900), 195-96; 37 (Aug 15, 1900), 243-44; 37 (Sep 1, 15, 1900), 258, 274-75.

21. E.g., Hartzler and Kauffman (1905: C2-87), 244-45; Hershberger (1970: C2-93), 222; Bender, as reprinted in Wenger (1966: C2-246), 180; *ME*, III, 614. For a more ample statement of the label issue, *see* my (1977: C1-18), 214-15.

22. Jos. Funk in Burkholder (1837: B1-5), 461; Brunk (1959: C2-30), I, 276ff., 286-87; Schlabach (1980: C2-172), 30-31.

23. John M. Brenneman to Peter Nissley, Mar 10, 1865, (A2-30). *HT*: 2 (Apr, Sep 1865), 30-31, 68-69; 4 (Jun, Aug 1867), 89-90, 120; 13 (Sep 1876), 159. *GH*, 16 (Feb 14, 1924), 941; *ME*, III, 755; Schlabach (1980: C2-172), 35-37.

24. *HT*: 2 (Sep 1865), 69; 4 (Jun, Aug 1867), 89-90, 120; Ind-Mich conf. (B2-48), Oct 14, 1897, p. 12. *See also* Virginia conf. (B2-86), Oct 1891, p. 37. *HT*, 29 (Apr 1, 1892), 99.

25. *HT*, 31 (Feb. 1, 15, 1894), 36-37, 51-52. On the basis of sources such as in these last two notes I hold that throughout most of the nineteenth century Mennonites kept a perception that peace and nonresistance were at the very heart of the gospel, not only a mandate that followed after forensic conversion. *See also* frequent references to Christians being part of Christ's kingdom of peace, as they appear in Christian Burkholder's and Peter Burkholder's and other early-nineteenth-century writings. [*See* chs. 4 and 5 above, and also Brenneman (1863: B2-9), discussed in ch. 6 at n. 32 and ch. 7 at n. 73-78.] In my past writings (*see* n. 3) I may have overstated the appearance of the phrases "gospel of peace" and "nonresistant gospel." But I believe thorough acquaintance with nineteenth-century sources will support my overall interpetation. For a closely related discussion *see* Weaver (1987: C1-22-2).

26. Schlabach (1980: C2-172), 43, 49, 56-59. *HT*: 29 (Nov 1, 15, and Dec 15, 1892), 326-27, 370-72; 30 (Nov 1, Dec 1, 1893), 338, 370-71.

27. *HT* items n. 26.

28. *HT*: 29 (Dec 15, 1982), 370; 30 (Dec 1, 1893), 371.

29. Schlabach (1980: C2-172), 56-68; Emma Oyer, *What God Hath Wrought in a Half Century at the Mennonite Home Mission* (Elkhart, Ind., 1949), 1-46; Lamb (1978: C2-122), 11-13.

30. Schlabach (1980: C2-172), 70-74.

31. Ibid.

32. Jacob Hildebrand to John F. Funk, Jan 10, 1873, box 7, f. 1, (A1-2). There were two ordained Jacob Hildebrands, and it is not clear which wrote to Funk—*see* Brunk (1959: C2-30), I, 393-98, 408-11, 418-19; John Gehman expense records at Jun 17, 1837, p. 24; Jun 15, 28, 1861, p. 48, (A2-13); Gibbons (1872: C2-74), 19; re camp meeting preacher, *see* ch. 3 at n. 47.

33. *HT*: 34 (Jan 15, 1897), 19.

34. *HT*: 26 (Nov 15, 1889), 341-43; 27 (Mar 1, 1890), 74-75.

35. *ME*, I, 475; *HT*, 29 (Apr 1, 1892), 99.

36. I have no absolute evidence of Lancaster Mennonite wealth, but *see*: MacMaster (1985: C1-10), 91ff.; Robertson (1980: C2-166), 76-81, 84-85, 87, 96-99.

37. Schlabach (1980: C2-172), 74-76.

38. *HT*, 15 (Aug 15, 1898), 246; Schlabach (1980: C2-172), 29; John A. Lapp, *The Mennonite Church in India, 1897-1962* (Scottdale, Pa., 1972), 27.

39. Lapp (n. 38), ch. 1; Schlabach (1980: C2-172), 78-80. Geo. L. Bender to: Herman Dirks, Apr 1, 1897; Cressman and Hallman, Apr 8, 1897; J. J. Warner, Apr 9, 1897; and *passim*; box 2, (A1-6). Bender to: D. H. Bender, Apr 16, 1897; Louis Klopf, Mar 16, 1897; G. L. Bender letterbook, box 2, (A2-28). Re Armenian aid *see* MEBB papers of 1896-1897, (A2-28), *passim*, and, e.g., *HT*, 33 (Feb 15, 1896), 49. Hershberger (1970: C2-93), 223-24—or more ample version in ms. Hershberger wrote as background for the article, (1976: C2-92), 172-176. Primary sources of the HFRC are esp. in collections just mentioned and in (A2-18); for HFRC certificate to supporters *see* f. 9, box 2, (A2-32); also, the *HT* printed HFRC-related articles and reports.

40. G. L. Bender to D. S. Sprunger, Mar 24, 1897, and to John E. Bontrager (Borntreger), Mar 31, 1897, (A2-28); to J. A. Sprunger, Apr 7, box 2, (A1-6); *ME*, IV, 605.

41. *ME*, IV, 1101; II, 274, 797. Lambert (1898: B2-57). John E. Borntreger to Geo. Bender, Mar 29, 1897; Bender to Cressman and Hallman, Mar 31, 1897; (A2-28).

42. *HT*, 35 (May 15, Jun 15, Aug 1, Sep 1, 1898), 145, 177, 225, 257—quot. from 257. *TM*, 13 (Jun 1898), 65; A. B. Shelly to D. F. Jansen (Janzten), Jun 18, 1898, box 25, (A1-2).

43. *TM*, 13 (Apr, Jun 1898), 55, 65; D. H. Bender to M. S. Steiner, May 25, 1898, (A1-9). Re "old" Mennonite gen. conf. origin, *see* n. 20.

44. Schlabach (1977: C1-18), 226.

45. Lapp (n. 35), 41.

46. *HT*, 28 (Dec 1, 1891), 358-59.

47. *HT*: 31 (Nov 1, 1894), 331; 28 (Dec 1, 1891), 358-59; 30 (Dec 1, 1893), 365. *See also* Schlabach (1980: C2-172), chs. 2-3. For background of this institution-building, *see* Hostetler (1977: C2-98-8), ch. 6.

48. G. L. Bender to M. S. Steiner, May 6, 1893; Andrew Rosenberger to Steiner, Nov 13, 1899; (A1-9). For an interpretation of such restructuring, *see* Hostetler (1977: C2-98-8), esp. ch. 8, and Hostetler (C2-98-4).

49. *HT*, 28 (Dec 1, 1891), 358; E. J. Berkey to M. S. Steiner, (A1-9).

50. C. K. Hostetler to M. S. Steiner, Sep 7, 1892; John S. Coffman to M. S. Steiner, Oct 17, 1893; (A1-9). Schlabach (1980: C2-172), 56-59, 64-65, chs. 2-3. *HT*: 30 (Nov 15, Dec 1, 1893), 361, 370-71; 32 (Jul 15, 1895), 210. John F. Funk to M. S. Steiner, Jan 5, 1893 (from internal evidence, really 1894), (A1-9).

51. *HT*, quot. 31 (May 1, 1894), 140; *see also*, e.g., 31 (Jun 1, Nov 15, 1894), 189, 346; 30 (Jul 1, 1893), 211-12.

52. For three books with biographical sketches of Mennonite women, including some from the 19th century, *see*: Cummings (1978: C2-43), Rich (1983: C2-164), and Wiebe (1979: C2-251).

53. *See esp.* Mathews (1969: C2-138); Schlabach (1979: C2-174). *See* ch. 4 of this book at n. 84. Barrett (1975: C2-9). However, the evidence on Anab. women is scanty; *see* Bainton (1971: C2-6), 145-58; and Sprunger (1985: C2-197). Cross (1965: C2-41), 177-78; Gilbert H. Barnes, *The Anti-Slavery Impulse, 1830-1844* (New York and London, 1933), 12-13; Smith (1967: C2-192), 82, 124, 133, 144-45, 169-71, 212.

54. E.g.: Sunday school record, 1868, West Swamp Menno. church papers, MCA 8-40, orig. in EPMHL; *TM*, 11 (Sep 1896), 93. *HT*, 29 (Nov 1, 15, 1892), 326, 338; 30 (Oct 15, Nov 1 and 15, Dec 1, 1893), 324, 325, 332, 354, 355, 369, 370. Klinglesmith (1980: C2-113), 166, citing ms. by Melvin Gingerich, in MCA.

55. Gingerich (1963: C2-77), 113-14; *CB*, 1 (Feb 1, 1882), 21; Women's Missionary Assoc. (1935: C2-258), 7, 14, 22.

56. *TM*: 4 (Nov, Dec 1888), 25, 34-35; 6 (Jan 1891), 52-53; 10 (Apr 1895), 52-53. *ME*: IV, 605; II, 24. Menn. Breth. church (B1-10), 3rd source: 1897, pp. 197, 203; 1898, p. 206.

57. A. D. Wenger to G. L. Bender, Feb 3, 1897; Bender to Wenger, Feb 9, 1897; (A2-28). *HT*, 34 (Dec 1, 1897), 364; 36 (Aug 15, Jul 1, 1899), 247, 199. Ira D. Landis, *The Missionary Movement Among the Lancaster Conference Mennonites* (Scottdale, Pa, 1938), 42-43. *HT*, 36 (Jun 15, Jul 15, Aug 1, Aug 15, Sep 1, Oct 15, 1899), 177, 215, 231, 247, 263, 311, quot. p. 215.

58. Many letter collections demonstrate this. *See*, e.g., (A2-19) and many letters published in Hoover (1982: B1-9).

59. Kans.-Nebr. conf. (1914: B2-52), Apr 27, 1877, p. 12; Ind.-Mich. conf. (1929: B2-48), Oct 9, 1891, p. 45; M. S. Steiner to G. L. Bender, Feb 23, 1892, box 6, (A2-1); Bender to Steiner, Apr 6, 1893, (A1-9).

60. Bender (1937: B2-6), 166-67; Bender (1934: B1-2), 92, 94, 96. Doc. printed in Lehman (1978: C2-126), 110-11.

61. Zook: *HT*, 34 (Apr 15, 1897), 116. Anti-higher criticism—e.g., *HT*, 32 (Jul 1, 1895), 194; 34

(May 1, 1897), 130-31; 35 (Apr 1, 1898), 98. These sources show little effort to understand higher criticism; for de facto use of it, *see*, e.g., Daniel Kauffman's remarks on baptism as noted in Coffman (1898: B2-17), 15-18.

62. *TM*: 13 (Nov 1897), 12; 5 (Oct 1889), 5; 4 (May 1889), 120; 7 (Nov 1891), 9.

63. *TM*, 4 (Nov, Dec 1888), 21, 33-35.

64. Coffman (1891:B2-16), 2-3; Lamb (1978:C2-122), 13-14; Klinglesmith (1980:C2-113).

65. *YPP*, 1 (Jan 6, 20, 1894), 7, 13.

66. *See* Barbara Welter's classic, oft-reprinted article (1966: C2-239). Since its appearance there has been much discussion and some refinement of its basic framework of piety, purity, domesticity, and submission. A good place to start for an updated reading is Woloch (1984: C2-257), ch. 6; *see esp.* its paragraph on sources for women and religion, 148-49. The present book cannot offer a full testing of 19th-century Mennonite materials against the current literature and paradigms of women's history; but I do not find that Mennonites laid the burden of maintaining piety and purity as heavily on women as the literature suggests for American culture at large. Among Mennonites there surely were elements of a "feminization" of religion such as authors suggest for America at large and for evangelicals in particular—*see esp.* Welter (1974: C2-240). Mennonites at least sang some of the hymns Welter cited as evidence; and N. B. Grubb of Philadelphia appointed twelve female "Associate Pastors"—*see TM*, 4 (May 1889), 120. Yet I doubt that further research will find feminization to have gone very far among Mennonites. Traditional Mennonites and Amish emphasized humility and submissiveness for men *and* women; and the aggressive mode of the quickening, by Welter's criteria, would be "masculinization." In 1893 M. S. Steiner preached on the "Manliness of God"—*see* his diary, Mar 12, 1893, (A1-9). Needed is much further testing of Mennonite materials against present-day women-studies literature. *See* e.g., the following, *CB*, 1 (Jul 1, 1882), 97. *TM:* 1 (Feb, Apr, Jun 1886), 68-69, 100, 133; 3 (Jun 1888), 133:4 (Dec 1888; Jan, May 1889), 33-34, 54, 119; 5 (Apr 1890), 109. *YPP:* 1 (Feb 17, Jun 9, Nov 24, 1894), 27, 89, 188; 3 (Jan 4, Jun 20, Aug 15, 1896), 4-5, 99, 101, 132, 135.

67. Re Anabaptists, *see esp.* Klaassen (1973: C2-111), 19-33; re Mennonites, I generalize from the many 19th-century sources herein cited.

68. Weaver (1987: C1-22-2). From my immersion in 19th-century Mennonite sources I fully concur with Weaver's analysis.

69. *HT*, 21 (Jan 1, 1884), 9.

70. Weaver (1987: C1-22-2), 25-28.

71. Ibid., 8, 42-43.

72. *See*, e.g.: Coffman (1898: B2-17); Kauffman (1898: B2-53); *YPP*, 3 (Mar 14, 1896), 44-45.—the *YPP* pages bring together a series of statements on salvation and assurance from a variety of people, and offer an excellent glimpse of mid-1890s' thought among "old" and Amish Mennonites concerning salvation.

73. Coffman (1894: B2-15); John S. Coffman diary, Jun 24, 1898, box 2, (A1-1); *HT*, 35 (Aug 15, 1898), 243.

74. Weaver (1987: C1-22-2), 31-39; Coffman (1891: B2-16); *HT*, 32 (Mar 1, 1895), 68; Coffman (1898: B2-17); M. D. Wenger to M. S. Steiner, Feb 20, 1898, (A1-9).

75. Coffman (1896: B2-18);Coffman (1894: B2-15).

76. Kauffman (1898: B2-53), 11-14, 205-07; Kauffman (1914: B2-54), *esp.* 535-49.

77. Kauffman (1928: B2-55), 442, 448, 510, 505, and *passim*. *See also* Weaver (1987: C1-22-2), 34-39, 43-44.

78. Weaver (1987: C1-22-2), 31-33; and I simply see no evidence that before his death Coffman was making progress to integrate the parts of his theology, or even that he saw the problem. Of course his contributions and gifts were those of an evangelist, not of a systematic theologian.

79. *HT*, 33 (Feb 15, 1896), 50: M. D. Wenger to M. S. Steiner, Feb 20, 1898, (A1-9). *HT*, 32 (Feb 15, Mar 1, 1895), 60-61, 67.

80. *HT*, 32 (Feb 15, 1895), 60: M. D. Wenger to M. S. Steiner, Feb 20, 1898, (A1-9).

81. *HT*, 29 (Nov 1, 1892), 321-22.

82. *HT*, 29 (Nov 1, 1892), 322; *TM*, 5 (Mar 1890), 84; *HT*, 35 (Mar 1, 1898), 65-66.

83. *HT*, 22 (Mar 15, 1885), 88. M. S. Steiner diary, Mar 12, 1983; "George" (G. L. Bender) to Steiner. May 6, 1893; Isaac Hershey to Steiner, Nov. 24, 1894; (A1-9).

84. For my fuller treatment of the change *see* (1978: C1-17).

85. M. S. Steiner diary, Feb 25 and 27, 1895, (A1-9).

BIBLIOGRAPHY

A1. EXCEPTIONALLY IMPORTANT COLLECTIONS OF PAPERS

A1-1. Coffman, John S. papers. Hist. Mss. 1-19, AMC. About three linear feet; primarily letters and, for years 1871 and 1876-1899, insightful diaries; invaluable for studying the "old" Mennonite "quickening." Coffman was an associate editor of the *Herald of Truth* and from about 1880 until death in 1899 was pioneer evangelist of the "old" Mennonite church. As his life touched many people he built up a wide correspondence, especially among "old" and Amish Mennonite church leaders and activist youth.

A1-2. Funk, John F. papers. Hist. Mss. 1-1, AMC. Funk, who began publishing the *Herald of Truth* and *Herold der Wahrheit* in 1864, was the foremost "old" Mennonite church leader from then until century's end; his collection is vast (35 linear feet) and includes especially diaries, correspondence with many Mennonite leaders and others, drafts of articles submitted to his publications, and materials on Mennonite immigration from the Russian empire in the 1870s and 1880s and the Mennonite Board of Guardians which helped facilitate and subsidize that immigration. In some categories the papers are far from complete; yet hardly any other collection anywhere offers as much on latter-nineteenth-century American Mennonite affairs.

A1-3. Gross, William papers. Hist. Mss. 8-39, AMC (on microfilm, three reels; originals in EPMHL). Interesting especially for deep pietism not of the revivalist variety and for Mennonite views and news from various places, including frontier Nebraska. Closely related are the John Gross (A2-15) and the Benjamin Weber (A2-38) papers.

A1-4. Jansen, Cornelius papers. MLA. Extensive collection of a Prussian resident of the Ukraine who emigrated to the U.S. in the 1870s and was a leader of Russian and Prussian Mennonite immigration; includes valuable diaries by his wife and children which offer women's perspectives.

A1-5. Mennonite Board of Guardians papers. MLA.

A1-6. Mennonite Board of Missions and Charities (MBMC) papers. Hist. Mss. IV-4, AMC.

A1-7. Mensch, Jacob papers. Hist. Mss. 8-36, AMC (on microfilm; originals in EPMHS). Extensive collection of letters, 1860-1911, of a conservative-minded, historically sensitive minister of the Franconia "old" Mennonite conference; also includes notes on harvest meetings of various Franconia congregations, 1880-1911.

Mensch also kept private minutes of Franconia conference sessions from 1880 until public minutes began in 1907—*see* A2-9. *See also*: Ernest G. Gehman, trans. and ed., "The Mensch-Oberholtzer Papers," *MQR*, 46 (Oct 1972), 329-83.

A1-8. Schwarzendruber, Jacob collection, in Daniel B. Swartzendruber papers. Hist. Mss. 1-144, AMC. For inventory of the papers, *see* John Umble, "Catalog of an Amish Bishop's 'Library,'" *MQR*, 20 (Jul 1946), 230-39. Items range from handwritten copies of old Amish *Ordnungsbriefe* to a tribute to Schwarzendruber's wife. Many documents are in old German handscript but are accompanied by transcriptions or translations. *See also* Bender (1946: B2-5).

A1-9. Steiner, Menno S. papers. Hist. Mss. 1-33, AMC. 4.5 linear feet. Letters (from 1884 and especially from 1889 to Steiner's early death in 1911) and diaries (1890, 1893-1897, 1899-1904, 1906, 1907) plus some clippings, notebooks, sermon notes, etc. Steiner was a key young evangelist and activist in beginning new programs and institutions, and a protégé of John F. Funk and John S. Coffman; his papers are a crucial source especially for studying the "old" and Amish Mennonite "quickening" of the 1890s and early twentieth century.

A1-10. Warkentin, Bernard papers. MLA. Bernard Warkentin was a young Mennonite of the Ukraine who came to North America in 1872 and soon settled in Kansas; he went on to become a wealthy businessman, mainly as a miller. Especially valuable for this book was extensive correspondence with David Goerz, a young schoolteacher who also immigrated and who became a churchman, editor, and key person in founding Mennonite institutions in Kansas from 1874-1900. The Goerz-Warkentin correspondence (trans. and typed) is a very revealing set of letters between two able young men who became central figures in the Russian Mennonite immigration to North America in 1873-1876. The letters give insight into what Mennonites in the Ukraine were hearing, how they developed their emigration strategy, and especially what impressions Warkentin communicated, as he arrived early and sent information back. Since after immigrating both Goerz and Warkentin became officials of the Mennonite Board of Guardians, the letters offer much insight into the immigrant aid machinery. Some of the letters from 1873 are printed in Cornelius Krahn, ed., "Some Letters of Bernhard Warkentin Pertaining to the Migration of 1873-1875," *MQR*, 24 (Jul 1950), 248-63.

A2. FURTHER PRIMARY COLLECTIONS AND MANUSCRIPTS

A2-1. Bender, George L. and Elsie Kolb papers. Hist. Mss. 1-392, AMC.

A2-2. Brenneman, John M. papers. Hist. Mss. 1-276, AMC.

A2-3. Brenneman, Moses papers. Hist. Mss. 1-467, AMC.

A2-4. Buller, Jakob letters. Available in typed trans. at MLA.

A2-5. Burkholder, Peter box. MSHL.

A2-6. Driver family box. MSHL.

A2-7. "Early Correspondence and Papers." Hist. Mss. 1-10, AMC. A miscellaneous collection.

A2-8. "Exposition on Sunday schools Between John F. Funk Editor of the herald of truth of Elkhart Indianna [*sic*] and The Antisundayschool Mennonites of Virginia." Handwritten folio, file 1 MS 5, in Harry A. Brunk Sr. materials box, Abraham Blosser papers. MSHL.

A2-9. Franconia Mennonite conference proceedings, 1880-1907. Privately recorded by Jacob Mensch, trans. by Raymond Hollenbach. Originals at EPMHL, microfilm at AMC.

A2-10. "From I[saac]. B. Tyson's Book to R. W. Tyson 1877." Schwenkfelder Library, Pennsburg, Pa. Copies at EPMHL and elsewhere.

A2-11. Funk, Joseph papers. MSHL.

A2-12. Funk, Salome Kratz, and Martha Funk and Phoebe Funk Kolb papers. Hist. Mss. 1-1, AMC. Papers of the spouse and the daughters of publisher John F. Funk.

A2-13. Gehman, Johannes, and Gehman family papers. Trans. by Raymond Hollenbach. EPMHL.

A2-14. Good, John S. papers. Hist. Mss. 1-424, AMC.

A2-15. Gross, John papers. Hist. Mss. 8-39, AMC. Originals. in EPMHL.

A2-16. Guengerich, Samuel D. papers. Hist. Mss. 1-2, AMC.

A2-17. Hershey, David papers. Hist. Mss. 1-194, AMC.

A2-18. Home and Foreign Relief Commission papers. Hist. Mss. VII-1-1 and VII-1-2.1, AMC.

A2-19. Hostetter, Jacob papers. Trans. by John Umble. LMHS.

A2-20. Kolb, Garrett diary. EPMHL.

A2-21. Krehbiel, Christian papers. MLA.

A2-22. Krehbiel, Susanna. "Autobiography of Susanna A. Krehbiel: Wife of Christian Krehbiel, April 22, 1840 - April 1920." Typed; copy in Hist. Mss. 1-551 SC, AMC; also now reproduced in multilith, 54 pp.

A2-23. Kurtz, Joseph papers. Hist. Mss. 1-10, AMC.

A2-24. Landis, John papers. Hist. Mss. 8-39, AMC. Originals in EPMHL.

A2-25. Lehman, J. Irvin papers. MSHL.

A2-26. Liechty, Jacob papers. Hist. Mss. 1-514, AMC.

A2-27. Mast, Samuel papers. Hist. Mss. 1-346, AMC.

A2-28. Mennonite Evangelizing and Benevolent Board (MEBB) papers. Hist. Mss. IV-4, AMC.

A2-29. Mennonite Executive Aid Committee of Pennsylvania selected records. Copies in MLA. Made from documents at LMHS, in: Peter Nissley papers, Metzler Mennonite Church papers, Slate Hill Mennonite Church papers, Kraybill Mennonite Church papers.

A2-30. Nissley, Peter papers. Hist. Mss. 1-293, AMC.

A2-31. Nold, Jacob papers. Hist. Mss. 1-442, AMC.

A2-32. Plank, David papers. Hist. Mss. 1-5, AMC.

A2-33. Ressler, J[acob]. A. and Lina Zook Ressler papers. Hist. Mss. 1-117, AMC.

A2-34. "Salford Congregation Record Book, 1830-1898." Trans. by Raymond Hollenbach. EPMHL.

A2-35. [Sudermann, Leonard]. "Abschiedsrede Gehalten am 20st. July [*sic*] vor des Jahres 1876 vor der Mennonitengemeine [*sic*] in Berdyansk, Sud-Russland [*sic*] von L. Sudermann." Typed farewell address to Mennonite congregation, Jul 20, 1876, at Berdyansk, the Ukraine; f. 25, A2-37.

A2-36. ________. "How a Mennonite Congregation was Founded in the Port City of Berdjansk in South Russia." Typed trans. of a mss., from internal evid. by Sudermann; f. 31, A2-37.

A2-37. Sudermann, Leonard papers. MLA.

A2-38. Weber, Benjamin papers. Hist. Mss. 1-10, AMC.

A2-39. Yoder, Christian Z. papers. Hist. Mss. 1-88, AMC.

A2-40. Zimmerly, John papers. Hist. Mss. 1-10, AMC.

B1. PRINTED PRIMARY SOURCES OF SPECIAL VALUE

B1-1. Beiler, David. *Das wahre Christenthum: Eine Christliche Betrachtung nach den Lehren der Heiligen Schrift* (Lancaster, Pa.: printed by Johann Bär's Söhnen, 1888 [but written much earlier; foreword says written by April 1857]).

B1-2. Bender, Harold S., trans. and ed. "Some Early American Amish Mennonite Disciplines," *MQR*, 8 (Apr 1934), 90-98.

B1-3. Brenneman, John M. *Pride and Humility: A Discourse, Setting Forth the Characteristics of the Proud and the Humble* (Elkhart, Ind.: John F. Funk, 1867). In German: *Hoffart und Demuth: einander gegenüber gestellt* (Elkhart, Ind.: John F. Funk, 1867). More English or German editions 1868, 1873, 1875.

B1-4. Burkholder, Christian. *Useful and Edifying Address to the Young.....* Bound with [Gerrit Roosen,] *Christian Spiritual Conversation on Saving Faith, for the Young, in Questions and Answers ...* 179-257 (Lancaster, Pa.: John Baer and Sons, 1857). This is a translation of Burkholder's *Nützliche und Erbauliche Anrede an die Jugend, Von der wahren Busse, von dem Selig-*

machenden Glauben an Jesu Christo, und der reinen Worte Gottes, und der reinen übergab der Seelen, an die Hand Gottes: Vorgestellt in Frag and Antwort ([Ephrata, Pa.?], 1804); and second printing (Ephrata, Pa.: Bauman und Cleim, 1804). It is the most important primary source for studying nineteenth-century Mennonite humility theology; also good for studying Pietistic influence.

B1-5. Burkholder, Peter. *The Confession of Faith of the Christians Known by the Name of Mennonites, in Thirty-Three Articles: With a Short Extract from Their Catechism. Translated from the German, and Accompanied with Notes, to Which Is Added an Introduction, also, Nine Reflections from Different Passages of the Scriptures, Illustrative of Their Confession, Faith & Practice.* Trans. by Joseph Funk (Winchester, Va.: Robinson and Hollis, 1837). New version of Peter Jansz Twisk Dutch Mennonite confession of ca. 1600, plus other writings.

B1-6. Correll, Ernst, ed. "The Congressional Debates on the Mennonite Immigration from Russia, 1873-1874," *MQR*, 20 (Jul 1946), 178-221.

B1-7. ________________, ed. "President Grant and the Mennonite Immigration from Russia," *MQR*, 9 (Jul 1935), 144-47.

B1-8. Godshalk, Abraham. *A Description of the New Creature: From Its Birth until Grown up "unto a Perfect Man"* ... (Doylestown, Pa.: printed by William M. Large, 1838). In German: Abraham Gottschall, *Wahre Gerechtigkeit verteidigt: oder ein Beweis, wie man durch den Glauben wirklich soll gerecht werden* (Doylestaun, Pa.: J. Jung u. Krapf, 1837).

B1-9. Hoover, Amos B, comp. and ed. *The Jonas Martin Era: Presented in a Collection of Essays, Letters and Documents that Shed Light on the Mennonite Churches During the 50 Year Ministry (1875-1925) of Bishop Jonas H. Martin* (Denver, Pa.: The Author, Rte. 3, Denver, Pa., 1982), pp. 1128. A remarkable collection of letters, newspaper clippings, etc., invaluable for studying Old Order Mennonite (although not Amish) outlook, hopes, origins, and early life. The focus is on the Weaverland church district of Lancaster County, Pa., but there is much information and evidence about like-minded movements and people in other locations, e.g., Jacob Wisler and his supporters in Elkhart County, Ind. All materials are translated (if necessary) into English; many items appear in German as well. The compilation is an archive in itself.

B1-10. [Mennonite Brethren Church of North America.] Mennonite Brethren church general conference minutes, 1878-1899, found in three sources: 1) "Minutes of the First Four Sessions of the M. B. General Conference 1879-1882. (Also the first meeting held in 1878, which was not recognized as being official)" (Typed transcript of notes compiled by J. F. Harms). 2) "Konferenzbeschluesse der Mennoniten Bruedergemeinde von Nord Amerika 1879-1882"

(Mimeographed document, 1949). 3) *Konferenzberichte der Mennoniten Brüdergemeinde von Nord Amerika, 1883-1919, Nebst Konstitution der Mennoniten Brüdergemeinde von Nord Amerika* (Hillsboro, Kans.: Mennonite Brethren Publishing House, 1920). Copies of the unpublished items may be found at the Center for Mennonite Brethren Studies, Fresno Pacific College, Fresno, Calif., and in MHL.

B1-11. Musser, Daniel. *The Reformed Mennonite Church: Its Rise and Progress, with Its Principles and Doctrines* (Lancaster, Pa.: Elias Barr and Co., 1873).

B1-12. [Oberholtzer, John H.] "Constitution of the Mennonite Brotherhood," trans. with intro. by Elizabeth Bender, *MQR*, 46 (Oct 1972), 384-97 (part of an "Oberholtzer Division" issue—*see* B1-13). The constitution is available in various other translations.

B1-13. "The Oberholtzer Division," *MQR*, 46 (Oct 1972), 326-430. This *MQR* issue contains the best primary sources on the Oberholtzer affair. Four of its items are listed individually in this bibliography: B1-12, B2-20, B2-65, B2-77.

B1-14. St[auffer]., J[acob or akob]. Part One: *Eine Chronik oder Geschicht-Büchlein von der sogenannten Mennonisten Gemeinde* ..., pp. 1-254, "By J. St., written in the year 1850." Part Two: *Glaubens-Grund und Bekenntniss der alten Wehrlosen Taufs-Gesinnten, nämlich der Gemeine Gottes, oder Mennonisten genannt* ..., pp. 255-399, "Written in the year 1848, by J. S." Part Three: *Noch ein Bekenntniss von der Entziehung oder Meidung der gefallenen und abgesonderten Glieder*, pp. 400-21. (Lancaster, Pa.: printed by Johann Baer und Söhnen, 1855).

B1-15. *Verhandlungen* [or *Bericht der Verhandlungen*—title varies] *der ... Diener-Versammlung der Deutschen Täufer oder Amischen Mennoniten* ... (1862-1878). Proceedings of the historic series of Amish ministers' meetings at the time of the sorting out of Old Order Amish from Amish Mennonite. Copy is in MHL. For this study, an unpublished trans. by Paton Yoder was used—in Yoder's possession, 1608 S. 14th St., Goshen Ind.

B2. OTHER PRINTED PRIMARY SOURCES

B2-1. Arndt, Johann. *Sechs Bücher vom Wahren Christenthum* ... (Philadelphia: J. Kohler, 1866).

B2-2. [JFB.] "Research Note: Ordnung," *MQR*, 56 (Oct 1982), 382-84. I also have a photocopy of JFB's handwritten draft incl. author's name, address, and date of writing "about June 14, 1974."

B2-3. Balzer, Heinrich. "Verstand und Vernunft ..." (Understanding and Reason: Simple Opinions Regarding the Difference Between Understanding and Reason, Discussed According to the Bible); mss. written ca. 1833, published in John G. Stauffer's periodical *Die Gemeinde unterm Kreuz* May 1886 - Jan 1887 in five installments; copy of mss. in A1-2; trans. with comments by Robert Friedmann in "Faith and Reason: The Principles of Mennonitism Reconsidered in a Treatise of 1833," *MQR*, 22 (Apr 1948), 75-93.

B2-4. [Beiler, David.] "Memoirs of an Amish Bishop," trans. and ed. with comments by John Umble, *MQR*, 22 (Apr 1948), 94-115.

B2-4-2. Bekker, Jacob P. *Origin of the Mennonite Brethren Church: Previously Unpublished Manuscript by One of the Eighteen Founders*, trans. by D. E. Pauls and A. E. Jansen ([Hillsboro, Kan.?:] The Mennonite Brethren Historical Society of the Midwest, 1973).

B2-5. Bender, Harold S., trans. and ed. "An Amish Bishop's Conference Epistle of 1865," *MQR*, 20 (Jul 1946), 222-29.

B2-6. ________________, trans. and ed. "An Amish Church Discipline of 1779," *MQR*, 11 (Apr 1937), 163-68.

B2-7. ________________, trans. and ed. "The Correspondence of Martin Mellinger: Translations of the Correspondence of Martin Mellinger with Relatives in the Rhenish Palatinate, 1807-1839," *MQR*, 5 (Jan 1931), 42-64.

B2-8. Boehm, Henry. *The Patriarch of One Hundred Years: Being Reminiscences, Historical and Biographical, of Rev. Henry Boehm*, J. B. Wakeley, ed. (New York: Nelson & Phillips, 1875).

B2-9. [Brenneman, John M.]. *Christianity and War: A Sermon Setting Forth the Suffering of Christians, . . . by a Minister of the Old Mennonite Church* (Chicago: printed by Chas. Hess, 1863); reprints, 1868, 1915. In German: *Das Christenthum und der Krieg . . .* (Lancaster, Pa.: printed by Johann Bär's Söhnen, 1864); reprints, 1868, 1920.

B2-10. ________________. "Civil War Petition to President Lincoln," *MHB*, 34 (Oct 1973), 2-3. Mss. printed therein are in f. 5, box 7, Hist. Mss. 1-442, AMC.

B2-11. Brenneman, John M. *Plain Teachings, or Simple Illustrations and Exhortations from the Word of God* (Elkhart, Ind.: Mennonite Publishing Co., 1876).

B2-12. Cassel, Daniel Kolb. *History of the Mennonites: Historically and Biographically Arranged. . . . More Particularly from the Time of their Emigration to America* (Philadelphia: The Author, 1888). Includes "A Historical Sketch of the Early Mennonites in Virginia, Communicated by Abraham Blosser, editor of *Watchful Pilgrim*."

B2-13. *Catechism, or Plain Instructions from the Sacred Scriptures: In Questions and Answers for Children* (Elkhart, Ind.: J. F. Funk and Bro., 1874).

B2-14. *Christlicher Ordnungen or Christian Discipline: Being a Collection and Translation of Anabaptist and Amish-Mennonite*

Church Disciplines, William McGrath, comp. and ed. (Aylmer, Ont.: Pathway Publishing Co., 1966).

B2-15. Coffman, J[ohn]. S. *Christianity Teaches Peace* (Elkhart, Ind.: Mennonite Book and Tract Society, n.d. [1894?]). An 8-page tractlike pamphlet adapted from Quaker materials; copy in MHL.

B2-16. ________. *Fundamental Bible References* (n.p., 1891), pp. 4; copy in MHL.

B2-17. ________. *Outlines and Notes Used at the Bible Conference Held at Johnstown, Pennsylvania from December 27, 1897 - January 7, 1898* (Elkhart, Ind.: Mennonite Publishing Co., 1898).

B2-18. ________. "The Spirit of Progress," *YPP*, 3 (Feb 29, Mar 14 and 28, 1896), 35, 42-43, 51. Reprinted as a booklet, *The Spirit of Progress: A Lecture, Delivered at the Exercises held at the Opening of the First School Building of the "Elkhart Institute" (Elkhart, Ind., Feb. 11, 1896)*, and as "The Spirit of Progress," *MHB*, 57 (Jul 1986), 1-6.

B2-19. Correll, Ernst, ed. "Mennonite Immigration into Manitoba: Sources and Documents, 1872, 1873," *MQR*, 11 (Jul, Oct 1937), 196-227, 267-83.

B2-20. [East Pennsylvania Mennonite Conference.] "History of the Division Among the Mennonites in 1847-1848," trans. by Elizabeth Horsch Bender, *MQR*, 46 (Oct 1972), 406-11 (part of an "Oberholtzer Division" issue—*see* B1-13). For further documents on this conference, *see*: B1-12, B2-21, B2-65.

B2-21. [Eastern District Conference.] Printed minutes are available in German (e.g., in MHL). For English, *see*: "Minutes of the Eastern District Conference of the General Conference of Mennonites of North America, 1847-1902," trans. by S[ilas]. M. Grubb; and "Minutes of the Eastern District Conference of the General Conference of Mennonites of North America, 1847-1902," trans. by N[athaniel]. B. Grubb; both typed; copies in MHL and other Mennonite archives. At the outset it was "East Pennsylvania" Mennonite conference.

B2-22. Friesen, Heinrich B. *The Autobiography of H. B. Friesen, 1837-1926*, trans. by August Schmidt (Newton, Kans.: A. Schmidt, 1974).

B2-23. Funck, Heinrich [Funk, Henry]. *A Mirror of Baptism, with the Spirit, with Water, and with Blood; in Three Parts, from the Holy Scriptures of the Old and New Testament* . . . (Mountain Valley, Va.: Joseph Funk and Sons, 1851). A trans. of his *Ein Spiegel der Tauffe, mit Geist, mit Wasser, und mit Blut*, ([Germantown, Pa.: Christoph Saur,] 1744).

B2-24. ________. *Restitution, or an Explanation of*

Several Principal Points of the Law (Elkhart, Ind.: Mennonite Publishing Co., 1915). A trans. of his *Eine Restitution, Oder eine Erklärung einiger Haupt-puncten des Gesetzes* (Philadelphia: Anton Armbrüster, 1763).

B2-25. Funk, John F. *Biographical Sketch of Preacher John Geil* (Elkhart, Ind.: Mennonite Publishing Co., 1897).

B2-26. ________. *Warfare. Its Evils, Our Duty: Addressed to the Mennonite Churches Throughout the United States, And All Others Who Sincerly* [sic] *Seek and Love the Truth* (Chicago: Chas. Hess, 1863), version herein used; also, (Markham, Ont.: printed at The Economist Office, 1863).

B2-27. Funk, Joseph, ed. *Die allgemein Nützliche Choral-Music* [sic]: *enthaltend auserlesene Melodien, welche bey allen Religions-Verfassungen gebräuchlich sind* . . . (Harrisonburg, Va.: printed by Laurentz Wartmann, ca. 1816).

B2-28. ________, ed. *A Compilation of Genuine Church Music* . . . (Winchester, Va.: published at the Office of the Republican, printed by J. W. Hollis, 1832).

B2-29. [General Conference Mennonite Church.] General conference minutes: *Verhandlungen der Allgemeinen Konferenz der Mennoniten von Nord-Amerika* (Berne, Ind.: Christlichen Central-Buchhandlung der Allgemeinen Konferenz der Mennoniten, [ca. 1888]); extensive excerpts of same are trans. in Krehbiel (1898: C2-119).

B2-30. [Grater, Abraham.] *An Explanation of Incidents that Took Place Among the So-Called Mennonites* ([Skippack, Pa.: J. M. Schueneman, 1854]).

B2-31. Gross, Leonard, ed. "The Coming of the Russian Mennonites to America: An Analysis by Johann Epp, Mennonite Minister in Russia, 1875," doc. trans. by Elizabeth Bender, *MQR*, 48 (Oct 1974), 460-75.

B2-32. Harms, John F. *Ein Lebensreise, von Anfang bis zum baldigen Ende* . . . (Hillsboro, Kans.: n.p., 1943).

B2-33. Hartman, Peter. "Civil War Reminiscences" (title varies). In Brunk (1937:C2-31), 45-73; and in *MQR*, 3 (Jan 1929), 203-19.

B2-34. Haury, S[amuel]. S. *Die Wehrlosigkeit in der Sonntagschule. Wie lehrt man sie: nur so im Allgemeinen oder direkt nach unserem (mennonitischen) Bekenntnis?* . . . (Dayton, Ohio: United Brethren Publishing House, [ca. 1894]).

B2-35. Herr, John. *John Herr's Complete Works, Comprising: The Way to Heaven, The Illustrating Mirror* . . . (Buffalo, N.Y.: Peter Paul and Bro., 1890).

B2-36. ________. *Life of John Herr* (LaSalle, N.Y.: David N. Long, 1890); printed from his *Complete Works* (1890: B2-35), 376-402.

B2-37. [Hoch, Daniel]. *Kurz gefasste Kirchen-Ordnung der Mennoniten oder Wehrlosen Christen in Canada* [Concise Church Regulations . . .] (Presston, [Waterloo Co.] Canada West: printed by Martin Rudolph, 1850). Copy in MHL.

B2-38. [________ or High, Daniel]. *Matters of Fact: Or, A Defence of His Views of the Gospel* (St. Catherines, Ont.: E. S. Leavenworth's Book and Job Printing Establishment, 1870).

B2-39. ________. *Wichtige Begebenheit auf gewisse Zeiten, in Bezug der Trennung unserer Gemeinde* (Jordan, Ont.: The Author, 1868), 4 pp.; copy in MHL.

B2-40. Hoch, Daniel; Bauman, Samuel B.; and Oberholtzer, John H. *Aufschluss der Verfolgungen gegen Daniel Hoch, Prediger der Mennonitten* [sic] *Gemeinschaft in Ober Canada* ([Milford Square?], Pa.: J. H. Oberholtzer, 1854). The first part is by Hoch with no separate title. Part II is by Bauman with its own pagination and the title "Eine Erleiterung, geschrieben von Samuel B. Bauman, an Benjamin Eby, über die Unruhen und Schwierigkeiten in den Mennoniten Gemeiden in Canada." Publisher Oberholtzer wrote short introductory and concluding pieces.

B2-41. Holdeman, John. *A History of the Church of God, As It Existed from the Beginning, Whereby It May Be Known, and How It Was Propagated until the Present Time* (Lancaster, Pa.: printed by John Baer's Sons, 1876).

B2-42. ________. *The Old Ground and Foundation, Taken from the Word of God* (Lancaster, Pa.: printed for the author by John Baer's Sons, 1863). First published in German, 1862.

B2-43. ________. *A Treatise on Redemption, Baptism, and the Passover and the Lord's Supper* (Carthage, Mo.: Press Book and Job Printing House, 1890).

B2-44. Hostetler, Pius. *Life, Preaching and Labors of John D. Kauffman: A Short Sketch . . .* (Shelbyville, Ill.: The Author, 1916).

B2-45. Hough, Samuel S., ed. *Christian Newcomer: His Life, Journal and Achievements* (Dayton, Ohio: Board of Administration, Church of the United Brethren in Christ, 1941).

B2-46. Huber, Samuel. *Autobiography of the Rev. Samuel Huber, Elder in the Church of the United Brethren in Christ . . .* , John Denig, ed. (Chambersburg, Pa.: M. Kieffer & Co., 1858).

B2-47. Hunsicker, Abraham. *A Statement of Facts, and Summary of Views on Morals and Religion: As Related with Suspension from the Mennonite Meeting* (Philadelphia: G. S. Harris, 1851).

B2-48. [Indiana-Michigan Mennonite Conference]. *Minutes of the Indiana-Michigan Conference, 1864-1929* (Scottdale, Pa.: Mennonite Publishing House, [1929?]). Variously the Indiana Conference; also includes Ind.-Mich. Amish Mennonite conference minutes.

B2-49. [Jansen, Cornelius, ed.]. *Sammlung von Notizen über*

Amerika (Danzig: printed by Paul Thieme, 1872). A 56-page pamphlet printing letters from several persons in North America; foreword by "C. Janzen," i.e. Jansen, its presumed editor.

B2-50. Jansen, Peter. *Memoirs of Peter Jansen: The Record of a Busy Life, An Autobiography* (Beatrice, Nebr.: The Author, 1921).

B2-51. Jutzi, George. *Ermahnungen von George Jutzi in Stark County, Ohio, an seine Hinterbliebenen* . . . (Somerset, Pa.: Alexander Stutzman, 1853).

B2-52 [Kansas-Nebraska Mennonite Conference], *Conference Record of . . . 1876-1914* (n.p., 1914).

B2-53. Kauffman, Daniel. *Manual of Bible Doctrines, Setting Forth the General Principles of the Plan of Salvation, Explaining . . . Ordinances . . . and . . . Restrictions* . . . (Elkhart, Ind.: Mennonite Publishing Co., 1898).

B2-54. __________, ed. *Bible Doctrine: A Treatise on the Great Doctrines of the Bible* . . . (Scottdale, Pa.: Mennonite Publishing House, 1914).

B2-55. __________, ed. *Doctrines of the Bible: A Brief Discussion of the Teachings of God's Word* (Scottdale, Pa.: Herald Press, 1928).

B2-56. Krehbiel, Christian. *Prairie Pioneer: The Christian Krehbiel Story* (Newton, Kans.: Faith and Life Press, 1961).

B2-57. Lambert, George. *India: The Horror-Stricken Empire: Containing a Full Account of the Famous Plague and Earthquake of 1896-7, Including a Complete Narration of the Relief Work Through the Home and Foreign Relief Commission* (Elkhart, Ind.: Mennonite Publishing Co., 1898; or Berne, Ind.: Mennonite Book Concern, 1898).

B2-58. [Lancaster Mennonite Conference]. *Bible Class Question Book* . . . (Elkhart, Ind.: Mennonite Publishing Co., 1881, 1882, 1888, 1891); *Intermediate Question Book* . . . (Elkhart, Ind.: Mennonite Publishing Co., 1880, 1881, 1883, 1887, 1891); *Primary Question Book* . . . (Elkhart, Ind.: Mennonite Publishing Co., 1880, 1883, 1887, 1891). All appeared in German also.

B2-59. __________. *Rules and Discipline of the Lancaster Conference, Approved Oct. 7, 1881* (n.p., n.d.). 4-page flyer. Warning: later revised editions are not clearly designated as revisions. Printed copy at LMHS.

B2-60-1. Luthy, David, ed. "Ohio Amish in 1862: Testimony Against War," *MHB*, 38 (Apr 1977), 8. A newspaper article originally published in the Holmes County *Farmer*, 1862.

B2-60-2. Miller, Harvey J., ed. "Proceedings of Amish Ministers Conferences, 1826-31," *MQR*, 33 (Apr 1959), 132-42.

B2-61. [Muhlenberg, Henry M.] *The Journals of Henry Melchoir Muhlenberg: In Three Volumes* (Philadelphia: Muhlenberg Press, 1942-1958).

B2-62. Musser, Daniel. *Non-Resistance Asserted: Or the Kingdom of Christ and the Kingdom of this World Separated* (Lancaster, Pa.: Elias Barr and Co., 1864). Also pp. 415-522 of 2nd ed. of his *Reformed Mennonite Church* (Lancaster, Pa.: Inquirer Printing and Publishing Co., 1878)—1st ed. B1-11.

B2-63. [Nafziger, Johannes (or Hans)]. Doc. publ. as "An Amish Church Discipline of 1781," *MQR*, 4 (Apr 1930), 140-48.

B2-64. Newcomer, Christian. *The Life and Journal of the Rev'd Christian Newcomer, Late Bishop of the Church of the United Brethren in Christ, Written by Himself, Containing His Travels and Labours in the Gospel from 1795 to 1830* . . ., ed. and trans. by John Hildt (Hagers-Town, Md.: F.G.W. Kapp, Book Printer, 1834). For an abridged, more available version, *see* Hough (1941: B2-45).

B2-65. Oberholtzer, John H. "A Letter of John H. Oberholtzer to Unnamed Friends in Germany, 1849," trans. by Elizabeth Bender, *MQR*, 46 (Oct 1972), 398-405; part of an "Oberholtzer Division" issue—*see* B1-13.

B2-66. Plett, Delbert F., ed., annot., and trans. *History and Events: Writings and Maps Pertaining to the History of the Mennonite Kleine Gemeinde from 1866 to 1876* (Steinbach, Man.: D. F. Plett Farms, 1982).

B2-67. *Proceedings of the Mennonite General Conference Including Discussion Leading to Its Orgination* [*sic*] (n.p., 1921).

B2-68. Schmidt, C[arl]. B. *Reminiscences of Kansas Immigration Work* (n.p., n.d.). 32-page pamphlet.

B2-69. Schwarzendruber, Jacob. "Concerning Weddings" and "Concerning Bundling" (written 1863), *MHB*, 20 (Oct 1977), 2-5. Original and typed transcript versions of Jacob Schwarzendruber materials are in A1-8.

B2-70. *Sermons Delivered by Noah Troyer, a Member of the Amish Mennonite Church, of Johnson Co., Iowa, while in an Unconscious State* . . . (Elkhart, Ind.: Mennonite Publishing Co., 1880).

B2-71. *Sermons Delivered by Noah Troyer, the Noted Amishman, While in an Unconscious State: With a Brief Biographical Sketch of His Life* (Iowa City, Iowa: Daily Republican Job Print, 1879).

B2-72. Shantz, J[acob]. Y. *Narrative of a Journey to Manitoba: Together with an Abstract of the Dominion Lands Act; and an Extract from the Government Pamphlet on Manitoba* (Ottawa: The Department of Agriculture, 1873).

B2-73. Simons, Menno. *The Complete Writings of Menno Simons, c. 1496-1561*, trans. by Leonard Verduin, ed. by J. C. Wenger (Scottdale Pa., and Kitchener, Ont.: Herald Press, 1956).

B2-74. [Southwestern Pennsylvania Mennonite Conference.]

Southwestern Pennsylvania [Mennonite] *Conference Reports, 1876-1945* (n.p., [1945?]).

B2-75. Strong, Josiah. *Our Country: Its Possible Future and Its Present Crisis* (New York: Baker and Taylor, for the American Home Missionary Society, 1885). Or the same in a Mennonite-produced translation: *Unser Land: dessen mögliche Zukunft und gegenwürtige Crisis*, trans. by W. Horn (Berne, Ind.: Christliche Central-Buchhandlung, Welty and Sprunger, 1892).

B2-76. Sudermann, Leonard. *From Russia to America: In Search of Freedom*, trans. and intro. by Elmer Suderman (Steinbach, Man.: Derksen Printers, 1974). Original: Leonhard Sudermann, *Eine Deputationsreise von Russland nach Amerika vor vierundswanzig Jahren* (Elkhart, Ind.: Mennonitische Verlagshandlung, 1897).

B2-77. "Testimony from the Boyertown Case," *MQR*, 46 (Oct 1972), 412-30; part of an "Oberholtzer Division" issue—*see* B1-13.

B2-78. Tolstoy, Leo N. *The Kingdom of God Is Within You*, first published in 1893; numerous eds. since; notes from trans. by Leo Wiener (Boston: L. C. Page, 1951).

B2-79. Treyer, David A. *Ein unparteiischer Bericht von den Hauptumständen welche sich ereigneten in den sogennanten Alt-Amischen Gemeinden in Ohio, vom Jahr 1850 bis ungefähr 1861, wodurch endlich eine vollkommene Spaltung entstand* (pamphlet, 1898); copy with trans. by John Umble in A2-28.

B2-80. [Tschetter, Paul.] "The Diary of Paul Tschetter, 1873," trans. and ed. by J. M. Hofer; biog. sketch by Joseph W. Tschetter, *MQR*, 5 (Apr, Jul 1931), 112-27, 198-220.

B2-81 Umble, John, ed. "An Amish Minister's Manual," *MQR*, 15 (Apr 1941), 95-117.

B2-82. ________. "Amish Service Manuals," *MQR*, 15 (Jan 1941), 26-32.

B2-83. ________. "Manuscript Amish Ministers' Manuals in the Goshen College Mennonite Historical Library," *MQR*, 15 (Oct 1941), 243-53.

B2-84. *Unpartheyisches Gesang-Buch* (Lancaster, Pa.: printed by Johann Albrecht, 1804).

B2-85. [Unruh, Tobias.] *Great-Grandfather's Diary* (Montezuma, Kans.: [A. J. Unruh], n.d. [MHL copy penciled "1949"]). Unpaginated booklet, appearing also in Abe J. and Verney Unruh, *Tobias A. Unruh: Biography, Diary and Family Record, 1819-1969* (Newton, Kans.: [The Authors], 1970).

B2-86. [Virginia Mennonite Conference.] *Minutes of the Virginia Mennonite Conference (1835-1938): Including Some Historical Data* . . . (n.pl.: Virginia Mennonite Conference, 1939).

B2-87. *War of the Rebellion: A Compilation of the Official Records of the Union and Confederate Armies* (70 vols—Washington D.C.: Government Print Office, 1880-1901).

B2-88. Weber, Max. *Max Weber on Charisma and Institution Building*, ed. by S. N. Eisenstadt (Chicago: University of Chicago Press, 1968).

B2-89. ________________. *The Protestant Ethic and the Spirit of Capitalism* (available in various editions).

B2-90. Wenger, John C. [or J. C.] "The Schleitheim Confession of Faith," *MQR*, 19 (Oct 1945), 243-53.

B2-91. ________________, ed. "Documents on the Daniel Brenneman Division," *MQR*, 34 (Jan 1960), 48-56.

B2-92. [Western District Amish Mennonite Conference.] *Western District A[mish]. M[ennonite]. Conference Proceedings 1890-1912* (n.p., [1912?]).

B2-93. [Western District Conference.] *Abdruck der Gesamt-Protokolle der Kansas- und Westlichen Distrikt-Konferenz der Mennoniten von Nord-Amerika*, used herein in typed translation: "General Conference Mennonite Church Western District Conference Minutes, 1877-1892." Both German and English are in MHL.

B2-94. Wiebe, Jakob A. "The Founding of Gnadenau," in Krahn (1949: C1-7), 98-101.

B2-95. Zook, Shem. *Eine wahre Darstellung . . . woraus endlich die unchristlichen Spaltungen sind* (Mattawana, Mifflin Co., Pa.: The Author, 1880). Copy in MHL; English trans. is in Hostetler (1964: C2-102).

C1. SECONDARY SOURCES OF SPECIAL VALUE

C1-1. Dyck, Cornelius J., ed. *An Introduction to Mennonite History: A Popular History of the Anabaptists and the Mennonites* (Scottdale, Pa., and Kitchener, Ont.: Herald Press, 1981). Excellent as a quick, readable, general source for Mennonite history.

C1-2. Epp, Frank H. *Mennonites in Canada, 1786-1920: The History of a Separate People* (Toronto: Macmillan of Canada, 1974). Vol. I of a very able and readable survey.

C1-3. Friedmann, Robert. *Mennonite Piety Through the Centuries: Its Genius and Its Literature* (Goshen, Ind.: The Mennonite Historical Society, 1949). The classic study of Pietism's influence on Mennonites; for a critique of it, *see* Schlabach (1983: C2-173).

C1-4. Friesen, Peter M. *The Mennonite Brotherhood in Russia (1789-1910): Translated from the German*, trans. by J. B. Toews, Abraham Friesen, Peter J. Klassen, and Harry Loewen (Fresno, Calif.: Board of Christian Literature, General Conference of Mennonite Brethren Churches, 1978). A very comprehensive source, by a fine scholar, for study of Mennonite experience in the Russian empire until the early twentieth century; originally written there, in German; published at Halbstadt, 1911. Covers a wide range of subjects and prints translations of many key documents.

C1-5. Handy, Robert T. *A Christian America: Protestant Hopes and Historical Realities* (New York: Oxford University Press, 1971; 2nd, enlarged ed., 1984).

C1-6. Horst, Samuel. *Mennonites in the Confederacy: A Study in Civil War Pacifism* (Scottdale, Pa.: Herald Press, 1967).

C1-7. Krahn, Cornelius, ed. *From the Steppes to the Prairies: 1874-1949* (Newton, Kans.: Mennonite Publication Office, 1949).

C1-8. Lehman, James O. "Mennonites in the North Face the Crises of the Civil War" (unpublished manuscript, 1982), 562 typed pages. Copies at LMHS and in hands of Lehman, John L. Ruth of Harleysville, Pa., and myself. A very excellent culling of local newspapers and other primary sources regarding the U.S. civil war experiences of Mennonites and Amish; logical, readable synthesis of the findings, with many lengthy primary-source quotations. An invaluable source.

C1-9. Liechty, Joseph C. "Humility: The Foundation of Mennonite Religious Outlook in the 1860s," *MQR*, 54 (Jan 1980), 5-31. A foundational article for studying nineteenth-century Mennonite theology of humility.

C1-10. MacMaster, Richard K. *Land, Piety, Peoplehood: The Establishment of Mennonite Communities in America, 1683-1790* (Scottdale, Pa., and Kitchener, Ont.: Herald Press, 1985). Vol. I of this *Mennonite Experience in America series.*

C1-11. Pannabecker, Samuel Floyd. *Open Doors: The History of the General Conference Mennonite Church* (Newton, Kans.: Faith and Life Press, 1975).

C1-12. Rempel, David G. "From Danzig to Russia: The First Mennonite Migration," *ML*, 24 (Jan, 1969), 8-28. Probably the best succinct source on beginning of Mennonite migration to Russia.

C1-13. ________. "The Mennonite Colonies in New Russia: A Study of their Settlement and Economic Development from 1789 to 1914" (Stanford University Ph.D. dissertation, 1933). Pagination is by chapters, e.g., 3/2 designates ch. 3, p. 2.

C1-14. ________. "The Mennonite Commonwealth in Russia: A Sketch of Its Founding and Endurance, 1789-1919," *MQR*, 47 (Oct 1973), 259-308; 48 (Jan 1974), 5-54.

C1-15. Ruth, John L. *Maintaining the Right Fellowship: A Narrative Account of Life in the Oldest Mennonite Community in North America* (Scottdale, Pa., and Kitchener, Ont.: Herald Press, 1984).

C1-16. Saum, Lewis O. *The Popular Mood of Civil War America* (Westport, Conn.: Greenwood, 1980). With a thesis that ordinary Americans spoke far more in terms of humility and self-resignation than did the rhetoric of their national leaders, Saum offers excellent qualification for my emphasis that humility was an especially Mennonite outlook; however, I think a careful reading indicates Saum was describing a more subjective attitude whereas Mennonites put more emphasis on expressing humility objectively, in overt lifestyle and church discipline.

C1-17. Schlabach, Theron F. "The Humble Become 'Aggressive Workers': Mennonites Organize for Mission, 1880-1910," *MQR*, 52 (Apr 1978), 113-26.

C1-18. ______________. "Reveille for *Die Stillen im Lande*: A Stir Among Mennonites in the Late Nineteenth Century," *MQR*, 51 (Jul 1977), 213-26.

C1-19. Toews, John A. *A History of the Mennonite Brethren Church: Pilgrims and Pioneers* (Fresno, Calif.: Board of Christian Literature, General Conference of Mennonite Brethren Churches, 1975).

C1-20. Unruh, John D., Jr. "The Burlington and Missouri River Railroad Brings the Mennonites to Nebraska" (University of Kansas M.A. thesis, 1962).

C1-21. Urry, James. "The Closed and the Open: Social and Religious Change Amongst the Mennonites in Russia (1789-1889)" (Oxford University Ph.D. dissertation, 1978). 830 typed pages. This is the most complete study available of the late-eighteenth- and nineteenth-century experience of Mennonites in the Russian empire, told as a story of two perceptions, a "closed order" idea of maintaining highly separatist, communally oriented Mennonite colonies versus an "open order" idea that was far more progressivist and amenable to economic, cultural, and religious innovation—including to European Pietism which was basically individualist and ecumenical. The work might be criticized for wordiness, an occasional tendency to force the evidence into the author's scheme, and a missed opportunity to make obvious comparisons to Old Order patterns in America. Yet it is massively researched, thoughtful, and corrective of older scholarship at many points. Its use is very necessary for any deep study of Mennonite experience in the empire of the czars.

C1-22. Van Braght, Thieleman J. *The Bloody Theater or Martyrs Mirror of the Defenseless Christians* . . . . I.e., *Martyrs Mirror* (many eds.; current one—Scottdale, Pa., and Kitchener, Ont.: Herald Press, 1982). A large Dutch Mennonite book full of accounts of nonresistant Christian martyrs through history; compiled in the seventeenth century. Thoroughly known by nineteenth-century Mennonites in America, it was a very major source of their historical and theological outlook.

C1-22-2. Weaver, J. Denny. "The Quickening of Soteriology: Atonement from Christian Burkholder to Daniel Kauffman," *MQR*, 61 (Jan 1987), 5-45.

C1-23. Yoder, Paton. "The *Diener-Versammlungen* and the

Great Schism in the Amish Mennonite Church" (unpublished manuscript, 1983). In Yoder's possession, 1608 S. 14th St. Goshen, Ind.

C2. OTHER SECONDARY SOURCES

C2-1. Adrian, Victor. "The Mennonite Brethren Church (Born of Anabaptism and Pietism)" (unpublished paper, 1964). Copy in MHL.

C2-2. Amstutz, P[eter]. B. *Historical Events of the Mennonite Settlement in Allen and Putnam Counties, Ohio*, trans. by Anne Konrad Dyck ([Bluffton, Ohio?]: Swiss Community Historical Society, 1978). Original German: (Bluffton, Ohio: n.p., 1925).

C2-3. Anderson, Martin, and Honeger, Barbara, eds. *The Military Draft: Selected Readings on Conscription* (Stanford, Calif.: Hoover Institution Press, 1982).

C2-4. Apter, David. *The Politics of Modernization* (Chicago: University of Chicago Press, 1965).

C2-5. Augsburger, Myron S. "Conversion in Anabaptist Thought," *MQR*, 36 (Jul 1962), 243-55.

C2-6. Bainton, Roland H. *Women of the Reformation in Germany and Italy* (Minneapolis: Augsburg Publishing House, 1971).

C2-7. Banman, H. "Geschichte der Alexanderwohl Mennoniten Gemeinde bei Goessel, Kansas," *Bundesbote-Kalendar*, (1926), 29-34.

C2-8. Barrett, Lois. *The Vision and the Reality: The Story of Home Missions in the General Conference Mennonite Church* (Newton, Kans.: Faith and Life Press, 1983).

C2-9. ______________. "Women in the Anabaptist Movement," in Herta Funk, ed., *Study Guide on Women* (Newton, Kans.: Commission of Education of the General Conference Mennonite Church, and Faith and Life Press, 1975), 33-38.

C2-10. Bartel, Daniel J. "The Emmanuel Mennonite Church of Meade, Kansas," (n.p., 1975). Multilithed.

C2-11. Bartlett, Roger P. *Human Capital: The Settlement of Foreigners in Russia, 1762-1804* (Cambridge: Cambridge University Press, 1979).

C2-12. Belk, Fred Richard. *The Great Trek of the Russian Mennonites to Central Asia, 1880-1884* (Scottdale, Pa., and Kitchener, Ont.: Herald Press, 1976).

C2-13. Bender, Harold S. "The Literature and Hymnology of the Mennonites of Lancaster County, Pennsylvania," *MQR*, 6 (Jul 1932), 156-68.

C2-14. ______________. *Mennonite Sunday School Centennial, 1840-1940* (Scottdale, Pa.: Mennonite Publishing House, 1940). Booklet.

C2-15. ______________. " 'Walking in the Resurrection': The Anabaptist Doctrine of Regeneration and Discipleship," *MQR*, 35 (Apr 1961), 96-110.

C2-16. Bender, Lynn. "The Yellow Creek Mennonite Settlers: A Study of Land and Community," *MQR*, 46 (Jan 1972), 70-83.

C2-17. Berger, Daniel. *History of the Church of the United Brethren in Christ* (The American Church Histories series, vol. XII. Dayton Ohio, and New York: United Brethren Publishing House, 1897).

C2-18. *Bethel Mennonite Church, Mountain Lake, Minnesota: Historical Highlights, 1889-1943* (Mountain Lake, Minn.: Bethel Mennonite Church, [1943?]).

C2-19. Billington, Ray Allen. *Westward Expansion: A History of the American Frontier* (4th ed. New York and London: Macmillan, 1974).

C2-20. "Biography: Notices of the Life and Labours of Martin Boehm and William Otterbein; and Other Ministers of the Gospel among the United German Brethren [*sic*]," *Methodist Magazine*, 6 (Jun, Jul 1823), 210-14, 249-56.

C2-21. Borntreger, Hans E. *Eine Geschichte der ersten Ansiedelung der Amischen Mennoniten und die Gründing ihrer ersten Gemeinde im Staate Indiana* (Elkhart, Ind.: Mennonite Publishing Co., 1907).

C2-22. Bowman, Bernard. "John F. Funk and the Revival Movement" (Eastern Mennonite College baccalaureate paper, 1972). Copy in box 14, I-3-3.5, AMC.

C2-23. Bowman, Rufus D. *The Church of the Brethren and War, 1708-1941* (Elgin, Ill.: Brethren Publishing House, 1944).

C2-24. Braun, Peter. "The Educational System of the Mennonite Colonies in Russia," trans. by Amy E. Enss, *MQR*, 3 (Jul 1929), 169-82.

C2-25. Brock, Peter. *Pacifism in the United States: From the Colonial Era to the First World War* (Princeton: Princeton University Press, 1968).

C2-26. Brodie, Fawn. *Thaddeus Stevens, Scourge of the South* (New York: Norton, 1959).

C2-27. *Brosamen aus Erfahrungen der Mennoniten in u. um Mountain Lake, Minnesota* ([Mountain Lake, Minn.]: n.p., 1938). Multilithed, bilingual.

C2-28. Brown, Dale W. *Understanding Pietism*. Grand Rapids: W. B. Eerdmans Publishing Co., 1978).

C2-29. ______________. "The Problem of Subjectivism in Pietism: A Redefinition with Philipp Jakob Spener and August Hermann Francke" (Northwestern University Ph.D dissertation, 1962).

C2-30. Brunk, Harry A. *History of Mennonites in Virginia*: [I:] *1727-1900*; [II:] *1900-1960* (Vol. I: Staunton, Va.: McClure Printing Co., 1959. Vol. II: Verona, Va.: McClure Printing Co., 1972).

C2-31. ________________, ed. *Life of Peter S. Hartman* ([Harrisonburg, Va.]: The Hartman Family, 1937).

C2-32. Buchheit, Robert H. "Mennonite 'Plautdietsch': A Phonological and Morphological Description of a Settlement Dialect in York and Hamilton Counties, Nebraska" (University of Nebraska—Lincoln Ph.D. dissertation, 1978).

C2-33. Carleton, William G. "Raising Armies Before the Civil War," in Anderson and Honeger (1982: C2-3). Reprinted from *Current History*, 54 (Jun 1968), 327-32, 363.

C2-34. Cawelti, John G. *Apostles of The Self-Made Man* (Chicago: University of Chicago Press, 1965).

C2-35. Chase, Gilbert. *America's Music: From the Pilgrims to the Present* (2nd, rev. ed. Westport, Conn.: Greenwood Press, 1966).

C2-36. Clemens, James Wm. "Changes in the *Herald of Truth*'s Support for Temperance and Prohibition" (Goshen College baccalaureate seminar paper, 1976). Copy in MHL.

C2-37. Cochran, Thomas C. *Pennsylvania: A Bicentennial History* (New York: Norton, 1978).

C2-38. Cosco, Ethel Reeser. *Christian Reeser: The Story of a Centenarian* (n.p., n.d.).

C2-39. Cronk, Sandra. "*Gelassenheit*: The Rites of the Redemptive Process in Old Order Amish and Old Order Mennonite Communities" (University of Chicago Divinity School Ph.D. dissertation, 1977).

C2-40. ________________. "*Gelassenheit*: The Rites of the Redemptive Process in Old Order Amish and Old Order Mennonite Communities," *MQR*, 55 (Jan 1981), 5-44.

C2-41. Cross, Whitney R. *The Burned-Over District: The Social and Intellectual History of Enthusiastic Religion in Western New York, 1800-1850* (Ithaca: Cornell University Press, 1950).

C2-42. Crous, Ernst. "Anabaptism, Pietism, Rationalism and German Mennonites," in Guy F. Hershberger, ed., *The Recovery of the Anabaptist Vision: A Sixtieth Anniversary Tribute to Harold S. Bender* (Scottdale, Pa.: Herald Press, 1957), 237-48.

C2-43. Cummings, Mary Lou, ed. *Full Circle: Stories of Mennonite Women* (Newton, Kans.: Faith and Life Press, 1978).

C2-44. Current, Richard. *Old Thad Stevens: A Story of Ambition* (Madison: University of Wisconsin Press, 1942).

C2-45. Davis, Kenneth R. *Anabaptism and Asceticism: A Study in Intellectual Origins* (Scottdale, Pa., and Kitchener, Ont.: Herald Press, 1974).

C2-46. DeBenedetti, Charles. *The Peace Reform in American*

History (Bloomington and London: Indiana University Press, 1980).

C2-47. Diller, M. Marie. "An Historical Study of the Development and Growth of the Evangelical Mennonite Church, Formerly Known as the Defenseless Mennonite Church" (MRE thesis, Biblical Seminary in New York, 1951).

C2-47-2. Dolan, Jay P. *Catholic Revivalism: The American Experience, 1830-1900* (Notre Dame and London: University of Notre Dame Press, 1978).

C2-48. Dorpalen, Andreas. "The German Element and the Issues of the Civil War," *The Mississippi Valley Historical Review*. 29 (Jun 1942), 55-76.

C2-49. ________________. "The Political Influence of the German Element in Colonial America," *Pennsylvania History*, 6 (Jul and Oct 1939), 147-58, 221-39.

C2-50. Driedger, Leo. "Native Rebellion and Mennonite Invasion: An Examination of Two Canadian River Valleys," *MQR*, 46 (Jul 1972), 290-300.

C2-51. Drury, A. W. *History of the Church of the United Brethren in Christ* (Dayton, Ohio: Otterbein Press, 1924).

C2-52. Durnbaugh, Donald. "The Genius of the Brethren," *Brethren Life and Thought*, 4 (Winter 1959), 4-34.

C2-53. ________________. "The Genius of the Early Brethren," *Brethren Life and Thought*, 4 (Spring 1959), 4-18.

C2-54. Dyck, Cornelius J. "The Life of the Spirit in Anabaptism," *MQR*, 47 (Oct 1973), 309-26.

C2-55. Eby, Benjamin. *Kurzgefasste kirchen Geschichte und Glaubenslehre der Taufgesinnten-Christen oder Mennoniten* (Berlin, Can.: printed by Heinrich Eby, 1841. Lancaster, Pa.: printed by Johann Baer, 1853). Now in English as *A Concise Ecclesiastical History and Doctrinal Theology of the Baptists or Mennonites* [*sic*] (Floradale, Ont.: Daniel Bowman, 1940?). Unfortunately the publisher trans. and reproduced the title page of a 1901 German ed.; thus it appears as (Elkhart, Ind.: Mennonite Publishing Co., 1901).

C2-56. Eby, Ezra. *A Biographical History of Waterloo Township and Other Townships of the County* (Vol. I. Berlin, Ont.: n. p., 1895).

C2-57. Epp, D[avid]. H[einrich]. *Die Chortitzer Mennoniten: Versuch einer Darstellung des Entwickelungsganges derselben* (Odessa: A. Schultze, 1889).

C2-58. Erb, Ethel Cooprider. *Through Tribulation to Crown of Life: The Story of a Godly Grandmother* (Hesston, Kans.: The Book and Bible Room, n.d.). Booklet.

C2-59. Erb, J. Delbert. "Index of Mennonite and Amish Mennonite Conference Resolutions" (unpublished mss., 1951). Copy in MHL.

C2-60. Erb, Paul. *South Central Frontiers: A History of the South Central Mennonite Conference* (Scottdale, Pa., and Kitchener, Ont.: Herald Press, 1974).

C2-61. Esau, John A. "The Congregational Debates on the coming of the Russian Mennonites" (unpublished Mennonite Biblical Seminary term paper, 1961). Copy in MHL.

C2-62. Eshelman, Wilmer J. *A History of the Reformed Mennonite Church* (Rev. ed. Lancaster, Pa.: n.p., 1969).

C2-63. Frantz, John B. "The Awakening of Religion among the German Settlers in the Middle Colonies," *The William and Mary Quarterly*, 33 (Apr 1976), 266-88.

C2-64. Freeman, Harrop A. "The Constitutionality of Peacetime Conscription," *Virginia Law Review*, 31 (1944), 40-82. Also in offprint form.

C2-65. Friedman, Leon. "Conscription and the Constitution: the Original Understanding," in Anderson and Honeger (1982: C2-3). Reprinted from *Michigan Law Review*, 67 (May 1969), 1493-552.

C2-66. Friedmann, Robert. "Anabaptism and Protestantism," *MQR*, 24 (Jan 1950), 12-24.

C2-66-2. Friesen, Abraham, ed. *P. M. Friesen and his History: Understanding Mennonite Brethren Beginnings* (Fresno: Center for Mennonite Brethren Studies, Mennonite Brethren Biblical Seminary, 1979).

C2-67. Fritz, Henry E. *The Movement for Indian Reform, 1860-1890* (Philadelphia: University of Pennsylvania Press, 1963).

C2-68. Funk, John F. *The Mennonite Church and Her Accusers* (Elkhart, Ind.: Mennonite Publishing Co., 1878).

C2-69. Gaeddert, Albert. *Centennial History of Hoffnungsau Mennonite Church* (North Newton, Kans.: Mennonite Press, 1974).

C2-70. Gascho, Milton. "The Amish Division of 1693-1697 in Switzerland and Alsace," *MQR*, 11 (Oct 1937), 235-66.

C2-71. Gates, Helen Kolb. *Bless the Lord, O My Soul: A Biography of Bishop John Fretz Funk, 1835-1930* (Scottdale, Pa.: Herald Press, 1964).

C2-72. Gering, John J. *After Fifty Years: A Brief Discussion of the History and Activities of the Swiss-German Mennonites from Russia Who Settled in South Dakota in 1874* (n.pl.: Pine Hill Printery, 1924).

C2-73. Gibble, Phares. *History of the East Pennsylvania Conference of the Church of the United Brethren in Christ* (Dayton, Ohio: Otterbein Press, 1951).

C2-74. Gibbons, P[hebe]. E. *"Pennsylvania Dutch" and Other Essays* (Philadelphia: J. B. Lippincott and Co., 1872, 1874, 1882. "Pennsylvania Dutch" was published originally in the *Atlantic*

Monthly (Oct 1869).

C2-75. Gingerich, James N. "*Ordnung* and Amish Ministers Meetings of the 1860s" (baccalaureate thesis, Goshen College, 1980). Copy in MHL.

C2-76. Gingerich, Melvin. *Mennonite Attire Through Four Centuries* (Breinigsville, Pa.: The Pennsylvania German Society, 1970).

C2-77. ______________. "The Mennonite Women's Missionary Society: I," *MQR*, 37 (Apr 1963), 113-25.

C2-78. ______________. *The Mennonites in Iowa: Marking the One Hundredth Anniversary of the Coming of the Mennonites to Iowa* (Iowa City: State Historical Society of Iowa, 1939).

C2-79. ______________. "The Reactions of the Russian Mennonite Immigrants of the 1870's to the American Frontier," *MQR*, 34 (Apr 1960), 137-46.

C2-79-2. Goen, C. C. *Broken Churches, Broken Nation: Denominational Schisms and the Coming of the Civil War.* (Macon, Ga.: Mercer University Press, 1985).

C2-80. Graber, Robert. "The Sociocultural Differentiation of a Religious Sect: Schisms Among Pennsylvania German Mennonites" (University of Wisconsin—Milwaukee Ph.D. dissertation, 1979).

C2-81. Gratz, Delbert. *Bernese Anabaptists and their American Descendents* (Scottdale, Pa.: Herald Press, 1953).

C2-82. ______________. "Swiss Mennonites Come to Putnam County, Ohio," *ML*, 15 (Oct 1960), 165-67.

C2-83. Gray, Wood. *The Hidden Civil War: The Story of the Copperheads* (New York: The Viking Press, 1942).

C2-84. Grieser, Orland, and Ervin Beck, Jr. *Out of the Wilderness: History of the Central Mennonite Church, 1835-1960* (Grand Rapids, Mich.: Dean-Hicks Co., 1960).

C2-85. Harder, Leland. "The Oberholtzer Division: 'Reformation' or 'Secularization'?" *MQR*, 37 (Oct 1963), 310-331, 342.

C2-86. ______________. "The Russian Mennonites and American Democracy under Grant," in Krahn (1949: C1-7), 54-67.

C2-87. Hartzler, J. S., and Daniel Kauffman. *Mennonite Church History* (Scottdale, Pa.: Mennonite Book and Tract Society, 1905).

C2-88. Hartzler, John E. *Education among the Mennonites of America* (Danvers, Ill.: Central Mennonite Publication Board, 1925).

C2-89. Harvey, George. *Henry Clay Frick: The Man* (n.pl.: Charles Scribner's Sons, 1928).

C2-90. Haury, David. *Prairie People: A History of the Western District Conference* (Newton, Kans.: Faith and Life Press, 1981).

C2-91. Hayes, A. Reed, Jr. *The Old Order Amish Mennonites: A*

Survival of Religious Fundamentalism in a New World Environment (Lewistown, Pa.: Mifflin County Historical Society, 1947).

C2-91-2. Heitala, Thomas R. *Manifest Design: Anxious Aggrandizement in Late Jacksonian America* (Ithaca and London: Cornell University Press, 1985).

C2-92. Hershberger, Guy F. "The Founding of the Mennonite Central Committee" (unpublished, typed). In 1976 copy was in Hershberger's possession.

C2-93. ______. "Historical Background to the Formation of the Mennonite Central Committee," *MQR*, 44 (Jul 1970), 213-44.

C2-94. ______. "Mennonites in the Civil War," *MQR*, 18 (Jul 1944), 131-44.

C2-95. Hershey, Mary Jane. "A Study of the Dress of the (Old) Mennonites of the Franconia Conference 1700-1953," *Pennsylvania Folklife*, 9 (Summer 1958), 24-47.

C2-96 Hiebert, Clarence. *The Henderson Mennonite Brethren, 1878-1978: Some Recollections of the 100-Year History of the Mennonite Brethren Church, Henderson, Nebraska* (Henderson, Nebr.: Service Press, 1979).

C2-97. ______. *The Holdeman People: The Church of God in Christ, Mennonite, 1859-1969* (South Pasadena, Calif.: William Carey Library, 1973).

C2-97-2. Hine, Robert V. *Community on the American Frontier: Separate but Not Alone* (Norman: University of Oklahoma Press, 1980).

C2-98. *A Historical Sketch of the Churches of the Evangelical Mennonite Brethren* (Rosthern, Sask.: printed by D. H. Epp, [1939?]).

C2-98-4. Hostetler, Beulah Stauffer. "Defensive Structuring and Codification of Practice," *MQR*, 60 (Jul 1986), 429-44.

C2-98-8. ______. "Franconia Mennonite Conference and American Protestant Movements, 1840-1940" (University of Pennsylvania Ph.D. dissertation, 1977); now revised and published as *American Mennonites and Protestant Movements: A Community Paradigm* (Scottdale, Pa., and Kithener, Ont,, Herald Press, 1987).

C2-99. Hostetler, John A. *Amish Society* (3rd ed. Baltimore and London: The Johns Hopkins University Press, 1980).

C2-100. ______. *Hutterite Society* (Baltimore and London: The Johns Hopkins University Press, 1974).

C2-101. ______. "Joseph Funk: Founder of Mennonite Publication Work, 1847," *GH*, 40 (27 Dec 1947), 817-18, 831.

C2-102. ______. "Memoirs of Shem Zook (1798-1880): A Biography," *MQR*, 38 (Jul 1964), 280-99, 303. Trans. of Zook (B2-95).

C2-102-2. ______________. "The Old Order Amish on the Great Plains: A Study in Vulnerability," in Luebke (1980: C2-134), 92-108.

C2-102-3. ______________. "The Plain People: Historical and Modern Perspectives," in Trommler and McVeigh (1985: C2-223-2), 106-17.

C2-102-4. Hughes, Richard T. "A Comparison of the Restitution Motifs of the Campbells (1809-1830) and the Anabaptists (1524-1560)," *MQR*, 45 (Oct 1971), 312-30.

C2-103. Juhnke, James C. "General Conference Mennonite Missions to the American Indians in the Late 19th Century" (unpublished paper read at a Mennonite Experience in America conference, 1977). Copy in MHL.

C2-104. ______________. *A People in Mission: A History of General Conference Mennonite Overseas Missions* (Newton, Kans.: Faith and Life Press, 1979).

C2-105. ______________. *A People of Two Kingdoms: The Political Acculturation of the Kansas Mennonites* (Newton, Kans.: Faith and Life Press, 1975).

C2-106. Kadelbach, Ada. "Die Hymnodie der Mennoniten in Nordamerika (1742-1860): Eine Studie zur Verpflanzung, Bewahrung und Umformung europäischer Kirchenliedtradition" (University of Mainz, West Germany, Ph.D. dissertation, 1971).

C2-107. Kauffman, J. Howard, and Leland Harder. *Anabaptists Four Centuries Later: A Profile of Five Mennonite and Brethren in Christ Denominations* (Scottdale, Pa. and Kitchener, Ont.: Herald Press, 1975).

C2-108. Kaufman, Edmund G. *The Development of the Missionary and Philanthropic Interest Among the Mennonites of North America* (Berne, Ind.: The Mennonite Book Concern, 1931).

C2-108-2. Keller, Robert H., Jr. *American Protestantism and United States Indian Policy, 1869-1882* (Lincoln and London: University of Nebraska Press, 1983).

C2-109. Kern, Kathleen. "The Reformed Mennonite Self-Conception as Christ's Sole Church; or, Heaven Won't be Crowded" (unpublished Bluffton College term paper, 1983). Copy in AMC.

C2-110. King, Trennis. *History of the Maple Grove Mennonite Church, Belleville, Pennsylvania, 1806-1974* (n.p., n.d.).

C2-111. Klaassen, Walter. *Anabaptism: Neither Catholic Nor Protestant* (Waterloo, Ont.: Conrad Press, 1973; rev. ed., 1981).

C2-111-2. ______________. "The Anabaptist Understanding of the Separation of the Church," *Church History*, 46 (Dec 1977), 421-36.

C2-112. Klement, Frank. *The Copperheads in the Middle West* (Chicago: University Of Chicago Press, 1960).

C2-113. Klinglesmith, Sharon. "Women in the Mennonite Church, 1900-1930," *MQR*, 54 (Jul 1980), 163-207.

C2-114. Klippenstein, Lawrence. "Manitoba Metis and Mennonite Immigrants: First Contacts," *MQR*, 48 (Oct 1974), 476-88.

C2-114-2. Kloberdanz, Timothy J. "Plainsmen of Three Continents: Volga German Adaptation to Steppe, Prairie, and Pampa," in Luebke (1980: C2-134), 54-72.

C2-115. Koch, Fred C. *The Volga Germans: In Russia and the Americas, from 1763 to the Present* (University Park, Pa., and London: Pennsylvania State University Press, 1977).

C2-116. Krahn, Cornelius. "A Centennial Chronology," *ML*, 28 (Mar, Jun 1973), 3-9, 40-45.

C2-117. ________. "From Russia to Meade," *ML*, 6 (Jul 1951), 18-19.

C2-117-2. ________. "Some Social Attitudes of Russian Mennonites," *MQR*, 9 (Oct 1935), 165-77.

C2-118. Kraus, C. Norman. *Dispensationalism in America: Its Rise and Development* (Richmond, Va.: John Knox Press, 1958).

C2-119. Krehbiel, H[enry]. P. *The History of the General Conference of the Mennonites of North America* (Vol. I: Canton, O.: The Author, 1898. Vol. II: Newton, Kans.: The Author, 1938).

C2-120. Kremer, Russ. "Conscientious Objection in Antebellum America" (history term paper, Goshen College, 1974). Copy in MHL; heavily summarizes parts of Brock (1968: C2-25).

C2-121. Kroeker, N.J. *First Mennonite Villages in Russia, 1789-1943: Khortitsa—Rosenthal* [Vancouver, B.C.: The Author, 1981].

C2-122. Lamb, Barbara Bixler. "The Role of Women in the Mennonite Missionary Movement, 1890-1910" (Goshen College baccalaureate paper, 1978). Copy in MHL.

C2-123. Landing, James E. "Amish Settlement in North America: A Geographic Brief," Illinois Geographical Society *Bulletin*, 12 (Dec 1970), 65-69.

C2-124. Landis, Ira. "The Plain Dutch," *MRJ*, 9 (Apr 1968), 13, 19, 21.

C2-124-2. Lears, T. J. Jackson. "The Concept of Cultural Hegemony: Problems and Possibilities," *The American Historical Review*, 90 (Jun 1985), 567-93.

C2-125. Lehman, James O. "Conflicting Loyalties of the Christian Citizen: Lancaster Mennonites and the Early Civil War Era," *Pennsylvania Mennonite Heritage*, 7 (Apr 1984), 2-15.

C2-126. ________. *Creative Congregationalism: A History of the Oak Grove Mennonite Church in Wayne County, Ohio* (Smithville, Ohio: Oak Grove Mennonite Church, 1978).

C2-127. ________________. *Growth Amidst Struggle: A Sesquicentennial History of the Longenecker Mennonite Church* (Winesburg, Ohio: Longenecker Mennonite Church, 1980).

C2-128. ________________. *Seedbed for Leadership: A Centennial History of the Pike Mennonite Church* (Elida, Ohio: Pike Mennonite Church, 1974).

C2-129. ________________. *Sonnenberg: A Haven and a Heritage* (Kidron, Ohio: Kidron Community Council, 1969).

C2-130. ________________, ed. *Welcome to Ohio* (Kidron, Ohio: n.p., 1962).

C2-131. Lemon, James T. *The Best Poor Man's Country: A Geographical Study of Early Southeastern Pennsylvania* (Baltimore and London: The Johns Hopkins University Press, 1972).

C2-132. Liebbrandt, Georg. "The Emigration of the German Mennonites from Russia to the United States and Canada in 1873-1880," *MQR*, 6 (Oct 1932), 205-26; 7 (Jan 1933), 5-41.

C2-133. Luebke, Frederick C. *Immigrants and Politics: The Germans of Nebraska, 1880-1890* (Lincoln: University of Nebraska Press, 1969).

C2-134. ________________, ed. *Ethnicity on the Great Plains* (Lincoln and London: University of Nebraska Press, 1980).

C2-135. MacMaster, Richard K. "The Children of God and the Children of Men" (address at Mennonite Experience in America conference, Dec 1976, Goshen College, Goshen, Ind.).

C2-136. Marty, Martin E. *Righteous Empire: The Protestant Experience in America* (New York: Dial Press, 1970).

C2-137. Mast, C. Z. "The First Church Controversy Among the Amish in America," *MHB*, 15 (Jul 1954), 1-2.

C2-138. Mathews, Donald G. "The Second Great Awakening as an Organizing Process, 1780-1830: An Hypothesis," *American Quarterly*, 21 (Spring 1969), 23-43.

C2-138-2. ________________. *Slavery and Methodism: A Chapter in American Morality, 1780-1845* (Princeton: Princeton University Press, 1965).

C2-139. Miller, Betty. *Amish Pioneers of the Walnut Creek Valley* (Wooster, Ohio: Atkinson Printing, 1977).

C2-140. Miller, D. Paul. "An Analysis of Community Adjustment: A Case Study of Jansen, Nebraska" (University of Nebraska Ph.D. dissertation, 1953).

C2-141. Miller, John Stanley. "A Statistical Survey of the Amish Settlers in Clinton Township, Elkhart County, Indiana, 1841-1850" (Goshen College baccalaureate seminar paper, 1971). Copy in MHL.

C2-141-2. Miller, Perry. *The Life of the Mind in America: From the Revolution to the Civil War* (New York: Harcourt, Brace, 1965).

C2-141-3. Miner, H. Craig, and William E. Unrau. *The End of Indian Kansas: A Study of Cultural Revolution, 1854-1871* (Lawrence: The Regents Press of Kansas, 1978).

C2-142. Miyakawa, T. Scott. *Protestants and Pioneers: Individualism and Conformity on the American Frontier* (Chicago: University of Chicago Press, 1964).

C2-142-2. Moltmann, Günther. "The Pattern of German Emigration to the United States in the Nineteenth Century," in Trommler and McVeigh (1985:C2-223-2), 14-24.

C2-143. Mook, Maurice A. "The Amishman Who Founded A City," *Christian Living*, 2 (Jul 1955), 4-7.

C2-143-2. Moorhead, James H. *American Apocalypse: Yankee Protestants and the Civil War, 1860-1869* (New Haven and London: Yale University Press, 1978).

C2-144. Morgan, Edith Wenger. *Stories My Father Told Us* (n.p., n.d.).

C2-145. Mulder, John M., and John F. Wilson, eds. *Religion in American History: Interpretive Essays* (Englewood Cliffs, N.J.: Prentice-Hall, 1978).

C2-146. Murdock, Eugene C. *Patriotism Limited, 1862-1865: The Civil War Draft and the Bounty System* ([Kent, Ohio]: Kent State University Press, 1967).

C2-147. Neufeld, Vernon. "Mennonites Settle in Lee County, Iowa," *ML*, 8 (Oct 1953), 170-73.

C2-148. Nugent, Walter T. K. *The Tolerant Populists: Kansas, Populism and Nativism* (Chicago: University of Chicago Press, 1963).

C2-149. Nussbaum, Stan. *You Must Be Born Again: A History of the Evangelical Mennonite Church* (Ft. Wayne, Ind.: Evangelical Mennonite Church, 1976 or 1977.)

C2-150. Olshan, Marc A. "Modernity, the Folk Society, and the Old Order Amish: An Alternative Interpretation," *Rural Sociology*, 46 (Summer 1981), 297-309.

C2-151. O'Malley, J. Stephen. *Pilgrimage of Faith: The Legacy of the Otterbeins* (Metuchen, N.J.: Scarecrow Press, 1973).

C2-152. O'Sullivan, John, and Alan M. Meckler, eds. *The Draft and Its Enemies: A Documentary History* (Chicago: University of Chicago Press, 1974).

C2-153. Pannabecker, Samuel Floyd. *Faith in Ferment: A History of the Central District Conference* (Newton, Kans.: Faith and Life Press, 1968).

C2-154. ______________. "The Nineteenth Century Swiss Mennonite Immigrants and Their Adherence to the General Conference Mennonite Church," *MQR*, 21 (Apr 1947), 64-102.

C2-155. Pantle, Alberta. "A Mennonite Village in Kansas," *ML*, 4 (Oct 1947), 20-22.

C2-156. Penner, Lloyd. "The Mennonites on the Washita River: The Culmination of Four Centuries of Migrations" (Oklahoma State University D.Ed. dissertation, 1976).

C2-157. Pennypacker, Samuel W. *The Autobiography of a Pennsylvanian* (Philadelphia: John C. Winston Co., 1918).

C2-158. Peters, Frank C. "The Early Mennonite Brethren Church: Baptist or Anabaptist?" *ML*, 14 (Oct 1959), 176-78.

C2-159. Plett, C. F. *The Story of the Krimmer Mennonite Brethren* (Hillsboro, Kans., and Winnipeg, Man.: Kindred Press, 1985).

C2-160. Prieb, Wesley. Ms. of a P. C. Hiebert biography, loaned to me by its author, at Center for M.B. Studies, Tabor College, Hillsboro, Kans.

C2-161. Prucha, Francis Paul. *American Indian Policy in Crisis: Christian Reformers and the Indian, 1865-1900* (Norman, Okla.: University of Oklahoma Press, 1975).

C2-162. ______________. *American Indian Policy in the Formative Years: The Indian Trade and Intercourse Acts, 1790-1834* (Cambridge, Mass.: Harvard University Press, 1962).

C2-163. Renno, John D. *A Brief History of the Amish Church in Belleville* (n.p., [between 1973 and 1977]).

C2-164. Rich, Elaine Sommers. *Mennonite Women: A Story of God's Faithfulness* (Scottdale, Pa., and Kitchener, Ont.: Herald Press, 1983).

C2-165. Ritschl, Albrecht. *Geschichte des Pietismus* (3 vols. Bonn: Adolph Marcus, 1880).

C2-166. Robertson, Andrew. "The Idealist as Opportunist: An Analysis of Thaddeus Stevens' Support in Lancaster County, 1843-1866," *Journal of the Lancaster County Historical Society*, 84 (Easter 1980), 49-107.

C2-167. Rosenberger, Homer Tope, ed. *Intimate Glimpses of the Pennsylvania Germans, 1891-1965* (Lancaster, Pa.: Pennsylvania German Society, 1966).

C2-168. Ruth, John L. *A History of Indian Valley and Its Bank* ([Souderton, Pa.]: The Union National Bank and Trust Co., 1976).

C2-169. Sandeen, Ernest R. *The Roots of Fundamentalism: British and American Millenarianism, 1800-1930* (Chicago and London: University of Chicago Press, 1970).

C2-170. Schelbert, Leo. "Eighteenth Century Migration of Swiss Mennonites to America," *MQR*, 42 (Jul, Oct 1968), 163-83, 285-300.

C2-170-2. ______________. "Pietism Rejected: A Reinterpretation of Amish Origins," in Trommler and McVeigh (1985:C2-223-2), 118-27.

C2-171. Schlabach, Erv. "A History of the Walnut Creek Mennonite Church," in *A Century and a Half with the Mennonites at Walnut Creek* (Strasburg, Ohio: Walnut Creek Mennonite Church Historical Committee, 1978), 1-43.

C2-172. Schlabach, Theron F. *Gospel Versus Gospel: Mission and the Mennonite Church, 1863-1944* (Scottdale, Pa., and Kitchener, Ont.: Herald Press, 1980).

C2-173. ______________. "Mennonites and Pietism in America, 1740-1880: Some Thoughts on the Friedmann Thesis," *MQR*, 57 (Jul 1983), 222-40.

C2-174. ______________. "Mennonites, Revivalism, Modernity, 1683-1850," *Church History*, 48 (Dec 1979), 398-415.

C2-175. ______________. *A New Rhythm for Mennonites: The Mennonite Church and the Missionary Movement 1860-1890* (Elkhart, Ind.: Mennonite Board of Missions, 1975). Essentially ch. 1 of C2-172.

C2-176. Schlissel, Lillian, ed. *Conscience in America: A Documentary History of Conscientious Objection in America, 1757-1967* (New York: E. P. Dutton and Co., 1968).

C2-177. Schmidt, John F. "A Century Ago Mennonites Came to Kansas with Turkey Red Wheat" (typed mss. in MLA).

C2-178. Schmidt, Theodore. "The Mennonites of Nebraska" (University of Nebraska M.A. thesis, 1933).

C2-179. Schnell, Kempes. "John F. Funk, 1835-1930, and the Mennonite Migration of 1873-1875," *MQR*, 24 (Jul 1950), 199-229. This *MQR* issue is devoted to that migration, at its 75th anniversary.

C2-180. Schrag, Martin H. "The Brethren in Christ Attitude Toward the 'World': A Historical Study of the Movement from Separation to an Increasing Acceptance of American Society" (Temple University Ph.D. dissertation, 1967).

C2-181. ______________. "European History of the Swiss-Volhynian Mennonite Ancestors of Mennonites Now Living in Communities in Kansas and South Dakota" (Eastern Baptist Seminary Th.M. thesis, 1956).

C2-182. Schrag, Robert. "Newton, Kansas: A Center of Mennonite Businesses," *ML*, 15 (Apr 1960), 64-67.

C2-183. ______________. "Newton, Kansas: A Frontier Town on the Chisholm Trail," *ML*, 15 (Jan 1960), 26-29.

C2-184. Schroeder, William. *The Bergthal Colony* (Winnipeg, Man.: The Author, 1973). Multilithed.

C2-185. Schultz, Ferdinand P. *A History of the Settlement of*

German Mennonites from Russia at Mountain Lake, Minnesota (Minneapolis: the author, 1938).

C2-186 *Seventy-Five Years in Minnesota, 1874-1949: Mennonite Churches in the Mountain Lake Community* (n.p., [1950?)].

C2-187. Sheehan, Bernard W. *Seeds of Extinction: Jeffersonian Philanthropy and the American Indian* (Chapel Hill, N.C.: University of North Carolina, 1974).

C2-188. Shetler, Sanford G. *Two Centuries of Struggle and Growth, 1763-1963: A History of the Allegheny Mennonite Conference* (n.pl.: Allegheny Mennonite Conference, 1963).

C2-189. Smith, C. Henry. *The Coming of the Russian Mennonites: An Episode in the Settling of the Last Frontier* (Berne, Ind.: Mennonite Book Concern, 1927).

C2-190. Smith, Elmer L. *Bundling among the Amish: A Curious Courtship Custom* (Akron, Pa.: Applied Arts, 1961).

C2-191. Smith, Elwyn A., ed. *The Religion of the Republic* (Philadelphia: Fortress Press, 1971).

C2-191-2. Smith, Timothy L. "Religious Denominations as Ethnic Communities: A Regional Case Study," *Church History*, 35 (Jun 1961), 207-26.

C2-192. ________________. *Revivalism and Social Reform: American Protestantism on the Eve of the Civil War* (Harper Torchbook ed. New York, etc.: Harper and Row, 1967).

C2-193. Smith, Willard H. *Mennonites in Illinois* (Scottdale, Pa., and Kitchener, Ont.: Herald Press, 1983).

C2-194. Spayth, Henry G. *History of the Church of the United Brethren in Christ* (Circleville, Ohio: Conference Office of the United Brethren in Christ, 1851).

C2-195. *Springs Mennonite Church, Springs, Pennsylvania: One Hundred Years, 1878-1978* (St. Louis, Mo.: Pictorial Church Directories of America, 1978).

C2-196. Sprunger, Eva F. *The First Hundred Years: A History of the Mennonite Church in Adams County, Indiana, 1838-1938* (Berne, Ind.: n.p., 1938).

C2-197. Sprunger, Keith. "God's Powerful Army of the Weak: Anabaptist Women of the Radical Reformation," in Richard L. Greaves, ed., *Triumph over Silence: Women in Protestant History* (Westport, Conn.: Greenwood Press, 1985), 45-74.

C2-198. Stiles, Henry Reed. *Bundling: Its Origin, Progress, and Decline in America* (New York: Book Collectors' Association, 1934).

C2-199. Stoeffler, F. Ernest. *German Pietism During the Eighteenth Century* (Leiden: E. J. Brill, 1973).

C2-200-1. ________________. "Pietism: Its Message, Early Manifestation, and Significance," in *Contemporary Perspectives on*

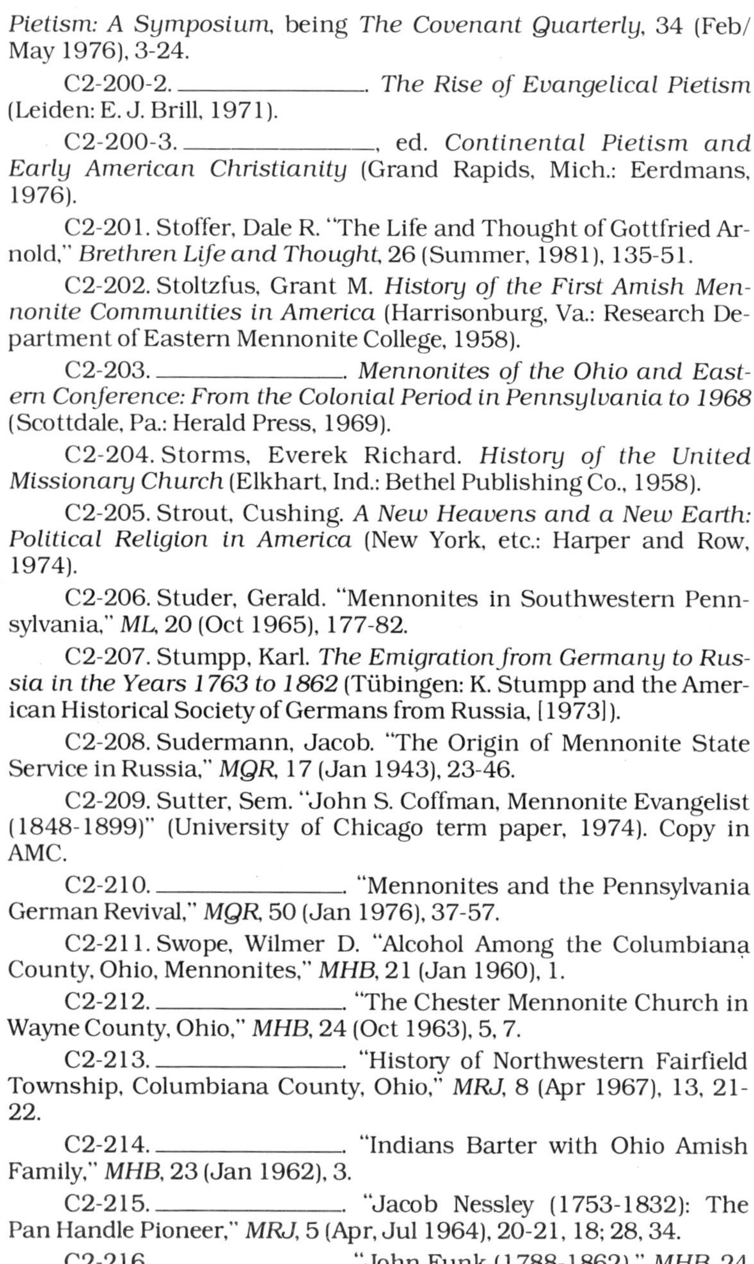

Pietism: A Symposium, being *The Covenant Quarterly*, 34 (Feb/May 1976), 3-24.

C2-200-2. ________________. *The Rise of Evangelical Pietism* (Leiden: E. J. Brill, 1971).

C2-200-3. ________________, ed. *Continental Pietism and Early American Christianity* (Grand Rapids, Mich.: Eerdmans, 1976).

C2-201. Stoffer, Dale R. "The Life and Thought of Gottfried Arnold," *Brethren Life and Thought*, 26 (Summer, 1981), 135-51.

C2-202. Stoltzfus, Grant M. *History of the First Amish Mennonite Communities in America* (Harrisonburg, Va.: Research Department of Eastern Mennonite College, 1958).

C2-203. ________________. *Mennonites of the Ohio and Eastern Conference: From the Colonial Period in Pennsylvania to 1968* (Scottdale, Pa.: Herald Press, 1969).

C2-204. Storms, Everek Richard. *History of the United Missionary Church* (Elkhart, Ind.: Bethel Publishing Co., 1958).

C2-205. Strout, Cushing. *A New Heavens and a New Earth: Political Religion in America* (New York, etc.: Harper and Row, 1974).

C2-206. Studer, Gerald. "Mennonites in Southwestern Pennsylvania," *ML*, 20 (Oct 1965), 177-82.

C2-207. Stumpp, Karl. *The Emigration from Germany to Russia in the Years 1763 to 1862* (Tübingen: K. Stumpp and the American Historical Society of Germans from Russia, [1973]).

C2-208. Sudermann, Jacob. "The Origin of Mennonite State Service in Russia," *MQR*, 17 (Jan 1943), 23-46.

C2-209. Sutter, Sem. "John S. Coffman, Mennonite Evangelist (1848-1899)" (University of Chicago term paper, 1974). Copy in AMC.

C2-210. ________________. "Mennonites and the Pennsylvania German Revival," *MQR*, 50 (Jan 1976), 37-57.

C2-211. Swope, Wilmer D. "Alcohol Among the Columbiana County, Ohio, Mennonites," *MHB*, 21 (Jan 1960), 1.

C2-212. ________________. "The Chester Mennonite Church in Wayne County, Ohio," *MHB*, 24 (Oct 1963), 5, 7.

C2-213. ________________. "History of Northwestern Fairfield Township, Columbiana County, Ohio," *MRJ*, 8 (Apr 1967), 13, 21-22.

C2-214. ________________. "Indians Barter with Ohio Amish Family," *MHB*, 23 (Jan 1962), 3.

C2-215. ________________. "Jacob Nessley (1753-1832): The Pan Handle Pioneer," *MRJ*, 5 (Apr, Jul 1964), 20-21, 18; 28, 34.

C2-216. ________________. "John Funk (1788-1862)," *MHB*, 24

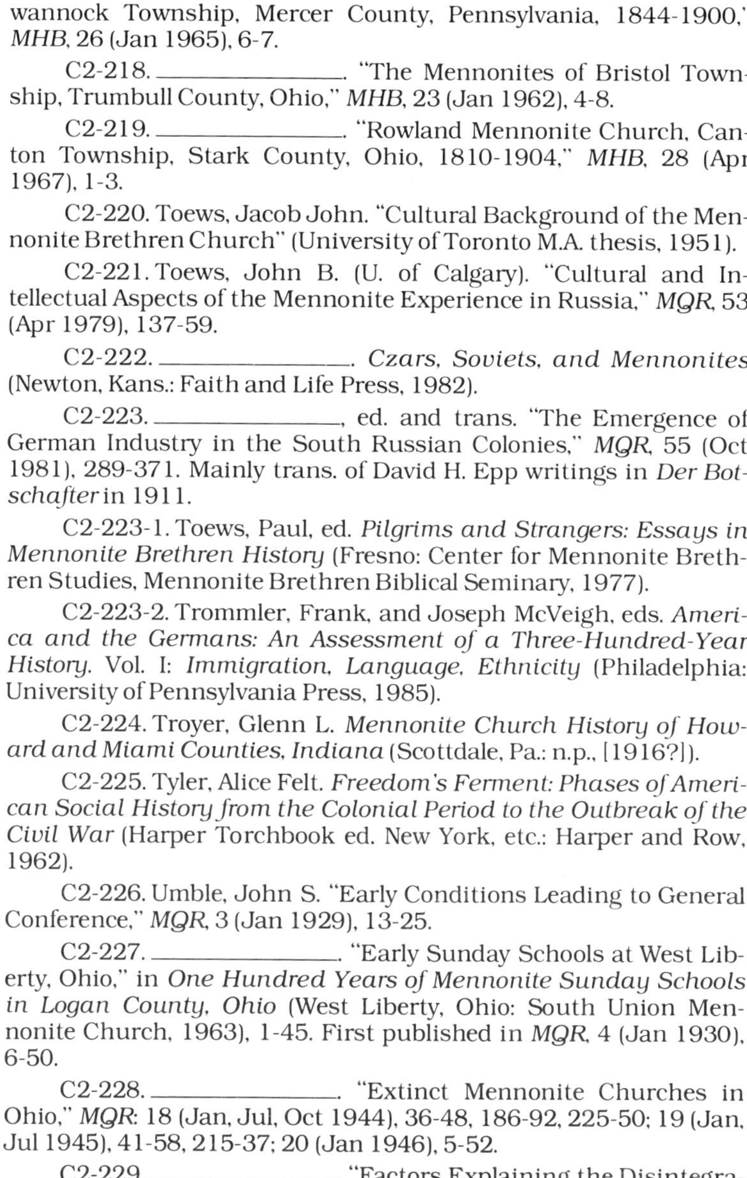

(Jan 1963), 4.

C2-217. ————————. "The Mennonite Church of Lackawannock Township, Mercer County, Pennsylvania, 1844-1900," *MHB*, 26 (Jan 1965), 6-7.

C2-218. ————————. "The Mennonites of Bristol Township, Trumbull County, Ohio," *MHB*, 23 (Jan 1962), 4-8.

C2-219. ————————. "Rowland Mennonite Church, Canton Township, Stark County, Ohio, 1810-1904," *MHB*, 28 (Apr 1967), 1-3.

C2-220. Toews, Jacob John. "Cultural Background of the Mennonite Brethren Church" (University of Toronto M.A. thesis, 1951).

C2-221. Toews, John B. (U. of Calgary). "Cultural and Intellectual Aspects of the Mennonite Experience in Russia," *MQR*, 53 (Apr 1979), 137-59.

C2-222. ————————. *Czars, Soviets, and Mennonites* (Newton, Kans.: Faith and Life Press, 1982).

C2-223. ————————, ed. and trans. "The Emergence of German Industry in the South Russian Colonies," *MQR*, 55 (Oct 1981), 289-371. Mainly trans. of David H. Epp writings in *Der Botschafter* in 1911.

C2-223-1. Toews, Paul, ed. *Pilgrims and Strangers: Essays in Mennonite Brethren History* (Fresno: Center for Mennonite Brethren Studies, Mennonite Brethren Biblical Seminary, 1977).

C2-223-2. Trommler, Frank, and Joseph McVeigh, eds. *America and the Germans: An Assessment of a Three-Hundred-Year History*. Vol. I: *Immigration, Language, Ethnicity* (Philadelphia: University of Pennsylvania Press, 1985).

C2-224. Troyer, Glenn L. *Mennonite Church History of Howard and Miami Counties, Indiana* (Scottdale, Pa.: n.p., [1916?]).

C2-225. Tyler, Alice Felt. *Freedom's Ferment: Phases of American Social History from the Colonial Period to the Outbreak of the Civil War* (Harper Torchbook ed. New York, etc.: Harper and Row, 1962).

C2-226. Umble, John S. "Early Conditions Leading to General Conference," *MQR*, 3 (Jan 1929), 13-25.

C2-227. ————————. "Early Sunday Schools at West Liberty, Ohio," in *One Hundred Years of Mennonite Sunday Schools in Logan County, Ohio* (West Liberty, Ohio: South Union Mennonite Church, 1963), 1-45. First published in *MQR*, 4 (Jan 1930), 6-50.

C2-228. ————————. "Extinct Mennonite Churches in Ohio," *MQR*: 18 (Jan, Jul, Oct 1944), 36-48, 186-92, 225-50; 19 (Jan, Jul 1945), 41-58, 215-37; 20 (Jan 1946), 5-52.

C2-229. ————————. "Factors Explaining the Disintegration of Mennonite Communities," in *Proceedings of the Seventh Annual Conference on Mennonite Cultural Problems* (North Newton, Kans.: Council of Mennonite and Affiliated Colleges, 1949), 113-28.

C2-230. ________________. *Ohio Mennonite Sunday Schools* (Goshen, Ind.: The Mennonite Historical Society, 1941).

C2-231. Unruh, Abe J. *The Helpless Poles* (Montezuma, Kans.: The Author, 1973).

C2-232-1. Unruh, John D. "A Century of Mennonites in South Dakota: A Segment of the German Russians," in *South Dakota Department of History: Report and Historical Collections* (Pierre, S.D.: South Dakota State Historical Society, 1972), XXXVI, 1-142. Also in offprint form.

C2-232-2. Urry, James. "Through the Eye of a Needle: Wealth and the Mennonite Experience in Russia" (paper presented at conference sponsored by the Institute of Anabaptist and Mennonite Studies, Conrad Grebel College, University of Waterloo, May 9-10, 1984).

C2-233. Voth, Stanley E., ed. *Henderson Mennonites: From Holland to Henderson* (Henderson, Nebr.: Henderson Centennial Committee, 1975).

C2-234. Wandel, Joseph. *The German Dimension in American History* (Chicago: Nelson-Hall, 1979).

C2-235. Washburn, Wilcomb E. *The Indian in America* (New York, etc.: Harper and Row, 1975).

C2-236. Wayland, John W. *Joseph Funk, Father of Song in Northern Virginia* (Dayton, Va.: Ruebush-Kieffer, [ca. 1911]). Reprint from *The Pennsylvania German*, 12 (1911), 580-94.

C2-236-2. Weaver, J. Denny. "The Work of Christ: On the Difficulty of Identifying an Anabaptist Perspective," *MQR*, 59 (Apr 1985), 107-29.

C2-237. Weaver, Martin G. *Mennonites of the Lancaster Conference . . .* (Scottdale, Pa.: Mennonite Publishing House, 1931).

C2-238. Wedel, David C. *The Story of Alexanderwohl* (Goessel, Kans.: Goessel Centennial Committee, 1974).

C2-239. Welter, Barbara M. "The Cult of True Womanhood: 1820-1860," *American Quarterly*, 18 (Summer 1966), 151-74.

C2-240. ________________. "The Feminization of American Religion, 1800-1860," in Mary Hartman and Lois Banner, eds., *Clio's Consciousness Raised: New Perspectives on the History of Women* (New York, etc.: Harper and Row, 1974), 137-57.

C2-241. Wenger, Eli D. *The Weaverland Mennonites . . . , 1766-1968* ([Manheim, Pa.: The Author], 1968).

C2-242. Wenger, John C. [or J. C.] "The Doctrinal Position of

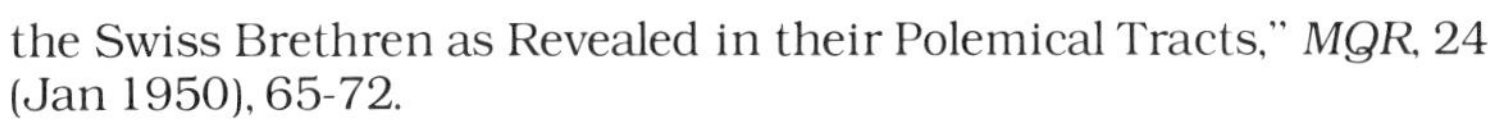

the Swiss Brethren as Revealed in their Polemical Tracts," *MQR*, 24 (Jan 1950), 65-72.

C2-243. ————. *Forks Mennonite Church: A Centennial History, 1857-1957* ([Middlebury, Ind.: Forks Mennonite Church], 1957).

C2-244. ————. *History of the Mennonites of the Franconia Conference* (Telford, Pa.: Franconia Mennonite Historical Society, 1937).

C2-245. ————. "Jacob Wisler and the Old Order Mennonite Schism of 1872 in Elkhart County, Indiana," *MQR*, 33 (Apr, Jul 1959), 108-31, 215-40.

C2-246. ————. *The Mennonite Church in America: Sometimes Called Old Mennonites* (Scottdale, Pa.: Herald Press, 1966).

C2-247. ————. *The Mennonites in Indiana and Michigan* (Scottdale, Pa.: Herald Press, 1961).

C2-248. Wenger, Samuel S. "The Mennonitism of Leo Tolstoy and His Reference to Daniel Musser," *MRJ*, 5 (Apr 1964), 13-14, 22.

C2-249. White, Ronald C., Jr., and C. Howard Hopkins. *The Social Gospel: Religion and Reform in Changing America* (Philadelphia: Temple University Press, 1976).

C2-250. Wiebe, David V. *Grace Meadow: The Story of Gnadenau and Its First Elder, Marion County, Kansas, With Illustrations* (Hillsboro, Kans.: Mennonite Brethren Publishing House, 1967).

C2-251. Wiebe, Katie Funk, ed. *Women Among the Brethren: Stories of Fifteen Mennonite Brethren and Krimmer Mennonite Brethren Women* (Hillsboro, Kans.: Mennonite Brethren Publishing House, 1979).

C2-252. Wiebe, P[eter]. A. *Kurze Biographie des Bruders Jakob A. Wiebe: seine Jugend, seine Bekehrung, und wie die Krimmer Menoniten Brüdergemeinde begründet wurde*, ed. by M. B. Fast (Hillsboro, Kans.: The Author, 1924).

C2-253. Williams, T. Harry. *Lincoln and the Radicals* (Madison: University of Wisconsin Press, 1941).

C2-254. Wilson, John F. *Public Religion in American Culture* (Philadelphia: Temple University Press, 1979).

C2-255. Wittke, Carl. *The Germans in America: A Students' Guide to Localized History* (New York: Teacher's College Press, 1967).

C2-256. ————. *We Who Built America: The Saga of the Immigrant* (New York: Prentice-Hall, 1939).

C2-257. Woloch, Nancy. *Women and the American Experience* (New York: Alfred A. Knopf, 1984).

C2-258. The Women's Missionary Association [of the] General Conference Mennonite Church. *History of the Women's Missionary Societies of the General Conference Mennonites* (n.p., 1935). Notes use pagination as penciled in MHL copy.

C2-259. Wood, Ralph, ed. *The Pennsylvania Germans* (Princeton: Princeton University Press, 1942).

C2-260. Wyllie, Irvin G. *The Self-Made Man in America: The Myth of Rags to Riches* (New Brunswick, N.J.: Rutgers University Press, 1954).

C2-261. Yoder, Don. *Pennsylvania Spirituals* (Lancaster, Pa.: Pennsylvania Folklife Society, 1961).

C2-262. Yoder, Don, *et al. Pennsylvania German Fraktur and Color Drawings* (Lancaster, Pa.: Landis Valley Associates, 1969.).

C2-263. Yoder, Edward. "The Mennonites of Westmoreland County, Pennsylvania," *MQR*, 15 (Jul, Oct 1941), 155-86, 219-42.

C2-264-1. Yoder, John H. "The Hermeneutics of the Anabaptists," *MQR*, 41 (Oct 1967), 291-308.

C2-264-2. ________________. *The Original Revolution: Essays on Christian Pacifism* (Scottdale, Pa., and Kitchener, Ont.: Herald Press, 1971).

C2-264-3. ________________. *The Politics of Jesus: Vicit Agnus Noster* (Grand Rapids, Mich.: Eerdmans, 1972).

C2-265. Yoder, Jonas J. *Locust Grove Conservative Mennonite Church Seventy-Fifth Anniversary, October 13, 14, 1973* (n.p., [1973?]). Copy in MHL.

C2-266. Yoder, Paul Marvin. "Nineteenth Century Sacred Music of the Mennonite Church in the United States" (Florida State University Ph.D. dissertation, 1961).

C2-267. Yoder, Richard B. "Nonresistance Among the Peace Churches of Somerset County, Pennsylvania During the Civil War" (Goshen Biblical Seminary term paper, 1959). Copy in MHL.

C2-268. Yoder, Sanford. "The Amish in Wright County [Iowa]," *The Palimpsest*, 43 (Sep 1962), 401-32.

C2-269. Zigler, D[avid]. H. *A History of the Brethren in Virginia* (Elgin, Ill.: Brethren Publishing House, 1908).

INDEX

••••

THE AUTHOR

Theron F. Schlabach has worked in both Mennonite and American history. In his writing we see how minority religious communities with distinctive beliefs and cultural traits have fared amid America's denominationalism and its national development. As an insider he understands the nuances of the Mennonite tradition. But with ample training and experience in the broad field of U.S. social history, he also puts Mennonite data into national perspective.

After graduate training at the University of Wisconsin, Schlabach established his career at Goshen College, Goshen, Indiana (the community where he was born in 1933, and reared). He worked with the history of American welfare reform, publishing two books in that field. Then in the 1970s he joined Goshen College's strong tradition of leadership in Mennonite studies.

Schlabach took up a relatively undeveloped topic, the Mennonite experience in America. By 1980 he had written several key articles and *Gospel Versus Gospel*, a book on mission history. With solid research *Gospel Versus Gospel* describes how Mennonites borrowed American Protestant traditions and fused them with their own. Its interpretation is one with which other scholars have had to come to terms.

Such strength now appears in the Mennonite Experience in America series, written for a rather wider circle. The series' four volumes cover many Mennonite groups and stories. They are designed for general readers as well as for scholars, yet the best qualities remain—fresh insight, thoughtful analysis, and the setting of the Mennonite story within the larger American one.

Schlabach is the series editor as well as author of this second volume. At Goshen College he teaches classes in general U.S. history and the history of Mennonites in America. In 1970-1971 and in

1986-1987 he and his wife, Sara, were leaders of Goshen's international studies program in Costa Rica. He is president of Goshen's Mennonite Historical Society and active in a local Mennonite congregation. He serves in the congregation's Witness and Service Commission, its Peace Committee, and its efforts to come to the aid of community people through a "Jubilee Fund." *Peace, Faith, Nation* is the product of a mature career.

Theron and Sara's three sons—Gerald, Carlyle, and Roderic—have grown up and begun careers (in church service, medicine, and engineering). Daughter Kristina is in high school. Two sons have married, and Theron and Sara Schlabach are three-time grandparents.